Atomic Structure of the Heaviest Elements

Atomic Structure of the Heaviest Elements

Editors

Mustapha Laatiaoui
Sebastian Raeder

MDPI • Basel • Beijing • Wuhan • Barcelona • Belgrade • Manchester • Tokyo • Cluj • Tianjin

Editors
Mustapha Laatiaoui
Johannes Gutenberg University
Germany

Sebastian Raeder
GSI Helmholtz Center for Heavy Ion Research
Germany

Editorial Office
MDPI
St. Alban-Anlage 66
4052 Basel, Switzerland

This is a reprint of articles from the Special Issue published online in the open access journal *Atoms* (ISSN 2218-2004) (available at: https://www.mdpi.com/journal/atoms/special_issues/AtomicStructure_HeaviestElements).

For citation purposes, cite each article independently as indicated on the article page online and as indicated below:

LastName, A.A.; LastName, B.B.; LastName, C.C. Article Title. *Journal Name* **Year**, *Volume Number*, Page Range.

ISBN 978-3-0365-5591-1 (Hbk)
ISBN 978-3-0365-5592-8 (PDF)

© 2023 by the authors. Articles in this book are Open Access and distributed under the Creative Commons Attribution (CC BY) license, which allows users to download, copy and build upon published articles, as long as the author and publisher are properly credited, which ensures maximum dissemination and a wider impact of our publications.

The book as a whole is distributed by MDPI under the terms and conditions of the Creative Commons license CC BY-NC-ND.

Contents

About the Editors vii

Preface to "Atomic Structure of the Heaviest Elements" ix

Mustapha Laatiaoui and Sebastian Raeder
New Developments in the Production and Research of Actinide Elements
Reprinted from: *Atoms* **2022**, *10*, 61, doi:10.3390/atoms10020061 1

Stephan Fritzsche
Level Structure and Properties of Open f-Shell Elements
Reprinted from: *Atoms* **2022**, *10*, 7, doi:10.3390/atoms10010007 11

Alexander Kramida
Update of Atomic Data for the First Three Spectra of Actinium
Reprinted from: *Atoms* **2022**, *10*, 42, doi:10.3390/atoms10020042 27

Ricardo F. Silva, Jorge M. Sampaio, Pedro Amaro, Andreas Flörs, Gabriel Martínez-Pinedo and José P. Marques
Structure Calculations in Nd III and U III Relevant for Kilonovae Modelling
Reprinted from: *Atoms* **2022**, *10*, 18, doi:10.3390/atoms10010018 57

Harry Ramanantoanina, Anastasia Borschevsky, Michael Block and Mustapha Laatiaoui
Electronic Structure of Lr^+ ($Z = 103$) from Ab Initio Calculations
Reprinted from: *Atoms* **2022**, *10*, 48, doi:10.3390/atoms10020048 67

Andrea Raggio, Ilkka Pohjalainen and Iain D. Moore
Observation of Collisional De-Excitation Phenomena in Plutonium
Reprinted from: *Atoms* **2022**, *10*, 40, doi:10.3390/atoms10020040 77

Felix Weber, Christoph Emanuel Düllmann, Vadim Gadelshin, Nina Kneip, Stephan Oberstedt, Sebastian Raeder, et al.
Probing the Atomic Structure of Californium by Resonance Ionization Spectroscopy
Reprinted from: *Atoms* **2022**, *10*, 51, doi:10.3390/atoms10020051 87

Jessica Warbinek, Brankica Anđelić, Michael Block, Premaditya Chhetri, Arno Claessens, Rafael Ferrer, et al.
Advancing Radiation-Detected Resonance Ionization towards Heavier Elements and More Exotic Nuclides
Reprinted from: *Atoms* **2022**, *10*, 41, doi:10.3390/atoms10020041 99

Danny Münzberg, Michael Block, Arno Claessens, Rafael Ferrer, Mustapha Laatiaoui, Jeremy Lantis, et al.
Resolution Characterizations of JetRIS in Mainz Using ^{164}Dy
Reprinted from: *Atoms* **2022**, *10*, 57, doi:10.3390/atoms10020057 111

Elisa Romero Romero, Michael Block, Biswajit Jana, EunKang Kim, Steven Nothhelfer, Sebastian Raeder, et al.
A Progress Report on Laser Resonance Chromatography
Reprinted from: *Atoms* **2022**, *10*, 87, doi:10.3390/atoms10030087 123

Benedict Seiferle, Daniel Moritz, Kevin Scharl, Shiqian Ding, Florian Zacherl, Lilli Löbell and Peter G. Thirolf
Extending Our Knowledge about the ^{229}Th Nuclear Isomer
Reprinted from: *Atoms* **2022**, *10*, 24, doi:10.3390/atoms10010024 135

Jekabs Romans, Anjali Ajayakumar, Martial Authier, Frederic Boumard, Lucia Caceres, Jean-François Cam, et al.
First Offline Results from the S^3 Low-Energy Branch
Reprinted from: *Atoms* **2022**, *10*, 21, doi:10.3390/atoms10010021 . . . . **141**

Julia Even, Xiangcheng Chen, Arif Soylu, Paul Fischer, Alexander Karpov, Vyacheslav Saiko, et al.
The NEXT Project: Towards Production and Investigation of Neutron-Rich Heavy Nuclides
Reprinted from: *Atoms* **2022**, *10*, 59, doi:10.3390/atoms10020059 . . . . **157**

About the Editors

Mustapha Laatiaoui

Mustapha Laatiaoui (Dr.) is a research group leader at the Department of Chemistry, University of Mainz, in Germany. His research activities include the study of atomic and nuclear structures of the heaviest chemical elements and the investigation of their transport properties in dilute gases. In 2018, he received an ERC Consolidator Grant for the development of a novel technique of optical spectroscopy to study the electronic structure of elements beyond nobelium (element 102).

Sebastian Raeder

Sebastian Raeder (Dr.) is a senior scientist at the GSI Helmholtzzentrum für Schwerionenforschung GmbH in Darmstadt, Germany. Working at the velocity filter SHIP (Separator for Heavy Ion reaction Products), his research topics revolve around the study of nuclear and atomic properties of the heaviest chemical elements. A special focus within this broad field lies in laser spectroscopic investigations of heavy elements for fundamental nuclear physics, trace analysis and ion source applications.

Preface to "Atomic Structure of the Heaviest Elements"

Actinides exhibit a remarkable transition in terms of applied and fundamental research as they comprise the heaviest naturally occurring and fully manmade chemical elements. They have attracted the attention of atomic spectroscopists since their discovery, as it was believed that many of their elemental properties could be deduced from knowledge of their electron configuration. The tiny quantity of these elements did not prevent scientists from performing elaborate and extensive spectroscopy, such as with huge spectrographs. Thus, essential data about the atomic structure up to element 99—einsteinium—were obtained, even if some spectral lines could not be (or not correctly) assigned back then.

Today, we are much farther along in atomic spectroscopy, although actinides are far from being fully explored. In addition to better model descriptions of the atom, recent developments and advances in the field of optical spectroscopy have not only led to a better understanding of the atomic structure of the already measured elements but also to tackling the superheavy elements previously considered experimentally inaccessible.

This Special Issue of *Atoms* covers recent theoretical and experimental work about the atomic structure of actinides, as well as related topics, such as nuclear properties, transport properties in gases and the production and separation of radionuclides. With the advancing technology for production and handling of actinides and transactinides, we hope that this issue will serve as a useful resource for future work in the field of optical spectroscopy and accelerator-based laser ion sources.

Mustapha Laatiaoui and Sebastian Raeder
Editors

Article

New Developments in the Production and Research of Actinide Elements

Mustapha Laatiaoui [1,2,3,*] and Sebastian Raeder [2,3,*]

1. Department Chemie—Standort TRIGA, Johannes Gutenberg-Universität Mainz, 55099 Mainz, Germany
2. Helmholtz Institut Mainz, 55099 Mainz, Germany
3. GSI Helmholtzzentrum für Schwerionenforschung, 64291 Darmstadt, Germany
* Correspondence: laatiaoui@uni-mainz.de (M.L.); s.raeder@gsi.de (S.R.)

Abstract: This article briefly reviews topics related to actinide research discussed at the virtual workshop *Atomic Structure of Actinides & Related Topics* organized by the University of Mainz, the Helmholtz Institute Mainz, and the GSI Helmholtz Centre for Heavy Ion Research, Darmstadt, Germany, and held on the 26–28 May 2021. It includes references to recent theoretical and experimental work on atomic structure and related topics, such as element production, access to nuclear properties, trace analysis, and medical applications.

Keywords: atomic structure theory; optical spectroscopy; actinides and transactinides; atomic and nuclear properties; thorium-229; trace analysis

Citation: Laatiaoui, M.; Raeder, S. New Developments in the Production and Research of Actinide Elements. *Atoms* **2022**, *10*, 61. https://doi.org/10.3390/atoms10020061

Academic Editor: Alexander Kramida

Received: 30 April 2022
Accepted: 1 June 2022
Published: 8 June 2022

Publisher's Note: MDPI stays neutral with regard to jurisdictional claims in published maps and institutional affiliations.

Copyright: © 2022 by the authors. Licensee MDPI, Basel, Switzerland. This article is an open access article distributed under the terms and conditions of the Creative Commons Attribution (CC BY) license (https://creativecommons.org/licenses/by/4.0/).

1. Introduction

The actinides refer to the series of elements at the bottom of the periodic table, which includes elements from actinium (Ac, $Z = 89$) to lawrencium (Lr, $Z = 103$). Apart from the current controversy about their positioning in the periodic table and about the composition of "Group 3" [1,2], the research on actinides is experiencing an upsurge with the development of sensitive and sophisticated spectroscopic techniques and regularly attracts attention in the scientific media. It is a multidisciplinary research area par excellence, encompassing experimental and theoretical atomic and nuclear physics, nuclear chemistry, and quantum chemistry, with links to astrophysics, nuclear medicine, nuclear forensics, trace analysis, and so on. A virtual workshop entitled *Atomic Structure of Actinides & Related Topics* was held on the 26–28 May 2021 and brought together many experts in the abovementioned areas to present and discuss their recent findings and outlooks. To commemorate this successful event, we have included the logo of the workshop in this article; see Figure 1. This current issue of the MDPI journal *Atoms* includes some of these scientific contributions for the same reason and in the hope of serving as a useful resource for future studies of the atomic structure of the heaviest elements. In this article we provide a brief overview of the topics presented at the workshop, focusing on aspects of atomic structure, without claiming completeness. For the various areas covered here, other review articles are available, to which we refer in the appropriate places.

Figure 1. Logo of the virtual workshop on the *Atomic Structure of Actinides & Related Topics*, 26–28 May 2021.

2. Element Production

The lack of availability and the radioactive nature of most actinide elements render their experimental investigation challenging. The lighter actinides up to uranium (U, Z = 92) are still found in the earth's crust today because they are either primordial, i.e., they were produced before the formation of the solar system and are not yet fully decayed due to their long half-lives, as is the case for ^{232}Th ($T_{1/2} = 1.405 \times 10^{10}$ a), and ^{238}U ($T_{1/2} = 4.468 \times 10^9$ a), or because they are continuously produced from the decay of the primordial ones [3]. The heavier actinides up to fermium can be produced in high flux reactors by breeding lighter actinide elements in successive chains of neutron capture reactions with subsequent β^-decays. Due to competing fission processes and the still-limited neutron flux, the quantities produced in such nuclear reactors become smaller and smaller with increasing atomic number. Although milligram quantities can still be obtained for californium (Cf, Z = 98), only microgram or even nanogram amounts are available (at most) for einsteinium (Es, Z = 99) and fermium (Fm, Z = 100), respectively [4,5]. The breeding chain ends as soon as the short-lived fission isotopes of the latter element are reached.

To produce elements beyond fermium, nuclear reaction mechanisms such as fusion evaporation reactions induced by accelerated heavy ion beams are exploited instead [6,7]. Often projectile currents in the range of one particle µA from large accelerator facilities are used in conjunction with thin-target production techniques. In this way, the heaviest actinides from mendelevium to lawrencium can be produced at rates of a few atoms per second at most, whereas heavier elements up to oganesson can be produced at much lower rates.

With multi-nucleon-transfer reactions at energies close or slightly above the Coulomb barrier, one may target the production of more exotic and rather neutron-rich isotopes of the heavy elements [8] at existing facilities such as the KISS facility at RIKEN, Japan [9], and the IGISOL facility at JYFL in Jyväskylä, Finland [10], or at upcoming ones such as the $N = 126$-factory at ANL in Argonne, USA [11], and the NEXT project at the AGOR cyclotron facility in Groningen, Netherlands [7].

Far away from earth-based accelerators, different scenarios are conceivable as to how these elements could have been or are being produced in nature. Currently, neutron star mergers are considered to be the most promising candidates for the so-called rapid neutron capture process [3] for the production of such elements due to the enormous neutron fluxes involved. Detection would therefore require multimessenger astronomy and a detailed spectral analysis of the light coming from these distant sources. However, in order to interpret these processes in terms of element abundances and production yields through comparison with the latest astrophysical models, a profound knowledge of the spectral light emissions of the elements and thus their atomic structure is essential [12–15].

3. Atomic Structure Modeling

In the second half of the last century, many experimentalists and theorists devoted increasing attention to the study of the atomic structure of the actinides, which until then had been a poorly explored area. It has been recognized that relativistic effects play an important role in the theoretical description of these atomic species [16]. Therefore, relativistic modeling of such atoms is indispensable today. Nevertheless, their accurate description remains a challenge, especially because they exhibit an open $5f$ shell, which provides space for a large number of valence electrons and thus access to numerous low-lying electron configurations. A prominent example of an actinide with a complex atomic structure is protactinium (Pa, Z = 91), for which a detailed analysis of its atomic level density already indicates quantum chaos behavior, as reported in [17,18]. Therefore, constraints on modeling these atomic systems are often direct implications of the greatly increased configuration space [19–22].

Meanwhile, various numerical approaches, such as multi-configuration Hartree–Dirac Fock (MCDHF), Fock-space coupled-cluster (FSCC), and configuration-interaction (CI), are constantly being developed to provide reliable predictions for ever more complex systems [22–24]. Only recently has progress been made in the ab initio framework, such that the atomic properties and spectra of actinium (Ac, Z = 89) [25], fermium (Fm, Z = 100) [26], mendelevium (Md, Z = 101) [27], lawrencium (Lr, Z = 103) [28–30], rutherfordium (Rf, Z = 104) [31,32], and dubnium (Db, Z = 105) [33] can be calculated with a relatively high degree of reliability.

These calculations guide and complement experimental studies of the atomic structure of the heavy actinides, as was accomplished several years ago for fermium [34,35] and nobelium (No, Z = 102) [36–41], and also predict the behavior of known superheavy elements that remain long out of the reach of experimental investigation, as is the case with oganesson (Og, Z = 118) [42–44]. In the recent years they have helped in pinning down the first ionization potential of the heaviest actinides that were measured utilizing surface ionization techniques [45,46] and in unveiling extraordinary possibilities for the realization of optical clocks based on highly charged actinide ions [47,48].

4. Experiments Targeting the Atomic Structure

Across the actinides, a wealth of information on their atomic structures can be obtained from databases such as NIST, albeit mainly for the lighter representatives of this series [49,50]. As the atomic number increases, the scarcity of information becomes apparent, not least because experimental investigations become increasingly complex and often tedious due to decreasing sample quantities. The methods used are often adapted to the element production process and optimized for studies on that specific element, and would usually need to be further developed to achieve higher sensitivity to cover other exotic or heavier radionuclides. We limit ourselves here to a few examples; for a detailed overview of some of these developments, the reader is referred to [51] and the references therein.

One example of contemporary experimental investigations of the heaviest actinides is the RADRIS technique. It is based on laser resonance ionization in a gas cell and was developed for atomic level searches on the element nobelium. The technique enabled the experimental observation and characterization of an optical transition of this element for the first time [41], which subsequently paved the way to extract the first ionization potential with high precision [52]. The RADRIS technique is constantly being optimized, with the focus now on spectroscopy of the next heavy element, lawrencium—the last member of the actinide series [53].

Another example is the novel method of laser resonance chromatography. Researchers have recently been proposed to extend laser spectroscopy to lawrencium and the refractory metals of the superheavy elements, enabling both atomic-level searches and subsequent high-resolution spectroscopy [54,55]. The method exploits optical pumping to change the transport properties of an ion as it drifts in helium gas, allowing optical resonances to be identified based on drift times alone, without using resonance ionization or fluorescence detection. A corresponding experimental setup is currently under construction [56]. Closely related to this, and due to the fact that transport properties are sensitive to electronic configurations, efforts are currently being devoted to making ion mobility spectrometry one of the useful tools for isobaric purification in actinide research [57].

5. Nuclear Properties

Another pertinent topic in this regard is the fact that optical spectroscopy can bridge atomic and nuclear physics. Because the interaction of the central nucleus with the atomic shell leads to subtle but measurable differences in the atomic line spectrum, hyperfine spectroscopy can be used to study nuclear properties such as nuclear electric and magnetic moments and changes in the mean square charge radii [58,59]. The question of which atomic transitions are most suitable for hyperfine spectroscopy depends essentially on the requirement that the sensitivity of the experimental method should not be greatly deteriorated and on the precision with which one can determine the nuclear parameters. Again, calculations based on atomic theory are often required, since some nuclear properties cannot be measured absolutely and—due to the scarcity of information—comparisons with isotopes already studied via other methods are only possible in particular cases.

Such studies are of paramount importance in the field of heavy elements. The fact that the actinides span from the closed spherical neutron shell with neutron number $N = 126$ to the deformed shell closure at $N = 152$ makes them an ideal experimental field for the study of shell effects and nuclear deformation, which are essential for understanding nuclear stability in the presence of the extreme repulsive Coulomb forces between the numerous protons in the nucleus.

Spectroscopically, interest in the study of actinides has increased in recent years due to the increasing sensitivity and selectivity of the applied techniques. Long-lived plutonium (Pu, $Z = 94$) isotopes were studied via laser spectroscopy in an atomic beam through resonance ionization spectroscopy and in a fast ion beam through collinear fluorescence techniques with high spectral resolution [60], and also for production in a buffer gas cell [61]. Actinium (Ac, $Z = 89$) was investigated via in-gas-jet, in-gas-cell, and hot cavity laser spectroscopy [62–65], whereas the latter technique could only recently be applied to californium (Cf, $Z = 98$) [66] and einsteinium (Es, $Z = 99$) isotopes [67].

For the study of even heavier elements, one may emphasize two examples. The RADRIS technique enabled experimental studies of $^{252-254}$No-isotopes, which, using atomic theory, allowed, for instance, the extraction of the charge radii changes [68]. In addition to level searches on lawrencium, RADRIS experiments are continuing, targeting heavy actinides to reach more exotic radionuclides with half-lives ranging from below one second up to more than one hour [53], given that the atomic transitions are known.

The other example is the in-gas-jet laser spectroscopy. This technique exploits laser resonance ionization in a low-temperature and low-density environment of a collimated gas jet emerging from a buffer gas stopping cell to enable high spectral resolution and maintain a high sensitivity at the same time [65,69–71]. Setups using his technique are planned for the S^3 separator at GANIL, Caen [72–74]; the MARA separator at JYFL, Jyväskylä [75]; and at the SHIP separator at GSI, Darmstadt [76,77]. Since the extraction of sample radionuclides occurs relatively quickly, one may gain access to short-lived nuclear isomers such as the K-isomer of ^{254}No. With the development of the in-gas-jet technique, the required laser systems are being further developed [78–80] to accommodate the needs of high-resolution spectroscopy.

Other research in relation to heavy elements includes the study of higher-order deformations of nuclei [81] and studies of radioactive molecules [82], which are motivated by the search for new particle physics beyond the standard model.

For more details on laser spectroscopy, we refer the reader to recent reviews [58,59] in a broader context and to [51] in the context of actinide research.

6. The Thorium-229 Nuclear Isomer

Another topic of particular interest for fundamental research is the low-lying nuclear isomer of thorium-229, the existence of which was demonstrated experimentally a few years ago [83]. The isomeric state is only 8.28 eV [84,85] above the ground state of the nucleus and thus within the VUV range of optical probing. Due to this singular property, several applications regarding a nuclear clock based on optical transitions of this isomer have been proposed [86], although several open questions concerning this isotope are still being investigated [87,88].

In many experiments the isomer is produced in the α-decay branch of ^{233}U. A promising new approach is currently being pursued to prepare the isomer online at increased efficiency via the β^- decay of ^{229}Ac [89]. In all experiments, however, the most important and urgent goal today is to determine the excitation energy with an accuracy that should allow much more precise spectroscopic studies in the future [90]. Since the energy of the nuclear isomer is in the range of atomic binding energies, internal conversion can dominate radiative decay, especially in a neutral atomic state [91,92]. This, along with the need for laser cooling in future applications, brings 2+ and 3+ cations of this isotope more into focus in this research field [93,94].

7. Trace Analysis and Medical Applications

As radionuclides of trans-uranium elements are artificially produced in nuclear reactors, their elemental and isotopic abundance in test samples depends on the fuel material and the neutron flux initially used. Therefore, quantitative analysis of these telltale isotopic abundances can be exploited to identify radioactive material and to determine the history of the sample for nuclear forensics, safeguards, and proliferation [95,96]. Some trace analysis techniques rely on laser resonance ionization or light absorption and therefore also require a thorough knowledge of atomic structure. For resonance ionization spectroscopy (RIS) of actinides, the development of efficient excitation and ionization schemes is ongoing [97–100], and recent reports attest to advances in the use of spatially resolved secondary neutral mass spectrometry combined with RIS on sample atoms [96,101,102].

Another technical application for actinide research arises from developments in targeted alpha-therapy, in which the locally released energy in alpha decay has been used for the treatment of cancer cells. For this medical application, alpha emitters such as ^{225}Ac are being studied in detail, which in turn requires an understanding of atomic properties, production and purification, and the underlying chemical behavior for selective binding to cancer cells [103,104].

8. Summary

The actinides in general, and the heaviest of them in particular, are very limited in availability. Because of this limitation and the lack of applications for most of them, even their basic physical properties have been scarcely studied. The increasing interest in the above-mentioned research aspects related to the atomic structure of actinides and the availability of increasingly sensitive spectroscopy techniques has recently pushed actinide research forward. Experimental and theoretical groups are jointly working on gradually filling in gaps in our knowledge regarding the atomic and nuclear properties of these fascinating elements at the bottom of the periodic table, so more exciting results can be expected in the near future.

Author Contributions: All authors contributed equally to this work. All authors have read and agreed to the published version of the manuscript.

Funding: M.L. acknowledges funding from the European Research Council (ERC) under the European Union's Horizon 2020 Research and Innovation Programme (Grant Agreement No. 819957).

Institutional Review Board Statement: Not applicable.

Informed Consent Statement: Not applicable.

Data Availability Statement: The data presented in this study are available on request from the corresponding author.

Conflicts of Interest: The authors declare no conflict of interest.

References

1. Vernon, R.E. The location and composition of Group 3 of the periodic table. *Found. Chem.* **2021**, *23*, 155–197. [CrossRef]
2. de Bettencourt-Dias, A. The Periodic Table and the f Elements. In *Rare Earth Elements and Actinides: Progress in Computational Science Applications*; ACS Publications: Washington, DC, USA, 2021; pp. 55–61.
3. Cowan, J.J.; Sneden, C.; Lawler, J.E.; Aprahamian, A.; Wiescher, M.; Langanke, K.; Martínez-Pinedo, G.; Thielemann, F.K. Origin of the heaviest elements: The rapid neutron-capture process. *Rev. Mod. Phys.* **2021**, *93*, 015002. [CrossRef]
4. Roberto, J.B.; Rykaczewski, K.P. Actinide Targets for the Synthesis of Superheavy Nuclei: Current Priorities and Future Opportunities. In Proceedings of the Fission and Properties of Neutron-Rich Nuclei Sixth International Conference on ICFN6, Sanibel Island, FL, USA, 6–12 November 2016; World Scientific: Singapore, 2017. [CrossRef]
5. Robinson, S.M.; Benker, D.E.; Collins, E.D.; Ezold, J.G.; Garrison, J.R.; Hogle, S.L. Production of Cf-252 and other transplutonium isotopes at Oak Ridge National Laboratory. *Radiochim. Acta* **2020**, *108*, 737–746. [CrossRef]
6. Moody, K.J. Synthesis of Superheavy Elements. In *The Chemistry of Superheavy Elements*; Springer: Berlin/Heidelberg, Germany, 2013; pp. 1–81. [CrossRef]
7. Even, J.; Chen, X.; Soylu, A.; Fischer, P.; Karpov, A.; Saiko, V.; Saren, J.; Schlaich, M.; Schlathölter, T.; Schweikhard, L.; et al. The NEXT project: Towards production and investigation of neutron-rich heavy nuclides. *Atoms* **2022**, *10*, 59. [CrossRef]
8. Münzenberg, G.; Devaraja, H.M.; Dickel, T.; Geissel, H.; Gupta, M.; Heinz, S.; Hofmann, S.; Plass, W.R.; Scheidenberger, C.; Winfield, J.S.; et al. SHE Research with Rare-Isotope Beams, Challenges and Perspectives, and the New Generation of SHE Factories. In *New Horizons in Fundamental Physics*; Schramm, S., Schäfer, M., Eds.; Springer International Publishing: Cham, Switzerland, 2017; pp. 81–90. [CrossRef]
9. Miyatake, H. KISS project. *AIP Conf. Proc.* **2021**, *2319*, 080006. Available online: https://aip.scitation.org/doi/pdf/10.1063/5.0036990 (accessed on 5 February 2022). [CrossRef]
10. Dickel, T.; Kankainen, A.; Spătaru, A.; Amanbayev, D.; Beliuskina, O.; Beck, S.; Constantin, P.; Benyamin, D.; Geissel, H.; Gröf, L.; et al. Multi-nucleon transfer reactions at ion catcher facilities—A new way to produce and study heavy neutron-rich nuclei. *J. Phys. Conf. Ser.* **2020**, *1668*, 012012. [CrossRef]
11. Savard, G.; Brodeur, M.; Clark, J.; Knaack, R.; Valverde, A. The N = 126 factory: A new facility to produce very heavy neutron-rich isotopes. *Nucl. Instrum. Methods Phys. Res. Sect. B Beam Interact. Mater. Atoms* **2020**, *463*, 258–261. [CrossRef]
12. Smartt, S.J.; Chen, T.W.; Jerkstrand, A.; Coughlin, M.; Kankare, E.; Sim, S.A.; Fraser, M.; Inserra, C.; Maguire, K.; Chambers, K.C.; et al. A kilonova as the electromagnetic counterpart to a gravitational-wave source. *Nature* **2017**, *551*, 75–79. [CrossRef]
13. Fontes, C.J.; Fryer, C.L.; Hungerford, A.L.; Wollaeger, R.T.; Korobkin, O. A line-binned treatment of opacities for the spectra and light curves from neutron star mergers. *Mon. Not. R. Astron. Soc.* **2020**, *493*, 4143–4171. Available online: https://academic.oup.com/mnras/article-pdf/493/3/4143/32920641/staa485.pdf (accessed on 27 May 2022). [CrossRef]
14. Tanaka, M.; Kato, D.; Gaigalas, G.; Kawaguchi, K. Systematic opacity calculations for kilonovae. *Mon. Not. R. Astron. Soc.* **2020**, *496*, 1369–1392. Available online: https://academic.oup.com/mnras/article-pdf/496/2/1369/33424936/staa1576.pdf (accessed on 27 May 2022). [CrossRef]
15. Silva, R.F.; Sampaio, J.M.; Amaro, P.; Flörs, A.; Martínez-Pinedo, G.; Marques, J.P. Structure Calculations in Nd III and U III Relevant for Kilonovae Modelling. *Atoms* **2022**, *10*, 18. [CrossRef]
16. Pyykkö, P. The RTAM electronic bibliography, version 17.0, on relativistic theory of atoms and molecules. *J. Comput. Chem.* **2013**, *34*, 2667. [CrossRef] [PubMed]
17. Naubereit, P.; Studer, D.; Viatkina, A.V.; Buchleitner, A.; Dietz, B.; Flambaum, V.V.; Wendt, K. Intrinsic quantum chaos and spectral fluctuations within the protactinium atom. *Phys. Rev. A* **2018**, *98*, 022506. [CrossRef]
18. Naubereit, P.; Gottwald, T.; Studer, D.; Wendt, K. Excited atomic energy levels in protactinium by resonance ionization spectroscopy. *Phys. Rev. A* **2018**, *98*, 022505. [CrossRef]
19. Eliav, E.; Borschevsky, A.; Kaldor, U. Electronic Structure at the Edge of the Periodic Table. *Nucl. Phys. News* **2019**, *29*, 16–20. [CrossRef]
20. Fritzsche, S. Symbolic Evaluation of Expressions from Racah's Algebra. *Symmetry* **2021**, *13*, 1558. [CrossRef]
21. Safronova, M.S.; Safronova, U.I.; Kozlov, M.G. Atomic properties of actinide ions with particle-hole configurations. *Phys. Rev. A* **2018**, *97*, 012511. [CrossRef]
22. Fritzsche, S. Level Structure and Properties of Open f-Shell Elements. *Atoms* **2022**, *10*, 7. [CrossRef]
23. Dzuba, V. Calculation of Polarizabilities for Atoms with Open Shells. *Symmetry* **2020**, *12*, 1950. [CrossRef]
24. Kahl, E.; Berengut, J. Ambit: A programme for high-precision relativistic atomic structure calculations. *Comput. Phys. Commun.* **2019**, *238*, 232–243. [CrossRef]
25. Dzuba, V.A.; Flambaum, V.V.; Roberts, B.M. Calculations of the atomic structure for the low-lying states of actinium. *Phys. Rev. A* **2019**, *100*, 022504. [CrossRef]
26. Allehabi, S.O.; Li, J.; Dzuba, V.; Flambaum, V. Theoretical study of electronic structure of erbium and fermium. *J. Quant. Spectrosc. Radiat. Transf.* **2020**, *253*, 107137. [CrossRef]
27. Li, J.; Dzuba, V. Theoretical study of the spectroscopic properties of mendelevium (Z = 101). *J. Quant. Spectrosc. Radiat. Transf.* **2020**, *247*, 106943. [CrossRef]
28. Kahl, E.V.; Berengut, J.C.; Laatiaoui, M.; Eliav, E.; Borschevsky, A. High-precision ab initio calculations of the spectrum of Lr^+. *Phys. Rev. A* **2019**, *100*, 062505. [CrossRef]

29. Kahl, E.V.; Raeder, S.; Eliav, E.; Borschevsky, A.; Berengut, J.C. Ab initio calculations of the spectrum of lawrencium. *Phys. Rev. A* **2021**, *104*, 052810. [CrossRef]
30. Ramanantoanina, H.; Borschevsky, A.; Block, M.; Laatiaoui, M. Electronic structure of Lr$^+$ (Z = 103) from *ab initio* calculations. *Atoms* **2022**, *10*, 48. [CrossRef]
31. Ramanantoanina, H.; Borschevsky, A.; Block, M.; Laatiaoui, M. Electronic structure of Rf$^+$ (Z = 104) from ab initio calculations. *Phys. Rev. A* **2021**, *104*, 022813. [CrossRef]
32. Allehabi, S.O.; Dzuba, V.A.; Flambaum, V.V. Theoretical study of the electronic structure of hafnium (Hf,Z = 72) and rutherfordium (Rf,Z = 104) atoms and their ions: Energy levels and hyperfine-structure constants. *Phys. Rev. A* **2021**, *104*, 052811. [CrossRef]
33. Lackenby, B.G.C.; Dzuba, V.A.; Flambaum, V.V. Calculation of atomic spectra and transition amplitudes for the superheavy element Db (Z = 105). *Phys. Rev. A* **2018**, *98*, 022518. [CrossRef]
34. Sewtz, M.; Backe, H.; Dretzke, A.; Kube, G.; Lauth, W.; Schwamb, P.; Eberhardt, K.; Grüning, C.; Thörle, P.; Trautmann, N.; et al. First Observation of Atomic Levels for the Element Fermium (Z = 100). *Phys. Rev. Lett.* **2003**, *90*, 163002. [CrossRef]
35. Backe, H.; Dretzke, A.; Fritzsche, S.; Haire, R.G.; Kunz, P.; Lauth, W.; Sewtz, M.; Trautmann, N. Laser Spectroscopic Investigation of the Element Fermium (Z = 100). *Hyperfine Interact.* **2005**, *162*, 3–14. [CrossRef]
36. Fritzsche, S. On the accuracy of valence–shell computations for heavy and super–heavy elements. *Eur. Phys. J. D* **2005**, *33*, 15–21. [CrossRef]
37. Borschevsky, A.; Eliav, E.; Vilkas, M.J.; Ishikawa, Y.; Kaldor, U. Predicted spectrum of atomic nobelium. *Phys. Rev. A* **2007**, *75*, 042514. [CrossRef]
38. Indelicato, P.; Santos, J.P.; Boucard, S.; Desclaux, J.P. QED and relativistic corrections in superheavy elements. *Eur. Phys. J. D* **2007**, *45*, 155–170. [CrossRef]
39. Liu, Y.; Hutton, R.; Zou, Y. Atomic structure of the super-heavy element No I (Z = 102). *Phys. Rev. A* **2007**, *76*, 062503. [CrossRef]
40. Dzuba, V.A.; Safronova, M.S.; Safronova, U.I. Atomic properties of superheavy elements No, Lr, and Rf. *Phys. Rev. A* **2014**, *90*, 012504. [CrossRef]
41. Laatiaoui, M.; Lauth, W.; Backe, H.; Block, M.; Ackermann, D.; Cheal, B.; Chhetri, P.; Düllmann, C.E.; van Duppen, P.; Even, J.; et al. Atom-at-a-time laser resonance ionization spectroscopy of nobelium. *Nature* **2016**, *538*, 495–498. [CrossRef]
42. Lackenby, B.G.C.; Dzuba, V.A.; Flambaum, V.V. Atomic structure calculations of superheavy noble element oganesson (Z = 118). *Phys. Rev. A* **2018**, *98*, 042512. [CrossRef]
43. Guo, Y.; Pašteka, L.F.; Eliav, E.; Borschevsky, A. Ionization potentials and electron affinity of oganesson with relativistic coupled cluster method. In *New Electron Correlation Methods and Their Applications, and Use of Atomic Orbitals with Exponential Asymptotes*; Elsevier: Amsterdam, The Netherlands, 2021; pp. 107–123. [CrossRef]
44. Smits, O.R.; Mewes, J.M.; Jerabek, P.; Schwerdtfeger, P. Oganesson: A Noble Gas Element That Is Neither Noble Nor a Gas. *Angew. Chem. Int. Ed.* **2020**, *59*, 23636–23640. [CrossRef]
45. Sato, T.; Asai, M.; Borschevsky, A.; Stora, T.; Sato, N.; Kaneya, Y.; Tsukada, K.; Düllmann, C.E.; Eberhardt, K.; Eliav, E.; et al. Measurement of the first ionization potential of lawrencium, element 103. *Nature* **2015**, *520*, 209–211. [CrossRef]
46. Sato, T.K.; Asai, M.; Borschevsky, A.; Beerwerth, R.; Kaneya, Y.; Makii, H.; Mitsukai, A.; Nagame, Y.; Osa, A.; Toyoshima, A.; et al. First ionization potentials of Fm, Md, No, and Lr: Verification of filling-up of 5f electrons and confirmation of the actinide series. *J. Am. Chem. Soc.* **2018**, *140*, 14609–14613. [CrossRef] [PubMed]
47. Kozlov, M.; Safronova, M.; López-Urrutia, J.C.; Schmidt, P. Highly charged ions: Optical clocks and applications in fundamental physics. *Rev. Mod. Phys.* **2018**, *90*, 045005. [CrossRef]
48. Porsev, S.G.; Safronova, U.I.; Safronova, M.S.; Schmidt, P.O.; Bondarev, A.I.; Kozlov, M.G.; Tupitsyn, I.I.; Cheung, C. Optical clocks based on the Cf^{15+} and Cf^{17+} ions. *Phys. Rev. A* **2020**, *102*, 012802. [CrossRef]
49. Kramida, A.; Ralchenko, Y.; Reader, J.; NIST ASD Team. *NIST Atomic Spectra Database (Ver. 5.9)*; National Institute of Standards and Technology: Gaithersburg, MD, USA, 2021. Available online: https://physics.nist.gov/asd (accessed on 26 April 2022).
50. Kramida, A. Update of Atomic Data for the First Three Spectra of Actinium. *Atoms* **2022**, *10*, 42. [CrossRef]
51. Block, M.; Laatiaoui, M.; Raeder, S. Recent progress in laser spectroscopy of the actinides. *Prog. Part. Nucl. Phys.* **2021**, *116*, 103834. [CrossRef]
52. Chhetri, P.; Ackermann, D.; Backe, H.; Block, M.; Cheal, B.; Droese, C.; Düllmann, C.E.; Even, J.; Ferrer, R.; Giacoppo, F.; et al. Precision Measurement of the First Ionization Potential of Nobelium. *Phys. Rev. Lett.* **2018**, *120*, 263003. [CrossRef]
53. Warbinek, J.; Andelic, B.; Block, M.; Chhetri, P.; Claessens, A.; Ferrer, R.; Giacoppo, F.; Kaleja, O.; Kieck, T.; Kim, E.; et al. Advancing Radiation-Detected Resonance Ionization towards Heavier Elements and More Exotic Nuclides. *Atoms* **2022**, *10*, 41. [CrossRef]
54. Laatiaoui, M.; Buchachenko, A.A.; Viehland, L.A. Laser Resonance Chromatography of Superheavy Elements. *Phys. Rev. Lett.* **2020**, *125*, 023002. [CrossRef]
55. Laatiaoui, M.; Buchachenko, A.A.; Viehland, L.A. Exploiting transport properties for the detection of optical pumping in heavy ions. *Phys. Rev. A* **2020**, *102*, 013106. [CrossRef]
56. Romero-Romero, E.; Block, M.; Kim, E.; Nothhelfer, S.; Raeder, S.; Ramanantoanina, H.; Rickert, E.; Schneider, J.; Sikora, P.; Laatiaoui, M. A progress report on Laser Resonance Chromatography. *Atoms* 2022. manuscript in preparation
57. Rickert, E.; Backe, H.; Block, M.; Laatiaoui, M.; Lauth, W.; Raeder, S.; Schneider, J.; Schneider, F. Ion Mobilities for Heaviest Element Identification. *Hyperfine Interact.* **2020**, *241*, 49. [CrossRef]

58. Cheal, B.; Flanagan, K.T. Progress in laser spectroscopy at radioactive ion beam facilities. *J. Phys. G Nucl. Part. Phys.* **2010**, *37*, 113101. [CrossRef]
59. Campbell, P.; Moore, I.; Pearson, M. Laser spectroscopy for nuclear structure physics. *Prog. Part. Nucl. Phys.* **2016**, *86*, 127–180. [CrossRef]
60. Voss, A.; Sonnenschein, V.; Campbell, P.; Cheal, B.; Kron, T.; Moore, I.D.; Pohjalainen, I.; Raeder, S.; Trautmann, N.; Wendt, K. High-resolution laser spectroscopy of long-lived plutonium isotopes. *Phys. Rev. A* **2017**, *95*, 032506. [CrossRef]
61. Raggio, A.; Pohjalainen, I.; Moore, I.D. Observation of Collisional De-Excitation Phenomena in Plutonium. *Atoms* **2022**, *10*, 40. [CrossRef]
62. Zhang, K.; Studer, D.; Weber, F.; Gadelshin, V.M.; Kneip, N.; Raeder, S.; Budker, D.; Wendt, K.; Kieck, T.; Porsev, S.G.; et al. Detection of the Lowest-Lying Odd-Parity Atomic Levels in Actinium. *Phys. Rev. Lett.* **2020**, *125*, 073001. [CrossRef]
63. Verstraelen, E.; Teigelhöfer, A.; Ryssens, W.; Ames, F.; Barzakh, A.; Bender, M.; Ferrer, R.; Goriely, S.; Heenen, P.H.; Huyse, M.; et al. Search for octupole-deformed actinium isotopes using resonance ionization spectroscopy. *Phys. Rev. C* **2019**, *100*, 044321. [CrossRef]
64. Ferrer, R.; Barzakh, A.; Bastin, B.; Beerwerth, R.; Block, M.; Creemers, P.; Grawe, H.; de Groote, R.; Delahaye, P.; Fléchard, X.; et al. Towards high-resolution laser ionization spectroscopy of the heaviest elements in supersonic gas jet expansion. *Nat. Commun.* **2017**, *8*, 14520. [CrossRef]
65. Granados, C.; Creemers, P.; Ferrer, R.; Gaffney, L.P.; Gins, W.; de Groote, R.; Huyse, M.; Kudryavtsev, Y.; Martínez, Y.; Raeder, S.; et al. In-gas laser ionization and spectroscopy of actinium isotopes near the N = 126 closed shell. *Phys. Rev. C* **2017**, *96*, 054331. [CrossRef]
66. Weber, F.; Düllmann, C.E.; Gadelshin, V.; Kneip, N.; Oberstedt, S.; Raeder, S.; Runke, J.; Mokry, C.; Thörle-Pospiech, P.; Studer, D.; et al. Probing the Atomic Structure of Californium by Resonance Ionization Spectroscopy. *Atoms* **2022**, *10*, 51. [CrossRef]
67. Nothhelfer, S.; Albrecht-Schönzart, T.E.; Block, M.; Chhetri, P.; Düllmann, C.E.; Ezold, J.G.; Gadelshin, V.; Gaiser, A.; Giacoppo, F.; Heinke, R.; et al. Nuclear structure investigations of Es253-255 by laser spectroscopy. *Phys. Rev. C* **2022**, *105*, L021302. [CrossRef]
68. Raeder, S.; Ackermann, D.; Backe, H.; Beerwerth, R.; Berengut, J.; Block, M.; Borschevsky, A.; Cheal, B.; Chhetri, P.; Düllmann, C.E.; et al. Probing Sizes and Shapes of Nobelium Isotopes by Laser Spectroscopy. *Phys. Rev. Lett.* **2018**, *120*, 232503. [CrossRef]
69. Kudryavtsev, Y.; Ferrer, R.; Huyse, M.; den Bergh, P.V.; Duppen, P.V. The in-gas-jet laser ion source: Resonance ionization spectroscopy of radioactive atoms in supersonic gas jets. *Nucl. Instrum. Methods Phys. Res. Sect. B Beam Interact. Mater. Atoms* **2013**, *297*, 7–22. [CrossRef]
70. Zadvornaya, A.; Creemers, P.; Dockx, K.; Ferrer, R.; Gaffney, L.; Gins, W.; Granados, C.; Huyse, M.; Kudryavtsev, Y.; Laatiaoui, M.; et al. Characterization of Supersonic Gas Jets for High-Resolution Laser Ionization Spectroscopy of Heavy Elements. *Phys. Rev. X* **2018**, *8*, 041008. [CrossRef]
71. Ferrer, R.; Verlinde, M.; Verstraelen, E.; Claessens, A.; Huyse, M.; Kraemer, S.; Kudryavtsev, Y.; Romans, J.; den Bergh, P.V.; Duppen, P.V.; et al. Hypersonic nozzle for laser-spectroscopy studies at 17 K characterized by resonance-ionization-spectroscopy-based flow mapping. *Phys. Rev. Res.* **2021**, *3*, 043041. [CrossRef]
72. Piot, J. Studying Nuclear Structure at the extremes with S3. *EPJ Web Conf.* **2018**, *178*, 02027. [CrossRef]
73. Ferrer, R.; Bastin, B.; Boilley, D.; Creemers, P.; Delahaye, P.; Liénard, E.; Fléchard, X.; Franchoo, S.; Ghys, L.; Huyse, M.; et al. In gas laser ionization and spectroscopy experiments at the Superconducting Separator Spectrometer (S3): Conceptual studies and preliminary design. *Nucl. Instrum. Methods Phys. Res. Sect. B Beam Interact. Mater. Atoms* **2013**, *317*, 570–581. [CrossRef]
74. Romans, J.; Ajayakumar, A.; Authier, M.; Boumard, F.; Caceres, L.; Cam, J.F.; Claessens, A.; Damoy, S.; Delahaye, P.; Desrues, P.; et al. First Offline Results from the S3 Low-Energy Branch. *Atoms* **2022**, *10*, 21. [CrossRef]
75. Papadakis, P.; Liimatainen, J.; Sarén, J.; Moore, I.; Eronen, T.; Partanen, J.; Pohjalainen, I.; Rinta-Antila, S.; Tuunanen, J.; Uusitalo, J. The MARA-LEB ion transport system. *Nucl. Instrum. Methods Phys. Res. Sect. B Beam Interact. Mater. Atoms* **2020**, *463*, 286–289. [CrossRef]
76. Raeder, S.; Block, M.; Chhetri, P.; Ferrer, R.; Kraemer, S.; Kron, T.; Laatiaoui, M.; Nothhelfer, S.; Schneider, F.; Duppen, P.V.; et al. A gas-jet apparatus for high-resolution laser spectroscopy on the heaviest elements at SHIP. *Nucl. Instrum. Methods Phys. Res. Sect. B Beam Interact. Mater. Atoms* **2020**, *463*, 272–276. [CrossRef]
77. Münzberg, D.; Block, M.; Claessens, A.; Ferrer, R.; Laatiaoui, M.; Lantis, J.; Nothhelfer, S.; Raeder, S.; Van Duppen, P. Resolution characterizations of JetRIS in Mainz using 164Dy. *Atoms* **2022**, *10*, 57. [CrossRef]
78. Verlinde, M.; Ferrer, R.; Claessens, A.; Granados, C.A.; Kraemer, S.; Kudryavtsev, Y.; Li, D.; den Bergh, P.V.; Duppen, P.V.; Verstraelen, E. Single-longitudinal-mode pumped pulsed-dye amplifier for high-resolution laser spectroscopy. *Rev. Sci. Instrum.* **2020**, *91*, 103002. [CrossRef] [PubMed]
79. Raeder, S.; Ferrer, R.; Granados, C.; Huyse, M.; Kron, T.; Kudryavtsev, Y.; Lecesne, N.; Piot, J.; Romans, J.; Savajols, H.; et al. Performance of Dye and Ti:sapphire laser systems for laser ionization and spectroscopy studies at S3. *Nucl. Instrum. Phys. Res. Sect. B Beam Interact. Mater. Atoms* **2020**, *463*, 86–95. [CrossRef]
80. Sonnenschein, V.; Ohashi, M.; Tomita, H.; Iguchi, T. A direct diode pumped continuous-wave Ti:sapphire laser as seed of a pulsed amplifier for high-resolution resonance ionization spectroscopy. *Nucl. Instrum. Methods Phys. Res. Sect. B Beam Interact. Mater. Atoms* **2020**, *463*, 512–514. [CrossRef]

81. Dobaczewski, J.; Engel, J.; Kortelainen, M.; Becker, P. Correlating Schiff Moments in the Light Actinides with Octupole Moments. *Phys. Rev. Lett.* **2018**, *121*, 232501. [CrossRef]
82. Ruiz, R.F.G.; Berger, R.; Billowes, J.; Binnersley, C.L.; Bissell, M.L.; Breier, A.A.; Brinson, A.J.; Chrysalidis, K.; Cocolios, T.E.; Cooper, B.S.; et al. Spectroscopy of short-lived radioactive molecules. *Nature* **2020**, *581*, 396–400. [CrossRef]
83. von der Wense, L.; Seiferle, B.; Laatiaoui, M.; Neumayr, J.B.; Maier, H.J.; Wirth, H.F.; Mokry, C.; Runke, J.; Eberhardt, K.; Düllmann, C.E.; et al. Direct detection of the 229Th nuclear clock transition. *Nature* **2016**, *533*, 47–51. [CrossRef]
84. Seiferle, B.; von der Wense, L.; Bilous, P.V.; Amersdorffer, I.; Lemell, C.; Libisch, F.; Stellmer, S.; Schumm, T.; Düllmann, C.E.; Pálffy, A.; et al. Energy of the 229Th nuclear clock transition. *Nature* **2019**, *573*, 243–246. [CrossRef]
85. Sikorsky, T.; Geist, J.; Hengstler, D.; Kempf, S.; Gastaldo, L.; Enss, C.; Mokry, C.; Runke, J.; Düllmann, C.E.; Wobrauschek, P.; et al. Measurement of the Th229 Isomer Energy with a Magnetic Microcalorimeter. *Phys. Rev. Lett.* **2020**, *125*, 142503. [CrossRef]
86. Peik, E.; Schumm, T.; Safronova, M.S.; Pálffy, A.; Weitenberg, J.; Thirolf, P.G. Nuclear clocks for testing fundamental physics. *Quantum Sci. Technol.* **2021**, *6*, 034002. [CrossRef]
87. Thirolf, P.G.; Seiferle, B.; Wense, L.V. The Thorium-Isomer: Heartbeat for a Nuclear Clock. *Nucl. Phys. News* **2021**, *31*, 13–18. [CrossRef]
88. Beeks, K.; Sikorsky, T.; Schumm, T.; Thielking, J.; Okhapkin, M.V.; Peik, E. The thorium-229 low-energy isomer and the nuclear clock. *Nat. Rev. Phys.* **2021**, *3*, 238–248. [CrossRef]
89. Verlinde, M.; Kraemer, S.; Moens, J.; Chrysalidis, K.; Correia, J.G.; Cottenier, S.; Witte, H.D.; Fedorov, D.V.; Fedosseev, V.N.; Ferrer, R.; et al. Alternative approach to populate and study the Th229 nuclear clock isomer. *Phys. Rev. C* **2019**, *100*, 024315. [CrossRef]
90. Seiferle, B.; Moritz, D.; Scharl, K.; Ding, S.; Zacherl, F.; Löbell, L.; Thirolf, P.G. Extending Our Knowledge about the 229Th Nuclear Isomer. *Atoms* **2022**, *10*, 24. [CrossRef]
91. Seiferle, B.; von der Wense, L.; Thirolf, P.G. Lifetime Measurement of the Th229 nuclear isomer. *Phys. Rev. Lett.* **2017**, *118*, 042501. [CrossRef] [PubMed]
92. Tkalya, E.V.; Si, R. Internal conversion of the low-energy Th229m isomer in the thorium anion. *Phys. Rev. C* **2020**, *101*, 054602. [CrossRef]
93. Campbell, C.J.; Radnaev, A.G.; Kuzmich, A. Wigner Crystals of ^{229}Th for Optical Excitation of the Nuclear Isomer. *Phys. Rev. Lett.* **2011**, *106*, 223001. [CrossRef] [PubMed]
94. Thielking, J.; Okhapkin, M.V.; Głowacki, P.; Meier, D.M.; von der Wense, L.; Seiferle, B.; Düllmann, C.E.; Thirolf, P.G.; Peik, E. Laser spectroscopic characterization of the nuclear-clock isomer 229mTh. *Nature* **2018**, *556*, 321–325. [CrossRef]
95. Hotchkis, M.; Child, D.; Zorko, B. Actinides AMS for nuclear safeguards and related applications. *Nucl. Instrum. Methods Phys. Res. Sect. B Beam Interact. Mater. Atoms* **2010**, *268*, 1257–1260. [CrossRef]
96. Bosco, H.; Hamann, L.; Kneip, N.; Raiwa, M.; Weiss, M.; Wendt, K.; Walther, C. New horizons in microparticle forensics: Actinide imaging and detection of 238 Pu and 242m Am in hot particles. *Sci. Adv.* **2021**, *7*, 44. [CrossRef]
97. Kneip, N.; Düllmann, C.E.; Gadelshin, V.; Heinke, R.; Mokry, C.; Raeder, S.; Runke, J.; Studer, D.; Trautmann, N.; Weber, F.; et al. Highly selective two-step laser ionization schemes for the analysis of actinide mixtures. *Hyperfine Interact.* **2020**, *241*, 45. [CrossRef]
98. Raeder, S.; Kneip, N.; Reich, T.; Studer, D.; Trautmann, N.; Wendt, K. Recent developments in resonance ionization mass spectrometry for ultra-trace analysis of actinide elements. *Radiochim. Acta* **2019**, *107*, 645–652. [CrossRef]
99. Liu, Y.; Stracener, D. High efficiency resonance ionization of thorium. *Nucl. Instrum. Methods Phys. Res. Sect. B Beam Interact. Mater. Atoms* **2020**, *462*, 95–101. [CrossRef]
100. Galindo-Uribarri, A.; Liu, Y.; Romero, E.R.; Stracener, D.W. High efficiency laser resonance ionization of plutonium. *Sci. Rep.* **2021**, *11*, 23432. [CrossRef]
101. Schönenbach, D.; Berg, F.; Breckheimer, M.; Hagenlocher, D.; Schönberg, P.; Haas, R.; Amayri, S.; Reich, T. Development, characterization, and first application of a resonant laser secondary neutral mass spectrometry setup for the research of plutonium in the context of long-term nuclear waste storage. *Anal. Bioanal. Chem.* **2021**, *413*, 3987–3997. [CrossRef]
102. Savina, M.R.; Isselhardt, B.H.; Trappitsch, R. Simultaneous Isotopic Analysis of U, Pu, and Am in Spent Nuclear Fuel by Resonance Ionization Mass Spectrometry. *Anal. Chem.* **2021**, *93*, 9505–9512. [CrossRef]
103. Dockx, K.; Cocolios, T.E.; Stora, T. ISOL Technique for the Production of 225Ac at CERN-MEDICIS. *J. Med Imaging Radiat. Sci.* **2019**, *50*, S92. [CrossRef]
104. Duchemin, C.; Ramos, J.P.; Stora, T.; Ahmed, E.; Aubert, E.; Audouin, N.; Barbero, E.; Barozier, V.; Bernardes, A.P.; Bertreix, P.; et al. CERN-MEDICIS: A Review Since Commissioning in 2017. *Front. Med.* **2021**, *8*. [CrossRef]

Article

Level Structure and Properties of Open f-Shell Elements

Stephan Fritzsche [1,2,3]

1. Helmholtz-Institut Jena, Fröbelstieg 3, D-07743 Jena, Germany; s.fritzsche@gsi.de
2. GSI Helmholtzzentrum für Schwerionenforschung, D-64291 Darmstadt, Germany
3. Theoretisch-Physikalisches Institut, Friedrich-Schiller-Universität Jena, D-07743 Jena, Germany

Abstract: Open f-shell elements still constitute a great challenge for atomic theory owing to their (very) rich fine-structure and strong correlations among the valence-shell electrons. For these medium and heavy elements, many atomic properties are sensitive to the correlated motion of electrons and, hence, require large-scale computations in order to deal consistently with all relativistic, correlation and rearrangement contributions to the electron density. Often, different concepts and notations need to be combined for just classifying the low-lying level structure of these elements. With JAC, the Jena Atomic Calculator, we here provide a toolbox that helps to explore and deal with such elements with open d- and f-shell structures. Based on Dirac's equation, JAC is suitable for almost all atoms and ions across the periodic table. As an example, we demonstrate how reasonably accurate computations can be performed for the low-lying level structure, transition probabilities and lifetimes for Th^{2+} ions with a $5f6d$ ground configuration. Other, and more complex, shell structures are supported as well, though often for a trade-off between the size and accuracy of the computations. Owing to its simple use, however, JAC supports both quick estimates and detailed case studies on open d- or f-shell elements.

Keywords: atomic structure; level and excitation energies; hyperfine splitting; isotope-shift; Jena Atomic Calculator; LSJ level notation; open d- and f-shell ion; relativistic; transition probability

---

Citation: Fritzsche, S. Level Structure and Properties of Open f-Shell Elements. *Atoms* 2022, 10, 7. https://doi.org/10.3390/atoms10010007

Academic Editors: Mustapha Laatiaoui and Sebastian Raeder

Received: 25 November 2021
Accepted: 1 January 2022
Published: 12 January 2022

Publisher's Note: MDPI stays neutral with regard to jurisdictional claims in published maps and institutional affiliations.

Copyright: © 2022 by the authors. Licensee MDPI, Basel, Switzerland. This article is an open access article distributed under the terms and conditions of the Creative Commons Attribution (CC BY) license (https://creativecommons.org/licenses/by/4.0/).

1. Demands of Open f-Shell Elements

The difficulties in calculating open f-shell elements have long been underrated in atomic theory. Apart from (i) strong relativistic and quantum-electrodynamical (QED) contributions to the level structure in all medium and heavy elements [1,2], difficulties arise especially from (ii) the nearly-degenerate and overlapping configurations, beside the spectroscopic nominated one, as well as (iii) the large *number* of electrons. All these difficulties have to be taken into account in *ab-initio* computations for explaining the low-lying levels of such elements. Therefore, the excitation energies and properties of open f-shell elements are not (yet) well understood, even if quite large computations have become feasible today. Figure 1 shows a simple man's view upon the fine-structure of open-shell elements with its overlapping configurations and strong relativistic contributions [3]. In particular, the actinides are known to exhibit very complex spectra owing to the presence of the open $5f$, $6d$, $7s$ and $7p$ shells whose fine-structure can be resolved only by high-resolution laboratory studies [4–6].

Laser spectroscopy on the (near) optical spectra of actinides has lead to renewed interest in the $4f$ and $5f$ elements. Especially, the resonance ionization spectroscopy (RIS) helped greatly improve the knowledge of the low-lying levels and absorption spectra of these heavy elements and to establish highly selective two-step laser excitation schemes [7–9]. For example, Chhetri and coworkers [10] applied laser spectroscopy on an *atom-at-a-time* scale in order to probe the optical spectrum of neutral nobelium with a $5f^{14}7s^2$ ground configuration near to its ionization threshold. Indeed, these and similar measurements [11–13] paved the way for high-precision spectroscopy of the atomic properties of heavy elements and also provide benchmarks for atomic computations, which include many-body, relativistic and QED contributions at an equal footing.

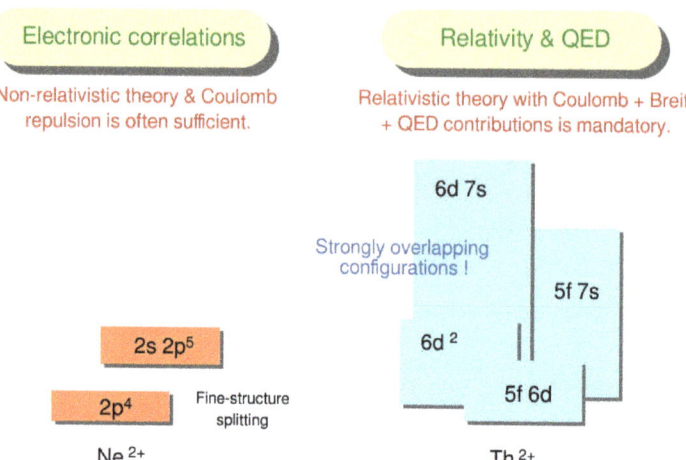

Figure 1. A simple man's view of the fine-structure of open-shell atoms and ions. For light elements, such as Ne^{2+} with a $2p^4$ ground configuration, the excitation of a valence-shell electron leads to levels that are energetically well separated, and whose configurations can be treated rather independently. For open d- and f-shell elements, in contrast, many configurations overlap with each other, and this even applies for the ground configuration. While the $2p^4$ fine-structure of Ne^{2+} is well separated by ~200,000 cm^{-1} from the $2s\,2p^5$ configuration, the $5f\,6d$ ground configuration of Th^{2+} 'overlaps' with the fine-structure levels of several and both, odd- and even-parity configurations. For any detailed *ab-initio* calculations, therefore, electronic correlations as well as relativistic and QED contributions need always to be taken into account for a quite large number of configurations.

While laser spectroscopy offers great precision ~μ eV, it usually requires prior knowledge about the level structure and the *allowed* transitions among the low-lying levels [14]. Until the present, most of these theoretical estimates are typically based on the configuration interaction (CI) or multiconfiguration Hartree-Dirac-Fock (MCDHF) methods, and which help incorporate all major contributions into the electronic structure calculations. When compared with the techniques from (relativistic) many-body perturbation theory (MBPT) [15,16] or coupled-cluster (CC) theory [17], these multi-configurational expansions are conceptional much simpler, especially if electrons occur in—either one or even several—open shells [18]. Successful multi-configuration calculations have been performed for selected low-lying levels of atomic fermium (Z = 100, [14,19]), nobelium [20], lawrencium [21,22] and copernicium [23], aside of a good number of much simpler calculations in the 1980s and 1990s [24–26]. For example, neutral fermium has a $5f^{12}7s^2\ ^3H_6$ ground-state and, because of the open f-shell, already a quite detailed fine-structure for just this single configuration. For similar elements with just one or two electrons (or holes) outside of closed shells, more advanced computations have been performed recently also in the framework of relativistic MBPT [27], its combination with fast CI methods [28] as well as by applying the relativistic Fock-space [29] or CC theory [30], to name just a few.

Beyond the level energies, the MCDHF method has been found versatile for dealing also with a rather wide range of atomic processes [18,31,32]. Despite of the frequent application of lanthanides and actinides in photonics, lighting industry or medical research, however, only a few limited tools are available to estimate or calculate the level structure and properties of these elements to good order. For the lanthanides, moreover, radiative transitions were observed in different solutions and doped crystals [33,34], and their emission spectra likely play a relevant role also for developing the next generation light sources for EUV lithography [35].

To fill the gap in dealing with open d- and f-shell elements, we recently developed JAC, the Jena Atomic Calculator [36], which help calculate the level structure and properties as well as a good number of excitation and decay processes for open-shell atoms and ions across the periodic table. This code aims to establish a general and easy-to-use toolbox for the atomic physics community. Below, we shall demonstrate how JAC can be applied to perform both, quick estimations as well as elaborate computations on the representation and properties of these elements. Indeed, a toolbox like JAC need to be developed (further) before the properties of open d- and f-shell elements can be studied with an accuracy comparable to that of simpler shell structures.

To set the background for these tools, the next section first provides a brief account on the theory of the MCDHF method with focus upon the d- and f-shell elements. Apart from the Hamiltonian and wave function expansion, this includes a short overview of JAC and its domain-specific language, the transformation of atomic levels into a LSJ coupling scheme as well as the computation of atomic level properties and processes. As an example, we then calculate in Section 3 the low-lying level structure, transition probabilities and lifetimes of Th^{2+} as widely discussed for developing a nuclear clock; for instance, see Ref. [37]. A few conclusions are finally given in Section 4.

2. Theory and Computations

2.1. Approximate Level Energies and Atomic State Functions

For open d- and f-shell elements, even the levels of the ground configuration can often not be described without that further configurations, nearby in their mean energy, are explicitly included into the representation of the approximate atomic states functions (ASF). In the MCDHF method, these ASF are typically written as superposition of symmetry-adopted configuration state functions (CSF) with well-defined parity P, total angular momentum J and projection M [18],

$$\psi_\alpha(PJM) \equiv |\alpha \mathbb{J} M\rangle = \sum_{r=1}^{n_c} c_r(\alpha) |\gamma_r PJM\rangle, \quad (1)$$

and where γ_r refers to all additional quantum numbers that are needed in order to specify the (N-electron) CSF uniquely. In most standard computations, the set $\{|\gamma_r PJM\rangle, r = 1, \ldots, n_c\}$ of CSF are constructed as antisymmetrized products of a common set of *orthonormal* (one-electron) orbitals. In the expansion (1), moreover, the notation $\mathbb{J} \equiv J^P$ has been introduced to just specify an (individual) level symmetry below by its total angular momentum and parity.

In the MCDHF method, the orbitals as well as expansion coefficients $\{c_r(\alpha)\}$ are typically both optimized on the *Dirac-Coulomb* Hamiltonian [2]

$$\mathbb{H}^{(DC)} = \sum_i h^{(Dirac)}(\mathbf{r}_i) + \sum_{i<j} \frac{1}{r_{ij}}, \quad (2)$$

in which the one-electron Dirac operator

$$h^{(Dirac)}(\mathbf{r}) = c\boldsymbol{\alpha} \cdot \mathbf{p} + \beta c^2 + V_{nuc}(r)$$

describes the kinetic energy of the electron and its interaction with the nuclear potential $V_{nuc}(r)$, and where the interaction among the electrons is given by the static Coulomb repulsion $1/r_{ij}$. For heavy elements, however, the pairwise interaction between the electrons is often better described by the sum of this Coulomb term and the (so-called) *transverse* Breit interaction b_{ij},

$$\sum_{i<j} v_{ij} = \sum_{i<j} \left(\frac{1}{r_{ij}} + b_{ij} \right), \qquad (3)$$

in order to account for the *relativistic* motion of the electrons. Typically, the Breit interaction is taken in its frequency-independent form as appropriate for most practical computations. For medium and heavy elements, furthermore, the decision about the particular form of the Hamiltonian, that is, of applying either the Dirac-Coulomb operator (2) or the Dirac-Coulomb-Breit operator $\mathbb{H}^{(DCB)} = \mathbb{H}^{(DC)} + \sum_{i<j} b_{ij}$, or any other approximation to the electron-electron interaction, is usually based upon physical arguments, such as the nuclear charge, the charge state of the ion or the shell structure of interest. In the JAC toolbox, the form of the Hamiltonian and the size of the wave function expansion can be specified quite flexibly in order to account for the relevant relativistic contributions in the representation of the ASF. While we shall refer the reader to the literature for all further details on relativistic atomic structure theory [1,2], let us mention especially the quasi-spin formalism that has been found crucial for systematically-enlarged MCDHF studies on open d- and f-shell elements [38], and which enables one to include single, double and (sometimes even) triple excitations into the wave function expansion (1). This feature is in fact relevant for most heavy and super-heavy ($Z \geq 104$) elements, and for which virtual excitations into $j = 9/2$ subshells are often inevitable.

Various proposals have been made in the literature to also incorporate the radiative, or (so-called) QED, corrections in terms of model potentials into the correlated many-electron methods, such as the MCDHF, many-body perturbation or coupled-cluster theories. Following the work by Shabaev et al. [39], these QED corrections can be taken into account by means of a (non-) local single-electron QED Hamiltonian

$$\mathbb{H}^{(QED)} = \mathbb{H}^{(SE)} + \mathbb{H}^{(VP)} = \sum_j h_j^{(QED)} = \sum_j \left(h_j^{(SE)} + h_j^{(VP)} \right),$$

that comprises *effective* self-energy (SE) and vacuum-polarization (VP) terms, and that can be treated like local operators. When compared to missing electronic correlations, these QED corrections are often less relevant as long as no inner-shell excitations are involved in any computed property or process [20,40]. For open d- and f-shell elements, indeed, these QED corrections are then considered to be negligible, at least at the present level of computational accuracy, though the CI computations in JAC can be carried out with and without including these QED estimates into the Hamiltonian matrix [41].

2.2. *Configuration-Interaction Expansions for Open f-Shell Elements*

Ansatz (1) seemingly provides an easy and straightforward way to the generation of atomic bound states. In practice, however, neither the choice of the Hamiltonian nor the construction of the CSF basis turns out to be as simple. For the sake of stability, moreover, the (relativistic) wave functions need often to be optimized layer-by-layer, that is, based on a set of *active* orbitals with the same principal quantum number n and a predefined maximum ℓ value. By starting from a given list of reference configurations, the wave function expansions are then generated by including single, double, or even triple excitations into ansatz (1). A quite similar concept is realized within the JAC toolbox [36] by means of a *configuration-interaction* (CI) representation; cf. the data type AtomicState.CiExpansion below. To specify such a representation of the many-electron wave function, use is made of different classes of excitations with regard to the given references and by just stipulating the set of active orbitals. Since all open d- and f-shell elements share quite complex shell structures, only a very limited number of active shells are typically feasible but concede a quick access to the relevant configurations. In general, the costs of ab-initio methods increases hereby very rapidly with the number of active electrons, at least until the open shells are half-filled.

2.3. The JAC Toolbox

2.3.1. Brief Overview of JAC

The JAC toolbox has been developed for calculating (atomic many-electron) interaction amplitudes, properties as well as a good number of excitation, ionization and capture processes for open-shell atoms and ions. This toolbox is based on the Dirac-Coulomb (-Breit) Hamiltonian and MCDHF method as briefly outline above. Figure 2 exposes the central features of this program and how it helps integrate different atomic processes within a single computational toolbox in order to ensure good self-consistency of all generated data. JAC is implemented in Julia , a new programming language for scientific computing, and which is known to include a number of (modern) features, such as dynamic types, optional type annotations, type-specializing, just-in-time compilation of code, dynamic code loading as well as garbage collection [42,43].

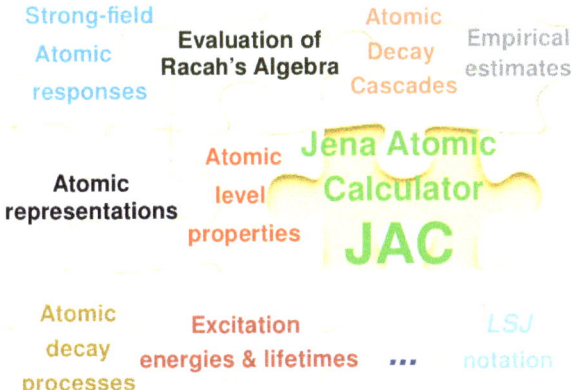

Figure 2. Overview of the JAC toolbox [36] for calculating atomic and ionic structures, processes and cascades, based on Dirac's equation and the MCDHF method. This toolbox facilitates a variety of relativistic computations as briefly shown in this jigsaw puzzle. In this work, JAC is especially applied to predict the excitation energies and level properties of open d- and f-shell elements.

Little need to be said about the design of JAC that has been described elsewhere [36,41] and can readily be downloaded from the web [44]. This toolbox can be utilized without much prior knowledge of the code. One of JAC's rather frequently applied *kind* of computation for medium and heavy elements refers to the (so-called) Atomic.Computations. These computation are based on explicitly specified electron configurations and (help) provide level energies, the representation of ASF or selected level properties. They also help evaluate the transition amplitudes (and rates) as the numerical *key* for predicting the fluorescence spectra and lifetimes of the low-lying excited levels. Below, we shall explain and discuss how this toolbox can be employed in order to estimate the level energies and lifetimes for the low-lying levels of Th^{2+}. For many (standard) computations, indeed, JAC provides an interface which is equally accessible for researchers from experiment, theory as well as for code developers. JAC's careful design enables the user to gradually approach different applications of atomic theory.

The JAC toolbox is internally built upon (the concept of) many-electron amplitudes that generally combine two atomic bound states of the same or of two different charge states, and may thus include *free* electrons in the continuum [45]. These amplitudes are then employed to compute the—radiative and nonradiative—rates, lifetimes or cross sections as shown below. Advantage of these tools is taken also to formulate (and implement) atomic cascade computations in a language that remains close to the formal theory [46,47]. The consequent use of these amplitudes is quite in contrast to most other atomic structure codes that are based on some further decomposition of these (many-electron) amplitudes into various one- and two-particle (reduced) matrix elements, or even into radial integrals, *well before* any coding is done.

2.3.2. Needs of a Descriptive Language for Atomic Computations

During the past decades, the demands to atomic structure and collision theory have changed distinctly from the accurate computation of a few low-lying level energies and properties towards (massive) applications in astro, plasma and technical physics, and at several places elsewhere. These demands make it desirable to develop a domain-specific and descriptive language, for instance built upon Julia, which not only reveal the underlying formalism but also avoids most technical details. Apart from a concise syntax, close to the formulation of atomic physics problems, such a domain-specific language should support access to different models and approximations as well as the decomposition of a given task into well-designed steps, similar to writing pseudo-code. Figure 3 points out several requirements for such a language of *doing* atomic physics, and for which JAC aims for. These requirements appear quite opposite to most previous—either FORTRAN or C—codes, for which simple extensions, a rapid proto-typing or the use of graphical interfaces often becomes cumbersome. Aside of these rather practical demands, such a language should as well support a transparent communication *with* and *within* the code, independent of the shell structure of the atoms or any particular application. For performing quantum many-particle computations, moreover, the language must be fast and flexible enough in order to implement all necessary building blocks. By using Julia with its deliberate language design, we therefore hope to bring over productivity and performance also to the JAC toolbox.

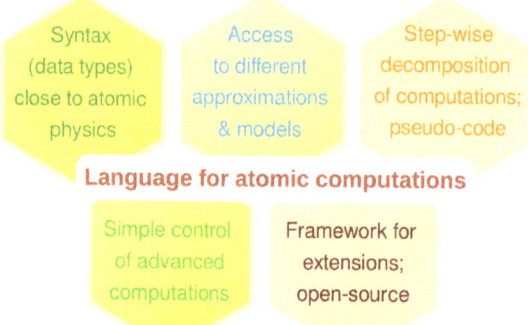

Figure 3. Requirements for establishing a domain-specific and *descriptive* atomic language as is implemented in JAC.

2.3.3. Combining Syntax and Semantics: JAC's Data Structures for Atomic Computations

Julia's type system is known as one of its strongest features, when compared with many other computing languages [42]. In Julia, all types are said to be *first-class* and are utilized to select the code dynamically by means of (so-called) multiple dispatch. While abstract data types are used to establish a hierarchy of relationships between data and actions, and are applied in order to model *behavior*, the actual data are always kept by concrete types, either as primitive and composite types. Moreover, abstract and concrete types can be both *parametric* to further enhance the dynamic code allocation. All these rather general concepts are also well adopted in JAC to facilitate the communication *with* as well as the data transfer *within* the program. In fact, the JAC toolbox is built upon ~250 such properly designed data structures. These structures define many useful and frequently recurring objects in order to deal with the level energies and processes of atoms and ions, and to make the implementation rather independent from the particular shell structure. Obviously, in addition, the (notion of most of these) data types should be readily understandable to any atomic physicist without much additional training. A few prominent examples of these data types are an Orbital to represent the quantum numbers and radial components of (one-electron) orbital functions, an atomic Basis to specify a set of CSF, or a Level for the full representation of a single ASF: E, $|\alpha \mathbb{J}M\rangle$ as shown in expansion (1). Frankly speaking, these data structures form the basic language elements in order to specify and describe the desired computations.

While most of JAC's data types (may) remain hidden to the user, this set typically needs to be enlarged in order to implement and explore new applications. Table 1 lists a few of these data types for predicting the properties of open d- and f-shell elements. For example, the AtomicState.Representation and its subtype AtomicState.CiExpansion have been found to be crucial to generate well-designed CI expansions for the computation of level energies and properties [48]. Figure 4 displays the definition of these data types together with the CiSettings in order to control the set of active orbitals and virtual excitation. Other wave function representations, which are partly supported by the JAC toolbox, refer to a MeanFieldBasis for generating a mean-field basis and a set of orbitals, a RasExpansion for dealing with restricted active-space (RAS) wave functions or a GreenExpansion for computing an approximate (many-electron) Green function [49]. These representations are subtypes of the AbstractRepresentationType from the same module. Although not all details of these data types will be explained here, Figure 4 shows how the data are communicated and maintained within the JAC program. Each representation and process (see below) usually comes with its own Settings in order to facilitate the detailed control of all computations, even if the default values are typically sufficient. Obviously, however, the careful design of these data types help keep the computations feasible.

```
struct   AtomicState.Representation  ...  a struct for defining an atomic state representation.
         Such representations often refer to approximate wave function approximations of one or
         several levels but may concern also a mean-field basis (for some multiplet of some
         configurations) or Green functions, etc.

+ name           ::String                     ... to assign a name to the given representation.
+ nuclearModel   ::Nuclear.Model              ... Model, charge and parameters of the nucleus.
+ grid           ::Radial.Grid                ... The radial grid to be used for the computation.
+ refConfigs     ::Array{Configuration,1}     ... List of references configurations, at least 1.
+ repType        ::AbstractRepresentationType ... Specifies the particular representation.


struct   AtomicState.CiExpansion  <:  AbstractRepresentationType  ...  a struct to represent (and
         generate) a configuration-interaction representation.

+ activeOrbitals ::Dict{Subshell, Orbital}    ... Set of active orbitals.
+ excitations    ::AtomicState.RasStep        ... Excitations to be included beyond refConfigs.
+ settings       ::AtomicState.CiSettings     ... Settings for the given CI expansion


struct   AtomicState.CiSettings  ...  a struct for defining the settings for a configuration-
         interaction (CI) expansion.

+ eeInteractionCI  ::AbstractEeInteraction    ... Specifies the treatment of the e-e interaction.
+ levelSelectionCI ::LevelSelection           ... Specifies the selected levels, if any.

AtomicState.CiSettings()  ...  constructor for setting the default values.

AtomicState.CiSettings(settings::AtomicState.CiSettings; eeInteractionCI = .., levelSelectionCI = ..)
    ... constructor for modifying the given CiSettings by ``overwriting'' the explicitly selected
        parameters.
```

Figure 4. Definition of the data types AtomicState.Representation (**upper panel**), AtomicState.CiExpansion (**middle panel**) and AtomicState.CiSettings (**lower panel**) to select and perform a configuration interaction computation as discussed in the text. CI wave functions utilize a single step of a restricted-active-space (RAS) expansion and the associated virtual excitations that are to be applied with regard to the given reference configurations.

Table 1. Selected data types of the JAC toolbox for predicting the properties of open d- and f-shell elements. Here, only a brief explanation is given, while further details can be found at Julia's REPL [50] by typing, for instance, ? Representation.

Struct	Brief Explanation
AbstractEeInteraction	Abstract type to distinguish between different electron-electron interaction operators; it comprises the concrete (singleton) types BreitInteraction, CoulombInteraction, CoulombBreit.
AbstractExcitationScheme	Abstract type to support different excitation schemes, such as DeExciteSingleElectron, ExciteByCapture, and several others.
AbstractScField	Abstract type for dealing with different self-consistent-field (SCF) potentials.
AsfSettings	Settings to control the SCF and CI calculations for a given multiplet.
Atomic.Computation	An atomic computation of one or several multiplets, including the SCF and CI calculations, as well as of selected properties or processes.
Basis	(Relativistic) many-electron basis, including the specification of the configuration space and all radial orbitals.
Configuration	(Nonrelativistic) electron configuration as specified by the shell occupation.
EmMultipole	A multipole (component) of the electro-magnetic field as specified by its electric or magnetic character and the multipolarity.
Level	Atomic level in terms of its quantum numbers, symmetry, energy and its (possibly full) representation.
LevelSelection	List of levels that is specified by either the level numbers and/or level symmetries.
LevelSymmetry	$\mathbb{J} = J^P$ specifies the (total) angular momentum and parity of a particular level.
LSjjSettings	Settings to control the $jj - LSJ$ transformation of the selected many-electron levels.
MeanFieldBasis	A simple representation of the electronic structure in terms of a mean-field orbital basis.
Multiplet	An ordered list of atomic levels, often associated with one or several configurations.
Nuclear.Model	A model of the nucleus to keep all nuclear parameters together.
Orbital	(Relativistic) radial orbital function that appears as *building block* in order to define the many-electron CSF; such an orbital comprises a large and small component and is typically given on a (radial) grid.
Radial.Grid	Radial grid to represent the (radial) orbital function and to perform all radial integration.
Radial.Potential	Radial potential function.
Representation	Representation of an atomic state in terms of either a mean-field basis, an approximate wave function, a many-electron Green function, or others.
RasExpansion	A restricted active-space representation of the levels from a given multiplet; cf. CiExpansion in Figure 3.
RasSettings	Settings to control the details of a RasExpansion.
RasStep	Single-step of a (systematically enlarged) restricted active-space computation.
Shell	Nonrelativistic shell, such as $1s$, $2s$, $2p$, ...
Subshell	Relativistic subshell, such as $1s_{1/2}$, $2s_{1/2}$, $2p_{1/2}$, $2p_{3/2}$, ...

2.4. LSJ Spectroscopic Notation for Open f-Shell Elements

Since relativistic computations are regularly based on jj-coupling, a (unitary) $jj - LS$ transformation need first to be carried out for determining the LSJ notation of the levels as usually applied in atomic spectroscopy. In JAC, such a transformation can be performed optionally for all or a selected number of levels. This is achieved by fixing LSjjSettings(true) in the AsfSettings as associated with any self-consistent-field computation for the wave functions of a given multiplet. Apart from the LSJ level assignment of the multiplet, JAC also supports a full transformation of the wave functions from a jjJ- to a LSJ-coupled basis by just setting the minWeight parameter to *zero* in the LSjjSettings. For open d- and f-shell elements, however, such a complete unitary transformation matrix is of little help and often results in just lengthy computations.

For open d- and f-shell atoms, a LSJ level notation is often needed already for classifying even the lowest part of the level structure owing to the very rich fine-structure. Indeed, the lack of providing a fast and proper spectroscopic notation in relativistic computations have hindered the spectroscopic level classification of heavy elements and the analysis of their (inner-shell) processes. If we formally express the wave function expansion (1) of atomic levels as [51,52]:

$$|\psi_\alpha\rangle = \sum_t c_t^{(NR)}(\alpha) \left| \gamma_t^{(NR)} LSJ \right\rangle = \sum_r c_r^{(R)}(\alpha) \left| \gamma_r^{(R)} J \right\rangle,$$

in the LSJ- and jjJ-coupled basis, the nonrelativistic Fourier coefficients $\{c_t^{(NR)}\}$ are implemented in JAC for up to two (nonrelativistic) open shells. Internally, this re-expansion of the jjJ-coupled levels into a LSJ basis makes use of the shell-dependent overlap integrals [53] as previously implemented already within the RATIP code [32]. Below, we shall discuss how this transformation can be utilized in order to classify the low-lying level structure of Th^{2+} ions.

2.5. Atomic Amplitudes and Properties

As mentioned before, the many-electron amplitudes between either CSF or approximate ASF are central to any implementation in atomic (structure) theory, from the set-up of the Hamiltonian matrix to the interaction of the electrons with the nuclear moments (hyperfine structure), to autoionization and electron capture processes, and up to the coupling of atoms to the radiation field. In JAC, three of these amplitudes refer to the electron–electron interaction, the multipole-moment and transition amplitudes as well as the momentum-transfer amplitudes, which can all be invoked by the user, if the atomic states (levels) and operators are properly specified. From these and a few other amplitudes, the fine and hyperfine splitting [54], isotope shifts [55,56], Lande g_J factors, atomic form factors, level-dependent fluorescence yields, or several other properties can be readily derived. Figure 5 displays selected applications of the JAC toolbox for predicting the properties and processes of atoms and ions, though not all of these processes have yet been implemented in full detail (as indicated by gray color).

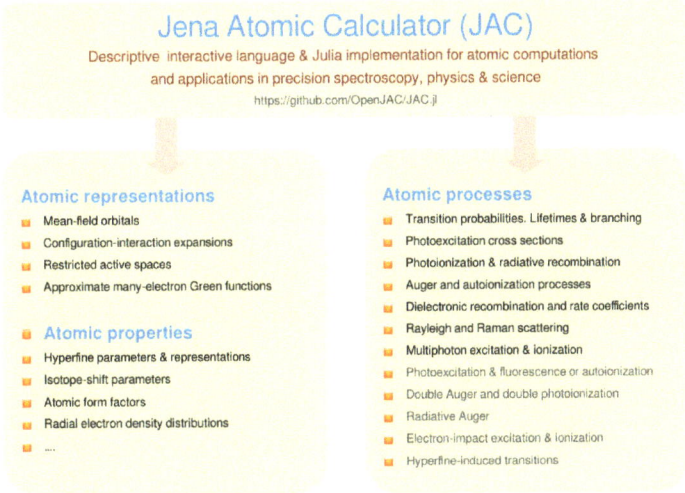

Figure 5. Selected applications of the JAC toolbox to generate atomic representations or to compute properties and processes. See Refs. [36,41] for a more detailed account of the various features of this toolbox.

The properties above can be examined by means of Atomic.Computations, a key data type of JAC that enables the user to *describe* the problem in sufficient detail. These computations are based on the levels (multiplets) as obtained from a set of configurations.

Two examples for such computations will be shown below for the low-lying level structure of Th^{2+}.

While atomic units are used throughout for all internal computations, the input and output of JAC is based on user-specified units, which can be overwritten interactively. The current (default) settings of the units are displayed on screen by typing Basics.display("settings"), and they can readily be modified by Defaults.setDefaults(), if the default settings are not appropriate. For example, the call Defaults.setDefaults("unit: energy", "Kayser") or Defaults.setDefaults("unit: energy", "Hartree") tells JAC that all further inputs and outputs are handled either in Kaysers or Hartrees (atomic units), if not stated otherwise.

2.6. Atomic Excitation and Decay Processes of Open f-Shell Elements

Today, several implementations of the MCDHF method support *correlated* expansions (1) also for open d- and f-shell elements. These approximate bound states can then be applied for obtaining the cross sections and rates of different atomic processes. In fact, a good number of such processes are known in atomic and plasma physics, including various excitation, ionization, recombination and scattering processes. Until the present, however, processes with—one or a few—electrons in the continuum still remain as a challenge for atomic theory, and this applies especially if atoms with open valence-shell structures are involved. Apart from the bare number of amplitudes and channels, difficulties in dealing with *free* electrons arise in particular from the rearrangement of the electron density, if the initial and final states are well separated in energy or simply belong to different charge states. Table 2 just lists a few of these processes; all of these computations can again be carried out by means of Atomic.Computations. Moreover, since each of these properties and processes is implemented by a separate module, this number can be readily enlarged in the future if needs arise from the user side.

Table 2. Selected excitation, capture and decay processes that can be calculated by means of the JAC toolbox. A^* refers to the excitation and $A^{(*)}$ to some possible excitation of an atom or ion with regard to its ground configuration.

Process & Brief Explanation
Photon emission $A^* \longrightarrow A^{(*)} + \hbar\omega$: Transition probabilities; oscillator strengths; lifetimes; angular distributions.
Photoexcitation $A + \hbar\omega \longrightarrow A^*$: Excitation cross sections, alignment parameters; statistical tensors.
Photoionization $A + \hbar\omega \longrightarrow A^{+*} + e_p^-$: Cross sections; angular parameters.
Photorecombination $A^{q+} + e^- \longrightarrow A^{(q-1)+} + \hbar\omega$: Recombination cross sections; angular parameters.
Auger emission or autoionization $A^{q+*} \longrightarrow A^{(q+1)+(*)} + e_a^-$: Auger rates; angular and polarization parameters.
Dielectronic recombination (DR) $A^{q+} + e^- \to A^{(q-1)+*} \to A^{(q-1)+(*)} + \hbar\omega$: Partial and total DR resonance strengths; DR plasma rate coefficients.
Photoexcitation with subsequent autoionization $A + \hbar\omega \longrightarrow A^* \longrightarrow A^{(*)} + e_a^-$: Rates.
Photo-double ionization $A + \hbar\omega \longrightarrow A^{+*} + e_1^- + e_2^-$: Energy-differential and total cross sections.
Rayleigh & Compton scattering of light $A + \hbar\omega \longrightarrow A^* + \hbar\omega'$: Angle-differential cross sections.

3. Low-Lying Level Structure of Th^{2+}

Computations of the electronic structure and properties of free atoms and ions have been found a powerful tool to explore the interaction of matter with light and particles of various kinds as well as in different—physical and chemical—environments. For open d- and f-shell atoms and ions, however, only a few *ab-initio* case studies exist because of the difficulties mentioned in the introduction. Accurate Fock-space and CC calculations have been carried out especially for the low-lying levels of selected atoms with just one or two electrons (or holes) outside of closed-shells. For most other lanthanide and actinide elements, in contrast, either restricted multiconfigurational calculations [25] have been performed or very little is still known at all until now. With the JAC toolbox, we wish to overcome these limitations and to facilitate—medium to large-scale—*ab-initio* computations also for these medium and heavy elements. Although further work is needed to make the code efficient, the variety of atomic level properties and processes, so far implemented in JAC, will support the spectroscopy of open d- and f-shell elements in the future, including the actinides. In this section, we therefore show how the low-lying level energies and lifetimes can (at least) be estimated.

3.1. Estimates on the Level Structure of Th^{2+}

Th^{2+} ions still have a simple odd-parity $5f\,6d$ ground configuration with a $^3H_4$ ground-state level. However, the low-lying even-parity configurations are nearby in energy and give rise to a $6d^2$ $^3F_2$ level just 63 cm^{-1} above of the $^3H_4$ ground state. For six even-parity levels of the $5f^2$, $5f\,7p$, $7s\,7p$ and $6d\,7p$ configurations at UV excitation energies, moreover, Biemont et al. [57] measured the lifetimes by using the time-resolved laser-induced fluorescence method. From observing the lines of Th^{2+} and other radio-active ions, the age of individual stars has been estimated in the Milky Way. At present, the NIST database [58] list $\lesssim 200$ low-lying levels of Th^{2+}, and to which we shall compare our computations below, though many of these levels are still unknown or not yet fully identified.

To demonstrate the easy use of the JAC toolbox, we here consider the level structure of the $5f\,6d + 5f\,7d + 5f\,7s + 5f\,8s + 6d\,6f + 6d\,7p$ odd-parity and $6d^2 + 5f^2 + 7s^2 + 5f\,7p + 5f\,6f + 6d\,7s$ even-parity configurations. For the odd-parity levels, Figure 6 displays the input for JAC that needs to be compiled prior to the computations. Apart from specifying a suitable radial grid and nuclear model, we need to provide the necessary configurations, and where [Rn] = $1s^2\,2s^2 2p^6\,3s^2 3p^6 3d^{10}\,4s^2 4p^6 4d^{10} 4f^{14}\,5s^2 5p^6 5d^{10}\,6s^2 6p^6$ just refers to the radon ground configuration. By re-specifying some fields of the *default* AsfSettings(), we furthermore tell the program to restrict the electron–electron interaction in the CI computations to the Coulomb repulsion [cf. Equation (2)] and to request for a $jjJ - LSJ$ transformation of all levels of interest. Indeed, this is all input that need to be provided to an Atomic.Computation in order to *overwrite* the default settings as obtained by the plain constructor Atomic.Computation(). Many more details could be specified but are omitted here for the sake of simplicity. Once an Atomic.Computation has been specified with just the essential physical information, that is, all the details to make the computational task explicit, it should be simply *performed* in order to return the results either tabulated or in a graphical form. Because of the complexity of open d- and f-shell elements, all other steps are then carried out automatically, making use of some default values. These steps especially refer to the computation of a self-consistent field, the setup and diagonalization of the Hamiltonian matrix based on the Dirac–Coulomb (–Breit) operator and, if requested, to the calculation of further transition amplitudes and probabilities. Since, moreover, we have demanded a $jjJ - LSJ$ transformation of all calculated levels in Figure 6, we also obtain the leading LSJ notation of these levels, together with their weights within the given representation.

Table 3 displays the excitation energies as obtained from the Atomic.Computation above. Results are shown for the 16 low-lying odd-parity levels with total angular momentum $J = 0, \ldots, 6$. These excitation energies can be compared with experiments [58,59] and the calculations by Safronova et al. [60], who combined the configuration-interaction and linearized coupled-cluster methods. These excitation energies agree within ~ 2000 cm^{-1} with the NIST tabulations, although larger deviations may occur for several highly-exited and even-parity levels. These deviations can be attributed to the rather limited set of active orbitals in the present computations. For the high-lying levels, indeed, the identification is typically less easy and requires the knowledge of the leading LSJ notations. To improve these energies, we could either include further configurations explicitly in the Atomic.Computation above or perform a more advanced AtomicState.RasExpansion. Such a restricted active space (RAS) expansion applies, analogous to a CI expansion, a user-specified excitation scheme to a given set of reference configurations in order to generate the requested configurations automatically and, hence, to ensure a systematic enlargement of the given basis. These RAS expansions are usually generated stepwise since, more often than not, the correlation orbitals need to be frozen before the next layer of orbitals can be optimized in addition to the pre-determined charge distribution. In practice, however, such RAS expansions are (much) less useful for open d- and f-shell elements because of their rich fine-structure. Some further gain in efficiency can be achieved by dividing the CSF basis into groups of CSF with the *same* symmetry $\mathbb{J} = J^P$, and where the rearrangement of the electron density retains partly included in the computation for levels of different symmetry.

```
# Calculate low-lying levels of Th^2+:
# odd-parity (5f 6d + 5f 7d + 5f 7s + 5f 8s + 6d 6f + 6d 7p)
grid        = Radial.Grid(Radial.Grid(false), rnt = 4.0e-6, h = 5.0e-2, hp = 0.6e-2, rbox = 10.0)
startOrbs   = multiplet.levels[1].basis.orbitals
subshells   = multiplet.levels[1].basis.subshells
asfSettings = AsfSettings(AsfSettings(), eeInteractionCI=CoulombInteraction(), jjLS=LSjjSettings(true),
                         startScfFrom=StartFromPrevious(startOrbs), frozenSubshells=subshells)
oddConfigs  = [Configuration("[Rn] 5f 6d"), Configuration("[Rn] 5f 7d"), Configuration("[Rn] 5f 7s"),
               Configuration("[Rn] 5f 8s"), Configuration("[Rn] 6d 6f"), Configuration("[Rn] 6d 7p")]
wa = Atomic.Computation(Atomic.Computation(), name="Th^2+ odd-partiy level energies", grid=grid,
                        nuclearModel = Nuclear.Model(90.),
                        configs = oddConfigs,   asfSettings = asfSettings)
wb = perform(wa, output=true)
```

```
pSettings   = PhotoEmission.Settings(PhotoEmission.Settings(), multipoles=[E1])
evenConfigs = [Configuration("[Rn] 6d^2"), Configuration("[Rn] 5f^2"), Configuration("[Rn] 7s^2"),
               Configuration("[Rn] 5f 7p"), Configuration("[Rn] 5f 6f"), Configuration("[Rn] 6d 7s")]

wa = Atomic.Computation(Atomic.Computation(), name="Th^2+: Lifetimes of even-partiy level energies",
                        grid=grid, nuclearModel=Nuclear.Model(90.),
                        initialConfigs  = evenConfigs, initialAsfSettings = asfSettings,
                        finalConfigs    = oddConfigs,  finalAsfSettings   = asfSettings,
                        processSettings = pSettings)
```

Figure 6. Input for the `Atomic.Computation` of the low-lying levels of Th^{2+}. In these calculations (**upper panel**), the orbitals of the [Rn] $5f\,6d$ configuration have first been optimized independently and then be kept frozen in the computation above. In the (**lower panel**), in addition, the transition probabilities and lifetimes are obtained by just specifying the even-parity configurations as well as the `Settings` for the photo emission.

While Figure 6 shows perhaps a surprisingly simple input to calculate and analyze the fine-structure of Th^{2+} ions, this "simplicity" becomes relevant especially if other open f-shell ions or their properties and processes need to be considered. Apart from the *standard* input, the user has extensive control about the interatomic interactions and the amount of correlations, if the defaults are carefully overwritten.

3.2. Transition Probabilities. Lifetimes and Branching Fractions

For open f-shell elements, the transition probabilities and lifetimes need often to be estimated in order to identify and characterize the low-lying level structure from the intensities of the observed line spectra. In JAC, such estimates can readily be done by just modifying a few lines in the input as shown in the lower panel of Figure 6.

Here, the (value of the) `processSettings` tells JAC to calculate the Einstein A and B coefficients as well as the oscillator strength for the photon emission from the even- to odd-parity levels, and as associated with the initial- and final-state configurations. In these computations, we just consider—in line with the defaults of the JAC toolbox—the electric-dipole transitions, although these *defaults* can also be readily modified within the code. Once the `Atomic.Computation` has been performed, all results are usually tabulated in a neat format, both at screen and within a summary file. In these tables, the atomic levels and transitions are then listed in terms of the level numbers as they arise from the diagonalization of the associated Hamiltonian matrix within the JAC program [32,40]. Moreover, the (full) representation of the initial and final-state multiplets as well as all the computed transition data can be obtained eventually if the optional argument `output=true` is given to the function `perform()`. Since the initial and final-state multiplets are determined independently in the computation of all atomic processes, the rearrangement of the electron density is partly taken into account, though no attempt has been made so far to deal with this non-orthogonality in the evaluation of the angular coefficients.

Table 3. Excitation energies [eV] and lifetimes [s] of Th^{2+}. Data from the JAC toolbox are compared with the NIST database ([58]), experiments and previous computations. Results are shown for 16 low-lying levels. These energetically low-lying levels can be identified uniquely using their energy and total symmetry despite of certain level crossings. In general, strong admixtures of other LSJ symmetries are typically found for these levels, which increase further as the valence-shell structure is "opened" further. See text for discussion.

Level		J^P	Energy [eV]			Lifetime [s]		
			This Work	Exp. [58]	Calc. [60]	This Work	Exp. [57]	Calc. [60]
$5f6d$	$^3H^o_4$	4^-	0	0	0			
$5f6d$	$^3F^o_2$	2^-	210	511	189			
$5f7s$	$^3F^o_3$	3^-	3686	2527	2436			
$5f7s$	$^3F^o_2$	2^-	4975	3182	2958			
$5f7s$	$^1G^o_4$	4^-	3026	3188	3207			
$5f6d$	$^3F^o_3$	3^-	5360	4827	4853			
$5f6d$	$^3H^o_5$	5^-	4863	4490	4802			
$5f6d$	$^3D^o_3$	3^-	6857	5060	5085			
$5f6d$	$^1D^o_2$	2^-	8466	6288	5797			
$5f7s$	$^3F^o_4$	4^-	6702	6311	6237			
$5f7s$	$^1F^o_3$	3^-	9279	7501	7609			
$5f6d$	$^3D^o_1$	1^-	8779	7921	8260			
$5f6d$	$^3G^o_4$	4^-	9192	8142	8197			
$5f6d$	$^3H^o_6$	6^-	8555	8437	8810			
$5f6d$	$^3P^o_1$	1^-	13,084	11,123	11,564			
$5f6d$	$^3P^o_0$	0^-	15,274	11,233	11,766			
$5f^2$	$^3P_2$	2^+	37,134	32,867	33,488	2.54 [−8]	2.58 ± 1.5 [−8]	2.12 [−8]
$5f7p$		4^+	43,256	38,581	38,980	1.86 [−8]	2.7 ± 0.2 [−9]	2.41 [−9]
$7s7p$	$^3P^o_0$	0^+	46,404	42,260	-	4.59 [−9]	6.6 ± 0.4 [−9]	6.19 [−9]
$7s7p$	$^3P^o_1$	1^+	47623	45,064	-	9.47 [−9]	2.4 ± 0.2 [−9]	2.22 [−9]
$6d7p$	$^3F^o_4$	4^+	55,884	53,052	-	4.36 [−9]	1.3 ± 0.2 [−9]	1.41 [−9]

We shall not display and compare here explicitly the transition probabilities with previous computations, and with typically a better agreement for the strong than the weak transitions. However, Table 3 compares the lifetime estimates from the present computations with the measurements by Biemont et al. [57] and recent calculations [60]. For these even parity levels with energies $\gtrsim 32,000$ cm^{-1}, both the energies and lifetimes still exhibit rather large uncertainties due to the limited configuration basis of the present computations. Again, the identification of these levels is possible by means of a $jjJ - LSJ$ transformation and the analysis of the leading LSJ terms. The lifetimes are shown here in velocity gauge and were found to differ by up to a factor of 3 from the corresponding length-gauge computations. Since we wish to demonstrated the simple use of the JAC toolbox, no further enlargement is shown for the wave-function expansion nor the derived properties. Our two examples however manifest how JAC can be employed to generate much larger surveys of fine-structure levels as well as the—radiative and nonradiative—decay branches of the resonantly excited ion.

4. Summary and Conclusions

While the difficulties with open d- and f-shell elements can hardly be overrated, we have shown how the JAC toolbox is utilized to perform reasonably accurate computations for these shell structures. In particular, we explain how these tools help estimate the energies and properties for complex fine-structures. Apart from such simple estimates, JAC can also be applied to approximate and systematically improve relativistic ASF by including different classes (schemes) of virtual excitations with regard to a given set of reference configurations. In addition, the JAC toolbox also facilitates the computation of atomic processes, cascades or even the symbolic simplification of expressions from Racah's algebra [61].

Numerical results are shown above for the low-lying level structure of Th^{2+} ions. These and similar computations for other actinide ions will be useful for developing new excitation schemes for heavy elements and for applications in medicine, radiation safety or elsewhere. Although, at present, the JAC program can often not immediately compete with its (numerical) accuracy with many-body perturbation or all-order techniques; these tools will help to go *beyond* the currently available applications of relativistic atomic structure theory.

Since JAC's very first design in 2017, the number of atomic properties and processes that can be handled by this code has grown steadily and it now supports the generation of (atomic) data for astro and plasma physics [62]. In fact, there are at present various demands to further advance the JAC toolbox: For open d- and f-shell elements, these requests mainly refer to efficiency and memory issues, the re-use of angular coefficients or the coupling of free electrons in ionization or capture processes. With the present version, however, a major step has already been made to obtain useful estimates and data for a large class of heavy and super-heavy elements.

Funding: This research received no external funding.

Conflicts of Interest: The author declares no conflict of interest.

References

1. Johnson, W.R. *Atomic Structure Theory: Lectures on Atomic Physics*; Springer: Berlin/Heidelberg, Germany, 2007.
2. Grant, I.P. *Relativistic Quantum Theory of Atoms and Molecules: Theory and Computation*; Springer: Berlin/Heidelberg, Germany, 2007.
3. Fritzsche, S. Large–scale accurate structure calculations for open–shell atoms and ions. *Phys. Scr.* **2002**, *T100*, 37. [CrossRef]
4. Raeder, S.; Ackermann, D.; Backe, H.; Block, M.; Cheal, B.; Chhetri, P.; Düllmann, C.E.; van Duppen, P.; Even, J.; Ferrer, R.; et al. Nuclear properties of nobelium isotopes from laser spectroscopy. *Phys. Rev. Lett.* **2018**, *120*, 232503. [CrossRef] [PubMed]
5. Raeder, S.; Kneip, N.; Reich, T.; Studer, D.; Trautmann, N.; Wendt, K. Recent developments in resonance ionization mass spectrometry for ultra-trace analysis of actinide elements. *Radiochim. Acta* **2019**, *107*, 1515. [CrossRef]
6. Rothe, S.; Andreyev, A.N.; Antalic, S.; Borschevsky, A.; Capponi, L.; Cocolios, T.E.; Witte, H.D.; Eliav, E.; Fedorov, D.V.; Fedosseev, V.N.; et al. Measurement of the first ionization potential of astatine by laser ionization. *Nat. Commun.* **2013**, *4*, 1835. [CrossRef]
7. Flanagan, K.T.; Lynch, K.M.; Billowes, J.; Bissell, M.L.; Budincevic V.; Cocolios, T.E.; de Groote, R.P.; Schepper, S.D.; Fedosseev, V.N.; Franchoo, S.; et al. Collinear resonance ionization spectroscopy of neutron-deficient francium isotopes. *Phys. Rev. Lett.* **2013**, *111*, 212501. [CrossRef] [PubMed]
8. Ferrer, R.; Barzakh, A.; Bastin, B.; Beerwerth, R.; Block, M.; Creemers, P.; Grawe, H.; de Groote, R.; Delahaye, P.; Fléchard, X.; et al. Towards high-resolution laser ionization spectroscopy of the heaviest elements in supersonic gas jet expansion. *Nat. Commun.* **2017**, *8*, 14520. [CrossRef]
9. Granados, C.; Creemers, P.; Ferrer, R.; Gaffney, L. P.; Gins, W.; de Groote, R.; Huyse, M.; Kudryavtsev, Y.; Martnez, Y.; Raeder, S.; et al. In-gas laser ionization and spectroscopy of actinium isotopes near the $N=126$ closed shell. *Phys. Rev. C* **2017**, *96*, 054331. [CrossRef]
10. Chhetri, P.; Ackermann, D.; Backe, H.; Block, M.; Cheal, B.; Droese, C.; Düllmann, C.E.; Even, J.; Ferrer, R.; Giacoppo, F.; et al. Precision measurement of the first ionization potential of nobelium. *Phys. Rev. Lett.* **2018**, *120*, 263003. [CrossRef] [PubMed]
11. Laatiaoui, M. On the way to unveiling the atomic structure of superheavy elements. *Eur. Phys. J. Conf.* **2016**, *131*, 05002. [CrossRef]
12. Laatiaoui, M.; Buchachenko, A.A.; Viehland, L.A. Exploiting transport properties for the detection of optical pumping in heavy ions. *Phys. Rev. A* **2020**, *102*, 013106. [CrossRef]
13. Sato, T.K.; Asai, M.; Tsukada, K.; Kaneya, Y.; Toyoshima, A.; Mitsukai, A.; Nagame, Y.; Osa, A.; Toyoshima, A.; Tsukada, K.; et al. First ionization potentials of Fm, Md, No, and Lr: Verification of filling-up of $5f$ electrons and confirmation of the actinide series. *J. Am. Chem. Soc.* **2018**, *140*, 14609. [CrossRef]
14. Sewtz, M.; Backe, H.; Dretzke, A.; Kube, G.; Lauth, W.; Schwamb, P.; Eberhardt, K.; Grüning, C.; Thörle, P.; Trautmann, N.; et al. First observation of atomic levels for the element fermium (Z = 100). *Phys. Rev. Lett.* **2003**, *90*, 163002. [CrossRef]
15. Morrison, J.C.; Rajnak, K. Many-body calculations for the heavy atoms. *Phys. Rev.* **1971**, *A4*, 536. [CrossRef]
16. Borschevsky, A.; Pershina, V.; Eliav, E.; Kaldor, U. Ab initio predictions of atomic properties of element 120 and its lighter group-2 homologues. *Phys. Rev. A* **2013**, *87*, 022502. [CrossRef]

17. Eliav, E.; Kaldor, U.; Ishikawa, Y. Transition energies of mercury and ekamercury (element 112) by the relativistic coupled-cluster method. *Phys. Rev.* **1995**, *52*, 2765. [CrossRef] [PubMed]
18. Grant, I.P. Relativistic Effects in Atoms and Molecules. In *Methods in Computational Chemistry*; Wilson, S., Ed; Plenum: New York, NY, USA, 1988; Volume 2, pp. 1–38.
19. Sewtz, M.; Backe, H.; Dong, C.Z.; Dretzke, A.; Eberhardt, K.; Fritzsche, S.; Grüning, C.; Haire, R.G.; Kube, G.; Kunz, P.; et al. Resonance ionization spectroscopy of fermium (Z = 100). *Spectrochim. Acta B* **2003**, *58*, 1077. [CrossRef]
20. Fritzsche, S. On the accuracy of valence–shell computations for heavy and super–heavy elements. *Eur. Phys. J. D* **2005**, *33*, 15. [CrossRef]
21. Zou, Y.; Froese Fischer, C. Resonance transition energies and oscillator strengths in lutetium and lawrencium. *Phys. Rev. Lett.* **2002**, *88*, 183001. [CrossRef] [PubMed]
22. Fritzsche, S.; Dong, C.Z.; Koike, F.; Uvarov, A. The low–ying level structure of atomic lawrencium (Z = 103): Energies and absorption rates. *Eur. Phys. J. D* **2007**, *45*, 107. [CrossRef]
23. Yu, Y.J.; Li, J.G.; Dong, C.Z.; Ding, X.B.; Fritzsche, S.; Fricke, B. The excitation energies, ionization potentials and oscillator strengths of neutral and ionized species of Uub (Z = 112) and the homologue elements Zn, Cd and Hg. *Eur. Phys. J. D* **2007**, *44*, 51. [CrossRef]
24. Fricke, B.; Greiner, W.; Waber, J.T. The continuation of the periodic table up to Z = 172. The chemistry of superheavy elements. *Theor. Chim. Acta* **1971**, *21*, 235. [CrossRef]
25. Johnson, E.; Pershina, V.; Fricke, B. Ionization potentials of Seaborgium. *J. Phys. Chem.* **1999**, *103*, 8458. [CrossRef]
26. Johnson, E.; Fricke, B.; Jacob, T.; Dong, C.Z.; Fritzsche, S.; Pershina, V. Ionization potentials and radii of neutral and ionized species of elements 107 (bohrium) and 108 (hassium) from extended multiconfiguration Dirac-Fock calculations. *J. Phys. Chem.* **2002**, *116*, 1862. [CrossRef]
27. Eliav, E.; Fritzsche, S.; Kaldor, U. Electronic structure theory of the superheavy elements. *Nucl. Phys. A* **2015**, *944*, 518. [CrossRef]
28. Kahl, E.V.; Berengut, J.C.; Laatiaoui, M.; Eliav, E.; Borschevsky, A. High-precision ab initio calculations of the spectrum of Lr^+. *Phys. Rev.* **2019**, *A100*, 062505. [CrossRef]
29. Oleynichenko, A.V.; Zaitsevskii, A.; Skripnikov, L.V.; Eliav, E. Relativistic Fock space coupled cluster method for many-electron systems: Non-perturbative account for connected triple excitations. *Symmetry* **2020**, *12*, 1101. [CrossRef]
30. Kumar, R.; Chattopadhyay, S.; Angom, D.; Mani, B.K. Relativistic coupled-cluster calculation of the electric dipole polarizability and correlation energy of Cn, Nh^+, and Og: Correlation effects from lighter to superheavy elements. *Phys. Rev. A* **2021**, *103*, 062803. [CrossRef]
31. Fritzsche, S.; Surzhykov, A.; Stöhlker, T. Dominance of the Breit interaction in the x-ray emission of highly charged ions following dielectronic recombination. *Phys. Rev. Lett.* **2009**, *103*, 113001. [CrossRef]
32. Fritzsche, S. The RATIP program for relativistic calculations of atomic transition, ionization and recombination properties. *Comp. Phys. Commun.* **2012**, *183* 1525. [CrossRef]
33. Judd, B.R. Correlation crystal fields for lanthanide ions. *Phys. Rev. Lett.* **1977**, *39*, 242. [CrossRef]
34. Dorenbos, P. Crystal field splitting of lanthanide $4f^n - 15d$ levels in inorganic compounds. *J. Alloys Comp.* **2002**, *341*, 156. [CrossRef]
35. Suzuki, C.; Koike, F.; Murakami, I.; Tamura, N.; Sudo, S. Systematic observation of EUV spectra from highly charged lanthanide ions in the large helical device. *Atoms* **2018**, *6*, 24. [CrossRef]
36. Fritzsche, S. A fresh computational approach to atomic structures, processes and cascades. *Comp. Phys. Commun.* **2019**, *240*, 1. [CrossRef]
37. Seiferle, B.; von der Wense, L.; Thirolf, P.G. Lifetime measurement of the ^{229}Th nuclear isomer. *Phys. Rev. Lett.* **2017**, *118*, 042501. [CrossRef]
38. Gaigalas, G.; Fritzsche, S.; Rudzikas, Z. Reduced coefficients of fractional parentage and matrix elements of the tensor $W^{(k_q k_j)}$ in jj-coupling. *At. D. Nucl. D. Tables* **2002**, *76*, 235. [CrossRef]
39. Shabaev, V.M.; Tupitsyn, I.I; Yerokhin, V.A. Model operator approach to the Lamb shift calculations in relativistic many-electron atoms. *Phys. Rev. A* **2013**, *88*, 012513. [CrossRef]
40. Indelicato, P.; Santos, J.P.; Boucard, S.; Desclaux, J.-P. QED and relativistic corrections in superheavy elements. *Eur. Phys. J. D* **2007**, *45*, 155. [CrossRef]
41. Fritzsche, S. JAC: User Guide, Compendium & Theoretical Background. Unpublished. Available online: https://github.com/OpenJAC/JAC.jl/blob/master/UserGuide-Jac.pdf (accessed on 10 October 2021).
42. Julia 1.7 Documentation. Available online: https://docs.julialang.org/ (accessed on 10 December 2021).
43. Bezanson, J.; Chen, J.; Chung, B.; Karpinski, S.; Shah, V.B.; Vitek, J.; Zoubritzky, L. Julia: Dynamism and performance reconciled by design. *Proc. ACM Program. Lang.* **2018**, *2*, 120. [CrossRef]
44. GitHub—OpenJAC / JAC.jl. Available online: https://github.com/OpenJAC/JAC.jl (accessed on 10 November 2021).
45. Fritzsche, S.; Fricke, B.; Sepp W.D. Reduced L_1 level-width and Coster-Kronig yields by relaxation and continuum interactions in atomic zinc. *Phys. Rev. A* **1992**, *45*, 1465. [CrossRef] [PubMed]
46. Fritzsche, S.; Palmeri, P.; Schippers, S. Atomic cascade computations. *Symmetry* **2021**, *13*, 520. [CrossRef]
47. Schippers, S.; Martins, M.; Beerwerth, R.; Bari, S.; Holste, K.; Schubert, K.; Viefhaus, J.; Savin, D.W.; Fritzsche, S.; Müller, A. Near L-edge single and multiple photoionization of singly charged iron ions. *Astrophys. J.* **2017**, *849*, 5. [CrossRef]

48. Fritzsche S.; Froese Fischer C.; Gaigalas G. A program for relativistic configuration interaction calculations. *Comput. Phys. Commun.* **2002**, *148*, 103. [CrossRef]
49. Fritzsche, S.; Surzhykov, A. Approximate atomic Green functions. *Molecules* **2021**, *26*, 2660. [CrossRef] [PubMed]
50. Julia Comes with a Full-Featured Interactive and Command-Line REPL (Read-Eval-Print Loop) That Is Built into the Executable of the Language. Available online: https://docs.julialang.org/en/v1/stdlib/REPL/ (accessed on 10 December 2021).
51. Gaigalas, G.; Zalandauskas, T.; Fritzsche, S. Spectroscopic *LSJ* notation for atomic levels as obtained from relativistic calculations. *Comput. Phys. Commun.* **2004**, *157*, 239. [CrossRef]
52. Gaigalas, G.; Fritzsche, S. Angular coefficients for symmetry-adapted configuration states in *jj*-coupling. *Comput. Phys. Commun.* **2021**, *267*, 108086. [CrossRef]
53. Gaigalas, G.; Fritzsche, S. Maple procedures for the coupling of angular momenta. VI. $LS - jj$ transformations. *Comput. Phys. Commun.* **2002**, *159*, 39. [CrossRef]
54. Fischer, A.; Canali, C.; Warring, U.; Kellerbauer, A.; Fritzsche, S. First optical hyperfine structure measurement in an atomic anion. *Phys. Rev. Lett.* **2010**, *104*, 073004. [CrossRef]
55. Cocolios, T.E.; Dexters, W.; Seliverstov, M.D.; Andreyev, A.N.; Antalic, S.; Barzakh, A.E.; Bastin, B.; Büscher, J.; Darby, I.G.; Fedorov, D.V.; et al. Early onset of ground state deformation in neutron deficient polonium isotopes. *Phys. Rev. Lett.* **2011**, *106*, 052503. [CrossRef]
56. Cheal, B.; Cocolios, T.E.; Fritzsche, S. Laser spectroscopy of radioactive isotopes: Role and limitations of accurate isotope-shift calculations. *Phys. Rev. A* **2012**, *86*, 042501. [CrossRef]
57. Biemont, E.; Palmeri, P.; Quinet, P.; Zhang, Z.G.; Svanberg, S. Doubly ionized thorium: Laser lifetime measurements and transition probability determination of interest in cosmochronology. *Astrophys. J.* **2002**, *567*, 1276. [CrossRef]
58. Kramida, A.; Ralchenko, Y.; Reader, J.; NIST ASD Team. NIST Atomic Spectra Database (ver. 5.8), [Online]. 2021 Available online: https://physics.nist.gov/asd (accessed on 25 October 2021).
59. Wyart, J.-F.; Kaufman, V. Extended analysis of doubly ionized thorium (Th III). *Phys. Scr.* **1981**, *24*, 941. [CrossRef]
60. Safronova, M.S.; Safronova, U.I.; Clark, C.W. Relativistic all-order calculations of Th, Th^+, and Th^{2+} atomic properties. *Phys. Rev. A* **2014**, *90*, 032512. [CrossRef]
61. Fritzsche, S. Symbolic evaluation of expressions from Racahs algebra. *Symmetry* **2021**, *13*, 1558. [CrossRef]
62. Fritzsche, S. Dielectronic recombination strengths and plasma rate coefficients of multiply-charged ions. *Astron. Astrophys.* **2021**, *656*, A163. [CrossRef]

Article

Update of Atomic Data for the First Three Spectra of Actinium

Alexander Kramida

National Institute of Standards and Technology, Gaithersburg, MD 20899, USA; alexander.kramida@nist.gov

Abstract: The present article describes a complete reanalysis of all published data on observed spectral lines and energy levels of the first three spectra of actinium (Ac I–III). In Ac I, three previously determined energy levels have been rejected, 12 new energy levels have been found; for six previously known levels, either the J values or the energies have been revised, and the ionization energy has been redetermined with an improved accuracy. In the line list of Ac I, three previous classifications have been discarded, 16 new ones have been found, and three have been revised. In Ac II, 16 new energy levels have been established, and 36 new identifications have been found for previously observed but unclassified lines. In both Ac I and Ac II, new sets of transition probabilities have been calculated. For all three spectra, complete datasets of critically evaluated energy levels, observed lines, and transition probabilities have been constructed to serve as recommended data on these spectra.

Keywords: atomic databases; standard reference databases; atomic spectroscopy; actinides; actinium; spectral lines; energy levels; transition probabilities; ionization energy

Citation: Kramida, A. Update of Atomic Data for the First Three Spectra of Actinium. *Atoms* **2022**, *10*, 42. https://doi.org/10.3390/atoms10020042

Academic Editors: Mustapha Laatiaoui and Sebastian Raeder

Received: 26 March 2022
Accepted: 14 April 2022
Published: 22 April 2022

Publisher's Note: MDPI stays neutral with regard to jurisdictional claims in published maps and institutional affiliations.

Copyright: © 2022 by the author. Licensee MDPI, Basel, Switzerland. This article is an open access article distributed under the terms and conditions of the Creative Commons Attribution (CC BY) license (https://creativecommons.org/licenses/by/4.0/).

1. Introduction

Strange as it may seem, the spectra of actinide atoms and ions are important for astrophysics, as all radioactive elements with atomic numbers $Z = 84$ through 99, except for At ($Z = 85$) and Fr ($Z = 87$), have been detected in chemically peculiar stars (see a good review of these observations in Quinet et al. [1]. In addition to that, spectra of atomic and ionized actinium have many important applications. The isotope ^{225}Ac is used in cancer radiotherapy, while ^{227}Ac is usable in radioisotope thermoelectric generators, neutron radiography, tomography, and other radiochemical investigations, as well as serving as a tracer for deep seawater circulation and mixing (see Zhang et al. [2] and references therein). Knowledge of the spectrum of atomic Ac helps in developing efficient laser-ionization methods for isotope separation. It also has potential applications in studies of atomic parity and time-reversal violation [3]. Spectra of Ac^+ and Ac^{2+}, along with other actinide ions, have good prospects in the search for variation of the fine-structure constant [4]. Ac^{2+} is also of interest in parity nonconservation research [5]. Thus, it is not surprising that many tens of papers have been published on these spectra. Comprehensive lists of these publications can be found in the bibliographic databases of National Institute of Standards and Technology (NIST) on atomic energy levels [6] and transition probabilities [7] accompanying the NIST Atomic Spectra Database (ASD) [8].

Despite the high interest in the spectra of actinium, the information on its spectra in the NIST ASD is rather scarce, and their theoretical interpretation is incomplete. Most of it is based on the comprehensive experimental work of Meggers et al. [9] on the first three actinium spectra (Ac I–III), which was a result of several years of work and was published in 1957. Meggers et al. have produced many tens of high-resolution spectrograms recorded on photographic plates archived at NIST. Since then, only a few fragmentary observations have been made using laser spectroscopy methods. Atomic theory has also made little progress in interpretation of these spectra. In 2020, the team supporting the NIST ASD [8] has critically evaluated all presently available data on these spectra and prepared updated datasets of energy levels and spectral lines for Ac I–III. The original purpose of the present work was to document these updated datasets. However, in the course of the work, new information on Ac I was obtained, which indicated that much of the original analysis that led to the 2020 revision of ASD was incorrect. This led to a complete reanalysis of both the Ac I and Ac II spectra, which is described here. The analysis of Ac III was found to be correct, and it is also described here.

2. Data of Meggers et al.

As described in Meggers et al. [9], those authors had only a few mg of actinium to conduct their spectral investigation. With that, they recorded about 150 photographic plates with spectrograms obtained with two different grating spectrographs, as well as a few Fabry–Perot spectrograms for analysis of hyperfine structure. Most of the spectrograms were taken with a hollow cathode light source, which produces mostly neutral-atom spectra. Several spectrograms were also taken with copper and silver spark discharges, where Ac II and especially Ac III lines were strongly enhanced. Still, the wavelength range was restricted to (2000–11,000) Å to target mostly the Ac I and Ac II spectra. The grating used in an initial study was blazed at 6000 Å, but the best spectrograms were obtained with a grating blazed at 4000 Å, so the intensities of observed lines greatly decreased towards the ultraviolet and infrared ends of the spectrum. The main source of standard wavelengths used to calibrate the spectrograms was iron, the spectrum of which was photographed on the same plates using masking of portions of the entrance slit of the spectrograph or a movable mask near the photographic plate. Auxiliary standards were also supplied by numerous impurities present in the light sources: boron, sodium, potassium, calcium, strontium, barium, magnesium, zinc, aluminum, silicon, iron, chromium, nickel, manganese, palladium, platinum, lanthanum, radium, and lead.

The wavelengths reported by Meggers et al. [9] are "the means of 2 to 13 measurements, except a few cases where the line was classified, although observed only once". These mean wavelengths were converted to vacuum wavenumbers. Although the air dispersion formula used was not specified, the present analysis revealed that it was the formula from Edlén 1953 [10]. The wavelength uncertainties were not specified for each line; instead, a general statement was made: "The probable error in any wavelength is usually less than 0.01 Å; this is shown by consistent agreement of different measurements and by the close fit of classified lines." Unfortunately, despite the high measurement precision, all wavelengths given by Meggers et al. [9] were rounded to two digits after the decimal point. However, in the tables of classified lines of Ac III, Ac II, and Ac I (Tables 3–7 of Meggers et al., respectively), the wavelengths are accompanied by wavenumbers, which are given with a greater relative precision, especially at longer wavelengths. In the present work, the wavenumbers of these classified lines were determined as weighted averages of the wavenumber values given in the tables and those obtained from the given air wavelengths with the air dispersion formula mentioned above. Then these mean wavenumbers were converted to air wavelengths using the now-standard five-parameter formula of Peck and Reeder [11]. Thus, the missing third digit in the wavelength was approximately restored in about half of all wavelengths.

Since detailed information about uncertainties of observed wavelengths is not available, these uncertainties have been evaluated by comparison of observed and Ritz wavelength values, as described in Ref. [12]. Figure 1 shows a comparison of wavelengths observed by Meggers et al. [9] with Ritz wavelengths calculated from these observed wavelengths in a least-squares level optimization procedure (see below). Only the meaningful spectral lines are shown in this figure, i.e., those for which upper and lower levels of the transition are not defined by a single observed line.

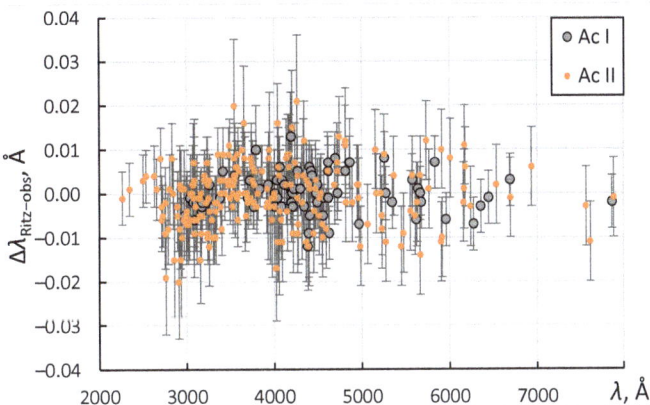

Figure 1. Observed wavelengths of Meggers et al. (1957) [9] compared with Ritz values. The error bars correspond to measurement uncertainties of Meggers et al. as assessed in the present work.

A few classified lines of Ac III are not shown in this plot, but their consistency with Ritz values is similarly good. For Ac I, the root-mean-square (rms) values of the differences $\Delta\lambda_{\text{Ritz}-\text{obs}}$ plotted in Figure 1 are about 0.004 Å for wavelengths shorter than about 4000 Å and 0.005 Å for longer wavelengths. For Ac II, the corresponding rms values are 0.006 Å and 0.009 Å. The lines marked with characters in the intensity values (such as "h"—hazy line, "c"—complex line, etc.) showed a somewhat greater rms values, 0.006 Å for Ac I and 0.008 Å for Ac II. These estimates were adopted as measurement uncertainties for most lines. For a few lines showing greater deviations of observed wavelengths from the Ritz values, the uncertainties have been increased. For wavelengths of unclassified lines, which were all rounded to two decimal places after the point and were not accompanied by wavenumbers in the tables of Meggers et al., an uncertainty of 0.013 Å was adopted.

In addition to the first three spectra of actinium, Meggers et al. [9] have observed six lines tentatively assigned to Ac IV (no attempts have been made to classify these lines) and several bands of the AcO molecule.

3. Ac I

3.1. Revisions and Extensions of Experimental Data on Ac I

Considering the lack of good computational resources at the time Meggers et al. [9] carried out their work, the quality of their measurements and analysis is amazingly good. Nevertheless, they made some mistakes.

One such mistake is a wrong $J = 3/2$ value assigned to the level at 22,801.11 cm^{-1}. This mistake was corrected by Ferrer et al. [13] (see also Granados et al. [14] and the earlier work of Sonnenschein [15]). These authors have analyzed the hyperfine structure (hfs) of the transition from this level to the ground level, which was observed by Meggers et al. [9] near 4384.5 Å (air wavelength). Their analysis of the observed hfs intervals unambiguously showed that this excited level has $J = 5/2$.

There are many other cases where the J values assigned by Meggers et al. [9] are not based on a unique choice allowed by observed combinations. A recent theoretical study by Dzuba et al. [3] suggested a number of possible revisions in those original J assignments. Some of them also involve a possible revision of excitation energy where the only observed transition could be associated not with the ground level 6d7s^2 ^{2}D$_{3/2}$ but with the first excited level with $J = 5/2$ of the same term.

On the other hand, the hfs study by Sonnenschein [15] has confirmed the J-values assigned by Meggers et al. [9] to three other low-excited levels at 25,729 cm^{-1} ($J = 1/2$), 26,066 cm^{-1} ($J = 3/2$), and 24,969 cm^{-1} ($J = 7/2$). For the latter level, the $J = 7/2$ assigned by Meggers et al. [9] is confirmed despite the fact that there is one line observed at 4003.79 Å (air wavelength; unclassified in the line list of Meggers et al. [9]) whose wave number (24,969.28 cm^{-1}) almost exactly coincides with this level's energy (24,969.294(17) cm^{-1}, according to the present analysis). This line cannot be due to a transition from the 24,969 cm^{-1} level ($J = 7/2$) to the ground level ($J = 3/2$), as it is optically forbidden. Thus, the wave number coincidence mentioned above must be treated as fortuitous.

Since the study of Meggers et al. [9] was restricted to the wavelength range below 7887 Å, they could not observe transitions from the lowest odd-parity levels ($7s^27p\ ^2P^\circ_{1/2,3/2}$) to the levels of the ground term. These transitions were recently observed and identified by the Mainz laser spectroscopy group in collaboration with several other institutions (see Zhang et al. [2]). Among the wavelengths measured in that work, there is one line in common with Meggers et al. [9], which allows an independent check of the measurement accuracy. The wavenumber of the $6d7s^2\ ^2D_{3/2}$– $6d7s(^3D)7p\ ^4F^\circ_{3/2}$ transition was reported by Zhang et al. [2] as 13,712.74(3) cm^{-1}, while it is 13,712.898(11) cm^{-1}, as follows from the measurements of Meggers et al. The difference is 0.16(3) cm^{-1}, corresponding to $-0.084(16)$ Å. As seen from Figure 1, this difference is much greater than the measurement uncertainty of Meggers et al., which means that there was a significant unaccounted source of error in the measurements of Zhang et al. [2]. As privately communicated by some of those authors [16], the Mainz group continues their investigations of the lowest odd-parity levels of Ac I. They have remeasured these levels with high resolution, which allowed them to study in detail the hfs structure of the three levels reported by Zhang et al. [2] and confirm the energy 13,712.898(11) cm^{-1} of the $6d7s(^3D)7p\ ^4F^\circ_{3/2}$ level following from the measurements of Meggers et al. [9]. The most probable cause of the error in the measurement of this level by Zhang et al. [2] is the large deviation of intensities of the hfs components of this level from those that assume theoretical line strengths and statistical populations of the hfs sublevels. Such large deviations were recently observed in other transitions of Ac I by Granados et al. [14], who used the same resonance ionization laser spectroscopy technique as Zhang et al. [2]. Granados et al. [14] gave detailed explanations for the reasons of these deviations. These deviations were ignored in the work of Zhang et al. [2], who assumed that the observed center of gravity of the transition corresponds to the difference between centers of gravity of the hfs structures of the two levels. On the other hand, the measurements of Zhang et al. [2] for the other two levels ($7s^27p\ ^2P^\circ_{1/2,3/2}$) have been confirmed by Raeder et al. [16].

Raeder et al. [16] have found that the transition observed at 4462.73 Å by Meggers et al. [9] originates not from the ground level, as classified by those authors, but from the metastable $6d7s^2\ ^2D_{5/2}$ level at 2231 cm^{-1}. Its observed hfs structure indicates the J-value of the upper level to be 7/2.

Another finding of Raeder et al. [16] is that the levels at 23,475.94 cm^{-1} and 26,533.16 cm^{-1}, which were assigned by Meggers et al. [9] to upper levels of transitions originating from the ground term $6d7s^2\ ^2D$, are impossible to observe by resonance excitation-ionization laser spectroscopy technique employed by the Mainz group. Thus, these levels are likely to be spurious, despite the very good agreement of the wave number difference of the lines at 3767.800 Å and 4113.769 Å (2231.40(3) cm^{-1}), which were assigned to the level at 26,533.16 cm^{-1} by Meggers et al. [9], with the splitting of the ground term (2231.432(8) cm^{-1}, according to the present work).

Besides the determination of the three energy levels ($7s^27p\ ^2P^\circ_{1/2,3/2}$ and $6d7s(^3D)7p\ ^4F^\circ_{3/2}$), the study of Zhang et al. [2] also includes a measurement of radiative lifetimes of these levels. They were found to be 668(11) ns, 255(7) ns, and 352(11) ns, respectively.

In addition to the studies discussed above, in 2012 Roßnagel et al. [17,18] experimentally determined the ionization energy (IE) of Ac I by analyzing three different Rydberg series in two-color resonant laser excitation. Their result, 43,394.45(19) cm^{-1}, is presently adopted as the recommended value of the ionization energy of Ac I. With the current values of fundamental constants [19], it corresponds to 5.380226(24) eV. In their work, Roßnagel et al. assumed the measurements of Meggers et al. [9] to have rather large uncertainties, namely, 0.11 cm^{-1} for both the Ac I and Ac II levels used in their analysis. From the present data described below, these uncertainties are much smaller (0.02–0.03) cm^{-1}, which calls for a repeated analysis of the measurements of Roßnagel et al. [17]. The value of the ionization energy can be improved with the present revised data of Meggers et al. [9]. This improvement is described below in Section 3.4.

All revisions and extensions discussed above have been incorporated in the present study and supplemented with several more new identifications. The complete line list with energy level classifications is presented in Table 1, and the list of energy levels (both the experimentally found and predicted ones) is given in Table 2 (both tables are placed at the bottom of this section to make reading of the text easier).

3.2. Theoretical Calculations for Ac I

The electronic structure of Ac I is very complex. The ground configuration is 6d7s^2, which involves only one open shell, 6d. However, excited levels involve many overlapping and strongly interacting configurations with up to three open shells: 6d7snl, 6d^2nl, 7s^2nl, and 7p^2nl. Meggers et al. [9] based their analysis on the supposed analogy with homologous spectra, Sc I, Y I, and La I. However, relative positions and widths of the interacting configurations $n'd(n'+1)snl$, $n'd^2nl$, $(n'+1)s^2nl$, and $(n'+1)p^2nl$ change with increasing n' ($n' = 3$ in Sc I, 4 in Y I, 5 in La I, and 6 in Ac I). This leads to redistribution of spectral line positions and strengths. Therefore, it is not surprising that many of the line classifications made by Meggers et al. [9] were erroneous. Luckily, the ground configuration of Ac I is still analogous to the homologous spectra, which simplified the initial analysis. The wavenumber difference of about 2231 cm^{-1} was seen in 20 pairs of observed lines and was readily identified as the fine-structure splitting within the ground term, 6d7s^2 ^{2}D. As one can see in the Periodic Table of the Elements [20], analogy of the ground configurations with those of the lighter homologous elements does not hold for the first spectra of the neighboring elements Th, Pa, U, and Np, making their analysis much more difficult.

The most extensive and accurate calculation of spectroscopic properties of Ac I was made in the above-mentioned work of Dzuba et al. [3]. This work used a combination of the configuration interaction and the linearized single-double–coupled-cluster methods (CI + SD). As seen from Table I of Dzuba et al., for levels below about 20,000 cm^{-1}, their calculated energies agree with experimental values of Meggers et al. [9] within a few hundred cm^{-1}. For higher energies, the discrepancies increase by an order of magnitude, and there are many ambiguities in association of the calculated levels with experimental ones. Dzuba et al. pointed out that many of the experimental energies could be wrong when they are determined by a single observed line. In those cases, the lower level of the corresponding transitions may differ from the interpretation of Meggers et al. There are also many cases where the J values assigned by Meggers et al. may be in error.

This illustrates the old problem: How do we establish a correspondence between the theoretical energy structure and that observed in experiments? A similar problem also occurs in comparisons of different theoretical models with each other. As explained by Kramida [12], the best method is to use the patterns of calculated transition probabilities from each level. In comparisons with experiments, these patterns should be matched with patterns of observed line intensities. This avoids the problem of unknown distributions of level populations in experimental spectra, since only the branching ratios are involved in the comparison. However, it requires the spectral variations of the registration sensitivity to be removed from the observed intensities, and relies on the assumption that the plasma is optically thin in the light source used. For establishing a correspondence between different theoretical models, the patterns of calculated transition probabilities can be directly compared. Energy level associations derived by this technique are much more reliable than associations based on energy ordering.

Table 1. Spectral lines of Ac I.

λ_{obs} [a] (Å)	λ_{Ritz} [a] (Å)	$\Delta\lambda_{O-R}$ [b] (Å)	σ_{obs} [c] (cm^{-1})	I_{obs} [d] (arb.u.)	Lower Level Configuration	Lower Level Term$_J$	Upper Level Configuration	Upper Level Term$_J$	E_{low} [e] (cm^{-1})	E_{upp} [e] (cm^{-1})	A [f] (s^{-1})	Acc. [g]	Type [h]	TP Ref. [i]	Line Ref. [i]	Notes [i]
2968.819(4)	2968.8142(15)	0.005	33,673.59	23	6d7s^2	$^2D_{3/2}$	6d^2(^{3}P)7p	$^4D^\circ_{3/2}$	0.000	33,673.650	9.e+06	E		TW	M	
3036.930(4)	3036.9294(16)	0.001	32,918.40	87	6d7s^2	$^2D_{3/2}$	6d^2(^{3}P)7p	$^2D^\circ_{3/2}$	0.000	32,918.416	6.e+06	E		TW	M	
3076.440(4)	3076.4385(18)	0.002	32,495.66	280	6d7s^2	$^2D_{3/2}$	6d^2(^{3}F)7p	$^2F^\circ_{5/2}$	0.000	32,495.679	5.e+06	E		TW	M	
3082.957(6)	3082.9507(16)	0.006	32,426.97	16	6d7s^2	$^2D_{3/2}$	6d^2(^{3}F)7p	$^4D^\circ_{5/2}$	2231.432	34,658.472		E			M	
3109.330(13)			32,151.94	83											M	
3111.570(4)	3111.5683(17)	0.001	32,128.80	420	6d7s^2	$^2D_{3/2}$	6d^2(^{1}G)7p	$^2G^\circ_{7/2}$	2231.432	34,360.247	1.0e+07	E		TW	M	
3140.720(13)			31,830.61	100											M	
3143.710(4)	3143.7088(18)	0.001	31,800.34	1100	6d7s^2	$^2D_{3/2}$	5d7s^2	$^2F^\circ_{5/2}$	0.000	31,800.350					M	
3171.170(4)	3171.1658(18)	0.004	31,524.98	1200	6d7s^2	$^2D_{3/2}$	6d^2(^{3}F)7p	$^2F^\circ_{7/2}$	2231.432	33,756.455	4.3e+07	D+		TW	M	
3174.224(4)	3174.2212(16)	0.003	31,494.65	160	6d7s^2	$^2D_{3/2}$	6d^2(^{3}F)7p	$^4F^\circ_{5/2}$	0.000	31,494.679					M	
...																
6340.100(13)	6340.104(11)	−0.004	15,768.26	200cs	6d7s(^{3}D)7p	$^4F^\circ_{7/2}$	6d7s(^{1}D)8s	$^4D_{5/2}$	17,683.869	33,452.12	1.52e+07	B		TW	M	N
...																
13,370.05(7)	13,370.05(7)		7477.36	1500	6d7s^2	$^2D_{3/2}$	7s^{2}7p	$^2P^\circ_{1/2}$	0.000	7477.36	1.497e+06	A+	M1	Z	Z	
44,814.27(16)			2231.432		6d7s^2	$^2D_{3/2}$	6d7s^2	$^2D_{5/2}$	0.000	2231.432	1.204e−01	AA	M1	TW		
85,321.3(11)			12,078.067		6d^2(^{3}F)7s	$^4F_{7/2}$	6d^2(^{3}F)7s	$^4F_{9/2}$	10,906.027	12,078.067	4.11e−02	A+	M1	TW		
95,929.0(11)			10,906.027		6d^2(^{3}F)7s	$^4F_{5/2}$	6d^2(^{3}F)7s	$^4F_{7/2}$	9863.589	10,906.027	4.53e−02	A+	M1	TW		
154,727(3)			9863.589		6d^2(^{3}F)7s	$^4F_{3/2}$	6d^2(^{3}F)7s	$^4F_{5/2}$	9217.288	9863.589	1.071e−02	A+		TW		

[a] Observed and Ritz wavelengths are given in standard air. Conversion between air and vacuum wavelengths was made with the five-parameter formula for the dispersion of air from Peck and Reeder [11].

[b] The difference between the observed and Ritz wavelengths. Blank for lines with unmeasured wavelength and for the lines that solely determine one of the energy levels of the transition.

[c] Transition wave number in vacuum.

[d] Observed intensity on an arbitrary scale, which is linear in terms of the energy flux under the line contour (see Section 6). The symbols after the numbers denote the character of the line: c—complex structure; D—double line; l—shaded on the long-wavelength side; m—masked by a stronger line; s—shaded on the short-wavelength side; :—the wavelength was not measured (the given value is a rounded Ritz wavelength).

[e] The optimized energies of the lower and upper levels of the transition. These values correspond to those given in Table 2.

[f] Transition probability. Exponential notation is used (e.g., "9.e+06" means "9. × 10^6").

[g] Accuracy of the transition probability. The code symbols for the accuracy are defined in the NIST ASD [8] (see https://physics.nist.gov/PhysRefData/ASD/Html/lineshelp.html#OUTACC, accessed on 25 March 2022).

[h] Transition type: blank—electric dipole; M1—magnetic dipole; E2—electric quadrupole; M1 + E2—mixed type (both types contribute more than 2% to the total A value given here).

[i] Code for references: D—Dzuba et al. [3]; Dn—values of Ref. [3] renormalized using the radiative lifetimes of Ref. [2]; M—Meggers et al. [9], Z—Zhang et al. [2]; TW—this work.

[i] Notes: D—the previous classification (of Ref. [9]) has been discarded; M—the line was masked by a much stronger Ac II line on the spectrograms of Ref. [9]; N—a newly classified line; R—the previous classification (of Ref. [9]) has been revised; T—a new tentative identification.

(Only a small portion of this table is given here for guidance to its content. The full version is available in machine-readable format in Table S1 of the Supplementary Online Materials, file Table S1.txt. The format of the supplementary table is slightly different: the uncertainties of λ_{obs} and λ_{Ritz} are given in separate columns instead of parentheses; the J-values of the lower and upper levels are given in separate columns; all notation is given inline with no superscripts or subscripts; the odd-parity symbol is replaced with the asterisk).

Table 2. Energy levels of Ac I.

E_{exp} (cm^{-1})	Unc. (cm^{-1})	Configuration	Term	J	Leading Percentages [a]				E_{calc} [b] (cm^{-1}) TW	E_{calc} [b] (cm^{-1}) [3]	g_{calc} [c] TW	g_{calc} [c] [3]	τ [d] (ns) TW	τ [d] (ns) u,%	Other [d]	Ref. [e]	Notes [f]
0.000	0.000	$6d7s^2$	^2D	3/2	94				87	0	0.799	0.8001				M	
2231.432	0.008	$6d7s^2$	^2D	5/2	93				2157	2339	1.200	1.2002	8.30e+09	1.0		TW,M	
7477.36	0.04	$7s^27p$	$^2P°$	1/2	90				7422	7565	0.664	0.6626	690	10	668(11)^Z	Z	
9217.288	0.013	$6d^2(^3F)7s$	^4F	3/2	93	6	$6d7s(^3D)7p$	$^2P°$	8766	8989	0.425	0.4088	1.0e+07	50		TW,M	
9863.589	0.012	$6d^2(^3F)7s$	^4F	5/2	91	5	$6d^2(^1D)7s$	^2D	9659	9288	1.036	1.0298	9.7e+09	38		TW,M	
10,906.027	0.014	$6d^2(^3F)7s$	^4F	7/2	98				11,111	9974	1.235	1.2333	1.27e+10	11		TW,M	
12,078.067	0.019	$6d^2(^3F)7s$	^4F	9/2	93	6	$6d^2(^1G)7s$	^2G	12,564	11,726	1.320	1.3143	1.5e+10	24		TW,M	
12,276.591	0.020	$7s^27p$	$^2P°$	3/2	84	10	$6d7s(^3D)7p$	$^2P°$	12,443	12,345	1.334	1.3332	280	10	255(7)^Z	Z	
		$6d^2(^3P)7s$	^4P	1/2	91	6	$6d^2(^1S)7s$	^2S	12,404	12,583	2.601	2.6295	2.7e+05	160			
		$6d^2(^3P)7s$	^4P	3/2	92	5	$6d^2(^1D)7s$	^2D	13,361	12,847	1.676	1.6841	4.5e+05	210			
21,195.870	0.018	$6d7s(^1D)7p$	$^2F°$	5/2	41	29	$6d7s(^3D)7p$	$^4P°$	21,313	21,170	1.129	1.0394	23	10		TW,M	
21,232.31	0.05	$6d7s(^3D)7p$	$^4D°$	7/2	81	9	$6d7s(^3D)7p$	$^4F°$	20,537	20,288	1.391	1.3858	160	10		TW	T
		$6d^2(^1S)7s$	^2S	1/2	81	5	$6d^2(^3P)7s$	^4P	22,088	21,918	1.962	1.9806	8.e+04	2300			
35,870.009	0.022	$6d^2(^3F)7p$	$^4D°$	7/2	32	24	$6d^2(^3F)7p$	$^2F°$	35,313		1.249		8.1	10		TW,M	J
		$6d7s(^3D)7d$	^4G	62	21	$6d7s(^3D)7d$	^2F	36,102	36,150	0.723	0.6868	19.0	10			
		$6d7s(^3D)7d$	^4D	1/2	76	17	$6d7s(^3D)7d$	^2P	36,248		0.171		17.7	10			
		$6d7s(^1D)8s$	^2D	3/2	32	13	$6d^2(^1D)8s$	^2D	36,322	36,218	0.850	0.8778	20.9	10			
43,394.52	0.10	Ac II ($6p^67s^2$ $^1S_0$)	Limit													TW,R	

[a] The first percentage pertains to the configuration and term given in the columns "Configuration" and "Term"; the second one pertains to the configuration and term specified in the next two columns.

[b] In this work (TW), the energies were calculated in a least-squares fit with Cowan's codes [21,22]. In the fitting, the calculated energies of Dzuba et al. [3] were used as "experimental" ones, where no experimental values are available.

[c] Landé g_J-factors (dimensionless) calculated in this work (TW) and in Ref. [3].

[d] Radiative lifetimes calculated in this work (TW) and those calculated or measured in other works. Exponential notation is used in some of the τ values (e.g., "8.30e+09" means "8.30 × 10^{9}"). For the values from this work, estimated percentage uncertainties are given in the next column. Reference values from other work are given with uncertainties specified in parentheses after the value in units of the last digit of the value. Their sources are specified as letter superscripts: D—Dzuba et al. [3] (theoretical); Z—Zhang et al. [2] (experimental).

[e] Code for references: F—Ferrer et al. [13]; M—Meggers et al. [9]; Z—Zhang et al. [2]; R—Roßnagel et al. [17]; TW—this work.

[f] Notes: J—the J-value (of Meggers et al. [9]) has been revised; N—a level newly identified in this work; R—revised identification; T—a new tentative identification of this work.

(Only a small portion of this table is given here for guidance to its content. The full version is available in machine-readable format in Table S2 of the Supplementary Online Materials, file Table S2.txt. The format of the supplementary table is slightly different. See footnotes to Table 1).

Table 3. Parameters of the least-squares fit for Ac I.

Parity	Configurations		Parameter	LSF [a] (cm^{-1})	Δ [b] (cm^{-1})	Group [c]	HFR [a]	LSF/HFR [a]
e	6d7s^2		E_{av}	3646.1	268		0.0	
e	6d7s^2		ζ_{6d}	855.0	126	6	1171.2	0.7300
e	6d7s7d		E_{av}	40,623.1	459		33,548.7	1.2109
e	6d7s7d		ζ_{6d}	991.7	146	6	1358.5	0.7300
e	6d7s7d		ζ_{7d}	63.6	9	6	87.1	0.7302
e	6d7s7d		$F^1(6d,7d)$	0.0	fixed		0.0	
e	6d7s7d		$F^2(6d,7d)$	2499.6	fixed		3570.9	0.7000
e	6d7s7d		$F^3(6d,7d)$	0.0	fixed		0.0	
e	6d7s7d		$F^4(6d,7d)$	1079.6	fixed		1542.3	0.7000
e	6d7s7d		$G^2(6d,7d)$	13,953.6	fixed		19,933.7	0.7000
...								
e	6d^{2}7s	6d^3	R_d^2(6d7s,6d6d)	−13,229.4	1040	9	−20,926.0	0.6322
e	6d^{2}8s	6d^3	R_d^2(6d8s,6d6d)	−3654.5	287	9	−5780.6	0.6322
...								
o	6d7s7p		E_{av}	23,249.1	239		16,467.7	1.4118
o	6d7s7p		ζ_{6d}	1015.9	140	6	1272.5	0.7983
o	6d7s7p		ζ_{7p}	2832.8	183	7	2195.9	1.2900
o	6d7s7p		$F^1(6d,7p)$	0.0	fixed		0.0	
o	6d7s7p		$F^2(6d,7p)$	8588.9	1001	5	14,362.0	0.5980
o	6d7s7p		$G^2(6d,7s)$	14,850.0	2470	3	19,062.1	0.7790
o	6d7s7p		$G^1(6d,7p)$	6443.2	482	2	9766.1	0.6597
o	6d7s7p		$G^2(6d,7p)$	0.0	fixed		0.0	
o	6d7s7p		$G^3(6d,7p)$	2519.3	1221	10	6894.4	0.3654
o	6d7s7p		$G^1(7s,7p)$	9196.1	774	4	20,369.4	0.4515
...								
o	6d7s7p	6d^{2}7p	R_d^2(6d7s,6d6d)	−14,498.5	2703	8	−22,138.2	0.6549
o	6d7s8p	6d^{2}8p	R_d^2(6d7s,6d6d)	−15,232.5	2840	8	−23,259.0	0.6549
...								

[a] Parameter values determined in the least-squares-fitted (LSF) and ab initio pseudo-relativistic Hartree–Fock (HFR) calculations and their ratio.
[b] Standard deviation of the fitted parameter. Parameters that were not varied in the fit are marked as "fixed".
[c] Parameters in each numbered group were linked together with their ratio fixed at the HFR level.

(Only a small portion of this table is given here for guidance to its content. The full version is available in machine-readable format in Table S3 of the Supplementary Online Materials, file Table S3.txt).

Dzuba et al. [3] provided their calculated transition probabilities for 66 lines originating from seven odd-parity levels. Intensities of the lines originating from these levels observed in experiments are compared in Figure 2 with those calculated by Dzuba et al. [3].

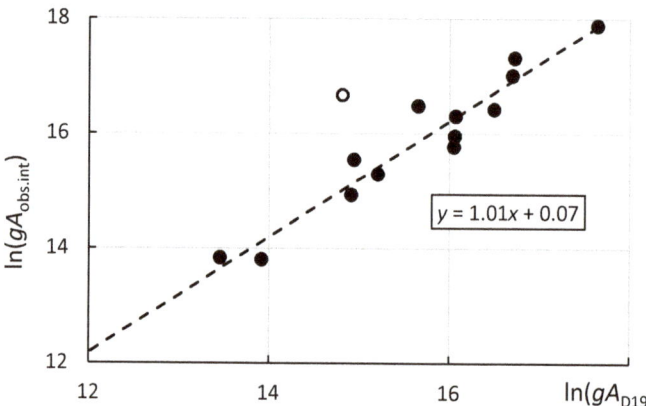

Figure 2. Comparison of observed line intensities with calculated transition rates (gA values) of Dzuba et al. [3]. The quantity $gA_{obs.int.}$ on the vertical axis represents the gA values derived from observed intensities reduced in the present work to a common linear scale (see Section 6). The empty circle represents the line at 5228.31 Å tentatively identified in this work as the transition from the 6d7s(^{3}D)7p ^{4}D$^°_{5/2}$ level to the ground level (see the text). This transition was excluded from the linear fit depicted by the dashed line.

The observed intensities used in this figure are the values that have been reduced in the present work to a common scale (see Section 6). The quantity $gA_{\text{obs.int.}}$ plotted in the figure is directly proportional to these intensities:

$$gA_{\text{obs.int.}} = \frac{I_{\text{obs}} \lambda}{\exp(-E_{\text{up}}/0.5121 + 3.693)}, \tag{1}$$

where I_{obs} is the observed intensity (in arbitrary units on the scale adopted here; see Section 6), λ is transition wavelength in angstroms, and E_{up} is the energy of the upper level in eV.

As one can see from Figure 2, agreement of the calculated gA values of Dzuba et al. [3] with observed intensities is very good (except for one tentatively identified line, which will be discussed further below in Section 3.3). Even more impressive is the agreement of the calculated lifetimes with the three experimental values of Zhang et al. [2]. After the A-values reported by Dzuba et al. [3] have been adjusted to experimental transition energies, the lifetimes calculated from these adjusted A-values agree with experiment within 10% on average. This estimate coincides with uncertainties given by Dzuba et al. [3] for their calculated lifetimes.

The other three published datasets of energy levels and transition rates for Ac I are those of Quinet et al. (2007) [1], Özdemir and Ürer (2010) [23], and Ürer and Özdemir (2012) [24]. Compared to the calculations of Dzuba et al. [3], those older ones are all of a relatively small scale. While all three older calculations account for only a limited amount of valence–valence electron correlations (by inclusion of 23/25 [1], 24/23 [23], and 13/5 [24] valence-excited configurations of even/odd parity), those of Dzuba et al. [3] effectively accounted for core–valence correlations (in the SD part of their method) and included a few hundred thousands of configurations in the CI part of their calculation. Consequently, the results of those older calculations are of very limited accuracy.

Calculations of Quinet et al. [1] were made with the pseudo-relativistic Hartree–Fock method with inclusion of core polarization (HFR+CPOL) implemented in a modified version of Cowan's atomic structure codes [21]. Addition of the core-polarization potential effectively accounts for core–valence interactions, which could potentially give reasonable results. Semiempirical adjustments were made to the average energies of configurations and spin–orbit interaction parameters in a least-squares fitting (LSF) of experimentally known energy levels. However, as noted by Quinet et al. [1], the odd-parity energy levels of Meggers et al. [9] could not be fitted with a reasonable accuracy. As discussed in the previous subsection, one of the reasons for that is presence of several incorrectly identified levels in Ref. [9].

In the present work, an attempt was made to calculate the Ac I spectrum with another modification of Cowan's codes [22]. As in the work of Quinet et al. [1], no configurations involving excitation from the Rn-like [Hg]$6p^6$ core were considered. The following configurations were included in these calculations: in even parity, [Rn]$6d(7s^2 + 7p^2 + 8s^2 + 7s5g + 7s7d + 7s8s + 7p8p + 7p5f + 8p5f + 7d8s)$, $7s(7p^2 + 8s^2 + 7p5f + 7p8p + 8p5f + 7d8s) + 6d^2(7s + 7d + 8s + 5g) + 6d^3 + 7s^2(5g + 8s + 7d) + 7p^2(8s + 7d) + 7p8s(8p + 5f) + 7p7d5f + 8s8p5f$ (30 configurations in total); in odd parity, [Rn]$6d7s(7p + 8p + 5f) + 6d7p(8s + 7d + 5g) + 6d8s(8p + 5f) + 6d^2(7p + 8p + 5f) + 6d7d(8p + 5f) + 7s7d(8p + 5f) + 7s^2(7p + 8p + 5f) + 8s^2(7p + 8p) + 7p^2(8p + 5f) + 7s7p(8s + 7d + 5g) + 7s8s(8p + 5f) + 7p^3 + 7p8p5f$ (29 configurations in total). These configuration sets are larger than those used in the study of Quinet et al. [1] (23 and 25 configurations in the even- and odd-parity sets, respectively). It should be noted that the present extension of the configuration sets included in the calculation does not replace the core-polarization corrections that were accounted for in the calculations of Quinet et al. [1], because no core-excited configurations were included here. Nevertheless, in the case of Ac I, a better account for interactions between the valence-excited configurations proved to be much more important than the effects of core excitations.

The calculation started with an attempt to reproduce the theoretical levels of Dzuba et al. [3] by adjusting the Slater parameters in a LSF. The immediate problem turned out to be with level designations of Dzuba et al. [3]. They did not calculate the eigenvector compositions. Instead, their level labels were assigned by using an ad hoc procedure involving a search for a combination of L and S quantum numbers that would give the best match between the Landé g-factor returned by a simple formula assuming pure LS coupling and the g-factor calculated by Dzuba et al. [3] with the CI + SD method. This method of labeling often results in unphysical term designations. For example, the level list of Dzuba et al. includes two $6d^3\ ^4D_{3/2}$ levels, one at 28,793 cm^{-1} and another at 34,409 cm^{-1}. Both designations are invalid, because there is no ^4D term in the $6d^3$ configuration (see, e.g., Martin et al. [25]). Configuration labels are also ambiguous because of strong CI (note that the level predicted at 33,551 cm^{-1} with $J = 3/2$ was wrongly designated by Dzuba et al. [3] as $7s^29p$. Most probably, it was just a misprint: it must be $7s^28p$, as follows from the present calculations). Thus, we are left with only two options available for matching the level structure calculated by Dzuba et al. [3] with that returned by Cowan's codes: (1) use the patterns of calculated transition rates (given by Dzuba et al. [3] for only a few lowest excited levels) and (2) use the Landé factors to identify the levels. By using these two methods, it turned out to be possible to make a reasonably good fit. It should be significantly better than an ab initio calculation with Cowan's codes, since this procedure effectively introduces corrections to Slater parameters, partially accounting for configuration interactions and relativistic effects missing in the ab initio Cowan-code calculation.

The LSF calculation then proceeded with replacement of theoretical levels of Dzuba et al. [3] with experimental values, where the identification was deemed reliable, and comparing the resulting predicted line intensities with the observed ones. Several sets of LSF calculations were made. In each set, all predicted levels and strong transitions were loaded into the input files for the visual line identification code IDEN2 [26], and the patterns of predicted intensities were compared with those present in the experimental line list of Meggers et al. [9]. If a level was found to be wrongly assigned to a set of observed lines (i.e., the observed intensities did not match the predicted ones for this level), or if a new, previously unknown level was found, the LSF was repeated with a corrected or expanded set of experimental levels, and a new session of work with IDEN2 was initiated. In total, several tens of LSF calculations were made, gradually extending the list of established levels and improving the match between observed and calculated line intensities.

For many odd-parity levels above 20,000 cm^{-1}, the calculated A-values were found to be very sensitive to small changes of Slater parameters. This is due to strong interactions between the configurations involved. It indicated that, to reliably predict the A-values, the positions of all strongly interacting configurations must be established with an error not exceeding a few hundred cm^{-1}. Fortunately, the calculations of Dzuba et al. [3] have provided enough sufficiently accurate data to make it possible.

In the end, a rather good agreement between the results of the present calculations with those of Dzuba et al. [3] has been achieved. The Landé g-factors calculated in the present LSF with Cowan's codes are compared with those of Dzuba et al. [3] in Figure 3.

As this figure shows, agreement between the two calculations is very good for the low-excited levels below about 15.1 kK (1 kK = 1000 cm^{-1}). The rms difference between the two sets of calculated g-values is 0.012 for these low-excited levels. For higher levels with energies between 15.1 kK and 32.9 kK, the rms difference is 0.05. For the levels above 32.9 kK, it grows to 0.12. In the absence of any experimental data for comparison, these estimates can be adopted as uncertainties for both sets of calculated data.

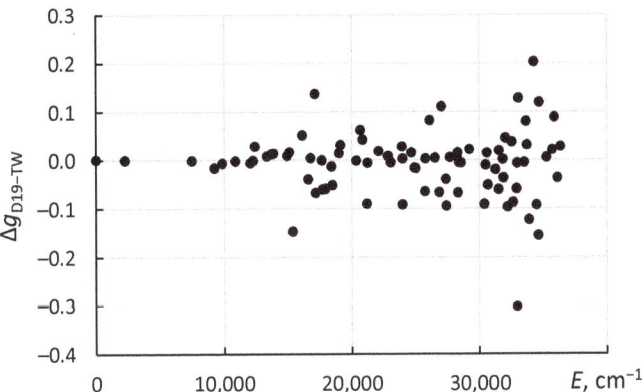

Figure 3. Differences of Landé g-factors calculated by Dzuba et al. [3] from those computed in the present work in a least-squares fitting with Cowan's codes.

A similar pattern is seen in comparison of the calculated energy levels with observed ones, shown in Figure 4.

For the even-parity levels, the rms difference of the presently calculated levels from experimental ones is 419 cm^{-1}, while for the calculation of Dzuba et al. [3] it is 531 cm^{-1}. For the odd-parity levels, the corresponding rms values are 411 cm^{-1} and 607 cm^{-1}. The one level that shows an outstandingly large difference between the calculation of Dzuba et al. [3] and experiment is $5f7s^2$ $^2F^\circ_{5/2}$. It is interesting to note that for the other $5f7s^2$ $^2F^\circ$ level with $J = 7/2$, the result of Dzuba et al. [3] is in rather good agreement both with the present calculation and with the experimental value. Both these levels are almost pure in LS coupling (with more than 90% of the leading term in their eigenvector compositions). The cause of the discrepancy in the calculation of Dzuba et al. is unclear.

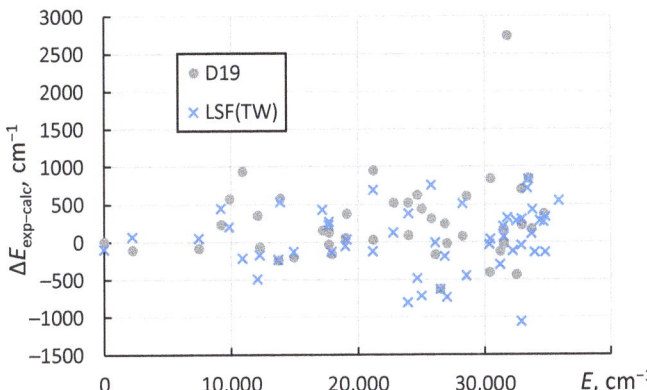

Figure 4. Differences of energy levels calculated by Dzuba et al. [3] (D19) and in the present LSF calculation (TW) from experimental values.

The calculated level values, their eigenvector compositions, and Landé factors found in the present LSF calculations are included in the level list given in Table 2 together with experimental energies and calculated radiative lifetimes (the latter are described in the following section). The final fitted values of the Slater parameters resulting from the present LSF are listed in Table 3.

3.3. Ac I Transition Probabilities

As mentioned in Section 3.1, radiative lifetimes of the lowest three odd-parity levels of Ac I were measured by Zhang et al. [2]. The measured lifetime of the $7s^27p\ ^2P^\circ_{1/2}$ level directly gives the $6d7s^2\ ^2D_{3/2}$–$7s^27p\ ^2P^\circ_{1/2}$ transition probability, as this is the only allowed channel of radiative decay of this level. For the two allowed electric dipole (E1) transitions from the $7s^27p\ ^2P^\circ_{3/2}$ level, as well as for two E1 transitions from the $6d7s(^3D)7p\ ^4F^\circ_{3/2}$ level, the present recommended values of transition probabilities (A-values) have been derived from the branching fractions computed by Dzuba et al. [3] combined with the lifetimes measured by Zhang et al. [2]. The five experimental and semiempirical A-values described above have been complemented by five A-values computed ab initio by Dzuba et al. [3], which have been assigned accuracy categories C+ (one transition), C (one transition), D+ (two transitions), and E (one transition). These accuracy categories correspond to uncertainties ≤18%, ≤25%, and ≤40%, and >50%, respectively. In addition to that, 85 A-values calculated in the present work (with Cowan's codes [22]) have been adopted. This selection was based on comparison of the present calculation with that of Dzuba et al. [3], as well as with observed line intensities. Eight of the presently computed A-values are for parity-forbidden transitions, which will be discussed further below. Of the 77 presently computed A-values of E1 transitions, 38 have been assigned to the accuracy category B (uncertainties ≤10%), 20 to the accuracy categories C, D+, and D (uncertainties ≤25%, ≤40%, and ≤50%), while the remaining 19 are estimated to be accurate only to a factor of about two, corresponding to the accuracy category E.

In the present calculation of allowed (E1) transitions, the reduced E1 transition matrix elements calculated by Cowan's codes [21,22] were reduced for s–p and p–d transitions by a factor of 0.811 to bring the calculated lifetimes of the lowest odd-parity levels in agreement with those observed by Zhang et al. [2] and calculated by Dzuba et al. [3] for Ac I. For the d–f and f–g transitions, the scaling factor was set at 0.8233 as determined in the analysis of Ac III data (see Section 5). The comparison of the presently calculated line strengths S with those calculated by Dzuba et al. [3] is depicted in Figure 5.

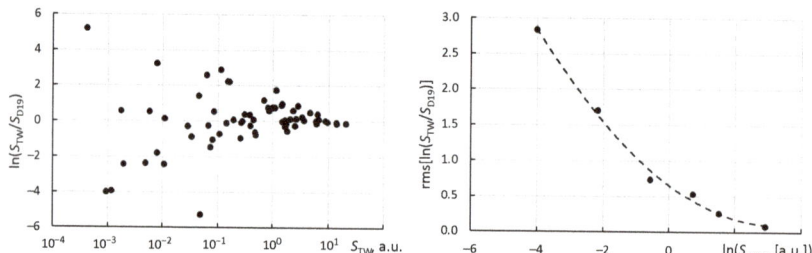

Figure 5. Left panel: Comparison of transition line strengths S (in atomic units, a.u.) calculated by Dzuba et al. [3] (D19) and in the present work (TW). **Right** panel: Derivation of the uncertainty estimate (see the text).

As seen in the left panel of Figure 5, the comparison shows a typical pattern of very small differences between the two calculations for the strongest transitions, while the agreement rapidly deteriorates with decreasing line strength S. To obtain numerical estimates of uncertainties as a function of S, following the method suggested by Kramida [12], the entire range of S-values available for comparison was divided into six intervals divided by the following values of S computed in this work (S_{TW}): 6.7 a.u., 3.0 a.u., 1.3 a.u., 0.18 a.u., and 0.06 a.u. In the right panel of Figure 5, the rms values of the natural logarithm of the ratio S_{TW}/S_{TW} are plotted against the average values of S_{TW} available for comparison in each interval. The quadratic interpolation depicted by the dashed line was then used to produce an estimate of uncertainty (in S) of the present calculation as a function of S.

As mentioned in the previous subsection, the earlier calculations of Refs. [1,23,24] were too inaccurate to be usable in such comparisons. Thus, in the absence of a better benchmark, the same function of S as described above was used to estimate the uncertainties of the calculation of Dzuba et al. [3]. For a few of the strongest transitions, even though the estimated uncertainties are similar, the data of Ref. [3] were given a higher preference. For weaker transitions, a comparison of calculated and observed line intensities was used as an additional selection tool. A few of the presently calculated A-values were found to better agree with the observations, so they were selected as recommended values.

In addition to E1 transitions, the A-values for the parity-forbidden magnetic dipole (M1) and electric–quadrupole (E2) transitions were calculated in the present work. No data on these transitions are currently available in the literature. Therefore, no comparisons with other data are available for estimation of uncertainties of these results. Thus, the Monte Carlo method suggested by Kramida [27] was used for this estimation. One hundred random trial calculations were made with the Slater parameters, and E2 transition matrix elements varied around their nominal values within the normal statistical distributions. The widths of these distributions for the Slater parameters were set by the standard deviations of the LSF, while for the E2 transition matrix elements, a variance of 15% was assumed. A transition was deemed to be of a "mixed" M1 + E2 type if the contribution of the E2 transition to the total A-value was found to be 2% or greater. A total of eight forbidden transitions are included in Table 1. Four of them are M1 transitions, for which the calculated A-values are very accurate (category A+ or AA). The accuracy is much worse for the E2 transitions and for the mixed-type transitions having a large E2 contribution. However, for the selected four transitions of this kind, the accuracy category is C+ or C (uncertainties $\leq$ 25%).

The radiative lifetimes included in Table 2 were calculated by summing up the A-values for all radiative decay branches of each level, including the E1, M1, and E2 transitions. Their uncertainties were calculated by a standard statistical formula for propagation of uncertainties of each participating A-value. Where the reference lifetime values are available experimentally [2] or theoretically [3], the present values agree with the reference values within 14% on average.

3.4. Ionization Energy of Ac I

As mentioned in Section 3.1, the ionization energy (IE) of Ac I was determined by Roßnagel et al. [17] to be 43,394.45(19) cm^{-1}. In that determination, those authors adopted the values of intermediate excited levels of Ac I from Meggers et al. [9] and assumed their uncertainties to be 0.11 cm^{-1}. The same assumption was made about the excitation energies of Ac II levels used to calculate the limit offsets for the Rydberg series converging to excited levels of Ac II. In the present work, the values of all these levels have been significantly refined. These new values are in agreement with those of [9], but their uncertainties are found to be much smaller, between 0.02 cm^{-1} and 0.03 cm^{-1}. Thus, a new determination of the IE was made here by using the data for the same Rydberg series as used by Roßnagel et al. [17]. The original measured wave numbers of the observed lines were taken from the master thesis of Roßnagel [18]. The IE was determined by a least-squares fit of the extended Ritz-type quantum-defect expansion formula (see, e.g., Ref. [12]). A recently written (by the present author) computer code *fit_Ritz*, which simultaneously fits multiple Rydberg series with a common IE value, was used. Unlike the multi-channel quantum defect formulas used by Roßnagel et al. [17], the formula used here cannot account for perturbations caused by configuration interactions. Therefore, the perturbed members of the series labeled as b and c in Roßnagel et al. [17], which converge to excited levels of Ac II, have been excluded from the fit. Namely, the levels with $n = 16$ to 25, 33, 36, and 46 have been excluded from the series b converging to the 6d7s $^3D_1$ level of Ac II at 4739.631(33) cm^{-1} (see Section 5). From the series c, converging to the 6d7s $^3D_2$ level of Ac II at 5267.147(32) cm^{-1}, levels with $n = 24$ to 34, 41, 47, 48, and 49 have been excluded. In the multi-channel quantum defect fit of Roßnagel et al. [17], the additional free variables pertaining to the perturbing levels have largely absorbed the additional degrees of freedom corresponding to the levels excluded here. Thus, these exclusions are not expected to significantly deteriorate the accuracy of the fit for the IE. Indeed, when each of the series b and c are fitted separately, their limits are found to be 43,394.39(6) cm^{-1} and 43,394.98(39) cm^{-1}, respectively, where the uncertainties are purely statistical. The corresponding values from Roßnagel et al. [17] are 43,394.25(27) cm^{-1} and 43,394.59(43) cm^{-1}. The present results agree with those of Roßnagel et al. [17], and the statistical uncertainties are even smaller. The most precise determination of the IE is provided by the unperturbed series a, for which 36 members were observed by Roßnagel [18]. The series limit derived here from this single series is 43,394.524(21) cm^{-1}. This agrees with the value of Roßnagel et al. [17] obtained for this series, 43,394.530(3) cm^{-1}. Here, the uncertainties are again purely statistical. However, it is evident that the meaning of "statistical" is different in the present work and in Roßnagel et al. [17]. The greater uncertainty of the present value stems from inclusion of the systematic part of the wavelength-measurement uncertainty (0.04 cm^{-1}, according to Raeder et al. [16]) in the uncertainties of the measured wave numbers, which are the input values for the present fit. Here, this systematic error was assumed to vary quasi-randomly in measurements of the different peaks. It makes little difference for the determination of the total uncertainty, since other systematic effects are estimated to be significantly larger. The most significant systematic error stems from the asymmetry of the observed peaks caused by unresolved fine and hyperfine structure. The largest of these errors is due to the hfs of the lower level, from which the Rydberg levels were excited. For the series a, it was the level at 31,800.350(18) cm^{-1}, which is presently identified as 5f7s^2 ^{2}F$^\circ_{5/2}$ (note that in the work of the Mainz group [17,18], this level was assumed to have $J = 3/2$, following Meggers et al. [9]). The possible effect of the asymmetry of this level caused by hfs is estimated to be about 0.1 cm^{-1}. This systematic error dominates the uncertainty of the final result of the present joint fit of the three series (a, b, and c), which is 43,394.52(10) cm^{-1}. With the present values of the fundamental constants [19], it corresponds to 5.380235(13) eV. This value agrees with the determination of Roßnagel et al. [17] but is about twice more precise.

3.5. Ac I: Discussion and Outlook

The experimental values of the energy levels given in Table 2 have been determined from the wavelengths of identified lines by the least-squares optimization procedure using the code LOPT [28]. Their uncertainties are estimated as the maximum of two values returned by LOPT, D_1, and D_2 (for definitions of these quantities, see Ref. [28]). This code also determines the uncertainties of the Ritz wavelengths, which include the covariances between the optimized values of the lower and upper levels of each transition. These uncertainties are also given in Table 2.

As can be seen in the last column of Table 2, the present level list includes 13 newly identified levels (eight of which are firmly established, and five are tentatively identified based on one observed line with a good match between the observed and calculated intensity). For another five levels, the J-values have been revised compared to the original assignment given by Meggers et al. [9].

All new identifications were made with the help of the IDEN2 code [26]. Most of them involve two or more transitions with wavelengths satisfying the arithmetic relations between the observed and Ritz wave numbers within or close to the combined measurement uncertainties. They are also supported by the closeness of the experimental energy to that calculated here in the LSF, as well as in Ref. [3], where available. In most cases, the observed intensities are in good agreement with the calculated ones. In a few cases, this agreement is poor, which can be explained by large uncertainties in the calculated transition rates.

Five of the new line identifications listed in Table 1 are considered as tentative, as they are the sole lines defining the corresponding upper levels. One of them is the 6d^2(^{3}F)7s ^{4}F$_{9/2}$–6d^2(^{3}F)7p ^{4}G$^\circ_{11/2}$ transition, which was previously identified by Meggers et al. [9], with the line observed at 4682.16 Å. It is now identified with a stronger line observed at 4705.782(6) Å, which was previously classified as the 6d7s^2 ^{2}D$_{5/2}$–6d^2(^{3}F)7p ^{4}D$^\circ_{7/2}$ transition [9] with the upper level at 23,475.94 cm^{-1}. As noted in Section 3.1, this level could not be observed in resonance excitation-ionization laser spectroscopy experiments [16] and thus was rejected here. The observed intensity of the 4705.782 Å line agrees much better with the present LSF calculation for the $^4F_{9/2}$–$^4G^\circ_{11/2}$ transition than the 4682.16 Å line. The predicted intensity is defined by the calculated A-value; its accuracy is estimated to be very good (accuracy category B, corresponding to uncertainty $\leq$10%). However, the difference by a factor of two between the intensities of the previously and newly identified lines is within the uncertainty of the present intensity modeling (see Section 6), so the revised identification is considered as tentative. The line at 4682.16 Å is now unclassified. It is the strongest unidentified line in the list of observed Ac I lines in Ref. [9].

Another tentative identification deserving discussion involves the 6d7s(^{3}D)7p $^4D^\circ_{5/2}$ level presently placed at 19,121.32 cm^{-1}. It is based on a single moderately strong line observed at 5228.31 Å. Its observed intensity agrees very well with the presently predicted one, but the accuracy of the present A-value is very low (category C, uncertainty > 50%). The A-value calculated by Dzuba et al. [3] is five times smaller, but its accuracy is estimated to be similarly low. For this level, transition with the largest predicted A-value is predicted to be to the 6d^2(^{3}F)7s $^4F_{7/2}$ level at 10,906.027(14) cm^{-1}. Its wavelength, 12,169.09 Å (in air) is outside of the wavelength range covered by the study of Meggers et al. M57. Pending the observation of this transition, the present identification remains questionable.

Meggers et al. [9] had listed three observed lines classified as transitions from the odd-parity level near 30,396.6 cm^{-1} with $J = 3/2$. This level was labeled as 6d7s(^{1}D)7p $^2P^\circ_{3/2}$. This level is now interpreted as 6d^2(^{3}F)7p $^4F^\circ_{3/2}$ (with 76% of this term in its composition; see Table 2). This interpretation seemed questionable at first, because the strongest transition from this level was predicted to occur at 4720.274(6) Å, well within the range of Ref. [9], but was not listed among observed lines. It was found here that this line must have been masked by the strong Ac II line at 4720.16 Å.

Percentage compositions given in Table 2 include only the two leading components of the eigenvectors in LS coupling. In the even-parity system, the average purity of the eigenvectors (i.e., the arithmetic mean of the leading percentage) is 76% and 60% for the even and odd parity, respectively. In the even parity, even though a few levels have leading percentages less than 50%, all level labels corresponding to the leading percentage are unambiguous. However, in the odd parity, mixing between different eigenstates with the same $J\pi$ symmetry (where π means parity) is much stronger. To provide unique labeling of all levels, in many cases it was necessary to use configuration and term designations of the second or third leading component of the eigenvector in the level labels given in the columns "Configuration" and "Term" of Table 2. These level labels have little physical meaning; they are used for bookkeeping only.

Table 2 includes all presently calculated levels up to the highest level tabulated in the work of Dzuba et al. [3], i.e., below 37 kK. As mentioned in Section 3.1, the two levels listed by Meggers et al. [9] at 23,475.94 cm^{-1} and 26,533.16 cm^{-1} have been rejected here. The first of them was already discussed above. As for the level at 26,533.16 cm^{-1}, the lines assigned to this level in Ref. [9] imply that the only J-values possible for this level are 3/2 and 5/2. As can be seen in Table 2, there is no place for this level in the present interpretation of the level system. The closest unobserved odd-parity levels are predicted at 20,864 cm^{-1} and 33,617 cm^{-1} (6d7s(^{3}D)7p $^4D^\circ_{3/2}$ and 6d^2(^{3}F)7p $^4D^\circ_{3/2}$, respectively). This is much too far from the position suggested by Meggers et al. [9].

It must be noted that there are two factors greatly influencing the efficiency of IDEN2 in new line identifications: (1) accuracy of the computed transition probabilities used in the input, and (2) abundance of observed lines. With the generally low accuracy of A-values computed with Cowan's codes and a small number of observed lines listed by Meggers et al. [9], it is very inefficient. A significant progress in the analysis of Ac I could be achieved if more observed lines were available. To estimate how many observed lines Meggers et al. [9] have omitted in their line list, I have scanned the top half of the portion of one photographic plate shown in Figure 2 of their paper. This endeavor was motivated by the figure caption stating that the very strong line at 4476 Å, marked on the figure, belongs to Ac I; no such line is listed in the tables of Meggers et al. [9]. Although the grainy and probably distorted photograph reproduced in the journal does not allow measuring the lines with high precision, the wavelengths could be determined with uncertainties of about 0.03 Å (0.003 nm). This was sufficient to identify numerous impurity lines of atomic iron (Fe I) and many lines that are probably due to Ac I. It turned out that the above-mentioned line at about 4476 Å, which is the strongest line in the figure, is the known strong line of atomic silver (Ag I) at 4476.040 Å [8]. This makes sense, as the figure displays a spectrum observed with an electric arc between silver electrodes with 0.5 mg of actinium implanted on the surface. This finding indicates that there are some errors in the paper of Meggers et al. [9]. Table 1 of Meggers et al. [9] contains 13 lines of Ac I within the region covered by their Figure 2, discussed here. A closer look reveals that, in this figure, the total number of lines having appearance similar to the known Ac I lines is 41. A few of them may be due to impurities, but most are probably due to Ac I. Thus, Meggers et al. [9] have listed only a quarter of all lines they observed. This suggests that the 150 photographic plates produced in the work of Meggers et al. [9] and stored in the NIST archives need to be reanalyzed.

4. Ac II

For Ra-like Ac II with the ground configuration [Rn]6d7s^2, Meggers et al. [9] have listed a total of 296 observed lines, 221 of which were interpreted as transitions between the 65 energy levels found by those authors. In 1992, Blaise and Wyart [29] published a collection of atomic data for actinide spectra, in which they included the results of unpublished theoretical work of J.-F. Wyart on Ac II. He used a parametric fitting with Cowan's computer codes [21] to interpret the energy structure. The [Rn](6d^2 + 6d7s + 7s^2 + 5f^2 + 5f7p) and [Rn](5f6d + 5f7s + 6d7p + 7s7p) even- and odd-parity configuration groups were included in these calculations. In that work, Wyart rejected two levels, 5f7p $^3G_5$ and 6d5f $^3H_5^\circ$, reported in Ref. [9]. While examining the several tens of unclassified Ac II lines observed by Meggers et al. [9], Wyart found four previously unknown levels, for which he could not find a theoretical interpretation. The principal ionization energy of Ac II was semiempirically determined by Martin et al. [30] to be 94,800(250) cm^{-1}. For this determination, they extrapolated to Ac II the known differences of the quantum defects of the baricenters of the 7s^2 and 7s8s configuration in the isoelectronic Ra I spectrum ($\Delta n^* = 1.053$) and of the 7s and 8s configurations in the somewhat less-similar Ra II spectrum ($\Delta n^* = 1.063$). The value of Δn^* they adopted for Ac II was 1.055 ± 0.006, yielding the IE value quoted above.

The most precise theoretical calculations of the energy structure and transition properties of Ac II were made by Roberts et al. [31]. Unfortunately, that work includes only a few of the lowest energy levels and transitions between them. It does not help much in resolving the questions remaining after the work of Wyart described above. The earlier work of Quinet et al. [1] was made using Cowan's suite of atomic codes [21] modified by inclusion of a model potential describing the effects of core polarization. In a semiempirical parametric fitting with these codes, those authors included the [Rn](6d^2 + 6d7s + 7s^2 + 7s8s) and [Rn](5f6d + 5f7s + 6d7p + 7s7p) even- and odd-parity configuration groups, i.e., the same sets of configurations as used by Wyart, except that instead of 5f^2 and 5f7p, they included 7s8s in the even parity. They motivated the omission of the 5f7p configuration, which is partially known from the experiment [9], by its strong mixing with unknown configurations, such as 7p^2, 6d8s, 6d7d, and 7s7d.

The small-scale multi-configuration Dirac–Fock calculations of Ürer and Özdemir [32] included only the 56 levels of the same eight configurations as considered by Quinet et al. [1]. Since these calculations were ab initio, i.e., they did not include any semiempirical adjustments or core-polarization corrections, they are very inaccurate and inferior to the calculations of Ref. [1].

To make some progress in the analysis, new parametric calculations were made in the present work with another version of Cowan's codes [22]. The following configuration sets were included: [Rn](6d^2 + 6d7d + 6d8d + 6d9d + 6d5g + 7s^2 + 7s8s + 7s9s + 7s7d +

7s8d + 7s9d + 7s5g + 6d7s + 6d8s + 6d9s + 5f^2 + 5f7p + 5f8p + 5f9p + 7p^2) and [Rn](7s7p + 7s8p + 7s9p + 6d7p + 6d8p + 6d9p + 5f7s + 5f8s + 5f9s + 5f6d + 5f7d + 5f8d + 5f9d + 7s6h + 6d6h + 5f5g) in the even- and odd-parity sets, respectively. The previous LSF calculations for neutral Ac made with the help of the data from the large-scale ab initio calculations of Dzuba et al. [3] provided vital clues about the locations of the experimentally unknown configurations. Their average energies have been adjusted from the ab initio HFR values by the same amounts as configurations involving similar subshells in Ac I. As in Ac I, similar Slater parameters in all configurations were linked in groups, so that fitting of the structure of experimentally known lowest excited configurations automatically improved predictions of internal structure of the unknown highly excited configurations. The LSF calculations were conducted in the same iterative manner as in Ac I, by transferring the fitted parameters to the RCG code, calculating the transition probabilities with these fitted parameters, loading them into the input files of the IDE2 code, and searching for new levels having predicted transition wavelengths and intensities agreeing with observed lines. If one or more new levels were found, they were introduced in the LSF, and the entire procedure was repeated.

In this way, it was possible to identify 16 new energy levels describing 33 observed, previously unclassified lines. Four of these new levels are tentative, as they are based on one observed line each. One new level (at 64,154.91 cm^{-1}), based on two observed lines, is also treated as questionable, because the strongest transition predicted to occur from it at 3249.366(9) Å (down to the level at 33,388.554 cm^{-1}) is not present in the tables of Meggers et al. [9]. Perhaps, it was mistaken for a La II line at 3249.35 Å [8], as lanthanum is listed in Ref. [9] as one of the many impurities. In addition, the original identification of the 5f7p ^{3}G$_5$ level [9], which was rejected by Wyart (see above), was found to be correct and has been reinstated. For 11 levels, the previous level designation (configuration, term, or J-value) from Blaise and Wyart [29] has been revised. One level listed by Meggers et al. [9] at 60,063.0 cm^{-1} and designated as $e\,^3D_1$ has been discarded, and the two lines attributed to it in Ref. [9] have been reclassified as transitions from other levels.

In the final LSF calculation, 45 experimentally known levels of even parity were fitted with an rms of the differences (observed minus calculated energies) of 128 cm^{-1}. For the 38 known levels of odd parity, this rms difference is 281 cm^{-1}. For the levels common with those tabulated by Roberts et al. [31] (13 even and 3 odd), the rms difference of the present LSF calculation from the experiment is 76 cm^{-1}, to be compared with the corresponding value from Roberts et al., 456 cm^{-1}. Compared to these numbers, the results of the LSF of Quinet et al. [1] are much worse: 1162 cm^{-1} for 18 even levels and 426 cm^{-1} for 37 odd levels. Note that, according to the present analysis, the two lowest experimental odd levels with $J = 2$ were interchanged in the calculations of Quinet et al. [1], as well as in the tabulated results of Roberts et al. [31], since their designations were interchanged in the works of Meggers et al. [9] and Blaise and Wyart [29]. In addition, note that, in the LSF of Quinet et al. [1], the experimental odd-parity level at 36,144.35 cm^{-1} [9] ($J = 3$) was mistaken as 35,144.35 cm^{-1}. From the above, it is evident that the present parametric calculation is superior to all previous calculations in the accuracy of predicted energy levels.

Transition probabilities have been calculated with Cowan's codes [22] by using the fitted Slater parameters from the LSF. In this calculation, the values of the s–p and p–d E1 transition matrix elements were scaled by a factor of 0.9284 to bring the calculated A-values in agreement with the calculation of Roberts et al. [31] for the strongest transitions. This scaling factor is comparable to the one used in the Ac I calculation (0.811; see Section 3.3). As in the Ac I calculation, the d–f and f–g E1 transition matrix elements were scaled by a factor of 0.8233 taken from the analysis of Ac III data (see Section 5). Since the calculations of Quinet et al. [1] and of Ürer and Özdemir [32] were found to be too inaccurate, the only available benchmark for comparison with the present calculation is the work of Roberts et al. [31]. Out of the total of 11 A-values tabulated by them, those of the four strongest transitions with the presently calculated line strengths $S > 2$ a.u. agree with the present ones within 11% on average. For the five weaker transitions with S between 0.1 a.u.

and 2 a.u., the average ratio to the present values is a factor of two, and for the two weakest transitions with $S \approx 0.04$ a.u., the average ratio is a factor of 9. The uncertainties of all presently calculated A-values were roughly estimated by extrapolating this trend to all transitions considered in the present work.

All 296 observed lines attributed to Ac II by Meggers et al. [9] are listed in Table 4. For 270 of these lines, the table includes the lower and upper level classifications and Ritz wavelengths (one of these lines is doubly classified). For 245 of these classified lines, the table also includes a critically evaluated A-value with its uncertainty expressed in terms of the NIST accuracy category. Most of these A-values are from the present calculations, only four being from Roberts et al. [31]. In addition to E1 transitions, all potentially important M1 and E2 transition probabilities have been calculated in this work. To the author's knowledge, no data for these transitions have been previously reported. For these transitions, as in the Ac I calculations described in Section 3.3, the method of Monte Carlo random trials [27] was used for estimation of uncertainties of the calculated A-values. As in Ac I, 100 random trials were used, in which the Slater parameters were randomly varied around their values from the LSF, and the variance of the E2 transition matrix elements was assumed to be 15%. In Ac II, unlike Ac I, there are two metastable or anomalously long-lived odd-parity levels with large J-values. However, these levels have not been found experimentally, so it was not possible to include the forbidden transitions from these levels in Table 4. Thus, all predicted forbidden transitions included in this table are between even-parity levels. These transitions have branching fractions greater than 2%. A transition is deemed to be of a mixed type (M1 + E2) if the contribution of one of the types to the total A-value exceeds 2%.

The experimental and calculated energy levels of Ac II are listed in Table 5. There are now 83 experimentally known Ac II levels (45 even and 38 odd). The uncertainties given for the level values in Table 5 pertain to the separations of the levels from the 6d^2 ^{3}F$_2$ level at 13,236.418 cm^{-1}. This level was chosen as the base for the determination of uncertainties, since it participates in the largest number of observed lines (19). The uncertainty of the excitation energy of any level from the ground level can be determined as a combination in quadrature of the uncertainty of this level given in Table 5 and the uncertainty of the ground level, 0.03 cm^{-1}.

Table 5 also includes all levels predicted below the highest experimentally known levels in each parity (68,692.14 cm^{-1} and 56,582.72 cm^{-1} for the even and odd parity, respectively). The data from the present LSF calculations are also included in the table: energies, percentage compositions (up to three leading terms with percentages greater than 5%), Landé g_J-factors, and radiative lifetimes. The latter were calculated by summing up all presently considered radiative decay branches, including E1, M1, and E2 transitions. According to the present calculation, the lowest excited state 6d7s ^{3}D$_1$ at 4739.631(33) cm^{-1} is extremely long-lived. Its radiative lifetime, determined by the M1 transition to the ground state at 21,098.69(15) Å, is about 3×10^6 years (with an estimated uncertainty of 50%). This value does not account for hyperfine-induced transitions that must substantially reduce it in odd isotopes of actinium. The longest-lived isotope of actinium is ^{227}Ac with a half-life of 22 years, which sets a practical limitation on the lifetime of any excited state. The lifetime of the 6d^2 ^{3}P$_2$ level at 19,202.962(33) cm^{-1}, which is of interest for studies of parity non-conservation [31], is presently calculated to be 0.215(10) s. This value agrees with the result of Roberts et al. [31], which is about 0.2 s.

Table 4. Spectral lines of Ac II.

λ_obs [a] (Å)	λ_Ritz [a] (Å)	Δλ_O-R [b] (Å)	σ_obs [c] (cm⁻¹)	I_obs [d] (arb.u.)	Lower Level Configuration	Lower Level Term_J	Upper Level Configuration	Upper Level Term_J	E_low [e] (cm⁻¹)	E_upp [e] (cm⁻¹)	A [f] (s⁻¹)	Acc. [g]	Type [h]	TP Ref. [i]	Notes [j]
2064.280(13)			48,427.6	14,000h											
2100.000(13)			47,603.9	27,000h											
2102.240(13)			47,553.2	3400h											
2261.749(6)	2261.7478(19)	0.001	44,199.89	12,000	$7s^2$	$^1S_0$	$7s7p$	$^1P^\circ_1$	0.00	44,199.914	2.04e+08	C+		TW	
2307.500(13)			43,323.62	9800h											
2316.060(13)			43,163.51	3500											
2344.871(6)	2344.8721(20)	−0.001	42,633.21	4100	$6d7s$	$^3D_3$	$5f6d$	$^3D^\circ_3$	7426.489	50,059.68	8.e+06	E		TW	
2501.391(6)	2501.3942(17)	−0.003	39,965.71	2500	$6d7s$	$^3D_1$	$5f6d$	$^1D^\circ_2$	4739.631	44,705.290	8.e+06	E		TW	
7567.652(9)	7567.647(7)	0.005	13,210.501	1800	$6d^2$	$^3F_2$	$6d7p$	$^3F^\circ_2$	13,236.418	26,446.928	5.5e+06	C+		TW	
7617.421(9)	7617.410(7)	0.011	13,124.190	320	$6d^2$	$^3F_4$	$6d7p$	$^3F^\circ_3$	16,756.847	29,881.055			M1 + E2	TW	
	7626.653(12)				$6d7s$	$^1D_2$	$6d^2$	$^1D^\circ_2$	9087.517	22,199.428	3.2e+00	D+		TW	
7886.822(9)	7886.821(7)	0.001	12,675.891	1200	$6d^2$	$^3P_2$	$6d7p$	$^1D^\circ_2$	19,202.962	31,878.854	1.46e+06	C+		TW	
...	58,385.5(4)				$6d^2$	$^3F_2$	$6d^2$	$^3F_3$	13,236.418	14,949.173	1.217e-01	AA	M1	TW	
	60,203.7(6)				$6d7s$	$^3D_3$	$6d7s$	$^1D_2$	7426.489	9087.517	1.47e-02	C+	M1	TW	
...	189,568(7)				$6d7s$	$^3D_1$	$6d7s$	$^3P_2$	4739.631	5267.147	3.11e-03	A+	M1	TW	

[a] Observed and Ritz wavelengths are given in standard air. Conversion between air and vacuum wavelengths was made with the five-parameter formula for the dispersion of air from Peck and Reeder [11]. All observed wavelengths are from the work of Meggers et al. [9].

[b] The difference between the observed and Ritz wavelengths. Blank for lines with unmeasured wavelength and for the lines that solely determine one of the energy levels of the transition.

[c] Transition wave number in vacuum.

[d] Observed intensity on an arbitrary scale, which is linear in terms of the energy flux under the line contour (see Section 6). The symbols after the numbers denote the character of the line: c—complex structure; h—hazy; l—shaded on the long-wavelength side; s—shaded on the short-wavelength side; *—the given intensity is shared by more than one transition.

[e] The optimized energies of the lower and upper levels of the transition. These values correspond to those given in Table 5.

[f] Transition probability. Exponential notation is used (e.g., "3.0e-01" means "3.0×10^{-1}").

[g] Accuracy of the transition probability. The code symbols for the accuracy are defined in the NIST ASD [8] (see https://physics.nist.gov/PhysRefData/ASD/Html/lineshelp.html#OUTACC, accessed on 25 March 2022).

[h] Transition type: blank—electric dipole; M1—magnetic dipole; E2—electric quadrupole; M1 + E2—mixed type (both types contribute more than 2% to the total A value given here).

[i] Code for references: R14—Roberts et al. [31]; TW—this work.

[j] Notes: N—a newly classified line; R—the previous classification (of Ref. [29]) has been revised; T—a new tentative identification.

(Only a small portion of this table is given here for guidance to its content. The full version is available in machine-readable format in Table S4 of the Supplementary Online Materials, file Table S4.txt. The format of the supplementary table is slightly different. See footnotes to Table 1).

Table 5. Energy levels of Ac II.

E_{exp} (cm^{-1})	Unc.[a] (cm^{-1})	Configuration	Term	J	Leading Percentages[b]					E_{calc}[c] (cm^{-1})	g_{calc}[d]	τ[e] (ns)	u%	Ref.[f]	Notes[g]
0.00	0.03	7s^2	^{1}S	0	95	^{1}S				0	0.000	1.0e+23	52	TW,M,BW	
4739.631	0.018	6d7s	^{3}D	1	99	^{3}D				4661	0.499	1.58e+11	19	TW,M,BW	
5267.147	0.015	6d7s	^{3}D	2	86	^{3}D	11	6d7s	^{1}D	5281	1.145	6.32e+09	1.7	TW,M,BW	
7426.489	0.016	6d7s	^{3}D	3	99	^{3}D				7498	1.334	1.61e+09	1.8	TW,M,BW	
9087.517	0.014	6d7s	^{1}D	2	68	^{1}D	16	6d^2	^{1}D	9087	1.015	1.96e+09	22	TW,M,BW	
13,236.418	0.000	6d^2	^{3}F	2	93					13,191	0.687			TW,M,BW	
...															
28,201.120	0.021	7s7p	^{3}P°	2	89	^{3}P°	7	6d7p	^{3}P°	28,324	1.480	25.2	9	TW,M,BW	C
		6d^2	^{1}S	0	83		6	6d^2	^{3}P	29,025	0.000	4.e+04	760		
64,154.91	0.08	6d7d	^{1}D	2	28	^{1}D	15	7p^2	^{3}P	64,487	1.121	2.21	7	TW	T
64,285.02	0.05	6d7d	^{3}F	4	72	^{3}G	18	6d7d	^{1}G	64,218	1.194	3.07	5	TW,BW	C,J
64,332.11	0.06	5f7p	^{3}D	3	47	^{3}D	17	5f7p	^{1}F	64,316	1.225	3.01	5	TW	N
		5f7p	^{1}D	2	13	^{1}D	27	6d7d		64,660	1.146	2.32	6		
		6d7d	^{3}P	1	64	^{3}S	29	6d7d		65,242	1.635	2.2	12		
65,392.37	0.04	5f7p	^{3}G	5	52	^{3}G	48			65,385	1.200	2.82	8	TW	RI
		6d7d	^{1}G	4	66	^{3}F	11	6d7d		65,799	1.040	4.2	7		
		5f7p	^{3}P	2	47	^{1}D	24	5f7p		65,894	1.284	2.64	8		
		6d7d	^{1}S	0	62	^{3}P	15	6d7d	^{3}P	66,901	0.000	5.2	25		
68,692.14	0.06	7p^2	^{1}D	2	34	^{1}D	14	5f7p		68,668	1.089	1.40	6	TW	N
[94,800][h]	250	Ac III (6p^{6}7s ^{2}S$_{1/2}$)	Limit											M74	

[a] Uncertainties are given for separations of the levels from the 6d^2 ^{3}F$_2$ level at 13,236.418 cm^{-1}.
[b] The first percentage pertains to the configuration and term given in the columns "Configuration" and "Term"; the second and third ones pertain to the configuration and term specified next to the number.
[c] The energies calculated in this work in a least-squares fit with Cowan's codes [21,22].
[d] Landé g_J-factors (dimensionless) calculated in this work.
[e] Radiative lifetimes calculated in this work. Their estimated percentage uncertainties are given in the next column. Some of the lifetimes are given in exponential notation (e.g., "6.e+04" means "6. × 10^4").
[f] Code for references: BW—Blaise and Wyart [29]; M—Meggers et al. [9]; M74—Martin et al. [30]; TW—this work.
[g] Notes: C—the configuration and/or term assignment (of Blaise and Wyart [29]) have been revised in this work; J—the J-value (of Blaise and Wyart [29]) has been revised; N—a level newly identified in this work; RI—the level established by Meggers et al. [9], previously rejected by Blaise and Wyart [29], has been reinstated in this work; T—a new tentative identification of this work.
[h] A semiempirical value.

(Only a small portion of this table is given here for guidance to its content. The full version is available in machine-readable format in Table S5 of the Supplementary Online Materials, file Table S5.txt. The format of the supplementary table is slightly different. See footnotes to Table 1).

The presently calculated Landé factors included in Table 5 agree with those previously calculated by Quinet et al. [1], with rms differences of 0.017 in the even parity and 0.06 in the odd parity. In the absence of a better benchmark for comparison, these rms differences can be adopted as the uncertainties of the present values.

No attempt was made here to re-evaluate the IE of Ac II. Thus, the recommended value of IE included in Table 5 is the semiempirical one quoted from Martin et al. [30].

The final fitted values of the Slater parameters resulting from the present LSF for Ac II are listed in Table 6.

Table 6. Parameters of the least-squares fit for Ac II.

Parity	Configurations		Parameter	LSF [a] (cm^{-1})	Δ [b] (cm^{-1})	Gr. [c]	HFR [a]	Ratio [a]
e	7s^2		E_{av}	2627.6	171		0.0	
e	7s8s		E_{av}	52,346.6	132	3	48,226.9	1.0854
e	7s8s		G^0(7s,8s)	833.9	127	9	1787.1	0.4666
e	7s9s		E_{av}	70,686.1	178	3	66,523.3	1.0626
e	7s9s		G^0(7s,9s)	274.6	42	9	588.4	0.4667
e	7s7d		E_{av}	58,920.4	262	6	54,156.8	1.0880
e	7s7d		ζ_{7d}	209.8	8	10	250.9	0.8362
e	7s7d		G^2(7s,7d)	1422.0	77	1	2076.6	0.6848
e	7s8d		E_{av}	74,175.2	330	6	69,239.0	1.0713
e	7s8d		ζ_{8d}	86.1	3	10	103.0	0.8359
e	7s8d		G^2(7s,8d)	535.5	29	1	782.0	0.6848
...								
e	7s7d	6d8s	R_d^2(7s7d,6d8s)	3323.0	164	15	5862.0	0.5669
e	7s7d	6d8s	R_e^0(7s7d,6d8s)	1420.4	70	15	2505.7	0.5669
e	7s7d	5f7p	R_d^3(7s7d,5f7p)	1174.0	58	15	2071.0	0.5669
e	7s7d	5f7p	R_e^1(7s7d,5f7p)	−1121.5	55	15	−1978.4	0.5669
e	6d7d	5f7p	R_e^1(6d7d,5f7p)	−3663.2	181	15	−6462.0	0.5669
e	6d7d	5f7p	R_e^3(6d7d,5f7p)	−1039.9	51	15	−1834.4	0.5669
e	6d7d	5f7p	R_d^1(6d7d,5f7p)	462.8	23	15	816.4	0.5669
e	6d7d	5f7p	R_e^5(6d7d,5f7p)	−15.8	1	15	−27.9	0.5672
e	6d7d	7p^2	R_d^1(6d7d,7p7p)	−3217.6	159	15	−5676.0	0.5669
e	6d7d	7p^2	R_d^3(6d7d,7p7p)	−1547.2	76	15	−2729.3	0.5669
e	5f7p	7p^2	R_d^2(5f7p,7p7p)	4234.6	209	15	7470.1	0.5669
o	7s7p		E_{av}	29,025.9	195		23,529.7	1.2336
o	7s7p		ζ_{7p}	5144.4	172	5	3795.7	1.3553
o	7s7p		G^1(7s,7p)	15,388.0	1104	4	25,295.3	0.6083
o	7s8p		E_{av}	63,502.9	fixed		58,060.7	1.0937
o	7s8p		ζ_{8p}	1646.7	55	5	1215.0	1.3553
o	7s8p		G^1(7s,8p)	2166.8	155	4	3561.9	0.6083
...								
o	6d7p	5f7s	R_d^1(6d7p,5f7s)	−11,247.3	517	9	−19,768.3	0.5690
o	6d7p	5f7s	R_e^2(6d7p,5f7s)	−4957.7	703	7	−7495.6	0.6614
o	6d7p	5f8s	R_d^1(6d7p,5f8s)	−574.6	26	9	−1009.9	0.5690
o	6d7p	5f8s	R_e^2(6d7p,5f8s)	−1105.3	157	7	−1671.1	0.6614
o	6d7p	5f9s	R_d^1(6d7p,5f9s)	−194.8	9	9	−342.4	0.5689
o	6d7p	5f9s	R_e^2(6d7p,5f9s)	−553.4	78	7	−836.7	0.6614
o	6d7p	5f6d	R_d^1(6d7p,5f6d)	8235.1	378	9	14,474.0	0.5690
o	6d7p	5f6d	R_d^3(6d7p,5f6d)	4374.5	201	9	7688.6	0.5690
...								

[a] Parameter values determined in the least-squares-fitted (LSF) and ab initio pseudo-relativistic Hartree–Fock (HFR) calculations and their ratio.
[b] Standard deviation of the fitted parameter. Parameters that were not varied in the fit are marked as "fixed".
[c] Parameters in each numbered group were linked together with their ratio fixed at the HFR level.

(Only a small portion of this table is given here for guidance to its content. The full version is available in machine-readable format in Table S6 of the Supplementary Online Materials, file Table S6.txt).

5. Ac III

The ground state of francium-like Ac III is [Rn]7s. Meggers et al. [9] have identified eight lines of Ac III, from which they determined the values of six excited levels. All these identifications have been confirmed here. The wavelengths reported by Meggers et al. [9] are internally consistent: they deviate from the Ritz values by less than 0.003 Å. However, the strong polar effect in the setup of Meggers et al. [9] may have led to a sizeable systematic shift in the measured wavelengths. Thus, the uncertainties of these measurements are conservatively estimated to be 0.013 Å for the lines above 3000 Å. For lines with shorter wavelengths, which are likely to have been measured in both the first and second orders of diffraction, a smaller uncertainty of 0.006 Å is assumed here. The list of observed lines of Ac III is given in Table 7.

As for Ac I and Ac II, the experimental energy levels have been redetermined here from the eight observed spectral lines by means of a least-squares level optimization with the code LOPT [28]. The list of the newly optimized energy levels of Ac III is given in Table 6. Separations of the optimized excited levels from the 6d $^2D_{5/2}$ level at 4203.89 cm^{-1} have uncertainties in the range from 0.04 cm^{-1} to 0.10 cm^{-1}. These uncertainties are given in Table 6. To obtain the uncertainties of excitation energies from the ground level (7s $^2S_{1/2}$), they must be combined in quadrature with the uncertainty of the ground level, 0.09 cm^{-1}.

On the theoretical side, the most precise reported calculations of energy levels and E1 transition rates are those of Roberts et al. [33], of Safronova et al. [34], and of Migdalek and Glowacz-Proszkiewicz [35]. For Ac III, E1 transition rates of Roberts et al. [33] and Safronova et al. [34] agree with each other within 3% on average. For only two longest-wavelength transitions (6d $^2D_{5/2}$–5f $^2F^\circ_{5/2,7/2}$), the difference between these two calculations reaches 5%. The A values of Roberts et al. [33] have been adopted here as recommended values. Their uncertainties are assigned according to the comparison outlined above. The A values of Migdalek and Glowacz-Proszkiewicz [35] deviate from those of Roberts et al. [33] by 5% on average. For the A values of Biémont et al. [36], the average deviations from Ref. [33] are slightly larger; 9% on average. For comparison, the A values computed by Ürer and Özdemir [37] are systematically lower than the reference values by (53 ± 30)% on average. These primitive Dirac–Fock calculations included only six configurations of even parity and five configurations of odd parity. The poor quality of the results speaks for itself.

Although Cowan-code calculations cannot compete in accuracy with the large-scale calculations of Roberts et al. [33] and Safronova et al. [34], such calculations were made in this work with the sole purpose of evaluation of systematic errors in the transition matrix elements computed with Cowan's codes. The scaling factors needed to bring the calculated E1 A values were 0.9510 for the s–p and p–d transitions and 0.8233 for the d–f and f–g transitions. The latter factor was used in the Ac I and Ac II calculations, where no reference values are available for an independent estimation.

Parity-forbidden E2 and M1 transition rates for transitions from the lowest two excited levels of Ac III have been reported by Safronova et al. [38]. These authors have included their estimated uncertainties for the A values and radiative lifetimes. These uncertainties are between 0.4% and 1.5%. The reference values taken from Ref. [38] have been used here to evaluate the systematic errors in the E2 transition matrix elements computed with Cowan's codes. It turned out that, unlike the E1 transitions, the E2 A values computed with Cowan's code agree with the reference values within a few percent with no discernible systematic difference. This observation in Ac III was extrapolated to the other Ac spectra, so that no scaling was applied to the E2 transition matrix elements in any of the spectra studied in this work.

The Landé g_J factors of the three lowest levels of Ac III were precisely calculated by Gossel et al. [39]. The rms difference of the g_J values calculated in that work from much more precise experimental values for Rb, Cs, Ba$^+$, and Fr is 3×10^{-5}, which can be adopted as an estimate of uncertainty for the Ac III values.

The currently recommended values of the principal ionization energy (IE) of Ac III, 140,590 cm^{-1} [8], is quoted from Migdalek and Glowacz-Proszkiewicz [35]. Its estimated uncertainty, 160 cm^{-1}, was derived from isoelectronic comparisons made in my unpublished research on the Fr isoelectronic sequence made in 2011. The newer calculations of Roberts et al. [33], as well as the calculations of Safronova et al. [34], which were overlooked in my early research, make it possible to establish a more precise value of the IE. A fairly extensive study of these data was undertaken in the present work. Unfortunately, the data of Migdalek and Glowacz-Proszkiewicz [35], as well as those of Safronova et al. [34], were found to contain errors that make them not smooth along the isoelectronic sequence.

The coefficient b given below Equation (5) of Migdalek and Glowacz-Proszkiewicz [35] has a misprint in the power of 10: it must be -1, not -2. However, even with the corrected b value, the values of the dipole polarizability α in Table 1 of that paper cannot be reproduced with the given equation. There is a discontinuity in the α values between Ac and Th, which is revealed in the residual differences between the α values of Table 1 of Ref. [35] and those computed with Equation (5) of that paper. The cause of this discontinuity may be in the values of the mean radii given in the same table, which are supposed to be fitted for Fr I through Th IV and extrapolated to the higher ions.

In the paper of Safronova et al. [34], there are several inconsistencies between their Table I and Table II. For example, for Fr I, the excitation energies of $6d_{3/2}$ and $6d_{5/2}$ given in Table II disagree with Table I by 286 cm^{-1} and 208 cm^{-1}, respectively. For the U VI $7p_{1/2}$ and $7p_{3/2}$ levels, the disagreement is much larger: 519 cm^{-1} and 1450 cm^{-1}, respectively. Table I of Ref. [34] lists the values of several computed quantities representing various contributions to the total binding energy. Some of these contributions are relatively small and are expected to vary smoothly along the isoelectronic sequence. However, this smoothness is disrupted by the abnormally large values of the parameters $E^{(3)}$ and $E^{(3)}_{extra}$ for the $7p_{3/2}$ level of Pa V. An isoelectronic comparison of the binding energies of the $6d_{3/2}$ and $6d_{5/2}$ levels computed with two methods by Safronova et al. [34] with those of Roberts et al. [33] reveals that the latter are likely to be too high by about 1000 cm^{-1} in Pa V.

Despite the problems discussed above, it was possible to interpolate the differences between the experimental and theoretical values of quantum defects for the $7s_{1/2}$, $6d_{3/2,5/2}$, $7p_{1/2,3/2}$, and $5f_{5/2,7/2}$ levels along the Fr isoelectronic sequence from Fr I to U VI and derive improved values of the IE for Ac III, Th IV, Pa V, and U VI. These values are 140,630(50) cm^{-1}, 230,973(14)) cm^{-1}, 361,690(200) cm^{-1}, and 506,400(50) cm^{-1}, equivalent to 17.436(6) eV, 28.6371(17) eV, 44.844(25) eV, and 62.786(6) eV, respectively. A detailed description of these isoelectronic interpolations will be the subject of a future paper. The above IE value for Th IV has been derived from a newly reoptimized set of experimental energy levels based on the wavelengths reported by Klinkenberg [40]. The series of the $ns_{1/2}$ ($n = 7$-10) energy levels was used in this determination, which employed a fitting of the extended Ritz quantum-defect expansion formula (see Kramida [12]) and comparisons with similar series in isoelectronic Fr I and Ra I.

A more precise determination of the IE could be made in the future, when more accurate calculations become available. Such calculations are desirable for the entire sequence from Fr I up to Np VII (for the latter spectrum, the only data available at present are those of Roberts et al. [33]). These calculations should be smooth along the isoelectronic sequence and include not only the levels listed above, but also 7d ($J = 3/2, 5/2$), 8p ($J = 1/2, 3/2$), and 8s ($J = 1/2$). These levels are precisely known experimentally for Fr I and Ra II, but in U VI their experimental values are provided with a rather low precision by the beam-foil study of Church et al. [41]. The abnormally large deviations of quantum defects of the 8p levels from the calculations of Roberts et al. [33] make the identifications of Church et al. [41] questionable. In terms of excitation energy, the discrepancy is about 4600(1600) cm^{-1} for the $8p_{1/2}$ level. More precise calculations could confirm or disprove this experimental identification.

The lists of observed spectral lines and energy levels of Ac III are given in Tables 7 and 8, respectively. Data for predicted forbidden transitions of Ac III are included in Table 7 for completeness. The lifetime values included in Table 8 are computed as sums of the E1, M1, and E2 radiative decay channels. The lifetime value for the 6d $^2D_{5/2}$ level, 2.305(34) s, differs slightly from the value originally reported by Safronova et al. [38], 2.326(34) s, possibly because in the present work the A values have been adjusted to experimental transition energies. The original values of the reduced transition matrix elements reported in Ref. [38] have been used here.

Table 7. Spectral lines of Ac III.

λ_{obs} [a] (Å)	λ_{Ritz} [a] (Å)	$\Delta\lambda_{O-R}$ [b] (Å)	σ_{obs} [c] (cm^{-1})	I_{obs} [d] (arb.u.)	Lower Level Configuration	Lower Level Term$_J$	Upper Level Configuration	Upper Level Term$_J$	E_{low} [e] (cm^{-1})	E_{upp} [e] (cm^{-1})	A [f] (s^{-1})	Acc. [g]	Type [h]	TP Ref. [i]
2626.440(6)	2626.439(5)	0.001	38,063.00	300,000 h	7s	$^2S_{1/2}$	7p	$^2P^\circ_{3/2}$	0.00	38,063.01	3.97e+08	A		R13,S07
2682.900(6)	2682.899(4)	0.001	37,262.03	23,000 h	6d	$^2D_{3/2}$	7p	$^2P^\circ_{3/2}$	800.97	38,063.01	2.89e+07	A		R13,S07
2952.550(6)	2952.551(5)	−0.001	33,859.13	230,000 h	6d	$^2D_{5/2}$	7p	$^2P^\circ_{3/2}$	4203.89	38,063.01	2.30e+08	A		R13,S07
3392.780(13)	3392.782(10)	−0.002	29,465.90	78,000 Dh	7s	$^2S_{1/2}$	7p	$^2P^\circ_{1/2}$	0.00	29,465.88	1.90e+08	A		R13,S07
3487.590(13)	3487.588(11)	0.002	28,664.89	99,000	6d	$^2D_{3/2}$	7p	$^2P^\circ_{1/2}$	800.97	29,465.88	1.58e+08	A		R13,S07
4413.090(11)	4413.093(11)	−0.003	22,653.50	34,000 h	6d	$^2D_{3/2}$	5f	$^2F^\circ_{5/2}$	800.97	23,454.45	1.85e+07	A		R13,S07
4569.870(13)	4569.870(13)		21,876.33	65,000 h	6d	$^2D_{5/2}$	5f	$^2F^\circ_{7/2}$	4203.89	26,080.22	2.11e+07	B+		R13,S07
5193.208(12)	5193.211(13)	0.003	19,250.55	710 h	6d	$^2D_{5/2}$	5f	$^2F^\circ_{5/2}$	4203.89	23,454.45	8.79e+05	B+		R13,S07
	23,787.5(5)				7s	$^2S_{1/2}$	6d	$^2D_{5/2}$	0.00	4203.89	3.748e-03	AA	E2	S17
	29,386.5(6)				6d	$^2D_{3/2}$	6d	$^2D_{5/2}$	800.97	4203.89	4.30e-01	A+	M1	S17
	124,849(14)				7s	$^2S_{1/2}$	6d	$^2D_{3/2}$	0.00	800.97	8.48e-07	AA	E2	S17

[a] Observed and Ritz wavelengths are given in standard air. Conversion between air and vacuum wavelengths was made with the five-parameter formula for the dispersion of air from Peck and Reeder [11]. All observed wavelengths are from the work of Meggers et al. [9].
[b] The difference between the observed and Ritz wavelengths. Blank for lines with unmeasured wavelength and for the lines that solely determine one of the energy levels of the transition.
[c] Transition wave number in vacuum.
[d] Observed intensity on an arbitrary scale, which is linear in terms of the energy flux under the line contour (see Section 6). The symbols after the numbers denote the character of the line: h—hazy; D—double line.
[e] The optimized energies of the lower and upper levels of the transition. These values correspond to those given in Table 8.
[f] Transition probability. Exponential notation is used (e.g., "3.97e+08" means "3.97×10^{8}").
[g] Accuracy of the transition probability. The code symbols for the accuracy are defined in the NIST ASD [8] (see https://physics.nist.gov/PhysRefData/ASD/Html/lineshelp.html#OUTACC, accessed on 25 March 2022).
[h] Transition type: blank—electric dipole; M1—magnetic dipole; E2—electric quadrupole.
[i] Code for transition probability references: R13—Roberts et al. [33]; S07—Safronova et al. [34]; S17—Safronova et al. [38].

Table 8. Energy levels of Ac III.

E_{exp} (cm^{-1})	Unc.[a] (cm^{-1})	Configuration	Term	J	Perc.[b]	TW	g_{calc}[c]	[39]	[35]	E_{calc}[d] (cm^{-1}) [33]	[34]	τ[e] (ns)
0.00	0.09	7s	^{2}S	1/2	99	2.002	2.005606	0	0	0	
800.97	0.06	6d	^{2}D	3/2	99	0.800	0.798662	562	435	825	1.171(6)e15^S
4203.89	0.00	6d	^{2}D	5/2	99	1.200	1.200627	4040	3926	4041	2.305(34)e9^S
23,454.45	0.04	5f	^{2}F	5/2	100	0.857		29,906	23,467	24,018	52(3)^R
26,080.22	0.06	5f	^{2}F	7/2	100	1.143		32,063	26,112	26,420	48(3)^R
29,465.88	0.10	7p	^{2}P$^\circ$	1/2	100	0.666		29,382	29,375	29,303	2.88(14)^R
38,063.01	0.06	7p	^{2}P$^\circ$	3/2	100	1.334		37,987	38,136	37,816	1.53(8)^R
[140,630][f]	50	Ac IV (6p^6 ^{1}S$_0$)	Limit					140,590	141,221	140,442	

[a] Uncertainties are given for separations of the levels from the 6d ^{2}D$_{5/2}$ level at 4203.89 cm^{-1}.
[b] Percentage of the configuration and term given in the columns "Configuration" and "Term" in the composition of the eigenvector (from the present Cowan-code calculation).
[c] Landé g_J-factors (dimensionless) calculated in this work (TW) and in Gossel et al. [39].
[d] The calculated energies from Migdalek and Glowacz-Proszkiewicz [35], Roberts et al. [33], and Safronova et al. [34].
[e] Radiative lifetimes calculated in the works denoted by the superscripts: R—Roberts et al. [33]; S—Safronova et al. [38]. The first two values are given in the exponential notation, e.g., 1.171(6)e15 means $(1.171 \pm 0.006) \times 10^{15}$.
[f] A semiempirical value derived in this work by isoelectronic interpolations (see the text of Section 5).

6. Reduction of Observed Line Intensities

Meggers et al. [9] have reported five sets of observed line intensities from the five types of light sources they used: an arc and a spark between silver electrodes, an arc and a spark between copper electrodes, and a hollow-cathode discharge. These light sources are denoted hereafter as "Ag arc", "Ag spark", "Cu arc", "Cu spark", and "HC", respectively. Small amounts of actinium were introduced into these light sources by soaking porous tips of the electrodes in a nitrate solution of Ac or by precipitating a similar solution on the bottom of the hollow cathode. No information was given by Meggers et al. [9] about the methods used in reduction of the observed intensities. They mentioned that several different types of photographic plates were used in different recordings: Eastman Kodak 103-F, 103-C, 103a-C, 103a-F, 103a-F (UV), I-N, and I-Q. For the most informative recordings, the 103a-F (UV) plates were used for the ultraviolet region, 103a-F for near ultraviolet and visible, I-N for red and adjacent infrared, and I-Q for longer wavelengths. It was noted that, in some exposures, "overlapping spectral orders were differentiated by supporting appropriate gelatine filters in front of the photographic plates to absorb portions of the slit images". The intensity values were given in the tables of Meggers et al. [9] on an apparently linear scale (in terms of exposure) with values between 1 and 5000. However, no information about the dependence of the overall sensitivity of the multiple setups on wavelength is available. The different light sources had notably different temperatures, which was manifested in enhanced intensities of Ac II and Ac III lines in sparks. Thus, reduction of all these intensity measurements to a common scale is a nontrivial task.

To achieve that, the present work uses the method suggested by Kramida [12] and described in more detail in later publications (see, e.g., Kramida et al. [42,43]). This method is based on the assumption of the Boltzmann distribution for the populations of excited levels and neglects self-absorption. The important prerequisite for this method to work is the availability of reliable A values for most of the lines throughout the entire spectral range of the observations. These requirements are likely to have have been met: extensive sets of fairly accurate A values are available for all three spectra (Ac I, Ac II, and Ac III; see Tables 1, 5 and 7), the tiny amounts of Ac introduced into the discharges make self-absorption to be unlikely, and the level populations in all types of the light sources used by Meggers et al. [9] are sufficiently close to local thermodynamic equilibrium.

The effective excitation temperatures determined from the slopes of Boltzmann plots (see [12,42,43]) in the various light sources used by Meggers et al. [9] are listed in Table 9 for each Ac spectrum. From the scatter of data points in the plots, uncertainties of these values are can be roughly estimated as about 20%.

Table 9. Effective excitation temperatures (in eV) in the light sources used by Meggers et al. [9], determined from Boltzmann plots.

Spectrum	Ag Arc	Ag Spark	Cu Arc	Cu Spark	HC
Ac I	0.51	0.60	0.53	0.59	0.41
Ac II	0.63	0.77	0.56	0.77	0.64
Ac III	1.06	2.18	–	1.07	–

As can be seen from Table 9, the observed spectra of different ions exhibit different excitation temperatures in the same light source. This is due to the different spatial origin of the spectra, which can be seen in Figures 2 and 3 of Meggers et al. [9]: lines of Ac I, Ac II, and Ac III have distinctly different distributions of intensities along the line height. For Ac III spectra taken with the Cu arc and HC discharges, it was not possible to determine the temperature, because only a few transitions with relatively close upper-level energies were observed in these spectra. For these spectra, the slope of the Boltzmann plots was fixed at zero in the intensity-reduction procedure.

The logarithmic inverse spectral response plots (see [12,42,43]) derived from the observed intensities are displayed in Figure 6. The inverse spectral response function $R(\lambda)$

is defined as $R(\lambda) = \ln(I_c/I_{obs})$, where λ is the observed wavelength, I_c is the calculated intensity, and I_{obs} is the observed intensity. To remove the wavelength-dependence of the spectral response of the instrument from the observed intensities, the latter are multiplied by $\exp(R(\lambda))$.

It was found that Meggers et al. [9] used different intensity-reduction procedures in the short-wavelength ($\lambda < 5000$ Å) and long-wavelength ($\lambda > 5000$ Å) regions. However, in each of these regions, the same reduction procedure was applied to certain groups of spectra. This can be seen, for example, in the top-left panel of Figure 6, showing the behavior of the observed Ac I intensities. There is no discernible difference in the shape of $R(\lambda)$ between the Ag arc, Ag spark, Cu arc, and Cu spark spectra, so they are all displayed with the same symbol (full rhombus). The ratios I_c/I_{obs} for the HC intensities may be perceived from the plot as slightly deviating from the overall fit shown by the dotted line, but these deviations are within the range of scatter of the data points. Thus, a common $R(\lambda)$ function shown by the dotted curve was used to correct the observed intensities in all these spectra.

A similar comparison is shown in the same wavelength range for the Ac II and Ac III spectra in the bottom-left panel of Figure 6. Again, the general behavior of the I_c/I_{obs} values is very similar for both Ac II and Ac III spectra recorded with Ag and Cu arcs and sparks and with HC. However, this behavior is very different from the one observed for the Ac I spectrum: at the shortest wavelengths below 3500 Å, the observed Ac II and Ac III intensities appear to be strongly suppressed, so that larger $R(\lambda)$ values are needed to bring them in agreement with the calculated intensities. This suppression may have been caused by the use of filters to suppress higher orders of diffraction. Again, a common $R(\lambda)$ function shown by the dotted curve was used to correct the observed intensities in all spectra included in this panel.

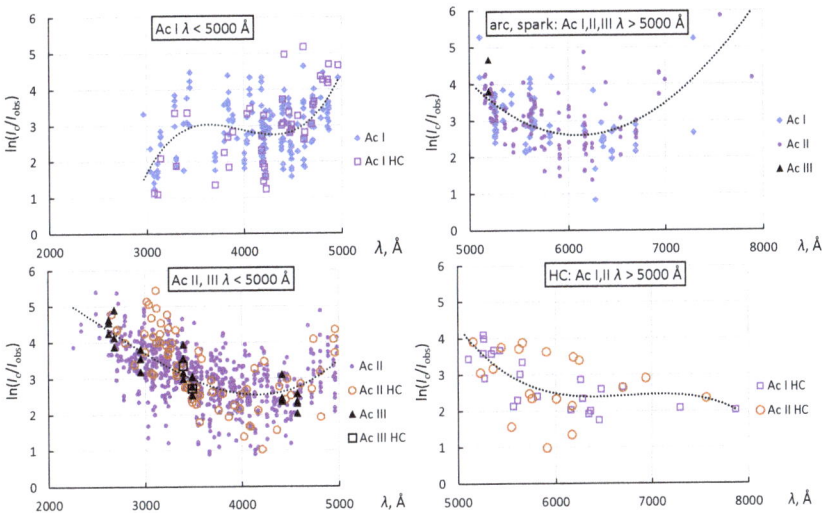

Figure 6. Inverse logarithmic spectral response functions for observations of Meggers et al. [9]. Top left: Observed Ac I short-wavelength line intensities in the Ag and Cu arc and spark spectra (labeled "Ac I") and in the HC spectrum (labeled "Ac I HC"). Bottom left: Observed Ac II and Ac III short-wavelength line intensities in the Ag and Cu arc and spark spectra (labeled "Ac II" and "Ac III") and in the HC spectrum (labeled "Ac II HC" and "Ac III HC"). Top right: Observed Ac I, Ac II, and Ac III long-wavelength line intensities in the Ag and Cu arc and spark spectra (labeled "Ac I", "Ac II", and "Ac III"). Bottom right: Observed Ac I and Ac II long-wavelength line intensities in the HC spectrum.

For the long-wavelength region above 5000 Å, a different division is observed between the various spectra. As shown in the top-right panel of Figure 6, all three actinium spectra appear to have the same scale of intensities observed in the arc and spark recordings. The overall shape of the $R(\lambda)$ function shown by the dotted curve, with a minimum near 6000 Å, is very reasonable, since the grating used in these recordings was blazed at this wavelength. However, the HC recordings (bottom-right panel of Figure 6) display a very different behavior of $R(\lambda)$ at the longest wavelengths above 6500 Å. Near 8000 ÅÅ, the observed HC relative intensities are much greater (by about two orders of magnitude) compared to the arc and spark intensities. The exact cause of the increased HC intensities at longer wavelengths is unknown. It might have been caused by the use of a different type of photographic plates in these recordings.

When the shapes of the $R(\lambda)$ function are established for each observed spectrum, and the effective temperatures are determined from Boltzmann plots, reduction of the observed intensities to a common scale corresponding to a chosen light source is straightforward (see a detailed description of this procedure in Kramida et al. [43]). For Ac I, the observed intensities given in Table 1 have been reduced to the same scale as established for the Ag arc recordings with an effective temperature of 0.51 eV. For Ac II and Ac III intensities given in Tables 4 and 7, respectively, the scale was based on the Ag spark observations with effective temperatures of 0.77 eV and 2.18 eV for Ac II and Ac III, respectively (see Table 9). Most of the tabulated intensity values are averages of several reduced intensity values from up to five observations in different light sources. These intensity values are expected to be accurate within a factor of two or three, on average. In principle, they allow the gA values to be derived from them (with that low accuracy) by constructing a Boltzmann plot with the temperatures given above (see Equation (1)). The scatter of the data points in Figure 6 suggests that a few of the intensity values may be in error by a factor of 10, or even more.

7. Conclusions

As a result of this work, several tens of new identifications have been made in the previously published Ac I and Ac II line lists of Meggers et al. [9] (16 in Ac I and 36 in Ac II). In Ac I, 16 new energy levels have been found, and the J values of 5 previously reported levels have been revised. In Ac II, 16 new energy levels have been established; one level listed by Meggers et al. [9] but discarded by Blaise and Wyart [29] has been reinstated, and one of the levels listed by Meggers et al. [9] has been discarded. New parametric least-squares fitting calculations with Cowan's codes [21,22] have been made for both Ac I and Ac II, providing eigenvector percentage compositions that involve revised classifications for several levels. These calculations have also provided a large number of new gA values in both Ac I and Ac II. The principal ionization energies (IE) of Ac I and Ac III have been redetermined with improved precision. As a byproduct, improved IE values have been determined for three other Fr-like actinide ions: Th IV, Pa V, and U VI.

The tables provided in this work represent the currently recommended reference data on energy levels, spectral lines, and transition probabilities of Ac I–III intended for inclusion in a future release of the NIST ASD [8].

Further progress in the knowledge of Ac spectra is impeded by scarcity of available experimental data. A partial analysis of a small part of photographic recordings of Meggers et al. [9] stored in the NIST archives indicates that only about a quarter of all Ac lines present on these plates are included in the published line lists. A reanalysis of these plates may be warranted. New laser-spectroscopy studies could test the validity of some tentative identifications in Ac I. Zeeman-effect patterns have never been experimentally studied in any Ac spectrum. Such studies could provide information on Landé factors, which are crucial in interpretation of energy levels. On the theoretical side, improved and extended large-scale calculations of all three first spectra of Ac could be useful in elucidating the intricate level structure of Ac I and Ac II riddled with strong configuration interactions and in precise determination of ionization energies of Ac III and other Fr-like ions.

Supplementary Materials: The following supporting information can be downloaded at: https://www.mdpi.com/article/10.3390/atoms10020042/s1; Table S1: Update of Atomic Data for the First Three Spectra of Actinium; Table S2: Update of Atomic Data for the First Three Spectra of Actinium; Table S3: Update of Atomic Data for the First Three Spectra of Actinium; Table S4: Update of Atomic Data for the First Three Spectra of Actinium; Table S5: Update of Atomic Data for the First Three Spectra of Actinium; Table S6: Update of Atomic Data for the First Three Spectra of Actinium.

Funding: This research received no external funding.

Institutional Review Board Statement: This manuscript has been approved by the NIST Editorial Review Board (ERB) for publication. ERB Control Number G2022-0825.

Informed Consent Statement: Not applicable.

Data Availability Statement: Data are contained within the article and its Supplementary Materials.

Acknowledgments: Fruitful communications with Sebastian Raeder, Klaus Wendt, and Dominic Studer of Johannes Gutenberg-University, Mainz, Germany, are gratefully acknowledged.

Conflicts of Interest: The author declares no conflict of interest.

Abbreviations

The following abbreviations are used in this manuscript:

ASD   Atomic Spectra Database
LTE   Local Thermodynamic Equilibrium
NIST   National Institute of Standards and Technology

References

1. Quinet, P.; Argante, C.; Fivet, V.; Terranova, C.; Yushchenko, A.V.; Biémont, É. Atomic Data for Radioactive Elements Ra I, Ra II, Ac I and Ac II and Application to their Detection in HD 101065 and HR 465. *Astron. Astrophys.* **2007**, *474*, 307–314. [CrossRef]
2. Zhang, K.; Studer, D.; Weber, F.; Gadelshin, V.M.; Kneip, N.; Raeder, S.; Budker, D.; Wendt, K.; Kieck, T.; Porsev, S.G.; et al. Detection of the Lowest-Lying Odd-Parity Atomic Levels in Actinium. *Phys. Rev. Lett.* **2020**, *125*, 073001. [CrossRef] [PubMed]
3. Dzuba, V.A.; Flambaum, V.V.; Roberts, B.M. Calculations of the Atomic Structure for the Low-Lying States of Actinium. *Phys. Rev. A* **2019**, *100*, 022504; Erratum in *Phys. Rev. A* **2020**, *101*, 059901. [CrossRef]
4. Berengut, J.C.; Dzuba, V.A.; Flambaum, V.V. Transitions in Zr, Hf, Ta, W, Re, Hg, Ac, and U Ions with High Sensitivity to Variation of the Fine-Structure Constant. *Phys. Rev. A* **2011**, *84*, 054501. [CrossRef]
5. Roberts, B.M.; Dzuba, V.A.; Flambaum, V.V. Nuclear-Spin-Dependent Parity Nonconservation in s-$d_{5/2}$ and s-$d_{3/2}$ Transitions. *Phys. Rev. A* **2014**, *89*, 012502. [CrossRef]
6. Kramida, A. *NIST Atomic Energy Levels and Spectra Bibliographic Database (Version 2.0)*; National Institute of Standards and Technology: Gaithersburg, MD, USA, 2010. Available online: https://physics.nist.gov/elevbib (accessed on 31 July 2020).
7. Kramida, A.; Fuhr, J.R. *NIST Atomic Transition Probability Bibliographic Database (Version 9.0)*; National Institute of Standards and Technology: Gaithersburg, MD, USA, 2010. Available online: https://physics.nist.gov/fvalbib (accessed on 31 July 2020).
8. Kramida, A.; Ralchenko, Y.; Reader, J.; NIST ASD Team. *NIST Atomic Spectra Database (Version 5.9)*; National Institute of Standards and Technology: Gaithersburg, MD, USA, 2021. Available online: https://physics.nist.gov/asd (accessed on 30 October 2020).
9. Meggers, W.F.; Fred, M.; Tomkins, F.S. Emission Spectra of Actinium. *J. Res. Natl. Bur. Stand.* **1957**, *58*, 297–315. [CrossRef]
10. Edlén, B. The Dispersion of Standard Air. *J. Opt. Soc. Am.* **1953**, *43*, 339–344. [CrossRef]
11. Peck, E.R.; Reeder, K. Dispersion of Air. *J. Opt. Soc. Am.* **1972**, *62*, 958–962. [CrossRef]
12. Kramida, A. Critical Evaluation of Data on Atomic Energy Levels, Wavelengths, and Transition Probabilities. *Fusion Sci. Technol.* **2013**, *63*, 313–323. [CrossRef]
13. Ferrer, R.; Barzakh, A.; Bastin, B.; Beerwerth, R.; Block, M.; Creemers, P.; Grawe, H.; de Groote, R.; Delahaye, P.; Fléchard, X.; et al. Towards High-Resolution Laser Ionization Spectroscopy of the Heaviest Elements in Supersonic Gas Jet Expansion. *Nat. Commun.* **2017**, *8*, 14520. [CrossRef]
14. Granados, C.; Creemers, P.; Ferrer, R.; Gaffney, L.P.; Gins, W.; de Groote, R.; Huyse, M.; Kudryavtsev, Y.; Martínez, Y.; Raeder, S.; et al. In-Gas Laser Ionization and Spectroscopy of Actinium Isotopes near the N = 126 Closed Shell. *Phys. Rev. C* **2017**, *96*, 054331. [CrossRef]
15. Sonnenschein, V. Laser Developments and High Resolution Resonance Ionization Spectroscopy of Actinide Elements. Ph.D. Thesis, University Jyväskylä, Jyväskylä, Finland, 2014. Available online: https://jyx.jyu.fi/handle/123456789/45033 (accessed on 25 March 2022).
16. Raeder, S.; Wendt, K.; Studer, K. (Johannes Gutenberg-Universität, Mainz, Germany). Personal communication, 2021.

17. Roßnagel, J.; Raeder, S.; Hakimi, A.; Ferrer, R.; Trautmann, N.; Wendt, K. Determination of the First Ionization Potential of Actinium. *Phys. Rev. A* **2012**, *85*, 012525. [CrossRef]
18. Roßnagel, J. Construction of an Atomic Beam Mass Spectrometer Apparatus for Resonant Laser Ionization. Master's Thesis, Johannes Gutenberg-Universität, Mainz, Germany, 2011.
19. Tiesinga, E.; Mohr, P.J.; Newell, D.B.; Taylor, B.N. *The 2018 CODATA Recommended Values of the Fundamental Physical Constants (Web Version 8.1). Database Developed by J. Baker, M. Douma, and S. Kotochigova*; National Institute of Standards and Technology: Gaithersburg, MD, USA, 2021. Available online: http://physics.nist.gov/constants (accessed on 28 October 2021).
20. Kramida, A.; Olsen, K.; Ralchenko, Y. *Periodic Table: Atomic Properties of the Elements (Version 14), NIST SP 966*; National Institute of Standards and Technology: Gaithersburg, MD, USA, 2019. Available online: https://physics.nist.gov/pt (accessed on 28 October 2021).
21. Cowan, R.D. *The Theory of Atomic Structure and Spectra*; University of California Press: Berkeley, CA, USA, 1981.
22. Kramida, A. *A Suite of Atomic Structure Codes Originally Developed by RD Cowan Adapted for Windows-Based Personal Computers*; National Institute of Standards and Technology: Gaithersburg, MD, USA, 2018.
23. Özdemir, L.; Ürer, G. Electric Dipole Transition Parameters for Low-Lying Levels for Neutral Actinium. *Acta Phys. Pol. A* **2010**, *118*, 563–569. [CrossRef]
24. Ürer, G.; Özdemir, L. Energy Levels and Electric Dipole Transitions for Neutral Actinium (Z = 89). *Arab. J. Sci. Eng.* **2012**, *37*, 239–250. [CrossRef]
25. Martin, W.C.; Zalubas, R.; Hagan, L. *Atomic Energy Levels—The Rare-Earth Elements*; National Standard Reference Data Series; National Bureau of Standards: Washington, DC, USA, 1978, Volume 60. [CrossRef]
26. Azarov, V.I.; Kramida, A.; Vokhmentsev, M.Y. IDEN2—A Program for Visual Identification of Spectral Lines and Energy Levels in Optical Spectra of Atoms and Simple Molecules. *Comput. Phys. Commun.* **2018**, *225*, 149–153. [CrossRef]
27. Kramida, A. Assessing Uncertainties of Theoretical Atomic Transition Probabilities with Monte Carlo Random Trials. *Atoms* **2014**, *2*, 86–122. [CrossRef]
28. Kramida, A.E. The Program LOPT for Least-Squares Optimization of Energy Levels. *Comput. Phys. Commun.* **2011**, *182*, 419–434. [CrossRef]
29. Blaise, J.; Wyart, J.-F. Energy Levels and Atomic Spectra of Actinides. In *International Tables of Selected Constants, Volume 20*; Centre National de la Recherche Scientifique: Paris, France, 1992; Numerical Data from This Compilation Web. Available online: http://www.lac.universite-paris-saclay.fr/Data/Database/ (accessed on 25 March 2022).
30. Martin, W.C.; Hagan, L.; Reader, J.; Sugar, J. Ground Levels and Ionization Potentials for Lanthanide and Actinide Atoms and Ions. *J. Phys. Chem. Ref. Data* **1974**, *3*, 771–780. [CrossRef]
31. Roberts, B.M.; Dzuba, V.A.; Flambaum, V.V. Strongly Enhanced Atomic Parity Violation Due to Close Levels of Opposite Parity. *Phys. Rev. A* **2014**, *89*, 042509. [CrossRef]
32. Ürer, G.; Özdemir, L. The Level Structure of Singly-Ionized Actinium. *J. Kor. Phys. Soc.* **2012**, *61*, 353–358. [CrossRef]
33. Roberts, B.M.; Dzuba, V.A.; Flambaum, V.V. Parity Nonconservation in Fr-like Actinide and Cs-like Rare-Earth-Metal Ions. *Phys. Rev. A* **2013**, *88*, 012510. [CrossRef]
34. Safronova, U.I.; Johnson, W.R.; Safronova, M.S. Excitation Energies, Polarizabilities, Multipole Transition Rates, and Lifetimes of Ions Along the Francium Isoelectronic Sequence. *Phys. Rev. A* **2007**, *76*, 042504. [CrossRef]
35. Migdalek, J.; Glowacz-Proszkiewicz, A. 'Dirac-Fock Plus Core-polarization' Calculations of E1 Transitions in the Francium Isoelectronic Sequence. *J. Phys. B* **2007**, *40*, 4143–4154. [CrossRef]
36. Biémont, E.; Fivet, V.; Quinet, P. Relativistic Hartree-Fock and Dirac-Fock Atomic Structure Calculations in Fr-like Ions Ra^+, Ac^{2+}, Th^{3+} and U^{5+}. *J. Phys. B* **2004**, *37*, 4193–4204. [CrossRef]
37. Ürer, G.; Özdemir, L. Excitation Energies and E1, E2, and M1 Transition Parameters for Ac III. *Chin. J. Phys.* **2011**, *49*, 1178–1187.
38. Safronova, U.I.; Safronova, M.S.; Johnson, W.R. Forbidden M1 and E2 Transitions in Monovalent Atoms and Ions. *Phys. Rev. A* **2017**, *95*, 042507. [CrossRef]
39. Gossel, G.H.; Dzuba, V.A.; Flambaum, V.V. Calculation of Strongly Forbidden M1 Transitions and g-factor Anomalies in Atoms Considered for Parity-Nonconservation Measurements. *Phys. Rev. A* **2013**, *88*, 034501. [CrossRef]
40. Klinkenberg, P.F.A. Spectral Structure of Trebly Ionized Thorium, Th IV. *Physica B+C* **1988**, *151*, 552–567. [CrossRef]
41. Church, D.A.; Druetta, M.; Dunford, R.; Liu, C.-J.; Froese-Fischer, C.; Idrees, M.; Umar, V.M. Collision Spectroscopy of Low-Energy-Beam U^{5+} Ions. *J. Opt. Soc. Am. B* **1992**, *9*, 2159–2162. [CrossRef]
42. Kramida, A.; Nave, G.; Reader, J. The Cu II Spectrum. *Atoms* **2017**, *5*, 9. [CrossRef]
43. Kramida, A.; Ryabtsev, A.N.; Young, P.R. Revised Analysis of Fe VII. *Astrophys. J. Suppl. Ser.* **2022**, *258*, 37. [CrossRef]

Article

Structure Calculations in Nd III and U III Relevant for Kilonovae Modelling

Ricardo F. Silva [1,2,*], Jorge M. Sampaio [1,2], Pedro Amaro [3], Andreas Flörs [4], Gabriel Martínez-Pinedo [4,5,6] and José P. Marques [1,2]

1. Laboratório de Instrumentação e Física Experimental de Partículas (LIP), Av. Prof. Gama Pinto 2, 1649-003 Lisboa, Portugal; jmsampaio@fc.ul.pt (J.M.S.); jmmarques@fc.ul.pt (J.P.M.)
2. Faculdade de Ciências, Universidade de Lisboa, Rua Ernesto de Vasconcelos, Edifíco C8, 1749-016 Lisboa, Portugal
3. Laboratory for Instrumentation, Biomedical Engineering and Radiation Physics (LIBPhys-UNL), Department of Physics, NOVA School of Science and Technology, NOVA University Lisbon, 2829-516 Caparica, Portugal; pdamaro@fct.unl.pt
4. GSI Helmholtzzentrum für Schwerionenforschung, Planckstraße 1, 64291 Darmstadt, Germany; a.floers@gsi.de (A.F.); g.martinez@gsi.de (G.M.-P.)
5. Institut für Kernphysik (Theoriezentrum), Fachbereich Physik, Technische Universität Darmstadt, Schlossgartenstraße 2, 64298 Darmstadt, Germany
6. Helmholtz Forschungsakademie Hessen für FAIR, GSI Helmholtzzentrum für Schwerionenforschung, Planckstraße 1, 64291 Darmstadt, Germany
* Correspondence: rfsilva@lip.pt

Abstract: The detection of gravitational waves and electromagnetic signals from the neutron star merger GW170817 has provided evidence that these astrophysical events are sites where the r-process nucleosynthesis operates. The electromagnetic signal, commonly known as kilonova, is powered by the radioactive decay of freshly synthesized nuclei. However, its luminosity, colour and spectra depend on the atomic opacities of the produced elements. In particular, opacities of lanthanides and actinides elements, due to their large density of bound–bound transitions, are fundamental. The current work focuses on atomic structure calculations for lanthanide and actinide ions, which are important in kilonovae modelling of ejecta spectra. Calculations for Nd III and U III, two representative rare-earth ions, were achieved. Our aim is to provide valuable insights for future opacity calculations for all heavy elements. We noticed that the opacity of U III is about an order of magnitude greater than the opacity of Nd III due to a higher density of levels in the case of the actinide.

Keywords: opacity; atomic data; kilonovae; oscillator strengths; neutron stars

1. Introduction

The production mechanisms of elements heavier than iron have been studied for many decades. They involve a sequence of neutron captures and beta-decays. Depending on the neutron density reached in the astrophysical environment, one distinguishes between the s-process (s for slow) and r-process (r for rapid). While it has been known for a long time that the s-process operates on the asymptotic giant branch (AGB) stars, only recently have we been able to identify one of the astrophysical sites where the r-process operates [1]. This has been made possible by the observation of a kilonova associated with the collision of two neutron stars. This observation took place in August 2017 after the detection of gravitational waves from a neutron star merger by the LIGO-Virgo experiment, the well-known GW170817 event [2]. Its electromagnetic counterpart, designated by AT2017gfo [3], exhibits a number of unique characteristics that set it apart from other transients, including an unusually high optical brightness in the days following the explosion and a long-lived infrared emission that lasted nearly two weeks. These characteristics, which are associated with the ejecta's rapid colour evolution, appear to be consistent with theoretical models of kilonovae, which consider them to be potential sites for the occurrence of heavy r-processes [4].

Numerous explanations have been put forward to account for the optical and near-infrared spectral features observed in this so-called kilonova. Due to a lack of information about the atomic properties of lanthanide and actinide ions, the majority of radiation transport simulations are based on grey opacity schemes in which the value of the opacity is adjusted to reproduce the colour of the emission. It is expected, however, that the opacities of the former ions are roughly 10 times higher than the ones associated with ironlike elements [5,6]. Regarding this lack of data, calculations for selected r-process elements [7–11] and for all lanthanide elements [12–14] have been published in recent years.

In this work, atomic structure and opacity calculations were carried out for two representative r-process ions, Nd III and U III. The expansion opacity is compared between these two ions in order to evaluate the possible impact of actinides. This is particularly significant given the scarcity of publications incorporating actinides into their opacity models. With this in mind, we discuss the effect of level density in the computation of expansion opacities and in particular how actinides can be prone to having a higher density of low-lying levels.

2. Methods

2.1. Expansion Opacities

Pinto & Eastman's previous work on the light curves of type Ia supernovae [15] have shown bound–bound transitions to be the major source of opacity, accounting for two orders of magnitude more than contributions from electron scattering, bound–free, and free–free transitions.

In rapidly evolving environments, such as those of SN Ia and of kilonovae, the velocity gradient of the expansion of the ejecta is much greater than thermal and turbulent motions responsible for Doppler broadening. When that is the case, and by also assuming the impact of the overlap of strong lines is negligible (as demonstrated by Tanaka et al. 2020 for the case of lanthanides [14]), we can use the expansion opacity formalism to compute the bound–bound opacity for a certain wavelength grid $\Delta\lambda$ [16,17]. Assuming homologously expanding ejecta with density ρ, the expansion opacity at the time t_{exp} after the explosion is given as

$$\kappa_{\exp}(\lambda_k) = \frac{1}{\rho c t_{exp}} \sum_k \frac{\lambda_k}{\Delta\lambda}(1 - e^{-\tau_k}), \tag{1}$$

where the sum is taken over all the lines within a wavelength interval of width $\Delta\lambda$. τ_k is the Sobolev's optical depth

$$\tau_k = \left(\frac{\pi e^2}{m_e c}\right) n_k t_{exp} f_k \lambda_k, \tag{2}$$

where n is the population of the lower level of the transition k with wavelength λ_k and f_k is the oscillator strength of the line.

2.2. Atomic Calculations

Most of the calculations for this work were performed using the open source and freely available Flexible Atomic Code (FAC) [18]. In particular, the forked version of the original code, cFAC (version 1.6.3a), was used [19]. The atomic structure fully takes into account relativistic effect as it is based on the diagonalization of the Dirac-Coulomb Hamiltonian:

$$H_{DC} = \sum_{i=1}^{N} \left(c\boldsymbol{\alpha}_i \cdot \boldsymbol{p}_i + (\beta_i - 1)c^2 + V_i\right) + \sum_{i<i}^{N} \frac{1}{r_{ij}}, \tag{3}$$

where α_i and β_i are the 4 × 4 Dirac matrices and V_i accounts for potential due to the nuclear charge. Higher order QED effects such as self-energy and vacuum polarization effects are included in the screened hydrogenic approximation, while the Breit interaction is only included in the zero energy limit for the exchanged photon. Relativistic configuration interaction (RCI) calculations are performed based on a set of atomic state functions (ASFs), Ψ, given by a superposition of $i = 1, \cdots, N_{CSF}$ configuration state functions (CSFs), ψ_i, with the same symmetries,

$$\Psi = \sum_i^{N_{CSF}} c_i \psi^i. \tag{4}$$

The CSFs used in the calculation are constructed from a linear combination of Slater determinants of one-electron orbitals, which are determined by solving self-consistently a set of Dirac–Fock–Slater differential equations for a local central potential which includes both nuclear field and electron–electron interactions. In this approach, the central potential is derived using a self-consistent method that minimizes the energy of a chosen mean configuration. In all the calculations provided with FAC, and as it is typically considered, the central potential was optimized for the ground configuration, [Xe] $4f^4$ in the case of Nd III and [Rn] $5f^4$ for U III.

3. Results and Discussion
3.1. Nd III

Starting with Nd III, a summary of the configurations used in each of the calculations, including the total number of levels and lines computed, is given in Table 1. For all calculations, a [Xe] ground configuration was used for the core of the ion. We performed two different FAC calculations (labelled accordingly as Calculations A and B) which are distinguished only by the inclusion in the basis set of the additional configuration $4f^3 6f$ in Calculation A.

Table 1. Summary of the different set of configurations used on different calculations for Nd III, including experimental results from NIST [20]. For the GRASP2K calculations [21], only the configurations from the multireference space are shown. The full active space of configurations used in that calculation is shown in Ref. [22].

Label	Configurations		All	
	Even	Odd	#Levels	#Lines
FAC (Calculation A)	$4f^4, 4f^3 6p, 4f^2 5d^2,$ $4f^2 5d 6s, 4f^3 5f, 4f^3 7p, 4f^3 6f$	$4f^3 5d, 4f^3 6s,$ $4f^3 6d, 4f^3 7s$	3206	708,077
FAC (Calculation B)	$4f^4, 4f^3 6p, 4f^2 5d^2,$ $4f^2 5d 6s, 4f^3 5f, 4f^3 7p$	$4f^3 5d, 4f^3 6s,$ $4f^3 6d, 4f^3 7s$	2702	542,264
GRAPS2K (Gaigalas et al.)	$4f^4, 4f^3 6p, 4f^2 5d^2,$ $4f^2 5d 6s, 4f^3 5f, 4f^3 7p$	$4f^3 5d, 4f^3 6s,$ $4f^3 6d, 4f^3 7s$	1453	148,759
NIST	$4f^4$	$4f^3 5d$	29	-

We compare our results with structure calculations performed with the GRASP2K code by Gaigalas et al. [22] as well with the NIST [20] database. As expected, however, the number of levels and lines measured experimentally is still very reduced.

For the data supplied by Gaigalas et al., MCDHF calculations were initially performed for the states of the ground configuration. The wave functions derived from these calculations were adopted as the initial ones to calculate the states of the multireference configurations (given in Table 1). Subsequent RCI calculations account for a larger number of configurations not included in the initial MCDHF self-consistent field. The Breit interaction and leading order QED effects are also included at this stage. The full details of the calculation and the construction of the active space used are given in [22]. As a result of the increased degree of optimization, MCDHF-RCI calculations are expected to be more precise than RCI calculations based on a central-field potential. Nonetheless, the latter has been used in calculations for lanthanides, with a typical precision for the lowest energy states of each configuration of 20% for neutral atoms and of less than 10% for the first ionization stages (see, for example, [14]).

A visual comparison of our results with those of Gaigalas et al. and with the NIST data is shown in Figure 1. We can clearly see that the FAC results for Calculation B appear to match reasonably well to the ones obtained with the GRASP2K code, especially for the lowest lying configurations. A worse match is achieved for the $4f^2\,5d^2$ and $4f^2\,5d\,6d$, as FAC seems to underestimate the energy values of those configurations. In order to compare our results, we have evaluated the difference in the lowest energy level of each configuration (normalized by the ionization potential) between our FAC calculations and the data from Gaigalas et al. and NIST. Agreement for Calculation A with the data from Gaigalas et al. and NIST is, on average, within 4.1% and 3.9%, respectively. Calculation B has an average agreement of 3.6% with Gaigalas et al. data and of 0.6% with NIST data. However, we also note that only data for the ground state and for $4f^3\,5d$ are available in the NIST database. No other experimental data were found for Nd III configurations beyond $4f^3 5d$.

In our particular case, the disparity of results between Calculations A and B of FAC points to the fact that the energy levels have not yet converged. Hence, although RCI codes can provide time-efficient calculations when only few configurations are included, which allow for systematic calculations of many ions (as achieved in [14]), one should note that the inclusion of a much higher number of configurations can have a considerable impact in the calculations.

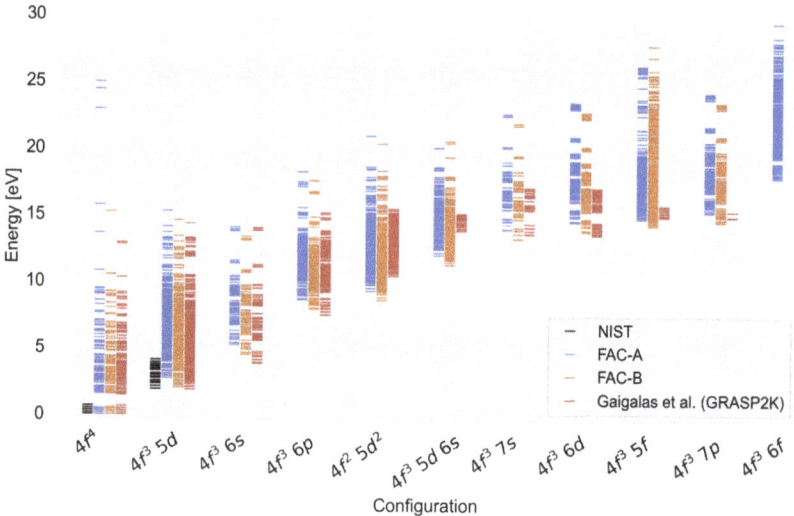

Figure 1. Energy levels for configurations of Nd III calculated with FAC and compared with the results from Gaigalas et al. [22] and with NIST data [20].

3.2. U III

As for the U III, the basis set for the FAC RCI calculations was determined by increasing the principal quantum number of the configurations used in Nd III by one. The set of configurations from Calculation B of Nd III was chosen because it produced the best results when compared to the experimental NIST data. At the time of writing, the only experimental data available for actinide ions are from Blaise et al. [23]. Furthermore, two independent groups from the *Los Alamos* institute have developed calculations for the first ionized states of uranium with the CI-MBPT code [24] and the ATOMIC codes [25]. Only the data from Savukov et al. [26], which used a hybrid configuration interaction (CI) plus linearized coupled cluster (LCC) methods described in [27], are publicly available. Sultana N. Nahar of the Ohio State University's Astronomy Department hosts and maintains the NORAD-Atomic-Data database [28], which contains calculations for a broad range of structure calculations for important astrophysical ions, including uranium, using the SUPERSTRUCTURE [29] algorithm. In that database, however, only highly ionized elements are available.

Table 2 provides an overview of the FAC calculation achieved in the work as well as the prior calculations for U III with the CI-MBPT code from Savukov et al. and of the experimental data from Blaise et al.

Table 2. Summary of the different set of configurations used on the FAC calculation for U III. An overview of the experimental data from Blaise et al. [23]. The calculations produced by Savukov et al. [26] using a hybrid configuration interaction (CI) plus linearized coupled cluster (LCC) methods (described in [27]) are also shown. For the CI+LCC calculations, we only show the configurations for which levels and lines data were published.

Label	Configurations		All	
	Even	Odd	#Levels	#Lines
FAC	$5f^4, 5f^37p, 5f^26d^2,$ $5f^26d7s, 5f^36f, 5f^38p$	$5f^36d, 5f^37s,$ $5f^37d, 5f^38s$	2702	542,264
CI+LCC-Savukov et al.	$5f^4, 5f^26d^2$ [a]	$5f^36d, 5f^37s$ [a]	192 [b]	3024 [c]
Exp.-Blaise et al.	$5f^4, 5f^37p, 5f^26d^2,$ $5f^26d7s$	$5f^36d, 5f^37s$	123	-

[a] Only configurations for published levels and lines are shown. [b] Only the energies for 96 levels are published. [c] Only the gf-values for 20 lines are published.

We can observe from Figure 2 that, as with Nd III, we were able to reproduce the lowest lying levels fairly accurately when compared to both experimental and computational data. From spectroscopic studies, Blaise et al. determined $5f^4$ to be the ground configuration for U III. On the other hand, the CI+LCC calculations suggest an electron in the $6d$ shell in the ion's lowest energy state. Our FAC calculations do provide better agreement with the experimental data in this regard, giving the even $5f^4$ configuration as the ground state of U III. Comparisons for the lowest energies levels of each configuration were evaluated in the same way as for NdIII. We found relative differences of 3.4%, on average, when comparing our FAC calculation with the experimental data from Blaise et al. The agreement for the lowest energy levels with calculations from Savukov et al. was within 2.2%, on average.

One important point to keep is the larger radius of the $5f$ shell when compared to the $4f$ shell [30]. As a result, $5f$ electrons tend to be less deeply buried in the core and less shielded from the effect of outer valence electrons than $4f$ electrons. This effect, associated with the higher Z of actinide elements can, in theory, contribute to a smaller gap between the ground state and the first few excited levels. In the particular case of U III, it is expected that the excitation energies of $5f$ and $6d$ are exceedingly close to each other.

The greater radius of $5f$ shells also contributes to a significantly higher level density in U III when compared to the previously discussed calculations for Nd III, as can be seen in more detail in Figure 3, despite the fact that the same number of levels was calculated in both cases. The number of levels is particularly high in the case of the actinide at energies below 10 eV. This is especially important to consider in the opacity calculations as the population of low-lying levels is favoured in LTE conditions. The gap between the two peaks that we find at roughly 12 eV is likely due to the limited set of configurations used in the calculation, as it was based from the calculation on Nd III. Therefore, contributions from 5g shells, for example, are not included, and can potentially contribute with energy levels at those energies.

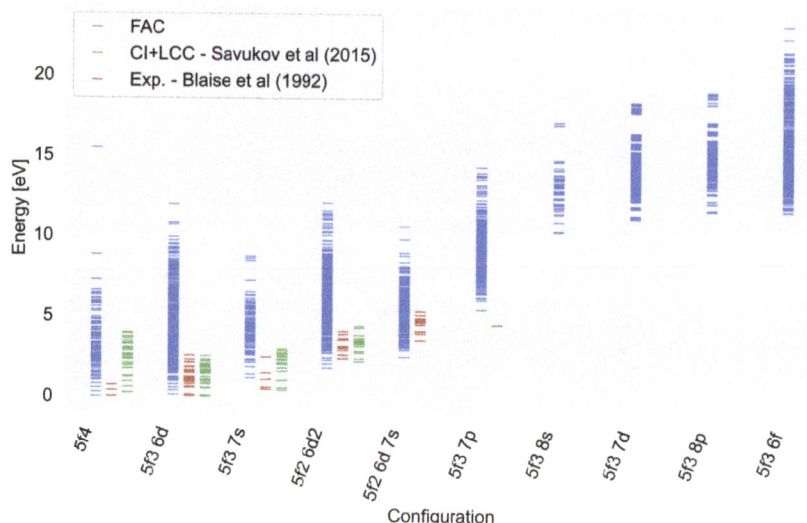

Figure 2. Energy levels for configurations of U III calculated with FAC. The excitation energies are compared with the experimental results from Blaise et al. [23] and the CI+LCC calculations from Savukov et al. [26].

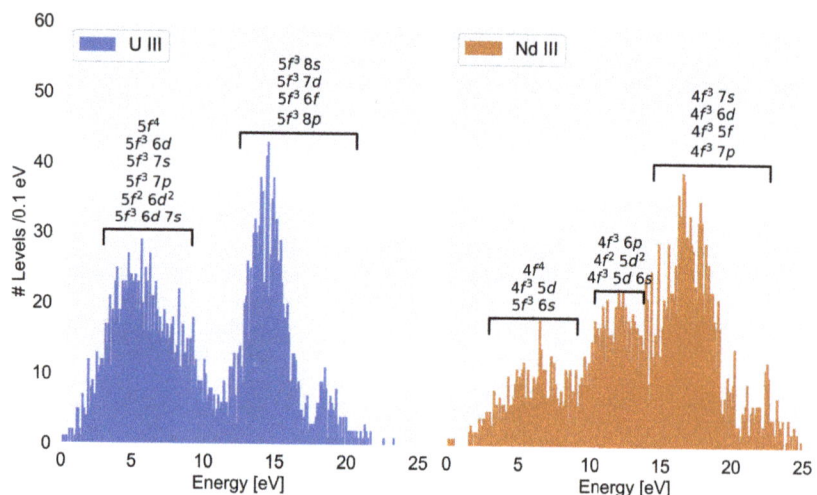

Figure 3. Level density distribution of U III and Nd III as calculated from FAC. The configurations with greater contribution for each peak are also highlighted.

3.3. Expansion Opacities

Following previous works, the expansion opacity of Nd III and U III was calculated individually for each ion, assuming a gas composition given just by those ions and thermal population of excited states. This allows us to investigate the effect of only the computed bound–bound transitions on the opacity. They were evaluated over a time period of one day following the explosion, when the medium density was about $\rho = 10^{-13}$ g cm^{-3} [12]. Additionally, a temperature of $T = 10{,}000$ K was specified based on prior estimates for doubly ionized ions [8,14]. The results are presented in Figure 4, including the expansion opacity calculated with the data provided by Gaigalas et al. [22] for Nd III (Strategy C). A good agreement was found between the opacity calculations using the data from Calculation B of Nd III and the data from Gaigalas et al., particularly at visible and infrared wavelengths (average deviations on the expansion opacity of 13% for $\lambda > 5000$ Å). Differences at lower energies are due to our opacity calculations taking into account a greater number of high energy levels than Gaigalas et al. The spectrum obtained with Calculation A for Nd III is overall similar to the one presented here for Calculation B (both in shape and magnitude), with only minor differences at very high energies (~1000 Å) due to the presence of more highly energetic levels.

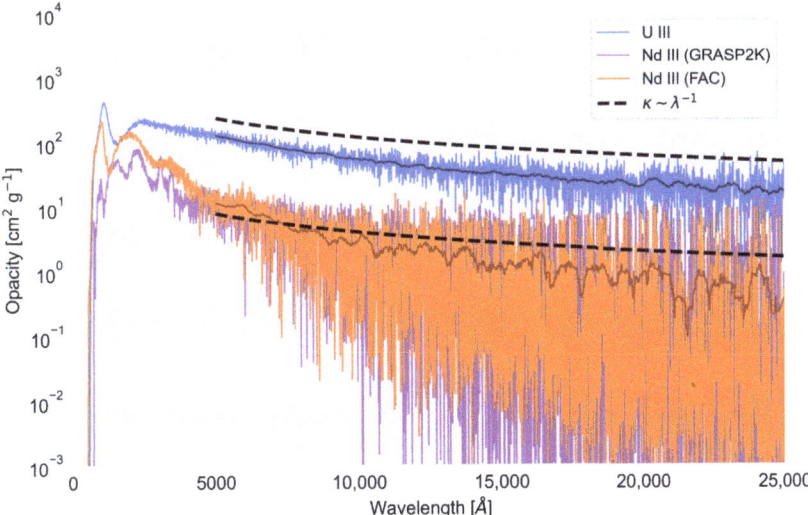

Figure 4. Expansion opacity for U III and Nd III (Calculation B) from the calculations performed with FAC. The expansion opacity of Nd III calculated using the data from Gaigalas et al. [22] is also to provide a more visual comparison between the two results. The opacity was evaluated at $t = 1$ day for the typical density and temperature values of $\rho = 10^{-13}$ g cm^{-3} and $T = 10{,}000$ K assumed by other calculations. A wavelength bin of $\Delta\lambda = 10$ Å was used. An average over a set of 10 bins is also shown in darker blue and orange lines. The black dashed line highlights the wavelength dependence of the opacity following approximately a λ^{-1} power law.

As it can be seen, the opacity of U III is nearly an order of magnitude greater than that of Nd III. This results can be explained by the higher density of low-lying levels in the case of U III, which have a greater contribution to the opacity in LTE than more excited ones. The difference is most noticeable in the visible range, and while it remains significant in the IR, it is less noticeable due to large fluctuations in the opacity of Nd III.

Another interesting observation is that the number of lines of both actinide and lanthanide elements seems to vary smoothly with the wavelength. In particular, we found that after the initial peak at $\lambda \sim 1000$ Å, the number of transitions decreases smoothly with $N \sim \lambda^{-2}$, especially at infrared wavelengths. This dependence is based on the low-energy tail seen empirically in the distribution of bound–bound transitions in Nd III and U III, that can be seen in Figure 5.

A parameterization of the opacities can, therefore, be obtained, when there is a high number of transitions with a high optical depth $(1 - e^{-\tau} \sim 1)$. In that case

$$\kappa_{exp} \approx \frac{1}{\rho c t_{exp}} \sum_k \frac{\lambda_k}{\Delta \lambda} \approx \frac{1}{\rho c t_{exp}} N \frac{\lambda}{\Delta \lambda} \sim \lambda^{-1}. \tag{5}$$

Equation 5 emphasizes the importance of the number of lines taken into account in these calculations. Given a high optical depth and LTE conditions, the primary source of opacity is the ion's line count per unit wavelength, rather than individual strong transitions. As a result, the precision of individual lines will be negligible in environments where the density of levels is sufficiently high enough to sustain local thermodynamical equilibrium and a high optical depth. These insights are particularly pertinent in the case of lanthanides and actinides, owing to their extremely complicated shell structure, which makes accurate computation extremely difficult to achieve within a reasonable amount of time and computational resources.

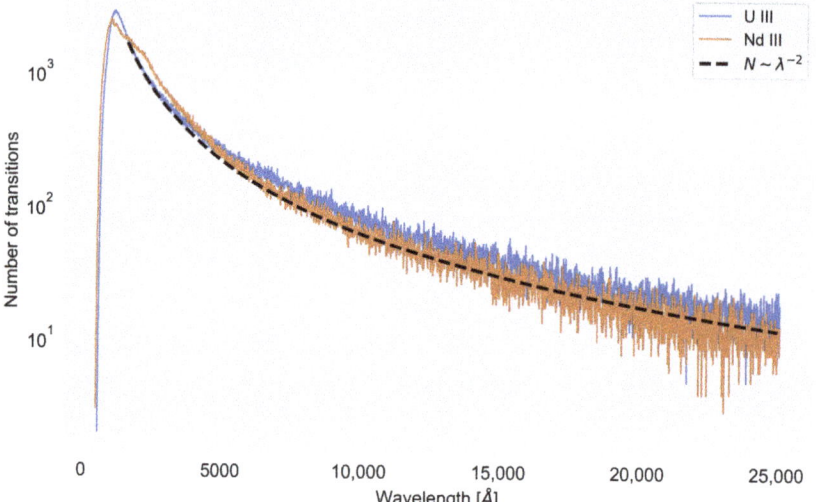

Figure 5. Total number of lines for Nd III and U III as a function of the wavelength. The $N \sim \lambda^{-2}$ inverse power law dependence on the wavelength is highlighted. A wavelength bin of $\Delta \lambda = 10$ Å was used.

4. Conclusions

In this work, the FAC code has been used to compute level energies, transition wavelengths and oscillator strengths for electric dipole (E1) transitions for Nd III and U III. We have noticed a reasonable agreement of the energies of low-lying levels with experimental data as well as with other theoretical calculations achieved for those ions. We predict the opacity of U III to be roughly an order of magnitude higher than of Nd III, in all wavelength ranges of interest. Moreover, the larger number of strong transitions of uranium makes the spectra extremely dependent on the number of transitions included, making the precision of individual lines negligible. Due to the higher density of levels expected for actinide elements when compared to lanthanides, we predict these differences to extend beyond Nd III and U III.

Author Contributions: Formal analysis, R.F.S., P.A. and A.F.; Project administration, G.M.-P. and J.P.M.; Supervision, J.M.S., G.M.-P. and J.P.M.; Validation, J.M.S., P.A., A.F. and G.M.-P.; Visualization, R.F.S.; Writing—original draft, R.F.S; Writing—review & editing, R.F.S., J.M.S., P.A., A.F., G.M.-P. and J.P.M. All authors have read and agreed to the published version of the manuscript.

Funding: This work was partially supported by the Fundação para a Ciência e Tecnologia (FCT), Portugal through the contract UIDP/50 0 07/2020 (LIP). R.F.S acknowledges the support from the ChETEC COST Action(CA16117) during his short-term scientific mission at GSI. A.F. and G.M.-P. acknowledge the support of the European Research Council (ERC) under the European Union's Horizon 2020 research and innovation program (ERC Advanced Grant KILONOVA No. 885281).

Data Availability Statement: The data presented in this study are available on request from the corresponding author.

Conflicts of Interest: The authors declare no conflict of interest.

References

1. Cowan, J.J.; Sneden, C.; Lawler, J.E.; Aprahamian, A.; Wiescher, M.; Langanke, K.; Martínez-Pinedo, G.; Thielemann, F.K. Origin of the heaviest elements: The rapid neutron-capture process. *Rev. Mod. Phys.* **2021**, *93*, 015002. [CrossRef]
2. Abbott, B. P. et al. Prospects for Observing and Localizing Gravitational-Wave Transients with Advanced LIGO and Advanced Virgo. *LRR* **2016**, *19*, 1. [CrossRef]
3. Abbott, B. P. et al. Multi-messenger Observations of a Binary Neutron Star Merger. *Astrophys. J.* **2017**, *848*, L12. [CrossRef]
4. Metzger, B.D.; Martínez-Pinedo, G.; Darbha, S.; Quataert, E.; Arcones, A.; Kasen, D.; Thomas, R.; Nugent, P.; Panov, I.V.; Zinner, N.T. Electromagnetic counterparts of compact object mergers powered by the radioactive decay of r-process nuclei. *Mon. Not. R. Astron. Soc.* **2010**, *406*, 2650–2662. [CrossRef]
5. Barnes, J.; Kasen, D. Effect of a high opacity on the light curves of radioactively powered transients from compact object mergers. *Astrophys. J.* **2013**, *775*, 18. [CrossRef]
6. Kasen, D.; Badnell, N.R.; Barnes, J. Opacities and spectra of the r-process ejecta from neutron star mergers. *Astrophys. J.* **2013**, *774*, 25. [CrossRef]
7. Wollaeger, R.T.; Korobkin, O.; Fontes, C.J.; Rosswog, S.K.; Even, W.P.; Fryer, C.L.; Sollerman, J.; Hungerford, A.L.; Van Rossum, D.R.; Wollaber, A.B. Impact of ejecta morphology and composition on the electromagnetic signatures of neutron star mergers. *Mon. Not. R. Astron. Soc.* **2017**, *478*, 3298–3334. [CrossRef]
8. Tanaka, M.; Kato, D.; Gaigalas, G.; Rynkun, P.; Radžiūtė, L.; Wanajo, S.; Sekiguchi, Y.; Nakamura, N.; Tanuma, H.; Murakami, I.; Sakaue, H.A. Properties of Kilonovae from Dynamical and Post-merger Ejecta of Neutron Star Mergers. *Astrophys. J.* **2018**, *852*, 109. [CrossRef]
9. Fontes, C.J.; Fryer, C.L.; Hungerford, A.L. A connection between atomic physics and gravitational wave spectroscopy. *AIP Conf. Proc.* **2017**, *1811*, 190. [CrossRef]
10. Mccann, M.; Bromley, S.; Loch, S.D.; Ballance, C.P. Atomic data calculations for Au i–Au iii and exploration in the application of collisional-radiative theory to laboratory and neutron star merger plasmas. *Mon. Not. R. Astron. Soc.* **2021**, *509*, 4723–4735. [CrossRef]
11. Pognan, Q.; Jerkstrand, A.; Grumer, J. On the validity of steady-state for nebular phase kilonovae. *Mon. Not. R. Astron. Soc.* **2022**, *510*, 3806–3837. [CrossRef]
12. Kasen, D.; Metzger, B.; Barnes, J.; Quataert, E.; Ramirez-Ruiz, E. Origin of the heavy elements in binary neutron-star mergers from a gravitational-wave event. *Nature* **2017**, *551*, 80–84. [CrossRef] [PubMed]
13. Fontes, C.J.; Fryer, C.L.; Hungerford, A.L.; Wollaeger, R.T.; Korobkin, O. A line-binned treatment of opacities for the spectra and light curves from neutron star mergers. *Mon. Not. R. Astron. Soc.* **2020**, *493*, 4143–4171. [CrossRef]
14. Tanaka, M.; Kato, D.; Gaigalas, G.; Kawaguchi, K. Systematic opacity calculations for kilonovae. *Mon. Not. R. Astron. Soc.* **2020**, *496*, 1369–1392. [CrossRef]
15. Eastman, R.G.; Pinto, P.A. Spectrum Formation in Supernovae: Numerical Techniques. *Astrophys. J.* **1993**, *412*, 731. [CrossRef]
16. Pinto, P.A.; Eastman, R.G. The Physics of Type Ia Supernova Light Curves. I. Analytic Results and Time Dependence. *Astrophys. J.* **2000**, *530*, 744–756. [CrossRef]
17. Pinto, P.A.; Eastman, R.G. The Physics of Type Ia Supernova Light Curves. II. Opacity and Diffusion. *Astrophys. J.* **2000**, *530*, 757–776. [CrossRef]
18. Gu, M.F. The flexible atomic code. *Can. J. Phys.* **2008**, *86*, 675–689. [CrossRef]
19. Stambulchik, E. cFAC—A Forked Version of FAC. 2020. Available online: https://github.com/fnevgeny/cfac (accessed on 20 December 2021).
20. Kramida, A.; Ralchenko, Y.; Reader, J. No Title. *NIST Atomic Spectra Database*, Version 5.8; National Institute of Standards and Technology: Gaithersburg, MD, USA, 2020. Available online: https://physics.nist.gov/asd (accessed on 9 April 2017).
21. Jönsson, P.; Gaigalas, G.; Bieroń, J.; Fischer, C.F.; Grant, I.P. New version: Grasp2K relativistic atomic structure package. *Comput. Phys. Commun.* **2013**, *184*, 2197–2203. [CrossRef]

22. Gaigalas, G.; Kato, D.; Rynkun, P.; Radžiūtė, L.; Tanaka, M.; Radžiūte, L.; Tanaka, M. Extended Calculations of Energy Levels and Transition Rates of Nd ii-iv Ions for Application to Neutron Star Mergers. *Astrophys. J. Suppl. Ser.* **2019**, *240*, 29. [CrossRef]
23. Blaise, J.; Wyart, J.F. *Energy Levels and Atomic Spectra of Actinides*; Tables Internationales de Constantes: Paris, France, 1992; p. 479.
24. Kozlov, M.G.; Porsev, S.G.; Safronova, M.S.; Tupitsyn, I.I. CI-MBPT: A package of programs for relativistic atomic calculations based on a method combining configuration interaction and many-body perturbation theory. *Comput. Phys. Commun.* **2015**, *195*, 199–213. [CrossRef]
25. Hakel, P.; Sherrill, M.E.; Mazevet, S.; Abdallah, J.; Colgan, J.; Kilcrease, D.P.; Magee, N.H.; Fontes, C.J.; Zhang, H.L. The new Los Alamos opacity code ATOMIC. *J. Quant. Spectrosc. Radiat. Transf.* **2006**, *99*, 265–271. [CrossRef]
26. Savukov, I.; Safronova, U.I.; Safronova, M.S. Relativistic configuration interaction plus linearized-coupled-cluster calculations of U^{2+} energies, g factors, transition rates, and lifetimes. *Phys. Rev. A* **2015**, *92*, 052516. [CrossRef]
27. Safronova, M.S.; Kozlov, M.G.; Johnson, W.R.; Jiang, D. Development of a configuration-interaction plus all-order method for atomic calculations. *Phys. Rev. A* **2009**, *80*, 012516. [CrossRef]
28. Nahar, S. Database NORAD-Atomic-Data for Atomic Processes in Plasma. *Atoms* **2020**, *8*, 68. [CrossRef]
29. Eissner, W. SUPERSTRUCTURE-An atomic code. *J. Phys. IV Proc.* **1991**, *1*, C1-3–C1-13.:1991101. [CrossRef]
30. Cowan, R.D. *The Theory of Atomic Structure and Spectra*; University of California Press: Berkeley, CA, USA, 1981; p. 731. [CrossRef]

Article

Electronic Structure of Lr$^+$ (Z = 103) from Ab Initio Calculations

Harry Ramanantoanina [1,2,*], Anastasia Borschevsky [3], Michael Block [1,2,4] and Mustapha Laatiaoui [1,2]

1. Department Chemie, Johannes Gutenberg-Universität, Fritz-Strassmann Weg 2, 55128 Mainz, Germany; m.block@gsi.de (M.B.); mlaatiao@uni-mainz.de (M.L.)
2. Helmholtz-Institut Mainz, Staudingerweg 18, 55128 Mainz, Germany
3. Van Swinderen Institute for Particle Physics and Gravity, University of Groningen, Nijenborgh 4, 9747 Groningen, The Netherlands; a.borschevsky@rug.nl
4. GSI Helmholtzzentrum für Schwerionenforschung, Planckstrasse 1, 64291 Darmstadt, Germany
* Correspondence: haramana@uni-mainz.de

Abstract: The four-component relativistic Dirac–Coulomb Hamiltonian and the multireference configuration interaction (MRCI) model were used to provide the reliable energy levels and spectroscopic properties of the Lr$^+$ ion and the Lu$^+$ homolog. The energy spectrum of Lr$^+$ is very similar to that of the Lu$^+$ homolog, with the multiplet manifold of the $7s^2$, $6d^17s^1$ and $7s^17p^1$ configurations as the ground and low-lying excited states. The results are discussed in light of earlier findings utilizing different theoretical models. Overall, the MRCI model can reliably predict the energy levels and properties and bring new insight into experiments with superheavy ions.

Keywords: MRCI; electronic structure; electric dipole transitions

Citation: Ramanantoanina, H.; Borschevsky, A.; Block M.; Laatiaoui, M. Electronic Structure of Lr$^+$ (Z = 103) from Ab Initio Calculations. *Atoms* **2022**, *10*, 48. https://doi.org/10.3390/atoms10020048

Academic Editor: Yew Kam Ho

Received: 14 April 2022
Accepted: 6 May 2022
Published: 9 May 2022

Publisher's Note: MDPI stays neutral with regard to jurisdictional claims in published maps and institutional affiliations.

Copyright: © 2022 by the authors. Licensee MDPI, Basel, Switzerland. This article is an open access article distributed under the terms and conditions of the Creative Commons Attribution (CC BY) license (https://creativecommons.org/licenses/by/4.0/).

1. Introduction

A new development in the field of atomic spectroscopy and ion mobility has been recently proposed under the name of Laser Resonance Chromatography (LRC) [1], a method that gained interest in particular because of its potential applicability to superheavy elements. In this method, optical resonances are identified based on resonant optical pumping of ions drifting in diluted helium [1,2]. The optical pumping process exploits strong ground state transitions to feed metastable electronic states, causing relative changes in the transport properties, which can be measured using drift time spectrometers [2]. However, in the perspective of an application of the LRC method in the field of superheavy elements, the question of how well optical lines are defined becomes important, because atomic levels are simply missing from conventional tables. In this context, theoretical models play a significant role in calculating the electronic structure and predicting energies. Additionally, calculations of the transport properties involving the interaction between metal ions and rare gas elements are very useful in assessing experimental parameters such as the required detector sensitivities and beamtimes [3,4].

High-accuracy theoretical predictions for the heaviest elements should be based on atomic calculations involving relativistic methods and the many-body theory. For spectra, these problems are often solved by using the Fock Space Coupled Cluster (FSCC) [5–7], configuration Interaction (CI) models based on multiconfigurational Dirac–Hartree–Fock (MCDHF) [8–11], a combination of CI and the many-body perturbation theory (CI+MBPT) [12,13], or multireference (MRCI) theory [14–16]. FSCC is one of the most powerful available approaches that provides very accurate results at a reasonable computational price, where applicable. The limitation of FSCC is in its formulation which, until recently, could only accommodate up to two holes or two electrons. Lately, this method has been extended to treat three valence electrons [17]. The use of MRCI techniques provides flexibility, allowing investigations of various configurations, and considerable effort has been invested in making the CI algorithm functional within realistic computational resources. The MRCI results for heavy and superheavy elements can be found in the literature [14–16,18–20].

In this work, calculations of the electronic structures and the properties of Lu$^+$ and Lr$^+$ ions using the MRCI model are reported. These results are compared with the experimental data [21,22] and earlier FSCC theoretical findings for the energy levels and earlier CI+MBPT data for the electronic transition rates [23]. These comparisons are used to evaluate the reliability of the calculated energy levels and to gain insight into the prospects of using this method to further study superheavy ions with multiple valence electrons (more than two) and also to evaluate the molecular systems of metal ions and rare gas elements.

2. Theoretical Method

The calculations were carried out using the 2019 release of the DIRAC code [24,25]. The electronic structure and wavefunctions were computed based on the four-component Dirac–Coulomb Hamiltonian to ensure full relativistic treatment of the superheavy elements. The nuclei were described within the finite-nucleus model in the form of a Gaussian charge distribution [26]. The Dyall basis set series of double- (cv2z), triple- (cv3z) and quadruple-zeta (cv4z) cardinal numbers for both the Lu and Lr elements [27,28] were used. All the properties were computed with these basis sets, thus allowing us to also extrapolate the energy levels at the complete basis set (CBS) limit. The small component wavefunctions were generated from the large component basis sets by strict kinetic balance [29]. Further augmentation of the basis sets with extra diffuse functions in an even-tempered manner would not significantly impact the results, as found in preliminary tests made with single- and double-augmented calculations.

We divided the theoretical procedure into three steps. The first step consisted of the atomic Dirac–Hartree–Fock (DHF) calculations that were conducted by using the average of configuration (AOC) method [30]. We considered the AOC-type calculation for consistency with an earlier study of Rf$^+$ ions [31]. We also note that based on the AOC electronic structure, we always obtained reliable energy levels and transitions in heavy metal ions and their molecular complexes [32–35]. The AOC method was used to distribute the two valence electrons of the Lu$^+$ and Lr$^+$ ions within 12 valence spinors of the s and d atomic characters. In other words, we used fractional occupation numbers (0.1667 = 2/12) for the merged Lu 6s and 5d orbitals as well as for the Lr 7s and 6d orbitals, allowing us to obtain a totally symmetrical wavefunction that was isomorphic with the configuration system under which the MRCI model (see below) was operated.

The second step consisted of the MRCI calculations that were conducted based on the AOC DHF wavefunctions. The MRCI calculations were performed by using the Kramers-restricted configuration interaction module in the DIRAC code [24]. Table 1 shows the theoretical scheme for the generalized active space (GAS) [15,18,19] that was defined in the model. In total, 34 electrons were activated that formed the basis of the valence 5d, 6s and 6p spinors of Lu (and similarly, 6d, 7s and 7p of Lr) and the semi-core 4d, 5s, 5p and 4f spinors of Lu (and similarly, 5d, 6s, 6p and 5f of Lr). No excitations were allowed in GAS 1 in order to reduce the computational demands, whereas single- and double-electron excitations were allowed in GAS 2 and GAS 3, respectively, to complete the CI expansion (see Table 1). Virtual spinors with energies below 30 atomic units were also added in the CI expansion. The numbers of the requested roots in the MRCI calculations were adjusted to contain all the multiplet manifolds of the Lu (and Lr) $6s^2$ ($7s^2$), $5d^1 6s^1$ ($6d^1 7s^1$) and $6s^1 6p^1$ ($7s^1 7p^1$) configurations. In order to correct the energy levels for the Breit (transverse photon interaction) and the lowest-order quantum electrodynamics (QED) contributions (vacuum polarization and the self-energy terms) [36,37], we used the GRASP program package [38], which is based on the Dirac–Coulomb–Breit Hamiltonian and the multiconfiguration Dirac–Hartree–Fock (MCDHF) model. Aside from that, in the GRASP program [38], the self-energy terms are treated within the Welton approach, where the screening coefficients are approximated by the ratio of the Dirac wavefunction density in a small region around the nucleus to the same density obtained for hydrogenoic orbitals [39]. The reference spaces for the MCDHF calculations were the $4f^{14}(5d6s6p)^2$ and $5f^{14}(6d7s7p)^2$ multiplet manifolds of Lu$^+$ and Lr$^+$, respectively. For Lu$^+$, the virtual space for the CI expansion consisted of one extra spinor for each l quantum number from 0 to 4 (i.e., $7s7p6d5f5g$). For Lr$^+$ on the other hand, the virtual space consisted of one extra spinor for each l quantum number from 0 to 2, together with two extra spinors for each l quantum number from 3 to 5 and the 6h function (i.e., $8s8p7d6f7f5g6g6h$). The Lu core 5s and 5p and Lr 6s and 6p electrons were also correlated. For each energy level, the quantities Δ_B and Δ_{B+QED} were calculated, representing the differences in the MCDHF energy without and with the Breit contributions and the differences in the MCDHF energy without and with the Breit+QED contributions, respectively.

Table 1. Specification of the generalized active space (GAS) scheme used for the calculations for the Lu$^+$ and Lr$^+$ ions (see the text for details).

GAS	Accumulated Electrons		Number of Spinors	Characters [a]
	Min [b]	Max		
1	$10 - x$	10	10	$(n-2)d$
2	$18 - y$	18	8	$(n-1)s, (n-1)p$
3	$32 - z$	32	14	$(n-2)f$
4	32	34	18	$ns, (n-1)d, np$
5	34	34	(<30 au) [c]	Virtual

[a] For Lu$^+$ and Lr$^+$, n = 6 and 7, respectively. [b] x, y and z are variables that control the electron excitation process attributed to the selective GAS. In the calculations, we defined the following: $x = 0$, $y = 2$ and $z = 1$, in line with the previous presentation [31]. [c] This includes all the virtual spinors up to an energy of 30 atomic units.

The third step consisted of the calculation of the spectroscopic properties based on the transition dipole moment between the levels. We used the relativistic transition moment operator within the MRCI method [40,41] to derive the oscillator strengths of the electronic transitions at the electric dipole (E_1) level. We considered the multiplet manifolds of the Lu $6s^2$ and $5d^16s^1$ (Lr $7s^2$ and $6d^17s^1$) configurations as the lower levels and the multiplet manifold of the Lu $6p^16s^1$ (Lr $7p^17s^1$) configurations as the upper ones. The calculations of the Einstein coefficients and branching ratios were also conducted by following the standard equations [42].

3. Results

Table 2 lists the energies of the ground and the low-lying excited states of the Lu$^+$ ions as obtained from the MRCI calculations. We used the natural orbital occupation numbers of the CI vectors to deduce the dominant electron configuration of each electronic state. The electronic states were predominantly the multiplet manifold of the $6s^2$, $5d^16s^1$ and $6s^16p^1$ configurations (see Table 2). Note that the multiplets that originated from configurations $5d^2$ or $5d^16p^1$ were omitted for convenience because they were found to be higher in energy. For comparison, Table 2 also shows the reference energies that were taken from the literature (i.e., the experimental data collected within the framework of the National Institute of Standards and Technology (NIST) atomic spectra database [21] and previous calculations based on the FSCC model [23]).

The four columns that are depicted in the MRCI results section of Table 2 show the calculated energy levels for the three different basis sets and, subsequently, the energy extrapolated to the MRCI complete basis set limit ($E(\infty)$). To derive ($E(\infty)$), we used the polynomial (n^{-3}) complete basis set scheme [43] for the correlation energies with cardinal number $n = 3$ and 4 for triple and quadruple zeta, respectively. In Table 2, the calculated energy corrections for the Breit and Breit+QED contributions are also listed, together with the final values that add up the MRCI CBS limit and the energy corrections. For these final values (see Table 2), the numbers in brackets indicate the likely uncertainties due to the computational protocol in the least significant digits of the energy values. The uncertainties consist of the absolute value of the difference in energy between the data obtained with the triple-zeta and quadruple-zeta basis sets. Table 3 lists the calculated energies for the ground and low-lying excited states of Lr$^+$ ion as obtained from the MRCI calculations, together with the energy corrections due to the Breit interactions and QED. Similar to Table 2, the final values also include the likely uncertainties due to the computational protocol. The energy spectrum of Lr$^+$ was very similar to that of the Lu$^+$ homolog. The ground and low-lying excited states belonged to the multiplet manifold of configurations $7s^2$, $6d^17s^1$ and $7s^17p^1$. For comparison, Table 3 also shows the earlier FSCC results [23].

Table 2. Calculated energies (in cm^{-1}) of the ground and the low-lying excited states of the Lu$^+$ ions obtained from the MRCI model using the double- (2), triple- (3) and quadruple-zeta (4) basis sets and the energy values derived at the complete basis set limit (∞), together with the final energy values (Final) that take into consideration the energy corrections obtained for the Breit (Δ_B) and QED (Δ_{B+QED}) contributions, compared with the experimental data (Exp.) and the FSCC results.

Levels			MRCI				Corrections		Final	Reference	
Config.	State	J	(2)	(3)	(4)	(∞)	Δ_B	Δ_{B+QED}		Exp.[a]	FSCC[b]
$6s^2$	^1S	0	0	0	0	0			0	0	0
$5d^16s^1$	^3D	1	12,227	12,213	12,172	12,145	92	−104	12,041 (41)	11,796	12,354
		2	12,698	12,669	12,626	12,598	91	−88	12,510 (43)	12,435	12,985
		3	13,946	13,907	13,866	13,838	88	−24	13,814 (41)	14,199	14,702
	^1D	2	16,817	16,656	16,583	16,535	98	−44	16,491 (73)	17,333	17,892
$6s^16p^1$	^3P	0	27,712	28,004	28,462	28,752	63	−88	28,664 (456)	27,264	27,091
		1	28,886	29,208	29,646	29,923	64	−77	29,846 (438)	28,503	28,440
		2	32,650	33,127	33,599	33,899	60	−36	33,863 (472)	32,453	32,294
	^1P	1	38,071	38,402	38,453	38,484	101	−51	38,433 (51)	38,223	38,464

[a] Taken from [21,22]. [b] Taken from [23].

Table 3. Calculated energies (in cm^{-1}) of the ground and the low-lying excited states of the Lr$^+$ ion obtained from the MRCI model using the double- (2), triple (3) and quadruple-zeta (4) basis sets, and the energy values derived at the complete basis set limit (∞), together with the final energy values (Final) that take into consideration the energy corrections obtained for the Breit (Δ_B) and QED (Δ_{B+QED}) contributions, compared with the FSCC results.

Levels			MRCI				Corrections		Final	Reference
Config.	State	J	(2)	(3)	(4)	(∞)	Δ_B	Δ_{B+QED}		FSCC[a]
$7s^2$	^1S	0	0	0	0	0			0	0
$6d^17s^1$	^3D	1	21,796	21,768	21,696	21,649	219	−86	21,563 (72)	20,265
		2	22,494	22,459	22,375	22,320	218	−61	22,259 (84)	21,623
		3	24,761	24,723	24,633	24,574	211	56	24,630 (90)	26,210
	^1D	2	28,883	28,721	28,570	28,472	230	32	28,504 (151)	31,200
$7s^17p^1$	^3P	0	29,825	30,072	31,006	31,600	144	−81	31,519 (934)	29,487
		1	32,114	32,360	33,222	33,770	150	−60	33,710 (862)	31,610
		2	43,428	43,809	44,783	45,402	152	49	45,451 (974)	43,513
	^1P	1	47,908	48,135	48,794	49,212	205	33	49,245 (659)	47,819

[a] Taken from [23].

Table 4 lists the spectroscopic properties obtained for the Lu$^+$ ions. The upper energy electronic states that belong to the configuration $6s^16p^1$ decayed via the electric dipole E_1 mechanism to the lower energy states from configurations $5d^16s^1$ and $6s^2$. To obtain the oscillator strengths, the Einstein coefficients and the branching ratios, we used the transition dipole moments obtained with the MRCI model [24,25], while we considered the extrapolated energy for the complete basis set limit in Table 2 for the ΔE between the upper and the lower energy levels. In Table 4, we also report the available experimental data for the Lu$^+$ ions for comparison [21,22].

Finally, Table 5 lists the spectroscopic properties obtained for the Lr$^+$ ions, alongside theoretical predictions that were taken from the literature (CI+MBPT model) [23]. Similar to the Lu$^+$ homolog, we show the transition rates for the multiplet manifolds of configuration $7s^17p^1$ that decay via the electric dipole E_1 mechanism to the multiplet manifolds of the configurations $6d^17s^1$ and $7s^2$. We observed that the calculated electronic transition rates of Lr$^+$ were slightly larger than those calculated for the Lu$^+$ homolog, and they were in good agreement with the earlier theoretical data taken from the literature [23].

Table 4. Calculated Einstein coefficients A_{E1} (in 1/s) and branching ratios β for the electric dipole's allowed transitions in Lu$^+$, obtained from the MRCI transition dipole moment matrix and the ΔE (in cm^{-1}) from the complete basis set limit, compared with the reference experimental values.

Levels			MRCI		Reference [a]
Upper	Lower	ΔE	A_{E1}	β	A_{E1}(NIST)
$^3P_1$ ($6s^16p^1$)	$^1S_0$ ($6s^2$)	29,924	6.10×10^6	0.08	1.25×10^7
$^1P_1$ ($6s^16p^1$)		38,474	3.74×10^8	0.90	4.53×10^8
$^3P_0$ ($6s^16p^1$)	$^3D_1$ ($5d^16s^1$)	16,609	4.38×10^7	1.00	
$^3P_1$ ($6s^16p^1$)		17,779	1.39×10^7	0.19	
$^3P_2$ ($6s^16p^1$)		21,750	1.14×10^6	<0.01	
$^1P_1$ ($6s^16p^1$)		26,329	4.00×10^5	<0.01	
$^3P_1$ ($6s^16p^1$)	$^3D_2$ ($5d^16s^1$)	17,326	5.36×10^7	0.72	9.90×10^6
$^3P_2$ ($6s^16p^1$)		21,297	2.06×10^7	0.16	
$^1P_1$ ($6s^16p^1$)		25,876	3.48×10^7	0.08	
$^3P_2$ ($6s^16p^1$)	$^3D_3$ ($5d^16s^1$)	20,058	1.09×10^8	0.82	
$^3P_1$ ($6s^16p^1$)	$^1D_2$ ($5d^16s^1$)	13,385	1.04×10^6	0.01	
$^3P_2$ ($6s^16p^1$)		17,356	1.82×10^6	0.01	
$^1P_1$ ($6s^16p^1$)		21,935	7.95×10^6	0.01	

[a] Taken from [21,22].

Table 5. Calculated Einstein coefficients A_{E1} (in 1/s) and branching ratios β for the electric dipole's allowed transitions in Lr$^+$, obtained from the MRCI transition dipole moment matrix and the ΔE (in cm^{-1}) from the complete basis set limit, compared with the reference theoretical data.

Levels			MRCI		Reference [a]
Upper	Lower	ΔE	A_{E1}	β	A_{E1}(CI+MBPT)
$^3P_1$ ($7s^17p^1$)	$^1S_0$ ($7s^2$)	33,783	2.97×10^7	0.49	6.36×10^7
$^1P_1$ ($7s^17p^1$)		49,221	7.93×10^8	0.87	8.34×10^8
$^3P_0$ ($7s^17p^1$)	$^3D_1$ ($6d^17s^1$)	9966	1.54×10^7	1.00	5.44×10^6
$^3P_1$ ($7s^17p^1$)		12,134	6.91×10^6	0.11	2.42×10^6
$^3P_2$ ($7s^17p^1$)		23,764	2.44×10^6	<0.01	9.41×10^5
$^1P_1$ ($7s^17p^1$)		27,572	1.07×10^6	<0.01	1.36×10^6
$^3P_1$ ($7s^17p^1$)	$^3D_2$ ($6d^17s^1$)	11,463	2.38×10^7	0.39	4.66×10^6
$^3P_2$ ($7s^17p^1$)		23,093	4.03×10^7	0.17	9.70×10^6
$^1P_1$ ($7s^17p^1$)		26,901	4.98×10^7	0.06	1.63×10^7
$^3P_2$ ($7s^17p^1$)	$^3D_3$ ($6d^17s^1$)	20,839	1.93×10^8	0.81	3.43×10^7
$^3P_1$ ($7s^17p^1$)	$^1D_2$ ($6d^17s^1$)	5307	2.51×10^4	<0.01	
$^3P_2$ ($7s^17p^1$)		16,937	2.68×10^6	0.01	3.19×10^5
$^1P_1$ ($7s^17p^1$)		20,745	6.60×10^7	0.07	1.68×10^7

[a] Theoretical values obtained by using CI plus many-body perturbation theory (MBPT) in [23].

4. Discussion

The Lu$^+$ and Lr$^+$ ions exhibited the same closed shell ground states and very similar energy spectra. The low-lying excited states of both the Lu$^+$ and Lr$^+$ ions belonged to the configurations $5d^16s^1$ and $6d^17s^1$, respectively. The multiplet manifolds of the Lu $6s^16p^1$ and

Lr $7s^17p^1$ configurations were higher in energy for both ions. The energy splitting in Lr$^+$ was larger than Lu$^+$ because of the larger spin–orbit interaction expected for the heavier element. We found that the Breit and QED corrections were relatively small, being to the order of 100 and 200 cm^{-1} for Lu$^+$ and Lr$^+$, respectively, with energy values comparable to the Breit and QED effects calculated for analogous elements [23,31,44].

The MRCI energies of the Lu$^+$ ions were in good agreement with the experimental data [21,22] and previous theoretical findings [23] (see Table 2). The relative errors of most of the tabulated energy levels with respect to the experimental values were less than 5%. For the $5d^16s^1$ configuration, the term with $J = 2$ (^{1}D) had the highest error (4.6%), making the term more susceptible to the interaction with the higher energy levels of the $5d^2$ configuration. For configuration $6s^16p^1$, the term with $J = 0$ (^{3}P) had the highest uncertainty (5.5%), which might also be due to mixing with higher energy-excited electronic states.

The MRCI energies of the Lr$^+$ ions were also in good agreement with the previous theoretical findings [23] (see Table 3), with slightly larger deviations than for Lu$^+$ within the range of 2.9 % to 8.7 %. For the $6d^17s^1$ configuration, the term with $J = 2$ (^{1}D) had the largest deviation (8.7%), a level which is more susceptible to interaction with the $6d^2$ configuration which, in its multiplet manifold, possesses a term with the same symmetry ($6d^2 \longrightarrow {}^1$S + ^{3}P + ^{1}D + ^{3}F + ^{1}G). For the $7s^17p^1$ configuration, the terms with $J = 0$ and 1 (^{3}P) had the highest deviations (7.2 % and 6.9 %, respectively).

We note that the discrepancies from the reference values were larger for the odd parity states (Lu $6s^16p^1$ and Lr $7s^17p^1$) than those for the even parity states (Lu $5d^16s^1$ and Lr $6d^17s^1$). These might result from the choice of the reference spinors for the MRCI calculation, since the Lu 6p (as well as Lr 7p) spinors were left outside of the AOC occupation scheme. A possible way to improve the odd parity energy levels would be to build another AOC occupation scheme by changing the occupation number to two electrons in the Lu 6s and 6p (as well as Lr 7s 7p) and therefore run the MRCI calculation of the even and odd parity energy levels individually. The calculated Einstein coefficients for the Lu$^+$ inter-configurational $6s^2 \longrightarrow 6s^16p^1$ transitions were in good agreement with the experimental data [21,22], where three electric dipole transitions were reported. The strongest transition corresponded to the ^{1}S$_0$ ($6s^2$) $\longrightarrow$ ^{1}P$_1$ ($6s^16p^1$), in line with the experimental data [21,22], but we noted the slight overestimation of the MRCI results (see Table 4). The calculated Einstein coefficients for the Lr$^+$ inter-configurational $7s^2 \longrightarrow 7s^17p^1$ transitions were also in agreement with the previously reported CI+MBPT values [23]. The strongest transition corresponded to the ^{1}S$_0$ ($7s^2$) $\longrightarrow$ ^{1}P$_1$ ($7s^17p^1$), as was previously predicted [23]. The second strongest transitions corresponded to the ^{3}D$_3$ ($6d^17s^1$) $\longrightarrow$ ^{3}P$_2$ ($7s^17p^1$) according to our MRCI calculation, unlike the ^{1}S$_0$ ($7s^2$) $\longrightarrow$ ^{3}P$_1$ ($7s^17p^1$) transition predicted in [23].

5. Conclusions

In this work, we calculated the electronic energy levels and spectroscopic properties of the Lr$^+$ ions and of the homolog Lu$^+$ ions. We used a multireference model and configuration interaction approach to obtain the electronic structure and to compute the transition probabilities. The theoretical results were compared with the experimental data for the Lu$^+$ ions and previous theoretical findings for the Lr$^+$ ions. For Lu$^+$, the results were remarkably very close to the experimental data, allowing us to translate the theoretical procedure to treat the heavier Lr$^+$ ions. For this, the calculated energy levels were also consistent later with the previous theoretical findings based on the Fock Space-coupled cluster method. We conclude that MRCI is a reliable theoretical model in computing energy levels for heavy and superheavy elements. MRCI is potentially of interest for systems with more than two valence electrons and also for the calculation of the interaction between the metal ions and rare gas atoms. The latter will be used to describe the transport properties of these ions in our next theoretical development.

Our results support the conclusions from previous theoretical work. (1) The energy spectrum of the Lr$^+$ ion was predicted to be similar to the one obtained for the Lu$^+$ homolog, and (2) both the Lr$^+$ and Lu$^+$ ions are good candidates for future Laser Resonance

Chromatography experiments. In fact, their energy spectra present a case for experiments based on a metastable electronic state that is too long-lived for spectroscopy experiments. A potential LRC route consists of pumping the ground state $^1S_0$ ($6s^2$ and $7s^2$) to the excited state $^3P_1$ ($6s^16p^1$ and $7s^17p^1$), which radiatively decays to the metastable $^3D_1$ ($5d^16s^1$ and $6d^17s^1$) state with a sizeable branching ratio.

Author Contributions: Conceptualization, H.R.; methodology, H.R. and A.B.; software, H.R. and A.B.; validation, H.R., A.B., M.B. and M.L.; formal analysis, H.R., A.B. and M.L.; investigation, H.R.; resources, A.B. and M.B.; data curation, H.R. and A.B.; writing—original draft preparation, H.R.; writing—review and editing, A.B., M.B. and M.L.; visualization, H.R.; supervision, A.B. and M.L.; project administration, M.B. and M.L.; funding acquisition, M.L. All authors have read and agreed to the published version of the manuscript.

Funding: This project received funding from the European Research Council (ERC) under the European Union's Horizon 2020 Research and Innovation Programme (Grant Agreement No. 819957).

Institutional Review Board Statement: Not applicable.

Informed Consent Statement: Not applicable.

Data Availability Statement: Data is contained within the article.

Acknowledgments: We gratefully acknowledge the high-performance computing (HPC) support, time and infrastructure from the Center for Information Technology of the University of Groningen (Peregrine), the Johannes Gutenberg University of Mainz (Mogon) and the HPC group of GSI. We are also indebted to the HPC-Europa3 program (host: Anastasia Borschevsky; guest: Harry Ramanantoanina) for HPC computer time (Netherlands) and for the funding of a short-term scientific mission in Groningen.

Conflicts of Interest: The authors declare no conflict of interest.

References

1. Laatiaoui, M.; Buchachenko, A.A.; Viehland, L.A. Laser Resonance Chromatography of Superheavy Elements. *Phys. Rev. Lett.* **2020**, *125*, 023002. [CrossRef] [PubMed]
2. Laatiaoui, M.; Buchachenko, A.A.; Viehland, L.A. Exploiting transport properties for the detection of optical pumping in heavy ions. *Phys. Rev. A* **2020**, *102*, 013106. [CrossRef]
3. Block, M.; Laatiaoui, M.; Raeder, S. Recent progress in laser spectroscopy of the actinides. *Prog. Part. Nucl. Phys.* **2021**, *116*, 103834. [CrossRef]
4. Visentin, G.; Laatiaoui, M.; Viehland, L.A.; Buchachenko, A.A. Mobility of the Singly-Charged Lanthanide and Actinide Cations: Trends and Perspectives. *Front. Chem.* **2020**, *8*, 438. [CrossRef] [PubMed]
5. Kaldor, U.; Eliav, E. High-Accuracy Calculations for Heavy and Super-Heavy Elements. In *Advances in Quantum Chemistry*; Academic Press: Cambridge, UK; 1998; Volume 31, pp. 313–336. [CrossRef]
6. Dzuba, V.A.; Safronova, M.S.; Safronova, U.I. Atomic properties of superheavy elements No, Lr, and Rf. *Phys. Rev. A* **2014**, *90*, 012504. [CrossRef]
7. Eliav, E.; Fritzsche, S.; Kaldor, U. Electronic structure theory of the superheavy elements. *Nucl. Phys. A* **2015**, *944*, 518–550. [CrossRef]
8. Radžiūtė, L.; Gaigalas, G.; Jönsson, P.; Bieroń, J. Electric dipole moments of superheavy elements: A case study on copernicium. *Phys. Rev. A* **2016**, *93*, 062508. [CrossRef]
9. Liu, J.; Shen, X.; Wang, K.; Sang, C. Ionization potentials of the superheavy element livermorium (Z = 116). *J. Chem. Phys.* **2020**, *152*, 204303. [CrossRef]
10. Fischer, C.F.; Senchuk, A. Numerical Procedures for Relativistic Atomic Structure Calculations. *Atoms* **2020**, *8*, 85. [CrossRef]
11. Fritzsche, S. Level Structure and Properties of Open f-Shell Elements. *Atoms* **2022**, *10*, 7. [CrossRef]
12. Porsev, S.G.; Safronova, M.S.; Safronova, U.I.; Dzuba, V.A.; Flambaum, V.V. Nobelium energy levels and hyperfine-structure constants. *Phys. Rev. A* **2018**, *98*, 052512. [CrossRef]
13. Allehabi, S.O.; Dzuba, V.A.; Flambaum, V.V. Theoretical study of the electronic structure of hafnium (Hf, $Z = 72$) and rutherfordium (Rf, $Z = 104$) atoms and their ions: Energy levels and hyperfine-structure constants. *Phys. Rev. A* **2021**, *104*, 052811. [CrossRef]
14. Visscher, L.; Saue, T.; Nieuwpoort, W.C.; Faegri, K.; Gropen, O. The electronic structure of the PtH molecule: Fully relativistic configuration interaction calculations of the ground and excited states. *J. Chem. Phys.* **1993**, *99*, 6704–6715. [CrossRef]

15. Fleig, T.; Olsen, J.; Visscher, L. The generalized active space concept for the relativistic treatment of electron correlation. II. Large-scale configuration interaction implementation based on relativistic 2- and 4-spinors and its application. *J. Chem. Phys.* **2003**, *119*, 2963–2971. [CrossRef]
16. Fleig, T. Invited review: Relativistic wave-function based electron correlation methods. *Chem. Phys.* **2012**, *395*, 2–15. [CrossRef]
17. Skripnikov, L.V.; Oleynichenko, A.V.; Zaitsevskii, A.V.; Maison, D.E.; Barzakh, A.E. Relativistic Fock space coupled-cluster study of bismuth electronic structure to extract the Bi nuclear quadrupole moment. *Phys. Rev. C* **2021**, *104*, 034316. [CrossRef]
18. Fleig, T.; Olsen, J.; Marian, C.M. The generalized active space concept for the relativistic treatment of electron correlation. I. Kramers-restricted two-component configuration interaction. *J. Chem. Phys.* **2001**, *114*, 4775–4790. [CrossRef]
19. Fleig, T.; Jensen, H.J.A.; Olsen, J.; Visscher, L. The generalized active space concept for the relativistic treatment of electron correlation. III. Large-scale configuration interaction and multiconfiguration self-consistent-field four-component methods with application to UO2. *J. Chem. Phys.* **2006**, *124*, 104106. [CrossRef]
20. Knecht, S.; Jensen, H.J.A.; Fleig, T. Large-scale parallel configuration interaction. II. Two- and four-component double-group general active space implementation with application to BiH. *J. Chem. Phys.* **2010**, *132*, 014108. [CrossRef]
21. Kramida, A.; Ralchenko, Y.; Reader, J.; NIST ASD Team. *NIST Atomic Spectra Database (Ver. 5.8)*; National Institute of Standards and Technology: Gaithersburg, MD, USA, 2022. Available online: https://physics.nist.gov/asd (accessed on 25 March 2022).
22. Sansonetti, J.E.; Martin, W.C. Handbook of Basic Atomic Spectroscopic Data. *J. Phys. Chem. Ref. Data* **2005**, *34*, 1559–2259. [CrossRef]
23. Kahl, E.V.; Berengut, J.C.; Laatiaoui, M.; Eliav, E.; Borschevsky, A. High-precision ab initio calculations of the spectrum of Lr^+. *Phys. Rev. A* **2019**, *100*, 062505. [CrossRef]
24. Saue, T.; Bast, R.; Gomes, A.S.P.; Jensen, H.J.A.; Visscher, L.; Aucar, I.A.; Di Remigio, R.; Dyall, K.G.; Eliav, E.; Fasshauer, E.; et al. The DIRAC code for relativistic molecular calculations. *J. Chem. Phys.* **2020**, *152*, 204104. [CrossRef] [PubMed]
25. DIRAC, a Relativistic Ab Initio Electronic Structure Program, Release DIRAC19 (2019). Available online: http://www.diracprogram.org (accessed on 17 March 2022).
26. Visscher, L.; Dyall, K. DIRAC–Fock Atomic Electronic Structure Calculations Using Different Nuclear Charge Distributions. *At. Data Nucl. Data Tables* **1997**, *67*, 207–224. [CrossRef]
27. Dyall, K.G. Relativistic double-zeta, triple-zeta, and quadruple-zeta basis sets for the 5d elements Hf–Hg. *Theor. Chem. Acc.* **2004**, *112*, 403. [CrossRef]
28. Dyall, K.G. Relativistic double-zeta, triple-zeta, and quadruple-zeta basis sets for the 6d elements Rf–Cn. *Theor. Chem. Acc.* **2011**, *129*, 603. [CrossRef]
29. Stanton, R.E.; Havriliak, S. Kinetic balance: A partial solution to the problem of variational safety in Dirac calculations. *J. Chem. Phys.* **1984**, *81*, 1910–1918. [CrossRef]
30. Slater, J.C. *Quantum Theory of Atomic Structure, Vol. 1, 2*; International Series of Monographs on Physics; McGraw-Hill: New York, NY, USA, 1960.
31. Ramanantoanina, H.; Borschevsky, A.; Block, M.; Laatiaoui, M. Electronic structure of Rf^+ (Z = 104) from ab initio calculations. *Phys. Rev. A* **2021**, *104*, 022813. [CrossRef]
32. Ramanantoanina, H. On the calculation of multiplet energies of three-open-shell $4f^{13}5fn6d^1$ electron configuration by LFDFT: Modeling the optical spectra of 4f core-electron excitation in actinide compounds. *Phys. Chem. Chem. Phys.* **2017**, *19*, 32481–32491. [CrossRef]
33. Ramanantoanina, H. A DFT-based theoretical model for the calculation of spectral profiles of lanthanide M4,5-edge X-ray absorption. *J. Chem. Phys.* **2018**, *149*, 054104. [CrossRef]
34. Ramanantoanina, H.; Studniarek, M.; Daffé, N.; Dreiser, J. Non-empirical calculation of X-ray magnetic circular dichroism in lanthanide compounds. *Chem. Commun.* **2019**, *55*, 2988–2991. [CrossRef]
35. Tobin, J.G.; Ramanantoanina, H.; Daul, C.; Roussel, P.; Yu, S.W.; Nowak, S.; Alonso-Mori, R.; Kroll, T.; Nordlund, D.; Weng, T.C.; et al. Unoccupied electronic structure of actinide dioxides. *Phys. Rev. B* **2022**, *105*, 125129. [CrossRef]
36. Indelicato, P.; Santos, J.P.; Boucard, S.; Desclaux, J.P. QED and relativistic corrections in superheavy elements. *Eur. Phys. J. D* **2007**, *45*, 155–170. [CrossRef]
37. Ginges, J.S.M.; Berengut, J.C. QED radiative corrections and many-body effects in atoms: Vacuum polarization and binding energy shifts in alkali metals. *J. Phys. B At. Mol. Opt. Phys.* **2016**, *49*, 095001. [CrossRef]
38. Fischer, C.F.; Gaigalas, G.; Jönsson, P.; Bieroń, J. GRASP2018—A Fortran 95 version of the General Relativistic Atomic Structure Package. *Comput. Phys. Commun.* **2019**, *237*, 184–187. [CrossRef]
39. Lowe, J.; Chantler, C.; Grant, I. Self-energy screening approximations in multi-electron atoms. *Radiat. Phys. Chem.* **2013**, *85*, 118–123. [CrossRef]
40. Knecht, S.R. *Parallel Relativistic Multiconfiguration Methods: New Powerful Tools for Heavy-Element Electronic-Structure Studies*; Heinrich-Heine-Universität: Düsseldorf, Germany, 2009.
41. Denis, M.; Nørby, M.S.; Jensen, H.J.A.; Gomes, A.S.P.; Nayak, M.K.; Knecht, S.; Fleig, T. Theoretical study on ThF, a prospective system in search of time-reversal violation. *New J. Phys.* **2015**, *17*, 043005. [CrossRef]
42. Cowan, R.D. *The Theory of Atomic Structure and Spectra*; International Series of Monographs on Physics; University of California Press, Ltd.: Berkeley, CA, USA, 1981.

43. Helgaker, T.; Klopper, W.; Koch, H.; Noga, J. Basis-set convergence of correlated calculations on water. *J. Chem. Phys.* **1997**, *106*, 9639–9646. [CrossRef]
44. Pašteka, L.; Eliav, E.; Borschevsky, A.; Kaldor, U.; Schwerdtfeger, P. Relativistic Coupled Cluster Calculations with Variational Quantum Electrodynamics Resolve the Discrepancy between Experiment and Theory Concerning the Electron Affinity and Ionization Potential of Gold. *Phys. Rev. Lett.* **2017**, *118*, 023002. [CrossRef]

 atoms

Article

Observation of Collisional De-Excitation Phenomena in Plutonium

Andrea Raggio *, Ilkka Pohjalainen and Iain D. Moore

Accelerator Laboratory, Department of Physics, University of Jyväskylä, FI-40014 Jyväskylä, Finland; ilkka.pohjalainen@jyu.fi (I.P.); iain.d.moore@jyu.fi (I.D.M.)
* Correspondence: andrea.a.raggio@jyu.fi; Tel.: +358-04-57-833-2669

Abstract: A program of research towards the high-resolution optical spectroscopy of actinide elements for the study of fundamental nuclear structure is currently ongoing at the IGISOL facility of the University of Jyväskylä. One aspect of this work is the development of a gas-cell-based actinide laser ion source using filament-based dispensers of long-lived actinide isotopes. We have observed prominent phenomena in the resonant laser ionization process specific to the gaseous environment of the gas cell. The development and investigation of a laser ionization scheme for plutonium atoms is reported, focusing on the effects arising from the collision-induced phenomena of plutonium atoms in helium gas. The gas-cell environment was observed to greatly reduce the sensitivity of an efficient plutonium ionization scheme developed in vacuum. This indicates competition between resonant laser excitation and collisional de-excitation by the gas atoms, which is likely being enhanced by the very high atomic level density within actinide elements.

Keywords: collisional de-excitation; actinide elements; resonance laser ionization; gas cell

Citation: Raggio, A.; Pohjalainen, I.; Moore, I.D. Observation of Collisional De-Excitation Phenomena in Plutonium. *Atoms* **2022**, *10*, 40. https://doi.org/10.3390/atoms10020040

Academic Editor: Mustapha Laatiaoui

Received: 27 March 2022
Accepted: 13 April 2022
Published: 20 April 2022

Publisher's Note: MDPI stays neutral with regard to jurisdictional claims in published maps and institutional affiliations.

Copyright: © 2022 by the authors. Licensee MDPI, Basel, Switzerland. This article is an open access article distributed under the terms and conditions of the Creative Commons Attribution (CC BY) license (https://creativecommons.org/licenses/by/4.0/).

1. Introduction

In radioactive ion beam (RIB) facilities based on the isotope separator on-line (ISOL) technique, laser resonance ionization is a widely used method for producing isobarically pure ion beams in combination with mass separation, thanks to its high efficiency and selectivity. Its implementation in facilities that use gas-cell-based techniques for ion thermalization and extraction, such as the ion guide isotope separator on-line (IGISOL) [1] technique at the University of Jyväskylä, the former Leuven isotope separator on-line (LISOL) in Louvain-La-Neuve [2], or the KEK isotope separation system at RIKEN [3], have led to the development of the in-gas-cell laser resonance ionization technique. The combination of this method with the fast gas-cell extraction time and the chemical non-selectivity of the used noble gasses allows for the production and study of refractory elements, which are notoriously challenging for the traditional ISOL technique. Laser resonance ionization is based on a multi-step excitation scheme, utilizing the unique atomic-level fingerprint of the desired element. Resonance ionization spectroscopy is a variant of the laser resonance ionization technique, whereby the mass-separated ion yield is measured as a function of the wavelength of one of the lasers used in the excitation process. By measuring the isotope shift and splitting (hyperfine structure) of the optical resonance, a comprehensive probe is provided into underlying nuclear properties, including nuclear spins, sizes and shapes [4].

When laser resonance excitation and ionization is applied in a gas-filled environment, a series of mechanisms start to play a detrimental role. For example, the spectral resolution of atomic resonance in a gas cell suffers from pressure broadening and shift due to collisions with the buffer gas atoms. Typical operating pressures of up to 500 mbar limit the resolution to a few GHz, sufficient to mask the hyperfine structure of lighter elements. Nevertheless, in-gas cell spectroscopy has the advantage of being a very sensitive method and optical spectroscopy can be performed on isotopes produced with small cross-sections. A recent highlight has been the successful demonstration of on-line, single-atom-at-a-time, resonance ionization spectroscopy of nobelium in an argon-filled gas cell [5]. A second, less-well-documented effect of the gas-filled environment, also arising from collisional interactions, is the potential reduction in the laser ionization efficiency through collisional de-excitation. This effect, which is of topical interest and the focus of this work, may be enhanced in elements with high atomic-level densities such as the lanthanides or actinides.

Collision-Induced Population Transfer

Collisions between atoms can cause changes in the electron population between atomic levels. A well known example of this is the Boltzmann-distributed population of low-lying levels in atoms emerging from thermal collisions with buffer gas atoms. Similarly, collisions with an excited atom can cause the excitation to be transferred to a different level or to the collision partner. In this work, we are interested in the collisional de-excitation of the resonantly excited states in plutonium and the competition with laser-induced resonant transitions. The dynamics of collisional de-excitation are examined below to give a qualitative understanding of the collision process in plutonium. However, as the atomic structure of heavy elements can be exceedingly complicated, the mechanism of collisional de-excitation is introduced here with the help of simpler systems.

Traditionally, collisional phenomena have been studied mostly in alkali and alkaline-earth atoms and ions with noble gasses [6–11], since only few loosely bound outer electrons participate in the collision, resulting in an easier theoretical modeling. Other elements studied in this context are reported, for example, in [12–16]. In general, it has been observed that the rate of population transfer is higher for heavier noble gasses.

A classic example and practical application of collisional excitation transfer is the helium–neon (HeNe) laser system. The helium atoms are excited from the ground state to higher-lying excited states by inelastic collisions with energetic electrons, among them the first two metastable states $1s2s\ ^3S_1$ and $1s2s\ ^1S_0$. Due to a fortuitous near degeneracy between the helium metastable states and excited states in neon atoms, collisions result in an efficient and selective transfer of excitation energy from the helium to neon, as reported, for example, in [17]. The subsequent decays of the excited states in neon are responsible for the characteristic emission wavelengths of the laser system.

Instead of transferring the energy of the colliding system to the collision partners, a second scenario is to convert the excitation energy of the colliding atoms into translational energy. This can be understood using the barium–argon system as an example, as barium has a rather simple electronic structure compared with heavier elements [18–21]. The collisional de-excitation process can be understood by looking at the potential curves of the diatomic system, illustrated in Figure 1, formed by barium configured in different excitation states and argon in the $^1S_0$ ground state. If such curves have crossing points at given interatomic distances, marked with a circle in Figure 1, and if the symmetry of the crossing states allows the formation of an avoided crossing, then an inelastic collision can occur, transferring the population to the lower excited state and converting the energy difference into the translational energy of the system. For this specific example, barium atoms, excited to the $6s6p\ ^1P_1^o$ state, for example, via laser excitation, are collisionally de-excited to the $6s6p\ ^3P_2^o$ level through inelastic collisions with argon atoms. The crossing happens between the attractive $^1\Pi_1$ potential curve and the repulsive $^3\Sigma_1^o$ potential curve, the latter adiabatically correlated with the $^3P_2^o$ barium level.

The rate of collisional de-excitation can be comparable to the optical de-excitation that occurs via spontaneous emission. For example, the rate of collisional de-excitation in barium of the $6s8p\ ^1P_1^o$ level by helium collisions at 833 K to the $6s7d\ ^3D_j$ multiplet has been measured to be $\sim 3 \times 10^{-9}$ cm^3/s [18], while the rate of de-excitation from the $3s^23p^4\ ^1D_2$ state in atomic sulphur in argon at 300 K has been measured to be 1.4×10^{-11} cm^3/s [22]. With a typical gas cell pressure (either helium or argon) of 100 mbar, these reaction rates result in depopulation rates of about 3.3×10^9 1/s and 4×10^7 1/s for barium and sulphur, respectively, comparable to a large A_{if} Einstein coefficient.

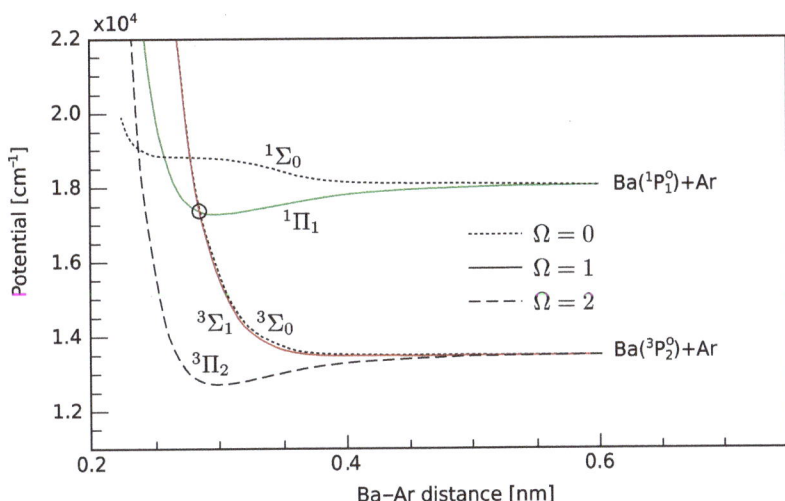

Figure 1. Diabatic potential curves in the barium–argon system. The level crossing indicated by a circle is responsible for the population transfer between the $^1P_1^o$ and $^3P_2^o$ levels of barium. Adapted with permission from [21]. 1992, American Physical Society.

In heavier elements, namely the actinide region, a non-negligible collisional de-excitation cross section is expected due to the high density of states compared with the simpler alkali or alkaline-like elements. Collisional phenomena have been observed in thorium [23] and exploited in laser spectroscopy measurements of singly ionized Th$^+$ ions [24,25]. The laser excitation of thorium from the ground state to a specific excited state can be inefficient as spontaneous decays increase the population of metastable (dark) states, which are not probed by the laser light. The use of buffer gasses such as hydrogen and helium in radiofrequency traps helps to redistribute the population of these states to the ground state via inelastic quenching collisions, improving the laser ionization rate.

Collisional phenomena were observed and also studied in nobelium and its chemical homologue ytterbium [26,27]. A two-step resonance ionization process was used in a buffer gas cell: the first excitation step to resonantly excite nobelium from the $^1S_0$ atomic ground state to the $^1P_1$ level, while the second step drove a transition to a Rydberg state, which was subsequently ionized either by residual laser light, black-body radiation or collisional processes. Importantly, analysis of the Rydberg states revealed contributions from two intermediate states, the singlet $^1P_1$ level and a longer-lived state lying ~300 cm^{-1} below the $^1P_1$ level. This lower-lying state, assigned as the $^3D_3$ level, was populated via a fast quenching from the $^1P_1$ level due to collisions with buffer gas atoms.

Here, we report evidence of such collision-induced phenomena for the case of plutonium via laser resonance ionization studies. Although collisional effects of actinide elements with noble gasses have been reported, especially for low-lying excited states, collisional de-excitation effects remain mostly unknown in the excited states.

2. Experimental Method

This work was performed in the context of the development of a new gas cell for the laser resonance ionization of long-lived actinide isotopes that can be produced in sufficient quantities at research reactors and transported to facilities elsewhere [28]. In collaboration with the Nuclear Chemistry Department of the University of Mainz, samples of $^{238-240,242}$Pu and ^{244}Pu isotopes were electrolytically deposited onto a tantalum substrate and delivered to Jyväskylä. The filaments, mounted within the gas cell filled with helium at a pressure of 80 mbar, were electrically heated to a temperature between 1000 and 1200 °C. The evaporated plutonium atoms were resonantly ionized with laser light provided by the FURIOS laser system [29], with broadband titanium–sapphire (Ti:sa) lasers operating at a repetition rate of 10 kHz in both the fundamental emission range as well as frequency doubled. Later, a dedicated grating-based Ti:Sapphire laser was employed in collaboration with Nagoya University, having the unique feature of intracavity second harmonic generation (SHG) [30]. This laser offers a wide-range scanning capability between 380 nm and 440 nm and thus is ideally suited for ionization scheme development.

The different lasers were spatially overlapped, transported to the front-end of the IGISOL target area and focused slowly into the gas cell through a quartz window. A maximum output power of ∼1 W of fundamental infrared (IR) light was available at the entrance to the gas cell. After intra-cavity frequency doubling, ∼660 mW from the standard broadband resonator was available, with ∼105 mW from the grating-based laser. In our studies of a two-step blue–blue ionization scheme, discussed below, both the JYFL Ti:sa laser and the grating-based laser were pumped by separate Nd:YAG lasers to allow for a precise timing control of the laser pulses to a few ns.

The resonant photo-ions were evacuated from the gas cell through an exit hole and guided towards the high-vacuum region of the mass separator using a radiofrequency sextupole ion guide (SPIG) [31]. The ions were accelerated to a potential of 30 kV, mass separated with a nominal mass resolving power of $M/\Delta M = 500$, and detected in the focal plane of the separator using a multichannel plate (MCP) detector. A schematic overview of the experimental setup is shown in Figure 2.

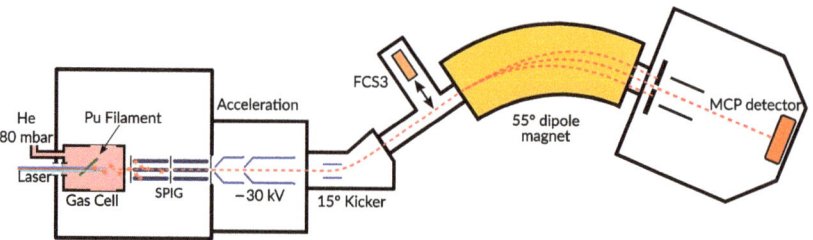

Figure 2. Schematic figure of the IGISOL beamline of relevance to this work. The gas cell is located inside the front-end vacuum chamber. Resonant laser ionization of plutonium atoms occurs along the gas cell axis; the ions are guided through a sextupole ion guide and accelerated towards the mass separator. The dipole magnet is set to mass-separate ^{244}Pu. An MCP detector in the separator focal plane is used to measure the ion counting rate. FC = Faraday cup.

Our earlier work [28] focused on the obtained mass spectra, which provided useful insight into the gas-phase chemistry exhibited by plutonium. The resulting monatomic yields of isotopes were sufficient for high-resolution collinear laser spectroscopy [32], with plutonium currently the heaviest element studied using this technique to date. Since the publication of Ref. [28], further investigations to elucidate a better understanding of the original ionization scheme have been made, using the same methodology as discussed in this section. As the isotopic composition of the samples was not of particular interest, the separator was tuned to the most abundant isotope, ^{244}Pu. The following section presents the results of the ionization scheme characterization.

3. Results and Discussion

Initially, a three-step ionization scheme was tested, using laser radiation at wavelengths of 420.76, 847.26, and 750.24 nm, with the final step resulting in the population of an auto-ionizing (AI) state at 48,898 cm^{-1} (Figure 3). This scheme was originally developed by Raeder and collaborators to selectively ionize plutonium isotopes under vacuum for trace analysis studies of environmental samples [33]. Surprisingly, in the gas-cell environment, the two IR steps did not contribute to the ion count rate. Nevertheless, a frequency scan of the first blue step wavelength presented a clear resonant signal and thus it was hypothesized that excitation and ionization proceeded via a Rydberg state located at around

47,532 cm^{-1}, with ionization occurring via atomic collisions with He gas atoms. Only at a substantially reduced first step laser power was a small response to the ion count rate observed, with the addition of the two IR steps.

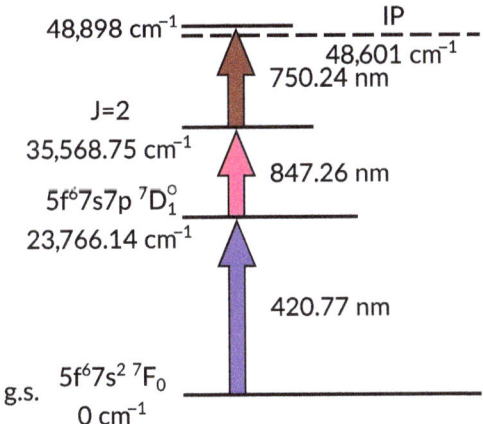

Figure 3. Resonance ionization scheme initially used in this work, developed for ultratrace analysis of environmental samples [33]. The three step blue-IR-IR scheme drives the electrons to an auto-ionizing state located at 48,898 cm^{-1}.

To explore this hypothesis, a second frequency-doubled Ti:Sapphire laser was implemented instead of the two IR lasers. The wavelength of the second laser was scanned in the vicinity of the first step 420.76 nm transition, with a resonance observed at a wavelength of 422.53 nm which, in combination with the original 420.77 nm, was found to considerably enhance the ionization rate. Interestingly, both transitions were found to ionize plutonium independently, albeit with much reduced count rates. Although there is no known level that can be populated from the ground state by the 422.53 nm laser, the low-lying first excited $^7F_1$ state at 2203.61 cm^{-1} is expected to be thermally populated due to the temperature of the hot filament (and the surrounding helium gas atoms). Excitation would then proceed from this J = 1 level to a known (J = 2) level at 25,870.69 cm^{-1}. Both 420.76 and 422.53 nm photons then drive the electron across the ionization potential. The population of the thermally excited state explains the ability of the two lasers to independently ionize plutonium, under the assumption that the ground-state transition is connected to the ionization potential via a high-lying Rydberg state, as previously hypothesized.

We note that the ionization rate with both blue laser transitions was found to be ∼5 times greater than the sum of the two ion rates obtained independently. This behavior suggests a connection between the two transitions and we postulate a population of the low-lying state at 2203.61 cm^{-1} from the $^7D_1^\circ$ level (Figure 3) through collisionally induced de-excitation. If this de-excitation process is fast compared with the original IR transitions or the AI-state lifetime, it could explain the negligible effect of the two IR steps in the original scheme when applied within the buffer gas environment.

To further study this behavior, a third experiment was carried out using the grating-based Ti:Sapphire laser from Nagoya University, combined with a standard broadband frequency-doubled Ti:Sapphire. The latter was tuned to the original ground-state transition at 420.77 nm, while the former was used to perform a wide-range wavelength scan around the region of the previously found 422.53 nm transition. The result of this scan is shown in Figure 4, illustrating the ion count rate in the case of the presence or absence of the 420.77 nm step. One can immediately see the effect of introducing the 420.77 nm laser transition, as the background ion rate is considerably enhanced, which we attribute to the laser constantly ionizing plutonium independent from the grating-based laser, postulated to occur via a potential Rydberg level, as noted earlier.

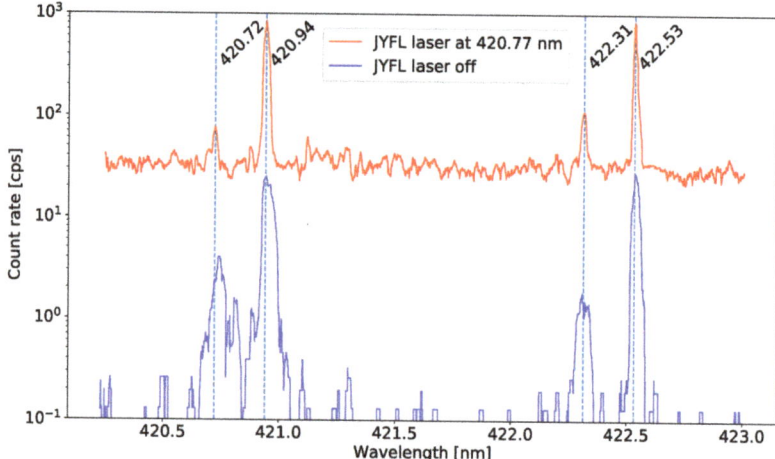

Figure 4. Wavelength scan of plutonium obtained from the grating-based Ti:Sapphire with (red) and without (blue) the 420.77 nm laser light produced by the JYFL broadband frequency-doubled Ti:Sapphire laser. The vertical dotted lines indicate the peak maxima according to the upper spectrum to allow for comparisons with the lower spectrum.

In addition to the previously detected transition at 422.53 nm, both spectra indicate the presence of new resonances. The centroid wavelengths were compared with available atomic level data [34], with all possible electric dipole transitions close to the detected resonances considered. A summary of the measured transitions is reported in Table 1 along with the literature assignment, the initial and final energy of the states involved, atomic spins and state configurations. Interestingly, the new transitions all originate from the first few low-lying states in plutonium. As the grating-based laser can excite and ionize the atoms without the presence of the 420.77 nm laser radiation, these low-lying levels must all be thermally populated due to the filament temperature. As an aside, we note that the resolution of the resonances in the lower spectrum of Figure 4 is slightly worse, likely indicating differences in the linewidths of the two lasers.

Table 1. List of the wavelengths λ_{meas} of the detected peaks obtained from the grating-based Ti:Sapphire scan as presented in Figure 4. Assignments from the literature are also given [34,35], along with level energies and configurations. The reported wavelengths are in vacuum.

$\lambda_{meas.}$ (nm)	$\lambda_{lit.}$ (nm)	E_i (cm^{-1})	Configuration	J_i	E_f (cm^{-1})	Configuration	J_f
420.72	420.712	6313.866	$5f^66d7s^2\ ^7K^o_4$	4	30,083.102	-	5
420.77	420.767	0	$5f^67s^2\ ^7F_0$	0	23,766.139	$5f^67s7p\ ^7D^o_1$	1
420.94	420.942	2203.606	$5f^67s^2\ ^7F_1$	1	25,959.849	$5f^66d^27s$	1
422.32	422.306	4299.659	$5f^67s^2\ ^7F_2$	2	27,979.161	$5f^67s7p$	2
422.53	422.528	2203.606	$5f^67s^2\ ^7F_1$	1	25,870.685	$5f^66d^27s$	2
	422.539	6144.515	$5f^67s^2\ ^7F_3$	3	29,810.974	$5f^67s7p$	3

The presence of both lasers not only results in a higher background count rate, but also considerably enhances the count rates of the three most intense peaks. Similar to the hypothesis made with regard to the observation of a considerably higher ionization rate seen in the second experiment (a potential enhancement of the population of the 2203.61 cm^{-1} state from the $^7D^o_1$ level), we suggest that these additional low-lying states are also populated via collisional de-excitation from higher-lying states, initially accessed via the ground-state transition.

In addition to the transitions mentioned in Table 1, a careful literature search revealed a candidate for excitation from the $5f^67s^2\ ^7F_6$ level at 10,238.473 cm^{-1} to the $5f^67s7p$ J = 5 level at 34,004.30 cm^{-1}. This energy difference would result in a resonance at a wavelength of 420.772 nm, which lies only 8 GHz from the the original 420.767 nm ground-state transition. Due to the convolution of the frequency-doubled laser linewidth (>5 GHz) with the Doppler broadening of atomic lines in the gas cell, we expect the atomic resonances to have a broadening of >8 GHz. Interestingly, if the $^7F_6$ level is populated through collisional de-excitations from the $^7D_1^o$ level, the non-resonant ionization of plutonium can then proceed from the 34,004.30 cm^{-1} level. This provides an alternative explanation to the ionization with a solely 420.77 nm laser light via an unknown Rydberg level. Due to the spectroscopic linewidth of the atomic transitions in the gas cell, we have a strong preference for this explanation.

Combining all of the additional spectroscopic information gathered with the grating-based Ti:sapphire laser, an extended ionization scheme for plutonium is presented in Figure 5.

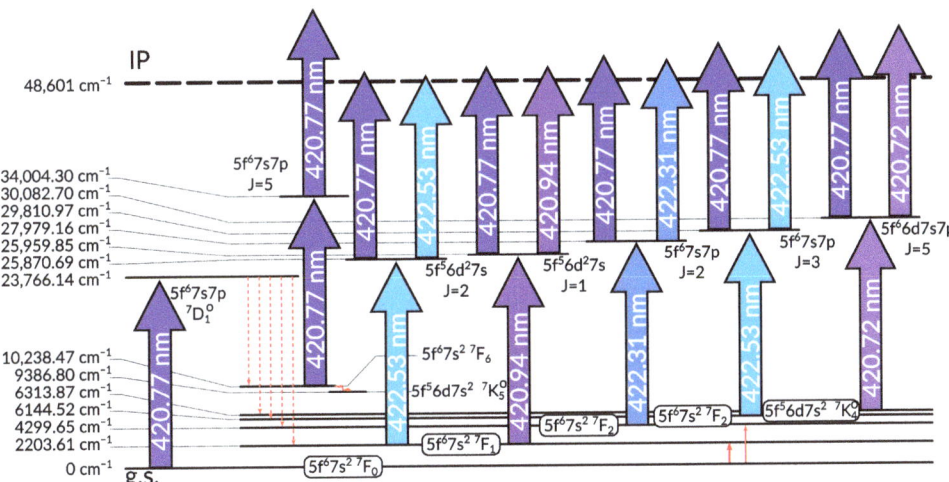

Figure 5. Plutonium atomic-level scheme developed with the grating-based Ti:Sapphire experiment. Thick arrows correspond to detected transitions, with the dashed arrows from the $^7D_1^o$ state representing the collisional de-excitation process to the low-lying states. The thin solid arrows starting from the atomic ground state indicate thermal excitation due to the hot filament.

4. Outlook

This work has shown evidence of collision-induced phenomena in plutonium through filament-based resonance ionization studies. A clear enhancement in the ionization rate of mass-separated ^{244}Pu is observed when the ground-state transition to the excited $^7D_1^o$ level is added to a laser resonance ionization scheme that relies on a single-color photon exciting (and subsequently ionizing) from thermally populated low-lying levels. The lifetime of the $^7D_1^o$ state in the gas-cell environment appears to be much shorter than the rate for the photoabsorption of an IR second step of the original three-step scheme that was dominant in a vacuum environment. There is strong evidence therefore that the $^7D_1^o$ state is de-excited by inelastic collisions.

The exact nature of this phenomena is difficult to fully characterize, in particular in actinide elements in which the electronic level density is high. Very similar effects to that discussed here were observed in our work on thorium, in which laser resonance ionization was performed in both vacuum and in a helium buffer gas environment [23]. Similar to plutonium, in a reported work of the laser ionization of actinium, a reduced in-gas-cell laser ionization efficiency was observed when compared with in-gas-jet ionization, which could partly be attributed to collisional quenching [36]. No experimental collisional cross section data for the quenching of excited levels for the actinides have been reported, to our knowledge. Nevertheless, in comparing the ionization schemes presented in this work, it is probable that the rate of collisional de-excitation is comparable to or greater than optical absorption rates.

In the near future, quantitative measurements will continue these investigations in neighboring uranium, both to be performed in vacuum and in the gas cell. Important information regarding the lifetimes of the excited state in the different environments will add to our understanding of the collisional processes. We note that despite the advantages of the gas-cell technique compared with the traditional ISOL method in terms of chemical non-selectivity, the buffer gas environment presents effects that need to be understood. Laser resonance ion sources using hot cavities have reported high efficiencies of ionization schemes for various elements. In the adaptation of these schemes for in-gas-cell resonance ionization, consideration should be given to the potential for very fast collisional channels that may well be detrimental to the efficiency of the method.

Author Contributions: Formal analysis, I.P.; Investigation, I.P.; Supervision, I.D.M.; Writing—original draft, A.R.; Writing—review & editing, A.R., I.P. and I.D.M. All authors have read and agreed to the published version of the manuscript.

Funding: This project has received funding from the European Union's Horizon 2020 research and innovation programme under grant agreement no. 861198–LISA–H2020-MSCA-ITN-2019, as well as from the Academy of Finland under project number 339245.

Institutional Review Board Statement: Not applicable.

Informed Consent Statement: Not applicable.

Data Availability Statement: The data presented in this study are available upon request from the corresponding author.

Conflicts of Interest: The authors declare no conflict of interest.

Abbreviations

The following abbreviations are used in this manuscript:

RIB	Radioactive Ion Beam
ISOL	Isotope Separator On-Line
IGISOL	Ion Guide Isotope Separator On-Line
LISOL	Leuven Isotope Separator On-Line
SHG	Second Harmonic Generation
SPIG	Sextupole Ion Guide
MCP	Multichannel Plate
FC	Faraday Cup
RIS	Resonance Ionization Scheme

References

1. Moore, I.; Dendooven, P.; Äystö, J. The IGISOL technique—three decades of developments. *Hyperfine Interact.* **2014**, *223*, 17–62. [CrossRef]
2. Van Duppen, P.; Bruyneel, B.; Huyse, M.; Kudryavtsev, Y.; Van Den Bergh, P.; Vermeeren, L. Beams of short lived nuclei by selective laser ionization in a gas cell. *Hyperfine Interact.* **2000**, *127*, 401–408. [CrossRef]
3. Hirayama, Y.; Watanabe, Y.; Imai, N.; Ishiyama, H.; Jeong, S.; Jung, H.; Miyatake, H.; Oyaizu, M.; Kimura, S.; Mukai, M.; et al. On-line experimental results of an argon gas cell-based laser ion source (KEK Isotope Separation System). *Nucl. Instrum. Methods Phys. Res. Sect. B Beam Interact. Mater. Atoms* **2016**, *376*, 52–56. [CrossRef]
4. Campbell, P.; Moore, I.; Pearson, M. Laser spectroscopy for nuclear structure physics. *Prog. Part. Nucl. Phys.* **2016**, *86*, 127–180. [CrossRef]
5. Laatiaoui, M.; Lauth, W.; Backe, H.; Block, M.; Ackermann, D.; Cheal, B.; Chhetri, P.; Düllmann, C.E.; Van Duppen, P.; Even, J.; et al. Atom-at-a-time laser resonance ionization spectroscopy of nobelium. *Nature* **2016**, *538*, 495–498. [CrossRef] [PubMed]

6. Edwards, M. The quenching of alkali fluorescence by rare gases. *J. Phys. B At. Mol. Phys.* **1969**, *2*, 719. [CrossRef]
7. Ehrlacher, E.; Huennekens, J. Excitation transfer among, and quenching of, the barium 6s5d 3 D J metastable levels due to collisions with argon, nitrogen, and barium perturbers. *Phys. Rev. A* **1994**, *50*, 4786. [CrossRef]
8. Knoop, M.; Vedel, M.; Vedel, F. Collisional quenching and j-mixing rate constants for the 3 D levels of Ca+. *Phys. Rev. A* **1998**, *58*, 264. [CrossRef]
9. Namiotka, R.; Ehrlacher, E.; Sagle, J.; Brewer, M.; Namiotka, D.; Hickman, A.; Streater, A.; Huennekens, J. Diffusion of barium atoms in the 6s5d 3 D J metastable levels and the 6 s 2 1 S 0 ground state through noble-gas perturbers. *Phys. Rev. A* **1996**, *54*, 449. [CrossRef]
10. Redondo, C.; Rayo, M.S.; Ecija, P.; Husain, D.; Castano, F. Collisional dynamics of low energy states of atomic strontium following the generation of Sr (5s5p1P1) in the presence of Ne, Kr and Xe. *Chem. Phys. Lett.* **2004**, *392*, 116–122. [CrossRef]
11. Church, D.A. Collision measurements and excited-level lifetime measurements on ions stored in Paul, Penning and Kingdon ion traps. *Phys. Rep.* **1993**, *228*, 253 358. [CrossRef]
12. Foo, P.; Wiesenfeld, J.; Husain, D. Collisional quenching of the spin-orbit states of atomic tin, Sn(5p23P2) and Sn(5p23P1). *Chem. Phys. Lett.* **1975**, *32*, 443–448. [CrossRef]
13. Czajkowski, M.; Bobkowski, R.; Krause, L. Depopulation of the 53P1 state of cadmium by collisions with ground-state Cd and noble-gas atoms. *Spectrochim. Acta Part B At. Spectrosc.* **1991**, *46*, 1–7. [CrossRef]
14. Czajkowski, M.; Bobkowski, R.; Krause, L. Depopulation of the Zn 43P1 state by collisions with ground-state Zn and noble-gas atoms. *Spectrochim. Acta Part B At. Spectrosc.* **1991**, *46*, 1161–1169. [CrossRef]
15. Nuñez-Reyes, D.; Kłos, J.; Alexander, M.H.; Dagdigian, P.J.; Hickson, K.M. Experimental and theoretical investigation of the temperature dependent electronic quenching of O (1 D) atoms in collisions with Kr. *J. Chem. Phys.* **2018**, *148*, 124311. [CrossRef]
16. Lara, M.; Berteloite, C.; Paniagua, M.; Dayou, F.; Le Picard, S.D.; Launay, J.M. Experimental and theoretical study of the collisional quenching of S (1 D) by Ar. *Phys. Chem. Chem. Phys.* **2017**, *19*, 28555–28571. [CrossRef]
17. Haberland, H.; Konz, W.; Oesterlin, P. Interaction potentials and energy transfer cross sections for collisions of metastable helium and neon. II. He (21S)+ Ne. *J. Phys. B At. Mol. Phys.* **1982**, *15*, 2969. [CrossRef]
18. Smedley, J.E.; Marran, D.F.; Peabody, M.R.; Marquis, C.N. Electronic energy transfer in Ba 6s8p1P rare gas collisions. *J. Chem. Phys.* **1993**, *98*, 1093–1100. [CrossRef]
19. Breckenridge, W.H.; Merrow, C.N. Exclusive production of Ba (6s6p3P2) in the collisional deactivation of Ba (6s6p1P1) by the rare gases. *J. Chem. Phys.* **1988**, *88*, 2329–2333. [CrossRef]
20. Visticot, J.P.; Berlande, J.; Cuvellier, J.; Mestdagh, J.M.; Meynadier, P.; de Pujo, P.; Sublemontier, O.; Bell, A.J.; Frey, J.G. Energy dependence of the inelastic process Ba(6s6p^{1}P$_1$)+Ar,He→Ba(6s6p^{3}P$_{1,2}$)+Ar,He. *J. Chem. Phys.* **1990**, *93*, 5354–5355. [CrossRef]
21. Visticot, J.P.; De Pujo, P.; Sublemontier, O.; Bell, A.; Berlande, J.; Cuvellier, J.; Gustavsson, T.; Lallement, A.; Mestdagh, J.; Meynadier, P.; et al. Polarization effects in the differential cross section of the Ba (1 P 1- 3 P 2) inelastic transition induced by argon. *Phys. Rev. A* **1992**, *45*, 6371. [CrossRef] [PubMed]
22. Black, G.; Jusinski, L.E. Rate coefficients for S(1D) removal at 300 K. *J. Chem. Phys.* **1985**, *82*, 789–793. [CrossRef]
23. Pohjalainen, I.; Moore, I.; Geldhof, S.; Rosecker, V.; Sterba, J.; Schumm, T. Gas cell studies of thorium using filament dispensers at IGISOL. *Nucl. Instrum. Methods Phys. Res. Sect. B Beam Interact. Mater. Atoms* **2020**, *484*, 59–70. [CrossRef]
24. Kälber, W.; Rink, J.; Bekk, K.; Faubel, W.; Göring, S.; Meisel, G.; Rebel, H.; Thompson, R. Nuclear radii of thorium isotopes from laser spectroscopy of stored ions. *Z. Phys. A At. Nucl.* **1989**, *334*, 103–108. [CrossRef]
25. Kälber, W.; Meisel, G.; Rink, J.; Thompson, R. Two-step optical excitation for doppler linewidth reduction and motion study of ions stored in a paul trap. *J. Mod. Opt.* **1992**, *39*, 335–347. [CrossRef]
26. Chhetri, P.; Ackermann, D.; Backe, H.; Block, M.; Cheal, B.; Düllmann, C.E.; Even, J.; Ferrer, R.; Giacoppo, F.; Götz, S.; et al. Impact of buffer gas quenching on the 1 S 0→ 1 P 1 ground-state atomic transition in nobelium. *Eur. Phys. J. D* **2017**, *71*, 1–7. [CrossRef]
27. Chhetri, P.; Ackermann, D.; Backe, H.; Block, M.; Cheal, B.; Droese, C.; Düllmann, C.E.; Even, J.; Ferrer, R.; Giacoppo, F.; et al. Precision Measurement of the First Ionization Potential of Nobelium. *Phys. Rev. Lett.* **2018**, *120*, 263003. [CrossRef]
28. Pohjalainen, I.; Moore, I.; Kron, T.; Raeder, S.; Sonnenschein, V.; Tomita, H.; Trautmann, N.; Voss, A.; Wendt, K. In-gas-cell laser ionization studies of plutonium isotopes at IGISOL. *Nucl. Instrum. Methods Phys. Res. Sect. B Beam Interact. Mater. Atoms* **2016**, *376*, 233–239. [CrossRef]
29. Reponen, M.; Moore, I.D.; Kessler, T.; Pohjalainen, I.; Rothe, S.; Sonnenschein, V. Laser developments and resonance ionization spectroscopy at IGISOL. *Eur. Phys. J. A* **2012**, *48*, 45. [CrossRef]
30. Tomita, H.; Nakamura, A.; Matsui, D.; Ohtake, R.; Sonnenschein, V.; Saito, K.; Kato, K.; Ohashi, M.; Degner, V.; Wendt, K.; et al. Development of two-color resonance ionization scheme for Th using an automated wide-range tunable Ti: Sapphire laser system. *Prog. Nucl. Sci. Technol.* **2018**, *5*, 97–99. [CrossRef]
31. Karvonen, P.; Moore, I.D.; Sonoda, T.; Kessler, T.; Penttilä, H.; Peräjärvi, K.; Ronkanen, P.; Äystö, J. A sextupole ion beam guide to improve the efficiency and beam quality at IGISOL. *Nucl. Instrum. Methods Phys. Res. Sect. B* **2008**, *266*, 4794–4807. [CrossRef]
32. Voss, A.; Sonnenschein, V.; Campbell, P.; Cheal, B.; Kron, T.; Moore, I.; Pohjalainen, I.; Raeder, S.; Trautmann, N.; Wendt, K. High-resolution laser spectroscopy of long-lived plutonium isotopes. *Phys. Rev. A* **2017**, *95*, 032506. [CrossRef]
33. Raeder, S.; Hakimi, A.; Stöbener, N.; Trautmann, N.; Wendt, K. Detection of plutonium isotopes at lowest quantities using in-source resonance ionization mass spectrometry. *Anal. Bioanal. Chem.* **2012**, *404*, 2163–2172. [CrossRef] [PubMed]
34. Blaise, J.; Fred, M.; Gutmacher, R.G. Term analysis of the spectrum of neutral plutonium, Pu i. *JOSA B* **1986**, *3*, 403–418. [CrossRef]

35. Richards, E.; Ridgeley, A. Preliminary classification in the plutonium I spectrum. *Spectrochim. Acta* **1965**, *21*, 1449–1466. [CrossRef]
36. Granados, C.; Creemers, P.; Ferrer, R.; Gaffney, L.P.; Gins, W.; de Groote, R.; Huyse, M.; Kudryavtsev, Y.; Martínez, Y.; Raeder, S.; et al. In-gas laser ionization and spectroscopy of actinium isotopes near the $N = 126$ closed shell. *Phys. Rev. C* **2017**, *96*, 054331. [CrossRef]

Article

Probing the Atomic Structure of Californium by Resonance Ionization Spectroscopy

Felix Weber [1,*], Christoph Emanuel Düllmann [2,3,4], Vadim Gadelshin [1], Nina Kneip [1], Stephan Oberstedt [5], Sebastian Raeder [3,4], Jörg Runke [4], Christoph Mokry [2,3], Petra Thörle-Pospiech [2,3], Dominik Studer [1], Norbert Trautmann [2] and Klaus Wendt [1]

1. Institut für Physik, Johannes Gutenberg-Universität Mainz, 55099 Mainz, Germany; gadelshin@uni-mainz.de (V.G.); nina.kneip@uni-mainz.de (N.K.); dstuder@uni-mainz.de (D.S.); kwendt@uni-mainz.de (K.W.)
2. Department Chemie—Standort TRIGA, Johannes Gutenberg-Universität Mainz, 55099 Mainz, Germany; duellmann@uni-mainz.de (C.E.D.); mokry@uni-mainz.de (C.M.); pthoerle@uni-mainz.de (P.T.-P.); ntrautma@uni-mainz.de (N.T.)
3. Helmholtz-Institut Mainz, 55099 Mainz, Germany; s.raeder@gsi.de
4. GSI Helmholtzzentrum für Schwerionenforschung GmbH, 64291 Darmstadt, Germany; runke@uni-mainz.de
5. European Commission, Joint Research Centre (JRC), 2440 Geel, Belgium; stephan.oberstedt@ec.europa.eu
* Correspondence: wfelix02@uni-mainz.de

Citation: Weber, F.; Düllmann, C.E.; Gadelshin, V.; Kneip, N.; Oberstedt, S.; Raeder, S.; Runke, J.; Mokry, C.; Thörle-Pospiech, P.; Studer, D.; et al. Probing the Atomic Structure of Californium by Resonance Ionization Spectroscopy. *Atoms* **2022**, *10*, 51. http://doi.org/10.3390/atoms10020051

Academic Editor: Kanti M. Aggarwal

Received: 20 April 2022
Accepted: 20 May 2022
Published: 24 May 2022

Publisher's Note: MDPI stays neutral with regard to jurisdictional claims in published maps and institutional affiliations.

Copyright: © 2022 by the authors. Licensee MDPI, Basel, Switzerland. This article is an open access article distributed under the terms and conditions of the Creative Commons Attribution (CC BY) license (https://creativecommons.org/licenses/by/4.0/).

Abstract: The atomic structure of californium is probed by two-step resonance ionization spectroscopy. Using samples with a total amount of about 2×10^{10} Cf atoms (ca. 8.3 pg), ground-state transitions as well as transitions to high-lying Rydberg states and auto-ionizing states above the ionization potential are investigated and the lifetimes of various atomic levels are measured. These investigations lead to the identification of efficient ionization schemes, important for trace analysis and nuclear structure investigations. Most of the measurements are conducted on ^{250}Cf. In addition, the isotope shift of the isotopic chain $^{249-252}$Cf is measured for one transition. The identification and analysis of Rydberg series enables the determination of the first ionization potential of californium to $E_{IP} = 50,666.76(5)$ cm^{-1}. This is about a factor of 20 more precise than the current literature value.

Keywords: californium; resonance ionization spectroscopy; ionization potential; atomic structure

1. Introduction

The radioactive element californium (Cf) with an atomic number of $Z = 98$ is one of the exotic heavier members of the actinide series. As a rare exception in this part of the nuclear chart, this element features a series of longer-lived isotopes that can be produced in high flux nuclear reactors. Nevertheless, only lower-lying atomic states of californium have been studied so far, while information on the higher-lying atomic states around the first ionization potential (IP) is almost completely missing [1]. Extending the available information is of fundamental relevance for the characterization of the element and will support the identification of efficient photo-ionization schemes, which are a precondition for, e.g., high resolution laser spectroscopy as well as ultra-sensitive trace analysis investigations in the range of the heavier actinides [2]. On top of that, detailed studies of the hyperfine structure and isotope shift will provide further insight into the nuclear structure in this region of the nuclear chart [3,4]. Californium, in particular, is of specific relevance for investigations of nuclei at the deformed sub-shell closure at neutron number $N = 152$, coinciding with ^{250}Cf. This shell structure has already been predicted by Seaborg in 1989 [5] and has been confirmed by high precision mass measurements [6] as well as decay spectroscopy [7], and updated in [8]. The californium isotopes in the vicinity, i.e., $^{249-252}$Cf, all have half-lives ($T_{1/2}$) in the order of 2 to 1000 years. They provide the only accessible isotope series around $N = 152$, which can be produced in mg quantities and thus easily be studied. Starting from curium as seed material, the californium isotopes are bred by successive neutron capture and subsequent β^--decays in the high flux isotope reactor (HFIR) at the Oak Ridge National Laboratory (ORNL) in Oak Ridge, TN, USA [9]. In particular, the isotope ^{252}Cf ($T_{1/2}$ = 2.64 a) is well recognized for its use as a starter neutron source in nuclear reactors, for medical applications and in the oil industry in well logging applications, based on its properties as a strong neutron emitter [10,11].

Californium was discovered in 1950 by Thompson et al. when it was produced by the irradiation of ^{242}Cm with 35 MeV helium ions at the Berkeley 60-inch cyclotron [12]. Its chemical behavior was found to be very similar to that of dysprosium, its isoelectronic homologue. First, investigations on the atomic spectrum of californium were performed in 1962 in a spark source [13], followed by the use of electrodeless lamps in the 1970s [14,15]. This work was extended in 1994 and led to a compilation of 136 even and 265 odd parity low-lying levels in neutral californium (Cf I), for which the angular momenta and even the electronic configurations were assigned for most levels [1].

In the current investigations, resonance ionization spectroscopy (RIS) was used as a versatile and highly sensitive technique to study the atomic structure by step-wise excitation and finally photo-ionization of the element of interest [16,17]. Due to the efficient generation and detection of ions, this method is extremely sensitive and can be applied on samples in the pg range with atom numbers well below 10^9 [18]. The first laser spectroscopic investigations on californium applying RIS were carried out in 1996 on a sample containing about 10^{12} atoms of ^{249}Cf ($T_{1/2}$ = 351 a). A resonant two-step laser excitation followed by a third ionization step using another tunable laser was used to determine the IP by electric field ionization, which led to a value of $E_{IP} = 50,665(1)$ cm^{-1} [19]. The analysis of the convergence limit of series of high-lying Rydberg levels is usually a more precise and reliable way to determine the IP of an element, although, in open f-shell elements like the lanthanides or actinides, this can be ambiguous due to the complex atomic spectra and the resulting variety of interactions and level mixings [20–22]. In californium, the complexity of the atomic spectrum around the IP is still unknown, as no studies are reported in this region. In this way, the present studies contribute to the understanding of these complex atomic structures with multiple open shells and acts as experimental support for the theoretical predictions of the entirely unknown atomic systems in the range of the super-heavy elements.

In this work, the investigation of the atomic structure of californium in this high-lying energy region around the first IP is presented. The studies include the search for strong auto-ionizing states (AIS) starting from six different odd-parity low-lying energy levels, which were populated through optical excitation steps from the ground-state. After the identification of efficient ionization schemes, some of these first excited states (FES) were investigated in more detail with respect to their lifetime and the saturation behaviour of the corresponding ground-state transition. The observed Rydbergs series converging to both the ionic ground-state and the lowest-lying excited state in the Cf$^+$-ion were analysed to determine the IP. In addition, the isotope shift for the ground-state transition at 419.91 nm was investigated in the isotopic sequence $^{249-252}$Cf with low resolution as preparation for future work.

2. Experimental Setup

A californium sample (isotopic composition: ^{249}Cf: 25.6%; ^{250}Cf: 31.4%; ^{251}Cf: 13.4%; ^{252}Cf: 29.6% at the time of the measurements) was purchased from Eckert & Ziegler Nuclitec GmbH (E & Z) as 0.1 M nitric acid solution and prepared at the Department of Chemistry's TRIGA Site at Johannes Gutenberg University Mainz (JGU). Two aliquots, each containing in total about 10^{10} atoms of $^{249-252}$Cf, were extracted from this solution and each aliquot was pipetted onto a 7 × 7 mm^2 zirconium foil of 25 µm thickness. After evaporation of the solution, the foils were folded for complete encasement of the samples, and then inserted into an atomizer tube. The RIS measurements were conducted at the RISIKO mass separator of the Institute of Physics at JGU. It offers a high efficiency, which is crucial for spectroscopy on minuscule samples. The principal layout of the RISIKO apparatus is depicted in Figure 1, while a more detailed description can be found in [23].

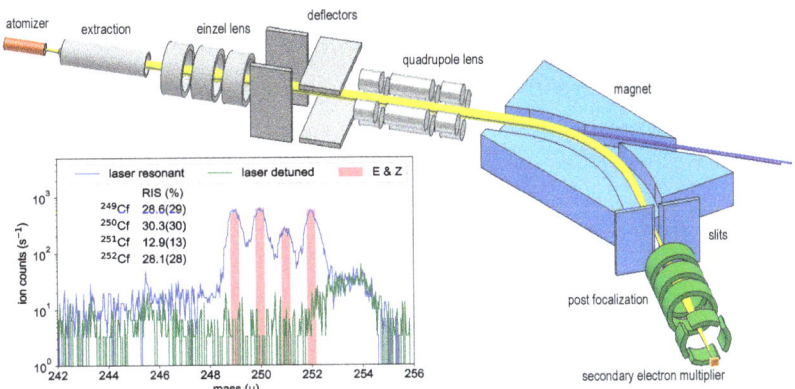

Figure 1. Sketch of the RISIKO mass separator with the ion trajectory indicated in yellow and the laser beams in blue. More details on the apparatus are given in [23]. The inset shows the mass spectrum of the californium sample measured with resonant ionization (blue trace) and with first-step laser detuned (green trace). The isotope ratio expected from the certificate of the material is shown in red. More details are given in the text.

The tantalum atomizer tube can be heated resistively to a maximum temperature of about 2000 °C. Already at atomizer temperatures around 800 °C, neutral californium atoms evaporate from the sample and an ion signal from resonant laser ionization is observed. This is in reasonable agreement with the evaporation behavior described in [24]. The ions are accelerated to 30 keV and guided as collimated ion beam through a 60°-sector-field dipole magnet, which separates them by their mass-to-charge ratio. An adjustable separation slit is used to select only a single mass, providing a mass resolution of $M/\Delta M \approx 600$. The mass-selected ions are re-focused by an einzel lens and counted by a secondary electron multiplier. The ionization process is induced by two custom-built pulsed Ti:sapphire lasers, both featuring automatic frequency scanning and tracked intra-cavity phase matching for second harmonic generation [25]. The average output powers range between 200 and 800 mW with a pulse repetition rate of 10 kHz, a pulse length of 30 to 50 ns and a continuous scanning range from 350 to 500 nm. Both Ti:sapphire lasers are individually pumped with up to 18 W power provided by commercial high repetition rate pulsed frequency-doubled Nd:YAG-lasers operating at 532 nm. A pulse generator is used to trigger the pump pulses for optimum synchronization required for efficient ionization. Alternatively, the pulse generator can be used to generate a variable time delay between the excitation steps to probe the lifetime of an excited state.

The inlay of Figure 1 shows the corresponding mass spectrum with all four californium isotopes being clearly visible as obtained by applying a two-step ionization with both lasers on resonance. For comparison, a spectrum was included with the first excitation laser detuned from the resonance. The latter was recorded to ensure that the signal obtained on resonance can be completely ascribed to californium and also in order to determine the remaining background conditions on the individual mass settings. Non-related mass peaks, like the structure at mass 254, show no dependence on the applied laser wavelength. The expected isotopic composition (certified by E & Z) is drawn as red bars and shows good agreement with the pattern obtained by RIS (*cf.* inlay Figure 1). Marginal uncertainties in the values determined by the RIS method can be ascribed to influences of the optical isotope shift, which was not taken into account during these measurement, to the different hyperfine structure patterns of the odd-mass isotopes or finally to minimal statistical fluctuations in the ion signal. For these reasons, an uncertainty of 10% of the determined value was adopted for each isotope.

3. Laser Spectroscopic Investigations

In the accessible energy range for the first excitation step from 23,000 to 28,720 cm^{-1}, 15 energy levels are listed in [1] that can be directly excited by electric dipole transitions, starting from the $5f^{10}7s^2\ ^5I_8$ ground-state. To confirm the completeness of optical ground-state transitions in this range, a frequency scan of the first excitation laser was performed, while keeping the second laser at a fixed wavelength of 360 nm with 400 mW average power to ensure photo-ionization from any resonantly excited level. In this scan, all known energy levels could be confirmed while no additional resonances were found. This measurement was performed using ^{249}Cf, which allowed a comparison to the data in [1]. Additionally, it created the opportunity to search for particularly broad resonance structures, which might be suitable candidates for future hyperfine structure measurements. The obtained results are in excellent agreement with the previous work. However, transitions that are prominent due to particularly large linewidths were not found in this broadband laser scan. In the next step, six different first excitation steps and the corresponding autoionizing structure have been measured on ^{250}Cf ($T_{1/2} = 13.08$ a), which was chosen to avoid possible influences of hyperfine structure in the spectra. The investigated ionization schemes are depicted in Figure 2 and discussed in the following.

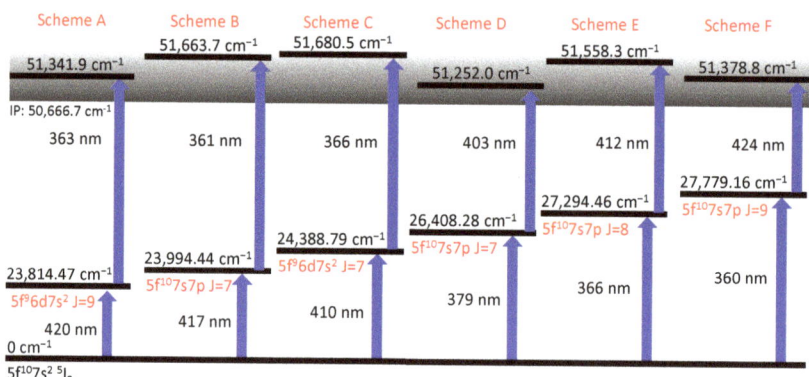

Figure 2. Sketch of the ionization schemes identified in this work. All energetic positions refer to ^{250}Cf. The electron configurations are taken from [1]. For all schemes, the ionization laser was scanned around the IP to search for AIS and Rydberg-levels. The AIS providing the highest ion count rate is given as a second step.

3.1. Ionization Schemes

To identify suitable ionization schemes, the laser driving the ionization step was scanned in the region of the IP starting from one of the six FES of Figure 2. Most scans were performed up to about the first excited level of the ion ($E_{IP} + 1180.52$ cm^{-1} [1]), while scheme C was deliberately extended up to an excitation energy of 52,000 cm^{-1} to map possible structures above. The obtained spectra show many AIS and Rydberg states, as visible in Figure 3. For each excitation scheme (Figure 2), the resonance resulting in the highest ion count rate is given to provide a collection of resonant two-step ionization schemes in californium. Depending on the first step, several AIS might produce similarly intense ion signals. Unfortunately, the ion count rate obtained from the different spectra cannot be compared directly to each other, due to varying ion source conditions. The laser scans for schemes D and E, e.g., were taken on a fresh, newly inserted californium sample and with a higher atomizer temperature, resulting in a higher ion count rate than the measurements of the other schemes. To compensate for that, an enhancement factor was determined by normalizing the ion signal to a baseline of non-resonant ionization. This allows for deducing the enhancement of the ion signal due to an AIS directly from the spectra shown in Figure 3. Nevertheless, this enhancement is somewhat biased because, for schemes D, E and F, the laser populating the FES could also provide ionization, which leads to an increased non-resonant baseline compared to the other schemes. Therefore, both types of information, i.e., the ion count rate during the scans and the enhancement compared to the non-resonant baseline, are provided in Figure 3. The distinct series of Rydberg states showing up in the spectra are evaluated in Section 3.4.

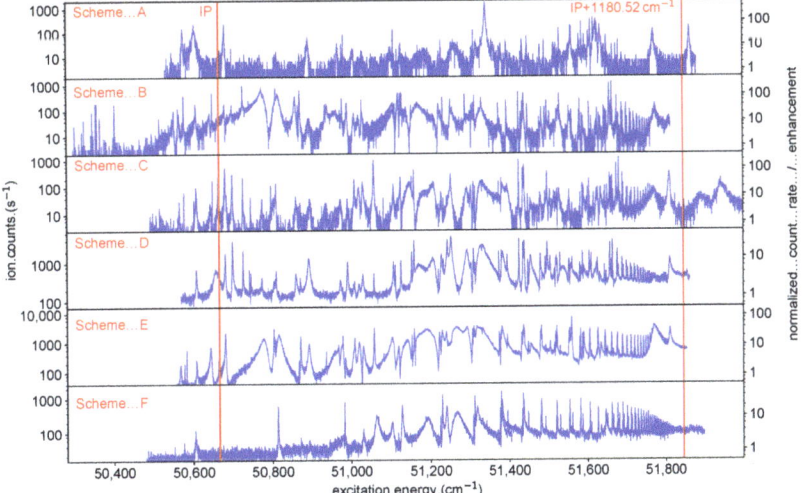

Figure 3. Spectra of neutral californium obtained by scanning the ionization laser around the IP starting from either one of the six different FES presented in Figure 2. On the left y-axes, the count rate during the measurement is displayed. On the right y-axes, an enhancement factor of the ion signal as determined by normalizing the ion signal to the individual baseline of non-resonant ionization is indicated. Distinct Rydberg series show up in nearly all spectra converging to the lowest-lying excited state in the Cf$^+$-ion, located at an excitation energy of 1180.52 cm^{-1} above the IP [1]. The resonance marked with an asterisk is discussed in Section 3.4

3.2. Lifetime and Saturation

The lifetime of an excited level is directly linked to the strengths of the involved optical channels for de-excitation. The ground-state transition should be one of the dominant ones in our case. Here, the decay of the FES population is probed by delaying the second, ionizing laser with respect to the first, exciting laser and monitoring the decline of the ion signal with increasing delay-times. The expected curve is a convolution of the nearly Gaussian-shaped laser pulse profile and the exponential decay of the level population [26]. In cases where the first transition is strongly saturated, the ionization rate increases notably when both laser pulses coincide. Then, the convolution cannot describe the complete shape of the decay curve, and an exponential decay is fitted on a subset describing the situation of temporally well separated laser interactions. The obtained results are shown in Figure 4 for schemes A, B and C, where the data in the left panel were measured with 130 mW to 160 mW laser power in the first step and in the right panel with a lower laser power of about 5 mW.

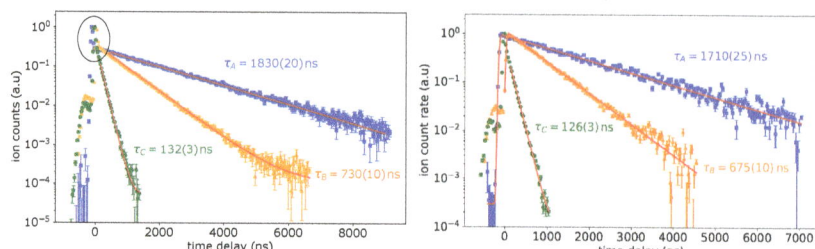

Figure 4. Left: lifetime measurement of the FES for schemes A, B and C with laser power of about 130 mW for scheme A, and 160 mW for scheme B and C in the excitation step. The area where both laser pulses overlap is highlighted. Right: same lifetime measurement with a laser power of about 5 mW for all schemes in the excitation step. More details are discussed in the text.

Both graphs show a small peak at the very beginning of the curve at negative time delay values. This is due to a weak second laser pulse following the main pulse of the ionization laser and can be neglected in the analysis. The additional strong peak in coincidence for a time delay of 0 ns (highlighted in the left panel in Figure 4) vanishes in the right panel for schemes A and B, as the laser power was decreased. Therefore, the convolution can be used here to describe the entire data set. In scheme C, the coincidence peak shows up even with reduced laser power, which indicates that the transition was still saturated. Here, the fit is applied to a subset of data only. The obtained lifetime values for schemes A and B differ somewhat between both measurements. The deviation is too large to be explained by statistics only. It is ascribed to varying temperature conditions within the atomizer during a measurement, which are induced by the change of laser power. This could be circumvented by waiting until the ion source conditions had stabilized before starting a new measurement. Future studies will allow for excluding systematic errors in these measurements. Correspondingly, the real value of the lifetime is expected in the range between the values given in Figure 4. It is obvious that the FES from schemes A and B are relatively long-lived.

Efficient ionization requires saturation of the excitation steps. The saturation power P_{sat} is measured by attenuating the laser power in the first excitation step and monitoring the ion signal. The lasers in both steps were focused on a beam spot size of $\approx 2.5(10)$ mm^2 in the atomizer tube. The expected ion signal curve can be expressed by

$$S(P) = C_1 \cdot \frac{1}{(1 + P/P_{sat})} + C_2 \cdot P + C_3, \quad (1)$$

with laser power P, saturation power P_{sat} and the coefficents for resonant ionization C_1, laser-induced background C_2, and laser-independent background C_3 [27]. In Figure 5, the saturation behavior is shown for the three ground-state transitions of schemes A, B and C.

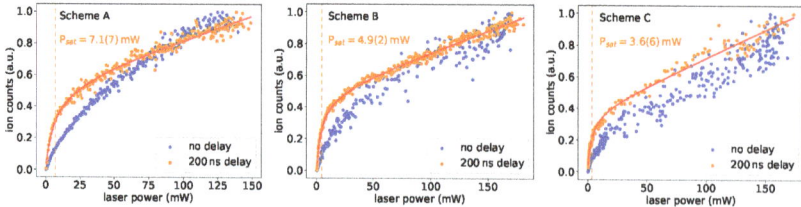

Figure 5. Saturation curves for the first excitation steps in schemes A, B and C. For all levels, the curve evolution differs when the ionization laser pulse was delayed. More details are given in the text.

The saturation behaviour differed significantly depending on whether the measurement was made with or without a time delay between excitation and ionization laser pulses. This was expected, as the strength of the primary peak for coincident laser pulses in the lifetime measurements was depending on the power of the excitation laser. In this case, a realistic saturation power of the transition can only be given for a sufficiently long delay between both pulses. The indicated saturation powers should only be seen as rough estimates, as the size of the laser beam overlapping with the second laser spot was not determined precisely, and power measurements were not performed directly at the point of interaction. Nevertheless, the values demonstrate that all three schemes can easily be saturated in common laser ion sources. As expected, the trend in P_{sat} follows the trend in lifetime, i.e., a longer lifetime corresponds to a higher saturation power.

3.3. Isotope Shift

The isotope shift is the frequency difference in an atomic transition between two isotopes with mass numbers A and A', defined as $\delta\nu^{A,A'} = \nu^{A'} - \nu^{A}$. Its sign provides hints about the configuration of the involved energy levels. A precise determination gives access to nuclear structure parameters such as the change in mean square charge radii and the incorporated nuclear deformation [4]. High-resolution measurements with linewidths of about 100 MHz, including evaluation of the hyperfine structure in ^{249,251}Cf, were performed by us on the californium samples in a more sophisticated experimental arrangement and will be discussed and published separately by the same authors. A detailed description of the required upgrade of the setup and the resulting high resolution spectroscopic data are beyond the scope of this publication. As preparation for these investigations, the isotope shift of the first step in scheme A was measured here with a spectral linewidth in the order of 2 GHz. The obtained data are shown in Figure 6. The linewidth is mainly determined by the Doppler broadening in the hot atomizer tube and by the laser bandwidth. For this measurement, an etalon was installed in the laser resonator. This reduced the laser bandwidth from the typical values of 5–7 GHz during the wide range scans to typical values of 1–2 GHz. Minor differences in the linewidths for the different isotopes are caused by different laser powers or laser operation conditions.

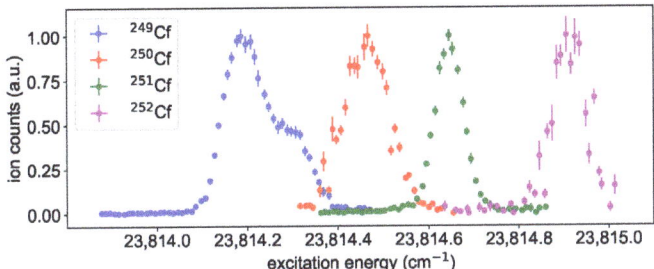

Figure 6. Isotope shift of $^{249-252}$Cf for the ground-state transition in scheme A with a linewidth of about 1.5 GHz. The isotope shift has a negative sign, which is in agreement with the assigned configuration of $5f^96d7s^2$ for the upper state.

The transition energy shown in Figure 6 is lower towards lighter isotopes, which indicates that none of the s-electrons in the $5f^{10}7s^2$ ground-state is involved in the transition. This is in agreement with the $5f^96d7s^2$ configuration assigned for the excited state in [1]. The transitions shows a sub-structure for ^{249}Cf caused by the hyperfine structure. However, due to the nuclear spin of $I = 9/2$ and the high angular momenta of $J = 8$ in the ground-state and $J = 9$ in the FES, 27 individual hyperfine structure components are expected, and therefore an analysis is not possible here. For ^{251}Cf, the nuclear spin of $I = 1/2$ leads to an expected splitting into just three hyperfine components, but no indication for hyperfine structure is visible in the corresponding peak at a linewidth of about 2 GHz. For these reasons, a quantitative analysis of the isotope shift is not attempted here and reference is given to the paper that will be published separately by the same authors.

3.4. Ionization Potential

Distinct Rydberg series converging to the lowest-lying excited state in the Cf$^+$-ion are observed for all schemes except of scheme A (cf. Figure 3). In some spectra, e.g., for scheme F, the series split at lower energies, i.e., at a larger distance from the convergence limit, into two or more series. Schemes B and E additionally exhibit series that converge to the ionic ground-state and thus directly allow the determination of the IP. In order to assign the resonances to individual series, all individual resonance peaks were fitted. All parts of the spectra containing Rydberg resonances were scanned twice, once with increasing and once with decreasing wavelength, in order to exclude systematic shifts in the resonances. These may occur due to the scanning speed of the laser and a possible marginal delay in the data acquisition. The mean value obtained from both scanning directions was taken as the energetic position of each peak. The observed shift of all peaks in a series between the two scanning directions was averaged and a common standard deviation was determined, which is taken as the uncertainty of the individual energies for a specific series. The average itself shows how strongly the peak positions are influenced by the scanning procedure and was used for correction if individual resonances could only be observed in one scan. The statistical uncertainty obtained in this way lies between 0.04 and 0.1 cm^{-1}, depending on the scanning speed and the statistical quality of the data. Afterwards, the obtained level energies were inserted into the Rydberg–Ritz formula

$$E_n = E_\infty - \frac{R_\mu}{(n - \delta(n))^2} = E_\infty - \frac{R_\mu}{(n^*)^2} \tag{2}$$

to obtain the effective principal quantum number n^*. Here, E_n is the energy of the Rydberg-level with the principal quantum number n, E_∞ the series limit, $\delta(n)$ the quantum defect and R_μ the Rydberg constant for finite nuclear mass. The fractional part of the quantum defect δ_frac is in first order constant and independent of n^* for a series, if the convergence limit is chosen properly. Minor variations as a function of n^* can be expressed with the Ritz expansion

$$\delta(n) \approx \delta_0 + \frac{\delta_1}{(n - \delta_0)^2} + \frac{\delta_2}{(n - \delta_0)^4} + (...), \tag{3}$$

where the higher orders are needed to account for alterations in $\delta(n)$ towards lower n^*. This is shown in Figure 7 with an assumed convergence limit $E_\infty = 51{,}847.20$ cm^{-1} for all schemes. Even for scheme A, Rydberg series can be recognised, although only a few levels could be measured. For this reason, no further analysis was carried out for this scheme. For many of the other schemes, two distinct series show up, which can be assigned to s- (green) and d-series (red), with the latter often exhibiting a significant fine structure splitting for lower n^*. In such cases, the dominant series of more prominent peaks in the spectrum was considered for the Rydberg fit.

It is noticeable that the plot for scheme F is much cleaner than, e.g., the plot for scheme D. The latter shows in addition a large perturbation around $n^* \approx 42$, so that the energy levels above this value are not taken into account in the further analysis. Specifically the s-series in scheme F shows a well localized perturbation caused by an interloper for $n^* \approx 22$, which can be described within the multi channel quantum defect theory as an additional contribution to the quantum defect [28]

$$\delta_\text{pert}(n) = \delta(n) - \frac{1}{\pi} \arctan\left(\frac{\Gamma_I/2}{E_n - E_I} \right). \tag{4}$$

Here E_I and Γ_I are the energy and the width of the interloper, respectively. It is also visible that, for scheme F, the s- and the d-series are not truly parallel, which results in slightly different convergence limits. This behaviour could be caused by a long range perturbation located close to the convergence limit, which however cannot be clearly identified here. All energy levels, which were used for the extraction of the IP, are highlighted in Figure 7 by the coloured dots. The schemes considered here, except for scheme C, have an 5f^{10}7s7p electron configuration in the first excited state so that s- or d-series can be excited. The fractional quantum defects of ≈0.4 and ≈0.7 in Figure 7 can be assigned to absolute quantum defects of ≈5.4 and ≈3.7 for s- and d-series, respectively, in agreement with theoretical expectations [29]. This allows for assigning the principal quantum number to each Rydberg level and to plot it against its excitation energy. The IP is extracted by fitting Equation (2) to this data as shown in Figure 8 for scheme E as an example.

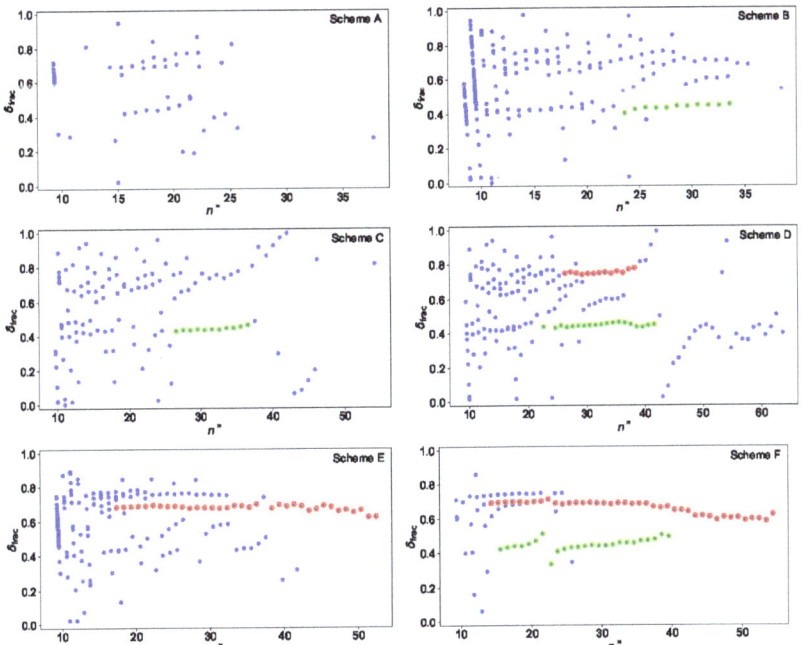

Figure 7. Plot of the fractional quantum defect δ_{frac} versus the effective quantum number n^* for all schemes with an assumed convergence limit of $E_\infty = 51{,}847.20$ cm^{-1}. Assigned resonances for the Rydberg-fits are highlighted in red for d-series and in green for s-series. Rydberg series converging directly to the IP appear in schemes B and E as nearly vertical lines around $n^* = 10$. More details are given in the text.

Here, two series were identified, one converging directly to the IP and the other one to the lowest-lying excited state in the Cf$^+$-ion. Below the IP, Rydberg-states were observed with principal quantum number from $n = 41$ to $n = 66$. Above, peaks were seen from $n = 21$ to $n = 56$, with a gap for $n = 41$, due to an underlying resonance (cf. the resonance marked with an asterisk, Figure 3, scheme E). To reduce systematic trends in the residuals, an interloper was included in the fit around $n = 26$. In this case, a definite identification was difficult, but the influence on the convergence limit with or without the consideration of an interloper is negligible here anyway. Table 1 summarizes the results for all series that were analysed in a similar way. Only those resonances for which a clear assignment to Rydberg series is possible are considered. If an interloper has to be taken into account as described in Equation (4), this is marked with an asterisk.

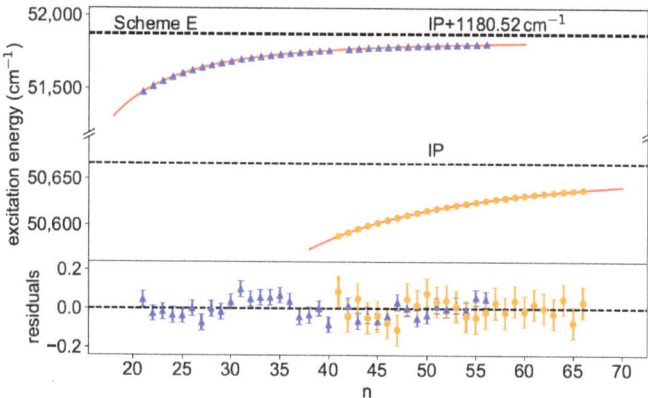

Figure 8. Rydberg–Ritz fits for scheme E towards the IP and the lowest-lying excited state in the Cf^+-ion. For the latter, an interloper is taken into account at $n = 26$. The residuals show that the model describes the data reasonably well for both cases. The extracted convergence limits are given in Table 1.

Table 1. Compilation of the results from the Rydberg-analysis of five different excitation schemes and altogether for nine series; two of them converge directly to the IP of ^{250}Cf, while the other converge to the lowest-lying excited state in the Cf^+-ion, which is located 1180.52 cm^{-1} above the IP [1]. The uncertainty of the mean value is calculated according to the Birge ratio. For series marked with an asterisk, an interloper is considered in the analysis. More details are given in the text.

E_1 (cm^{-1})	n	δ_0	δ_1	E_∞ (cm^{-1})	IP (cm^{-1})	χ^2_{red}
23,994.44(1)	41–70	3.64(2)	-	50,666.75(11)	50,666.75(11)	0.99
23,994.44(1)	29–39 *	5.42(4)	-	51,847.04(34)	50,666.52(34)	0.41
24,388.79(1)	32–42	5.42(1)	-	51,847.04(16)	50,666.52(16)	0.45
26,408.28(1)	30–42	3.74(2)	-	51,847.13(24)	50,666.61(24)	0.35
26,408.28(1)	28, 30–47	5.44(1)	-	51,847.14(16)	50,666.62(16)	0.25
27,294.46(1)	41–66	3.61(2)	-	50,666.78(13)	50,666.78(13)	0.39
27,294.46(1)	21–40, 42–56 *	3.70(4)	−3.6(13)	51,847.28(8)	50,666.76(8)	1.42
27,779.16(1)	18–58 *	3.72(1)	−4.5(6)	51,847.42(8)	50,666.90(8)	0.71
27,779.16(1)	21–43 *	5.46(1)	−10.0(15)	51,847.17(16)	50,666.65(16)	0.68
				weighted mean value	50,666.76(5)	

All series contain at least 11 Rydberg levels, with the longest sequence even consisting of 41 levels. The small values of χ^2_{red} show that the statistical uncertainties of the individual peaks might be somewhat overestimated. The fitting uncertainties for the convergence limit and the IP stated in Table 1 are increased by a factor of 2.6, resulting from analyzing the Birge ratio [30,31]. This factor leads to a good agreement of all values within their error bars, which would not be the case otherwise. One reason for such a slight deviation could be perturbations due to configuration mixing within some series, which are not accounted for by the Rydberg–Ritz formula. In this case, it is not possible to describe the course completely and the uncertainties can be underestimated, which justifies the procedure. An additional small uncertainty arises for all series converging to the lowest-lying excited state in the Cf^+-ion. Its energetic position is only known for ^{249}Cf, while all measurements here are conducted for ^{250}Cf. An isotope shift would result in a slight systematic deviation for those two studied series, which converge directly to the IP. Here, this uncertainty is assumed to be negligible. The final value

$$E_{IP} = 50,666.76(5) \text{ cm}^{-1}$$

is determined as the weighted mean value of all individual results with the overall statistical uncertainty according to the Birge ratio. This result is in good agreement with the current literature value of $E_{IP} = 50,665(1)$ cm^{-1} [19] and increases the precision by about a factor of 20.

4. Conclusions

Extensive studies on the atomic spectrum of neutral californium by laser resonance ionization spectroscopy were carried out and presented here. Based on six different first excitation steps, strong auto-ionizing resonances were identified, resulting in efficient two-step ionization schemes. Three of the first excitation steps and related intermediate levels were investigated in more detail by measuring their lifetimes as well as the saturation behavior of the corresponding ground-state transitions. As the saturation has a strong influence on the ion signal when both laser pulses overlap, a determination of saturation powers was only possible when a temporal delay between the two pulses was applied. The isotope shift of the isotopic chain $^{249-252}$Cf was measured for one ground-state transition with a spectral resolution of about 2 GHz, which was not sufficient for a detailed quantitative analysis of the isotope shift or the hyperfine structure in ^{249,251}Cf. This will be provided in upcoming high resolution studies the paper that will be published separately by the same authors. Rydberg-series converging to the ionic ground state and to the lowest-lying excited state in the Cf$^+$-ion were analysed to determine the IP of californium to $E_{IP} = 50,666.76(5)$ cm^{-1}. This value is in good agreement with the current literature value with an improvement in precision by about a factor of 20.

Author Contributions: Formal analysis, F.W.; investigation, F.W., V.G., N.K. and D.S.; project administration, C.E.D. and K.W.; resources, C.E.D., S.O., J.R., C.M., P.T.-P. and N.T.; writing—original draft preparation, F.W.; writing—review and editing, F.W., C.E.D., V.G., N.K., S.O., S.R., J.R., C.M., P.T.-P., D.S., N.T. and K.W.; visualization, F.W.; supervision, C.E.D, N.T. and K.W.; funding acquisition, K.W. All authors have read and agreed to the published version of the manuscript.

Funding: This research was funded by the Bundesministerium für Bildung und Forschung (BMBF, Germany) under Grant No. 05P18UMCIA.

Institutional Review Board Statement: Not applicable.

Informed Consent Statement: Not applicable.

Data Availability Statement: The data presented in this study are available upon reasonable request from the corresponding author.

Conflicts of Interest: The authors declare no conflict of interest.

References

1. Conway, J.G.; Worden, E.F.; Blaise, J. Energy levels of neutral californium (^{249}Cf I) and singly ionized californium (^{249}Cf II). *J. Opt. Soc. Am. B* **1995**, *12*, 1186–1202. [CrossRef]
2. Bosco, H.; Hamann, L.; Kneip, N.; Raiwa, M.; Weiss, M.; Wendt, K.; Walther, C. New horizons in microparticle forensics: Actinide imaging and detection of ^{238}Pu and ^{242m}Am in hot particles. *Sci. Adv.* **2021**, *7*. [CrossRef] [PubMed]
3. Ferrer, R.; Barzakh, A.; Bastin, B.; Beerwerth, R.; Block, M.; Creemers, P.; Grawe, H.; de Groote, R.; Delahaye, P.; Fléchard, X.; et al. Towards high-resolution laser ionization spectroscopy of the heaviest elements in supersonic gas jet expansion. *Nat. Commun.* **2017**, *8*, 14520. [CrossRef] [PubMed]
4. Campbell, P.; Moore, I.D.; Pearson, M.R. Laser spectroscopy for nuclear structure physics. *Prog. Part. Nucl.* **2016**, *86*, 127–180. [CrossRef]
5. Seaborg, G.T. Transuranium isotopes—An overview. *Trans. Am. Nucl. Soc.* **1989**, *60*, 275–276.
6. Ramirez, E.M.; Ackermann, D.; Blaum, K.; Block, M.; Droese, C.; Düllmann, C.E.; Dworschak, M.; Eibach, M.; Eliseev, S.; Haettner, E.; et al., Direct mapping of nuclear shell effects in the heaviest elements. *Science* **2012**, *337*, 1207–1210. [CrossRef]
7. Ackermann, D. Nuclear structure of superheavy nuclei—State of the art and perspectives (@ S^3). *EPJ Web Conf.* **2018**, *193*, 04013. [CrossRef]
8. Block, M.; Giacoppo, F.; Heßberger, F.-P.; Raeder, S. Recent progress in experiments on the heaviest nuclides at SHIP. *Riv. Nuovo C.* **2022**, *45*, 279–323. [CrossRef]

9. Ferguson, D.E. ORNL transuranium program—The production of transuranium elements. *Nucl. Sci. Eng.* **1963**, *17*, 435–437. [CrossRef]
10. Martin, R.C.; Knauer, J.B.; Balo, P.A. Production, distribution and applications of californium-252 neutron sources. *Appl. Radiat. Isot.* **2000**, *53*, 785–792. [CrossRef]
11. Boulogne, A.R.; Faraci, J.P. Californium-252 neutron sources for industrial applications. *Nucl. Technol.* **1971**, *11*, 75–83. [CrossRef]
12. Thompson, S.G.; Street, K., Jr.; Ghiorso, A.; Seaborg, G.T. The new element californium (atomic number 98). *Phys. Rev.* **1950**, *80*, 790. [CrossRef]
13. Conway, J.G.; Hulet, E.K.; Morrow, R.J. Emission spectrum of californium. *J. Opt. Soc. Am.* **1962**, *52*, 222. JOSA.52.000222. [CrossRef]
14. Worden, E.F.; Conway, J.G. Ground states and normal electronic configurations of californium I and II. *J. Opt. Soc. Am.* **1970**, *60*, 1144–1145. [CrossRef]
15. Conway, J.G.; Worden, E.F.; Blaise, J.; Vergfàs, J. The infrared spectrum of californium-249. *Spectrochim. Acta B* **1977**, *32*, 97–99. [CrossRef]
16. Hurst, G.S.; Payne, M.G.; Kramer, S.D.; Young, J.P. Resonance ionization spectroscopy and one-atom detection. *Rev. Mod. Phys.* **1979**, *51*, 767–819. [CrossRef]
17. Letokhov, V.S.; Mishin, V.I. Highly selective multistep ionization of atoms by laser radiation. *Opt. Commun.* **1979**, *29*, 168–171. [CrossRef]
18. Raeder, S.; Kneip, N.; Reich, T.; Studer, D.; Trautmann, N.; Wendt, K. Recent developments in resonance ionization mass spectrometry for ultra-trace analysis of actinide elements. *Radiochim. Acta* **2019**, *107*, 645–652. [CrossRef]
19. Köhler, S.; Erdmann, N.; Nunnemann, M.; Herrmann, G.; Huber, G.; Kratz, J.V.; Passler, G.; Trautmann, N. First experimental determination of the ionization potentials of berkelium and californium. *Chem. Int. Ed.* **1996**, *35*, 2856–2858. [CrossRef]
20. Fritzsche, S. Level structure and properties of open f-shell elements. *Atoms* **2022**, *10*, 7. [CrossRef]
21. Naubereit, P.; Gottwald, T.; Studer, D.; Wendt, K. Excited atomic energy levels in protactinium by resonance ionization spectroscopy. *Phys. Rev. A* **2018**, *98*, 022505. [CrossRef]
22. Studer, D.; Heinitz, S.; Heinke, R.; Naubereit, P.; Dressler, R.; Guerrero, C.; Köster, U.; Schumann, D.; Wendt, K. Atomic transitions and the first ionization potential of promethium determined by laser spectroscopy. *Phys. Rev. A* **2019**, *99*, 062513. [CrossRef]
23. Kieck, T.; Biebricher, S.; Düllmann, C.E.; Wendt, K. Optimization of a laser ion source for ^{163}Ho isotope separation. *Rev. Sci. Instrum.* **2019**, *90*, 053304. [CrossRef]
24. Eichler, B.; Hübener, S.; Erdmann, N.; Eberhardt, K.; Funk, H.; Herrmann, G.; Köhler, S.; Trautmann, N.; Passler, G.; Urban, F.-J. An atomic beam source for actinide elements: Concept and realization. *Radiochim. Acta* **1997**, *79*, 221–234. [CrossRef]
25. Raiwa, M.; Büchner, S.; Kneip, N.; Weiß, M.; Hanemann, P.; Fraatz, P.; Heller, M.; Bosco, H.; Weber, F.; Wendt, K.; et al. Actinide imaging in environmental hot particles from Chernobyl by rapid spatially resolved resonant laser secondary neutral mass spectrometry. *Spectrochim. Acta B* **2022**, *190*, 106377. [CrossRef]
26. King, G.C.; Read, F.H.; Imhof, R.E. The measurement of molecular lifetimes by the photon-photon delayed coincidence method. *J. Phys. B* **1975**, *8*, 665–673. [CrossRef]
27. Schneider, F.; Chrysalidis, K.; Dorrer, H.; Düllmann, C.E.; Eberhardt, K.; Haas, R.; Kieck, T.; Mokry, C.; Naubereit, P.; Schmidt, S.; et al. Resonance ionization of holmium for ion implantation in microcalorimeters. *Nucl. Instrum. Methods Phys. Res. B* **2016**, *376*, 388–392. [CrossRef]
28. Fano, U. Effects of configuration interaction on intensities and phase shifts. *Phys. Rev.* **1961**, *124*, 1866–1878. [CrossRef]
29. Fano, U.; Theodosiou, C.E.; Dehmer, J.L. Electron-optical properties of atomic fields. *Rev. Mod. Phys.* **1976**, *48*, 49–68. [CrossRef]
30. Birge, R.T. Probable values of the general physical constants. *Rev. Mod. Phys.* **1929**, *1*, 1–73. [CrossRef]
31. Bodnar, O.; Elster, C. On the adjustment of inconsistent data using the Birge ratio. *Metrologia* **2014**, *51*, 516–521. [CrossRef]

Article

Advancing Radiation-Detected Resonance Ionization towards Heavier Elements and More Exotic Nuclides

Jessica Warbinek [1,2,*], Brankica Anđelić [1,3,4], Michael Block [1,2,4], Premaditya Chhetri [1,4], Arno Claessens [5], Rafael Ferrer [5], Francesca Giacoppo [1,4], Oliver Kaleja [1,6], Tom Kieck [1,4], EunKang Kim [2], Mustapha Laatiaoui [2], Jeremy Lantis [2], Andrew Mistry [1,7], Danny Münzberg [1,2,4], Steven Nothhelfer [1,2,4], Sebastian Raeder [1,4], Emmanuel Rey-Herme [8], Elisabeth Rickert [1,2,4], Jekabs Romans [5], Elisa Romero-Romero [2], Marine Vandebrouck [8], Piet Van Duppen [5] and Thomas Walther [9]

1. Abteilung Superschwere Elemente Physik, GSI Helmholtzzentrum für Schwerionenforschung, 64291 Darmstadt, Germany; andjelicbrankica@gmail.com (B.A.); m.block@gsi.de (M.B.); premaditya.chhetri@kuleuven.be (P.C.); f.giacoppo@gsi.de (F.G.); o.kaleja@gsi.de (O.K.); tomkieck@uni-mainz.de (T.K.); a.k.mistry@gsi.de (A.M.); dmuenzbe@students.uni-mainz.de (D.M.); nothhelfer@uni-mainz.de (S.N.); s.raeder@gsi.de (S.R.); e.rickert@uni-mainz.de (E.R.)
2. Department Chemie—Standort TRIGA, Johannes Gutenberg-Universität Mainz, 55099 Mainz, Germany; eukim@uni-mainz.de (E.K.); mlaatiao@uni-mainz.de (M.L.); jlantis@uni-mainz.de (J.L.); eromeror@uni-mainz.de (E.R.-R.)
3. Faculty of Science and Engineering, University of Groningen, 9747 AG Groningen, The Netherlands
4. Sektion Superschwere Elemente Physik, Helmholtz Institut Mainz, 55099 Mainz, Germany
5. Department of Physics and Astronomy, KU Leuven, 3000 Leuven, Belgium; arno.claessens@kuleuven.be (A.C.); rafael.ferrer@kuleuven.be (R.F.); jekabs.romans@kuleuven.be (J.R.); piet.vanduppen@kuleuven.be (P.V.D.)
6. Institut für Physik, Universität Greifswald, 17489 Greifswald, Germany
7. Institut für Kernphysik, Technische Universität Darmstadt, 64289 Darmstadt, Germany
8. Irfu, CEA, Université Paris-Saclay, 91191 Gif-sur-Yvette, France; emmanuel.rey-herme@cea.fr (E.R.-H.); marine.vandebrouck@cea.fr (M.V.)
9. Institut für Angewandte Physik, Technische Universität Darmstadt, 64289 Darmstadt, Germany; thomas.walther@physik.tu-darmstadt.de
* Correspondence: j.warbinek@gsi.de

Citation: Warbinek, J.; Anđelić, B.; Block, M.; Chhetri, P.; Claessens, A.; Ferrer, R.; Giacoppo, F.; Kaleja, O.; Kieck, T.; Kim, E.; et al. Advancing Radiation-Detected Resonance Ionization towards Heavier Elements and More Exotic Nuclides. *Atoms* **2022**, *10*, 41. https://doi.org/10.3390/atoms10020041

Academic Editor: Alexander Kramida

Received: 28 March 2022
Accepted: 13 April 2022
Published: 21 April 2022

Publisher's Note: MDPI stays neutral with regard to jurisdictional claims in published maps and institutional affiliations.

Copyright: © 2022 by the authors. Licensee MDPI, Basel, Switzerland. This article is an open access article distributed under the terms and conditions of the Creative Commons Attribution (CC BY) license (https://creativecommons.org/licenses/by/4.0/).

Abstract: RAdiation-Detected Resonance Ionization Spectroscopy (RADRIS) is a versatile method for highly sensitive laser spectroscopy studies of the heaviest actinides. Most of these nuclides need to be produced at accelerator facilities in fusion-evaporation reactions and are studied immediately after their production and separation from the primary beam due to their short half-lives and low production rates of only a few atoms per second or less. Only recently, the first laser spectroscopic investigation of nobelium ($Z = 102$) was performed by applying the RADRIS technique in a buffer-gas-filled stopping cell at the GSI in Darmstadt, Germany. To expand this technique to other nobelium isotopes and for the search for atomic levels in the heaviest actinide element, lawrencium ($Z = 103$), the sensitivity of the RADRIS setup needed to be further improved. Therefore, a new movable double-detector setup was developed, which enhances the overall efficiency by approximately 65 % compared to the previously used single-detector setup. Further development work was performed to enable the study of longer-lived ($t_{1/2} > 1\,\mathrm{h}$) and shorter-lived nuclides ($t_{1/2} < 1\,\mathrm{s}$) with the RADRIS method. With a new rotatable multi-detector design, the long-lived isotope ^{254}Fm ($t_{1/2} = 3.2\,\mathrm{h}$) becomes within reach for laser spectroscopy. Upcoming experiments will also tackle the short-lived isotope ^{251}No ($t_{1/2} = 0.8\,\mathrm{s}$) by applying a newly implemented short RADRIS measurement cycle.

Keywords: laser spectroscopy; resonance ionization; atomic level scheme; gas cell; radiation detection; heavy actinides

1. Introduction

The study of the heaviest elements of the actinide series has recently gained much interest in the field of modern laser-based physics research [1]. Relativistic effects strongly influence the electronic configurations of these exotic elements, altering their atomic and chemical properties. Laser spectroscopy constitutes a powerful tool to study these effects, for example by measuring the ionization potential (IP) or by probing the atomic-level structure and optical transitions. Experimental data can benchmark theoretical predictions obtained through many-body methods such as relativistic coupled-cluster (RCC), the multi-configuration Dirac–Fock (MCDF), and the configuration interaction (CI) calculations [2]. In addition, laser spectroscopy can give access to nuclear structure observables, e.g., nuclear spin and nuclear moments or changes in the nuclear mean square charge radii, to validate and guide theoretical studies as for instance in the region of the heaviest elements around the $N = 152$ neutron shell closure [3].

To study these heavy elements, synthetic production of respective atoms is necessary as they do not naturally occur on earth. While the actinides up to fermium ($Z = 100$) can still be produced in macroscopic sample sizes from breeding processes in nuclear reactors [4], the transfermium elements ($Z > 100$) are exclusively produced in atom-at-a-time quantities in fusion-evaporation reactions at large-scale accelerator facilities. Therefore, measurements of their atomic properties are very challenging. Some of these properties can, for instance, be determined in gas- and liquid-phase chemistry experiments [5,6]. Only recently, the IPs of the heaviest actinides, ranging from fermium to lawrencium ($Z = 103$), were determined via a surface-ionization technique to meV precision [7,8]. However, the present accuracy of the IPs is limited by the applied technique, whereas the determination by laser spectroscopy can result in orders-of-magnitude higher precision. As of today, the heaviest element investigated by means of laser spectroscopy is the actinide element nobelium ($Z = 102$) [9]. The first ionization potential of this element was determined with a 50 µeV accuracy [10] to benchmark atomic theory and to probe relativistic effects on this property in the range of the heaviest elements.

The study of transfermium elements via common laser spectroscopy techniques such as collinear laser spectroscopy [11] or the hot-cavity technique [12] is often unfeasible. Due to the low production yield of only a few nuclei per second at most and the short half-lives, the application of laser spectroscopy requires a fast and extremely sensitive probing of the produced particles directly after their separation from the primary beam. The RAdiation-Detected Resonance Ionization Spectroscopy (RADRIS) method [13,14] is dedicated to the study of exotic, heavy elements, and was successfully applied to find a ground-state transition in nobelium [9].

To date, an isotopic chain of nobelium isotopes ranging from mass numbers 252 to 254 has been investigated by this method [15]. For the study of short-lived nuclides with half-lives of $t_{1/2} < 1\,\mathrm{s}$ such as the isotope ^{251}No ($t_{1/2} = 0.8\,\mathrm{s}$), additional improvements are required due to significant decay losses expected in the measurement scheme. Further limitations appear for nuclides with half-lives of $t_{1/2} > 1\,\mathrm{h}$. Moreover, a gain in the RADRIS efficiency could in general be decisive to identify resonance signals in future experiments such as for the search of yet experimentally undetermined atomic levels in elements heavier than nobelium.

Recent developments address these current limitations in terms of the range of accessible nuclides and the overall RADRIS efficiency. Here, the latest advances towards laser spectroscopy of longer-lived and shorter-lived transfermium nuclides are discussed, and corresponding results from on-line test experiments are presented. Additional development work towards an enhanced efficiency of RADRIS for the search for atomic levels in the heaviest actinide, lawrencium, will also be outlined.

2. Experimental Setup

2.1. RADRIS Technique

The RADRIS experimental setup consists of a stopping cell attached to the velocity filter SHIP at the GSI in Darmstadt [13,16]. A schematic drawing of the RADRIS setup is shown in Figure 1a. Recoil nuclei transmitted through the velocity filter enter the gas cell through an entrance window of 3.5 µm thin aluminum-coated mylar foil, supported by a stainless steel grid, and are stopped in 90 mbar argon buffer gas. A 1 mm × 25 µm Hf-strip filament positioned opposite the entrance window and biased with an attractive voltage allows collecting incoming ions which adsorb and neutralize on the filament surface. By resistive pulse-heating of the filament, collected fusion products are re-evaporated to form a cloud of neutral atoms in the vicinity of the filament. Here, the evaporation temperature is critical for an efficient desorption paired with a minimum ion background from surface ionization processes. For an optimal filament choice, the IP of the collected atom species, the work function of the filament material, and the filament temperature are key parameters to be considered. A more detailed description of the desorption from filaments can be found in [17].

After the successful evaporation from the filament, the created neutral atoms are illuminated with two lasers following a two-step resonance ionization spectroscopy (RIS) scheme. Here, a UV-pumped dye laser supplies the first excitation step while the second, non-resonant step for ionization is provided by a high-power excimer or Nd:YAG laser. Resulting laser ions are then guided via suitable electric fields towards the detection area where they are collected on a 200 nm thin aluminized kapton foil in front of a Passivated Implanted Planar Silicon (PIPS) detector. Finally, the laser-ionized fusion products are detected via their alpha-decay energy. In this way, registered signals can additionally be gated by their characteristic decay energy to discriminate contributions of decay signals from background ions and subsequent decays of daughter nuclides.

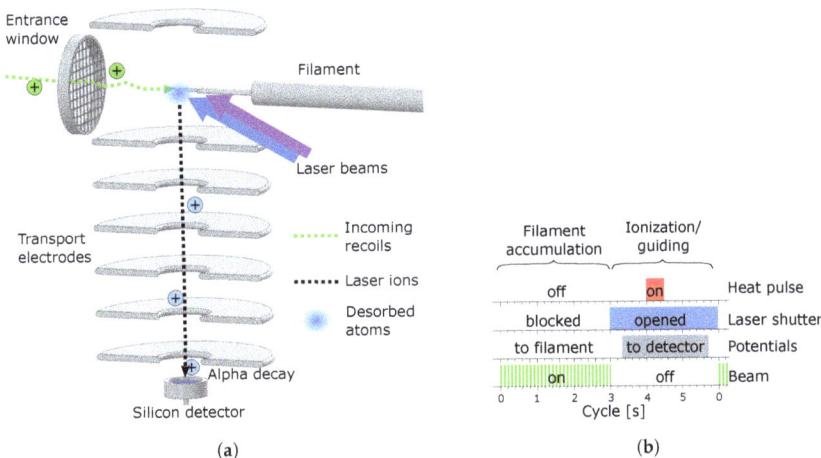

Figure 1. (a) Schematic drawing of the RADRIS setup. Incoming fusion products (green) enter the gas cell through the entrance window and thermalize in the 90 mbar argon buffer-gas environment. The recoils are collected on a Hf-strip filament, where they adsorb and neutralize. After desorption by pulse-heating the filament, an atomic cloud (blue) is formed around the filament which is illuminated with two lasers following a two-step RIS scheme. Resulting laser ions (blue) are guided towards a silicon detector by applying suitable transport electrode potentials where they are detected via their characteristic alpha-decay energy. (b) Previously applied RADRIS cycle for resonance ionization spectroscopy of ^{155}Yb. Delays between blocking the beam and changing the potentials, as well as applying the filament heat-pulse, are chosen to allow settling down of the stopped recoil ions and complete switching of the voltages, respectively [13].

2.2. RADRIS Measurement Cycle

The application of the RADRIS technique is cyclic, where each cycle is divided into the filament accumulation mode and the ionization/guiding mode. In the accumulation mode, fusion products enter the gas cell and are collected on the filament by applying an attractive potential compared to the surrounding electrodes and the chamber itself [13]. After the accumulation is completed, the setup is switched to the ionization/guiding mode in which the incoming primary beam is stopped, the laser shutters are opened to expose the stopping volume to laser light, and the potentials are set such that the created laser ions are guided towards the silicon detector. To change between the two modes, electrostatic potentials applied to the chamber, the filament, and the transport electrodes surrounding the filament need to be switched by giving an analog trigger to the power supplies after the primary beam is stopped. A time of approximately 0.3 s is required for the potentials to reach the set values. After switching the potentials, the filament is pulse-heated to desorb collected fusion products followed by laser ionization. Before starting the next cycle and unblocking the primary beam, both laser shutters are closed and the potentials are switched back for the next accumulation on the filament.

To ensure an optimum duty cycle, the beam break in the cycle should be as short as possible. However, the exact timing of the potential switching in the cycle is crucial to prevent any direct transport of incoming, positively charged fusion products onto the detector creating a background count rate independent of any laser interaction. Therefore, a delay of 0.3 s between beam blocking and the potential switching is considered in the cycle. An additional delay of 0.7 s between the switch of the potentials and pulse-heating the filament ensures a completed change to the guiding mode before the filament has reached the desorption temperature towards the end of the heat pulse. A typical RADRIS cycle for resonance ionization of incoming ^{155}Yb fusion products ($t_{1/2}$ =1.8 s) is shown in Figure 1b. For this isotope, the cycle features an accumulation on the filament for the accelerator beam-on period of 3 s and a beam break of 3 s.

3. New Detector Developments

The total RADRIS efficiency, which corresponds to the ratio of detected laser ions and incoming fusion products, does not only depend on the transport efficiency and the detection efficiency, but also on the duty cycle due to the cyclic application of the RADRIS technique. In the current setup, the detection efficiency is limited to 40% due to the covered solid angle by the detector for alpha decay on the foil [13]. For short-lived nuclides and respective short cycles, additional losses due to radioactive decay reduce the overall efficiency and hamper the study of nuclides with half-lives $t_{1/2} < 1$ s. For long-lived nuclides on the other hand, longer beam breaks after a completed measurement point are necessary, reducing the duty cycle and efficient beamtime usage. Thus, the RADRIS cycle needs to be adapted for each isotope depending on its half-life [18]. New developments were initiated to improve the overall efficiency for the application of RADRIS to different nuclides.

3.1. Rotatable Detector Setup

In the previously used design of the RADRIS setup [13], each measurement point required a waiting time long enough to detect subsequent decays of resonantly ionized products collected on the detector. To allow for a more efficient usage of beamtime when longer-lived (>1 h) nuclides are studied, a rotatable multi-detector setup was developed. This setup enables to parallelize multiple measurements on long-lived nuclides by decoupling the collection phase on the detector from the measurements of subsequent alpha decays. The new design combines three identical PIPS detectors with an active area of 450 mm^2 on a rotatable feedthrough, as shown in the schematic drawing in Figure 2a. The three detectors are positioned such that one of these detectors is placed on-axis with the transport electrodes to collect generated laser ions (the collection mode), while the other detectors are positioned off-axis to register residual alpha activity on their surfaces (the detection mode). After the collection is concluded on the on-axis detector, the detector setup is rotated such that the next detector is in the collection mode, now for laser ions produced by light of the excitation laser tuned to the next wavelength.

In this new setup, recoil ions are directly guided onto the detectors without an additional collection foil in front. In this way, the detection efficiency for each detector can be increased from 40% to 50%. The increased tailing in the alpha spectra due to the decay of collected nuclides on the detector surface itself does not impact alpha signals from decays that differ by more than 0.25 MeV, as can be seen in the spectrum in Figure 2a.

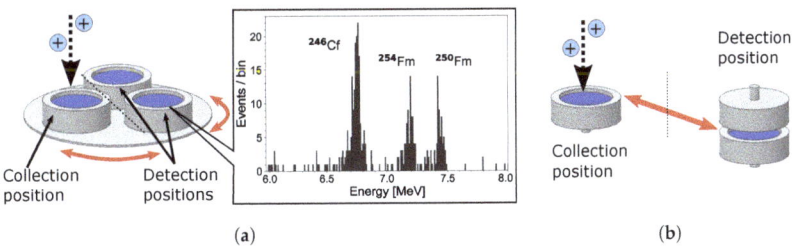

Figure 2. (**a**) Schematic drawing of the rotatable RADRIS detector setup. Laser ions (blue) are guided towards the PIPS detector in on-axis position in the collection mode. For the next collection, the detectors are rotated such that the next detector is placed on-axis with the chamber. Subsequent decays on the prior collection detector are registered in an off-axis detection position. An alpha spectrum on one of the detectors is shown for accumulated ^{254}Fm RIS signals of a measurement time of approximately 5 days. (**b**) Schematic drawing of the movable double-detector setup. Laser ions (blue) are guided towards the on-axis PIPS detector in the collection mode. For the detection mode, the detector is moved on top of a second PIPS detector to detect alphas emitted in the hemisphere opposite the active area of the collection detector.

The new detector arrangement was recently commissioned and tested in a first on-line laser spectroscopy of ^{254}Fm with a half-life of 3.2 h. These data are still under analysis and will be published independently. Figure 2a includes accumulated alpha spectra of the ^{254}Fm laser ions on one of the three detectors. With only a single detector, approximately one day per scan step of the excitation laser was expected to be required, while using the rotatable detector setup shortened the measurement time per detector and wavelength step to only seven hours. The resulting time gain allowed performing this experiment in 5.5 days with parasitic beam (5 ms long beam pulses with a repetition rate of 5 Hz) from the UNILAC accelerator at the GSI.

3.2. Movable Detector Setup

New challenges for the RADRIS technique arise when applying it to heavier and more exotic nuclei for which an enhancement in the overall efficiency can be of utmost importance. One of these challenges is the search for atomic levels in lawrencium, as for instance the production yield of ^{255}Lr ($\approx$437 nb) is approximately one order of magnitude lower than for ^{254}No ($\approx$2050 nb) [19,20] which was previously investigated for the search for atomic levels in nobelium [9]. In addition, predicted atomic levels accessible for laser spectroscopy range from 20,000 to 30,000 cm^{-1} [21–25], which would require an extended measurement time to identify a first atomic level. Thus, a combination of an enhancement in the sensitivity and efficiency of the detection method will benefit the search for atomic energy levels. To enhance the applicability of the RADRIS technique, a new setup with a movable detector was designed as shown in Figure 2b. This new detector system includes a double-PIPS detector setup, where both detectors have an active area of 600 mm^2. The collection PIPS detector is placed on rails, enabling the movement of this detector between an on-axis position for laser ion collection and an off-axis position located on top of the second detector, where the active areas of both detectors face each other. The swap between both positions occurs via a fast pneumatically-coupled linear feedthrough with a 50 mm stroke in less than 1 s. During accumulation on the filament for a next wavelength step, the collection detector is moved to rest on top of the second PIPS. The efficiency of detecting the alpha decay of collected nuclei is hence increased, as usually approximately 50% of the alphas emitted in the hemisphere opposite the active detector area would be lost. In this constellation, the second detector with a distance of approximately 4 mm between both active areas increases the rate of detected events. More than 65% of the fraction of alpha events seen by the collection detector can now be detected with the additional detector, which would usually be missed.

For future experiments on longer-lived species, the movable and rotatable detector designs can be combined by adding detectors opposite to those detectors in the detection mode on the rotatable setup.

4. Short RADRIS Cycle Development

With typical RADRIS cycles, laser spectroscopic investigations on short-lived nuclides ($t_{1/2} < 1$ s) are not feasible due to radioactive decay losses. Therefore, a new RADRIS cycle scheme for such nuclides was developed and applied to ^{154}Yb in recent on-line measurements. This isotope with a half-life of only $t_{1/2} = 0.4$ s and a relatively high production rate compared to the heavy actinides represents an ideal test case for the application of RADRIS to short-lived nuclei. This nuclide is produced in complete fusion-evaporation reactions of a ^{48}Ca beam at a beam energy of 4.55 MeV u^{-1} on a ^{112}Sn target in the ^{112}Sn(^{48}Ca,6n)^{154}Yb reaction channel at the SHIP separator. Figure 3a shows the alpha-decay spectrum of produced nuclides in this reaction after direct transport to a single PIPS detector. In addition to ^{154}Yb, other isotopes such as ^{155,156}Yb, and other radionuclides are present in the alpha spectrum as shown in Figure 3b, as different evaporation channels exist for the de-excitation of the compound nucleus ^{160}Yb*. In addition, decay daughters with significant alpha-branching ratios along the decay chains are present. As these nuclides from different evaporation channels have similar velocities, the velocity filter SHIP transports them to the focal plane. Thus, measured alpha-decay signals need to be carefully gated according to the respective alpha-decay energies for unambiguous identification.

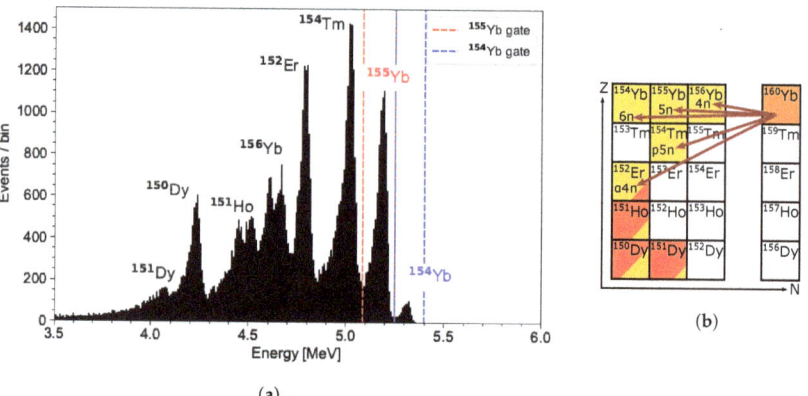

Figure 3. (a) Alpha spectrum of indirectly and directly produced nuclei in the ^{48}Ca+^{112}Sn fusion-evaporation reaction guided directly onto the PIPS detector after stopping inside of the gas cell. The signal strengths mostly reflect the respective production cross sections. Additionally, decay losses during ion transport through the gas cell impact the signal strength especially of the short-lived ^{154}Yb. Data for this spectrum were collected for 50 min with parasitic beam of 5 ms long beam pulses with a repetition rate of 5 Hz from the UNILAC accelerator at the GSI. (b) Observed evaporation channels of the ^{48}Ca+^{112}Sn fusion-evaporation reaction for a beam energy of 4.55 MeV u^{-1}. Shown are products and the subsequent daughter nuclides decaying via alpha decay which are mainly observed in the experiment.

To systematically understand the limitations of the cycles in terms of ion mobility in the gas cell, the transport time of ^{154}Yb through the cell to the detector was investigated. Therefore, reaction products were created during 5 ms long pulses of the UNILAC accelerator with a repetition rate of 1 Hz and entered the RADRIS gas cell, where they were stopped and transported directly to the detector. Figure 4a shows the time evolution of energy-gated and time-binned alpha events of ^{154}Yb as a function of the cycle time. Due to the limited mobility [6,26] of the Yb ions in the argon buffer gas, the ions reach the detector with a certain delay. The stopping distribution of the recoils in the gas cell [27] in addition to diffusion processes lead to an increased width of the distribution of the ions' arrival time at the detector. To determine the time required for the ions to reach the detector, one has to solve the differential equation describing the increasing number of ^{154}Yb ions on the detector after every accelerator beam pulse with respect to their successive decay as

$$\frac{dN}{dt} = A \cdot e^{\frac{-(t-t_c)^2}{(2 \cdot w^2)}} - \lambda \cdot N,$$

and fit the obtained solution for $N(t)$ to the measured distribution in Figure 4a. Here, N describes the number of ions, A the amplitude of the distribution, t the cycle time, t_c the center of the time distribution, w its width, and $\lambda = \frac{\ln(2)}{t_{1/2}}$ the decay constant of ^{154}Yb. For this model, a Gaussian time distribution for the ions reaching the detector was assumed. The transport time, defined as the time required for 84.13% of the ions in the arrival-time distribution to reach the detector (corresponding to the centroid t_c of the distribution plus $1w$), was determined to be 0.33 s in argon buffer gas at a pressure of 90 mbar and a potential gradient of approximately 29 V/cm from the filament to ground potential on the detector.

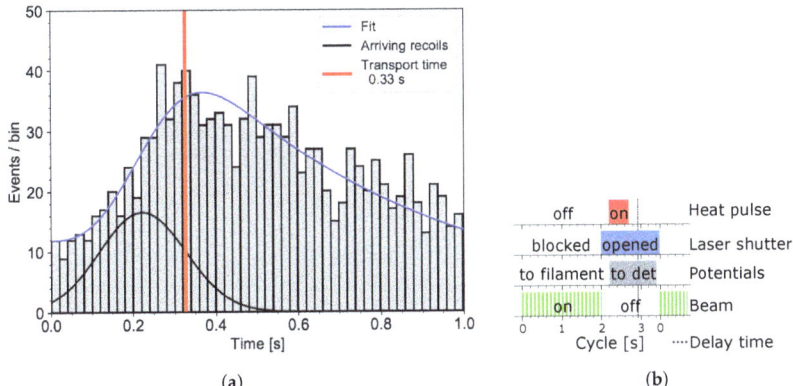

Figure 4. (a) Time structure of decay signals from incoming nuclei produced by 5 ms pulses from the accelerator with a repetition rate of 1 Hz. The incoming ions were directly transported to the detector. The transport time marked in red is determined as the time needed for 84.13% of the ions within the assumed Gaussian time distribution (black) to arrive on the detector. For more details, see text. (b) New, short RADRIS cycle for resonance ionization spectroscopy of ^{154}Yb. The overall cycle, as well as the beam break and the delay between beam stop and potential switch were generously shortened. The delay time between stopping of the accelerator beam and arrival of laser ions is marked in the cycle and needs to be considered for further decay losses.

Taking this boundary condition into account, a short RADRIS cycle as shown in Figure 4b was implemented. A simplified, faster configuration was tested in which only the filament potential is switched instead of switching the potential of multiple transport electrodes. To speed up the filament potential switching, a fast high-voltage switch (Behlke GHTS) was used, enabling a switching time of a few ms. With this rapid switching, the new, short RADRIS cycle features a waiting time between the potential switch and the pulse-heating of the filament reduced to 0.2 s to allow settling down of the stopped recoil ions, thus reducing further decay losses. With this modification and the new potential configuration for ion accumulation on the filament, no additional losses in the ion transport were observed.

To determine the RADRIS efficiency with the short cycle, the short-lived ^{154}Yb was resonantly laser-ionized together with the neighboring, longer-lived ^{155}Yb. Hereby, the ratio of ^{154}Yb/^{155}Yb was measured to be $R = 7.40(16)\%$ in the focal plane [28] as can be seen also in the alpha spectrum in Figure 3a. For laser spectroscopy of both isotopes, a two-step RIS scheme as shown in Figure 5b was employed. A grating dye laser was deployed in broadband configuration with approximately 6 GHz linewidth for the first excitation step (FES). The second excitation step (SES) was provided by a high-power excimer laser. By discriminating the registered alpha-decay energies, laser-induced signals stemming from the two investigated Yb isotopes could be individually identified.

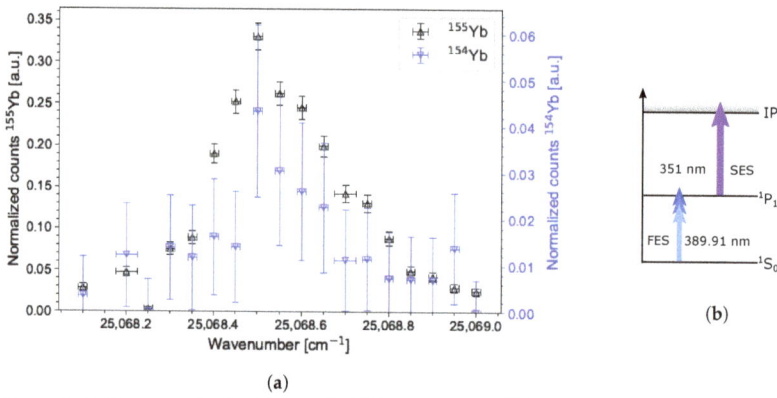

Figure 5. (a) Resonance ionization signal of ^{155}Yb (black) and ^{154}Yb (blue). Both rates are normalized to their respective count rates for a direct transport of produced recoil nuclei per accumulated charge integral of the primary beam. (b) RIS scheme for laser spectroscopy of ^{154,155}Yb. The first excitation step was provided by a dye laser, the second, non-resonant step for ionization by a high-power excimer laser.

5. Results with the Short RADRIS Cycle Implementation

For characterization of the short cycle, results from laser spectroscopy of the short-lived ^{154}Yb isotope were compared with those obtained for ^{155}Yb, providing information on the RIS efficiency for ytterbium isotopes of different half-lives. The energy-gated alpha-decay signal in dependence of the wavenumber of the FES is shown in Figure 5a, and the applied RIS scheme is presented in Figure 5b. The RIS count rates of ^{154}Yb and ^{155}Yb were normalized to the primary-beam integral for comparison with the respective rate of guiding ions directly to the detector. With the short cycle, it was possible to detect ^{154}Yb from resonant laser ionization for the first time. The limited resolution in the gas cell [27] did not allow resolving the hyperfine structure of three expected hyperfine components in ^{155}Yb with a nuclear spin of $I = 7/2$. In addition, the expected isotope shift of around 1 GHz [29–32] is much smaller compared to the spectral linewidth of the FES laser of approximately 6 GHz and has therefore not been properly determined with the available statistics. Due to the large linewidth, the expected hyperfine splitting has not been observed to additionally contribute to the broadening of the resonance.

To determine the respective RIS efficiency, a Gaussian fit was applied to both isotope spectra to extract the maximum normalized count rate on resonance. From the ratio of the obtained RIS signal rate to the signal rate from direct transport to the detector, a half-life-dependent efficiency was determined, which is depicted in Figure 6 as black symbols. In addition to ^{154,155}Yb, also the nuclides ^{254}No ($t_{1/2} = 51.2$ s) and ^{252}No ($t_{1/2} = 2.46$ s) were investigated with respect to RIS and direct transport count rates on the detector and respective efficiencies added to the results in Figure 6. It has to be noted that for ^{252}No and ^{254}No different cycles, optimized for the respective half-lives, were applied.

To conclude if the experimentally determined efficiency dependence is fully governed by the expected decay losses and to exclude additional losses due to other effects, the total efficiency ϵ_{Cycle} of the different cycles was calculated analogously to [18]. Decay losses during accumulation on the filament and the overall usage of beamtime were considered by using the equation

$$\epsilon_{\text{Cycle}} = \frac{t_{1/2}}{(t_{\text{beam}} + t_{\text{break}}) \cdot \ln(2)} \left[1 - e^{\frac{-\ln(2)}{t_{1/2}} \cdot t_{\text{beam}}} \right] \cdot e^{\frac{-\ln(2)}{t_{1/2}} \cdot t_{\text{delay}}}.$$

Here, $t_{1/2}$ is the half-life of the considered nuclide, t_{beam} (2 s in the case of the short cycle) is the beam-on time which equals the accumulation time on the filament, t_{break} (1.5 s for the short cycle) is the time of the beam break. For the calculation, a continuous production during the accumulation phase was assumed, followed by a decay of the collected population with the respective half-life. Additional losses during the beam break are considered by the last exponential function with $t_{\text{delay}} = 0.93$ s being the time between the beam shutoff and the ions reaching the detector in their required transport time after the desorption and resonant ionization. The calculated efficiencies for the respective cycles and nuclide half-lives are shown as red symbols in Figure 6. As the trend is of most importance in the comparison of experimental with calculated values, both values for ^{254}No were chosen to coincide in the graph. From the observed trend it becomes clear that the experimental behavior is fully described by decay losses. This enables forecasting the RADRIS performance for other exotic cases such as the isotope ^{251}No, for which a RIS-to-direct transport ratio of 0.053 was calculated for the new short cycle of 3.5 s duration with a break of 1.5 s shown in Figure 4b.

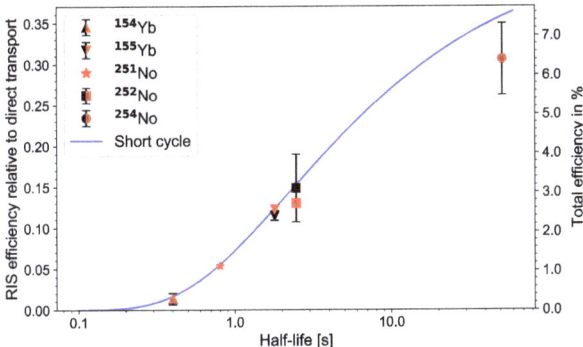

Figure 6. Comparison of efficiencies for rates of laser ions (with the laser frequency tuned on resonance) relative to direct transport rates. Experimentally determined efficiencies are shown in black. Red data points show estimated efficiencies of the RADRIS cycles in relation to the experimental RIS efficiency of ^{254}No. Overall efficiencies of the RADRIS setup are added with the right scale considering the known efficiency for ^{254}No [9].

From previous experiments on ^{254}No and ^{252}No, the total efficiency of the setup is known as number of detected laser ions in resonance relative to the number of respective recoil ions in the focal plane. The overall efficiencies were previously determined to 6.4% ± 1.0% and 3.3% ± 1.0% for ^{254}No and ^{252}No, respectively [9]. Comparing the expectation values for ^{251}No to ^{254}No, a total efficiency of 1.1% is expected for the performance of the setup with the short cycle. For a future RADRIS experiment on the nobelium isotope ^{251}No, with a production cross section of 30 nb [19], a RIS signal rate of approximately 2.5 ions per hour can be expected.

6. Conclusions and Outlook

Different aspects in improving the performance of the RADRIS technique were investigated in this work. A new rotatable detector assembly was successfully commissioned, extending the half-life range of nuclides accessible by RADRIS to half-lives of at least 3 h. With the newly implemented short RADRIS cycle, short-lived nuclides with half-lives of less than 1 s can now be studied, which was demonstrated on the short-lived isotope ^{154}Yb with $t_{1/2} = 0.4$ s. From comparison with calculations, the expected efficiency for the application of this new cycle to ^{251}No is sufficient to allow the first optical spectroscopy of this isotope. Further upcoming experiments will focus on the search for atomic levels in lawrencium, for which the newly developed movable double-detector design features an efficiency gain with the second detector giving a decisive benefit. For future experiments, a re-designed transport electrode structure in combination with the double-detector setup will soon be commissioned in the upcoming beamtimes at the GSI to further boost the overall efficiency of the RADRIS technique.

Author Contributions: Conceptualization, J.W., B.A., M.B., P.C., A.C., R.F., F.G., O.K., T.K., E.K., M.L., J.L., A.M., D.M., S.N., S.R., E.R.-H., E.R., J.R., E.R.-R., M.V., P.V.D. and T.W.; methodology, J.W., M.B., P.C., T.K., M.L. and S.R.; investigation, J.W., B.A., M.B., P.C., R.F., F.G., O.K., E.K., M.L., J.L., D.M., S.N., S.R., E.R.-H., E.R. and E.R.-R.; software, P.C.; formal analysis, J.W. and S.R.; data curation, J.W. and S.R.; writing—original draft preparation, J.W.; writing—review and editing, M.B. and S.R.; visualization, J.W.; supervision, M.B. and S.R.; project administration, M.B. and S.R.; funding acquisition, M.B., P.V.D. and T.W. All authors have read and agreed to the published version of the manuscript.

Funding: This work has been supported by the Bundesministerium für Bildung und Forschung (BMBF, Germany) under Project No. 05P18UMCIA. This project has received funding from the European Union's Horizon 2020 research and innovation programme under grant agreement No 861198–LISA–H2020-MSCA-ITN-2019. E.K., E.R.-R. and M.L. acknowledge funding from the European Research Council (ERC) under the European Union's Horizon 2020 Research and Innovation Programme (Grant Agreement No. 819957). P.V.D., A.C., R.F. and J.R. acknowledge funding from the Research Foundation – Flanders (FWO) and from the EOS (nr. 30468642) project of the FWO and F.R.S.-FNRS under the Excellence of Science (EOS) programme. T.W. acknowledges funding from the Bundesministerium für Bildung und Forschung (BMBF, Germany) under grant number 05P21RDFN1.

Data Availability Statement: The data presented in this study are available on request from the corresponding author.

Conflicts of Interest: The authors declare no conflict of interest.

Abbreviations

The following abbreviations are used in this manuscript:

RADRIS	RAdiation-Detected Resonance Ionization Spectroscopy
IP	Ionization Potential
RCC	Relativistic Coupled-Cluster
MCDF	Multi-Configuration Dirac–Fock
CI	Configuration Interaction
SHIP	Separator for Heavy Ion reaction Products
UNILAC	Universal Linear Accelerator
UV	Ultraviolet
SES	Second Excitation Step
FES	First Excitation Step
RIS	Resonance Ionization Spectroscopy
PIPS	Passivated Implanted Planar Silicon

References

1. Block, M.; Laatiaoui, M.; Raeder, S. Recent progress in laser spectroscopy of the actinides. *Prog. Part. Nucl. Phys.* **2021**, *116*, 103834.
2. Eliav, E.; Fritzsche, S.; Kaldor, U. Electronic structure theory of the superheavy elements. *Nucl. Phys. A* **2015**, *944*, 518–550.
3. Campbell, P.; Moore, I.; Pearson, M. Laser spectroscopy for nuclear structure physics. *Prog. Part. Nucl. Phys.* **2016**, *86*, 127–180.
4. Robinson, S.M.; Benker, D.E.; Collins, E.D.; Ezold, J.G.; Garrison, J.R.; Hogle, S.L. Production of Cf-252 and other transplutonium isotopes at Oak Ridge National Laboratory. *Radiochim. Acta* **2020**, *108*, 737–746.
5. Schädel, M.; Shaughnessy, D. *The Chemistry of Superheavy Elements*; Springer: Berlin/Heidelberg, Germany, 2013.
6. Backe, H.; Lauth, W.; Block, M.; Laatiaoui, M. Prospects for laser spectroscopy, ion chemistry and mobility measurements of superheavy elements in buffer-gas traps. *Nucl. Phys. A* **2015**, *944*, 492–517.
7. Sato, T.; Asai, M.; Borschevsky, A.; Stora, T.; Sato, N.; Kaneya, Y.; Tsukada, K.; Düllmann, C.E.; Eberhardt, K.; Eliav, E.; et al. Measurement of the first ionization potential of lawrencium, element 103. *Nature* **2015**, *520*, 209–211.
8. Sato, T.K.; Asai, M.; Borschevsky, A.; Beerwerth, R.; Kaneya, Y.; Makii, H.; Mitsukai, A.; Nagame, Y.; Osa, A.; Toyoshima, A.; et al. First ionization potentials of Fm, Md, No, and Lr: Verification of filling-up of 5f electrons and confirmation of the actinide series. *J. Am. Chem. Soc.* **2018**, *140*, 14609–14613.
9. Laatiaoui, M.; Lauth, W.; Backe, H.; Block, M.; Ackermann, D.; Cheal, B.; Chhetri, P.; Düllmann, C.E.; Van Duppen, P.; Even, J.; et al. Atom-at-a-time laser resonance ionization spectroscopy of nobelium. *Nature* **2016**, *538*, 495–498.
10. Chhetri, P.; Ackermann, D.; Backe, H.; Block, M.; Cheal, B.; Droese, C.; Düllmann, C.E.; Even, J.; Ferrer, R.; Giacoppo, F.; et al. Precision measurement of the first ionization potential of nobelium. *Phys. Rev. Lett.* **2018**, *120*, 263003.
11. Neugart, R.; Billowes, J.; Bissell, M.; Blaum, K.; Cheal, B.; Flanagan, K.; Neyens, G.; Nörtershäuser, W.; Yordanov, D. Collinear laser spectroscopy at ISOLDE: New methods and highlights. *J. Phys. G Nucl. Part. Phys.* **2017**, *44*, 064002.
12. Fedosseev, V.; Chrysalidis, K.; Goodacre, T.D.; Marsh, B.; Rothe, S.; Seiffert, C.; Wendt, K. Ion beam production and study of radioactive isotopes with the laser ion source at ISOLDE. *J. Phys. G Nucl. Part. Phys.* **2017**, *44*, 084006.
13. Lautenschläger, F.; Chhetri, P.; Ackermann, D.; Backe, H.; Block, M.; Cheal, B.; Clark, A.; Droese, C.; Ferrer, R.; Giacoppo, F.; et al. Developments for resonance ionization laser spectroscopy of the heaviest elements at SHIP. *Nucl. Instrum. Methods Phys. Res. Sect. B Beam Interact. Mater. At.* **2016**, *383*, 115–122.
14. Backe, H.; Kunz, P.; Lauth, W.; Dretzke, A.; Horn, R.; Kolb, T.; Laatiaoui, M.; Sewtz, M.; Ackermann, D.; Block, M.; et al. Towards optical spectroscopy of the element nobelium (Z = 102) in a buffer gas cell. *Eur. Phys. J. D* **2007**, *45*, 99–106.
15. Raeder, S.; Ackermann, D.; Backe, H.; Beerwerth, R.; Berengut, J.; Block, M.; Borschevsky, A.; Cheal, B.; Chhetri, P.; Düllmann, C.E.; et al. Probing sizes and shapes of nobelium isotopes by laser spectroscopy. *Phys. Rev. Lett.* **2018**, *120*, 232503.
16. Münzenberg, G.; Faust, W.; Hofmann, S.; Armbruster, P.; Güttner, K.; Ewald, H. The velocity filter SHIP, a separator of unslowed heavy ion fusion products. *Nucl. Instrum. Methods* **1979**, *161*, 65–82.
17. Murböck, T.; Raeder, S.; Chhetri, P.; Diaz, K.; Laatiaoui, M.; Giacoppo, F.; Block, M. Filament studies for laser spectroscopy on lawrencium. *Hyperfine Interact.* **2020**, *241*, 1–9.
18. Laatiaoui, M.; Backe, H.; Block, M.; Chhetri, P.; Lautenschläger, F.; Lauth, W.; Walther, T. Perspectives for laser spectroscopy of the element nobelium. *Hyperfine Interact.* **2014**, *227*, 69–75.
19. Oganessian, Y.T.; Utyonkov, V.; Lobanov, Y.V.; Abdullin, F.S.; Polyakov, A.; Shirokovsky, I.; Tsyganov, Y.S.; Mezentsev, A.; Iliev, S.; Subbotin, V.; et al. Measurements of cross sections for the fusion-evaporation reactions ^{204,206,207,208}Pb + ^{48}Ca and ^{207}Pb + ^{34}S: Decay properties of the even-even nuclides ^{238}Cf and ^{250}No. *Phys. Rev. C* **2001**, *64*, 054606.
20. Gäggeler, H.; Jost, D.; Türler, A.; Armbruster, P.; Brüchle, W.; Folger, H.; Heßberger, F.; Hofmann, S.; Münzenberg, G.; Ninov, V.; et al. Cold fusion reactions with ^{48}Ca. *Nucl. Phys. A* **1989**, *502*, 561–570.
21. Zou, Y.; Fischer, C.F. Resonance transition energies and oscillator strengths in lutetium and lawrencium. *Phys. Rev. Lett.* **2002**, *88*, 183001.
22. Borschevsky, A.; Eliav, E.; Vilkas, M.; Ishikawa, Y.; Kaldor, U. Transition energies of atomic lawrencium. *Eur. Phys. J. D* **2007**, *45*, 115–119.
23. Fritzsche, S.; Dong, C.; Koike, F.; Uvarov, A. The low-lying level structure of atomic lawrencium (Z = 103): Energies and absorption rates. *Eur. Phys. J. D* **2007**, *45*, 107–113.
24. Dzuba, V.; Safronova, M.; Safronova, U. Atomic properties of superheavy elements No, Lr, and Rf. *Phys. Rev. A* **2014**, *90*, 012504.
25. Kahl, E.; Raeder, S.; Eliav, E.; Borschevsky, A.; Berengut, J. Ab initio calculations of the spectrum of lawrencium. *Phys. Rev. A* **2021**, *104*, 052810.
26. Laatiaoui, M.; Backe, H.; Habs, D.; Kunz, P.; Lauth, W.; Sewtz, M. Low-field mobilities of rare-earth metals. *Eur. Phys. J. D* **2012**, *66*, 1–5.
27. Raeder, S.; Block, M.; Chhetri, P.; Ferrer, R.; Kraemer, S.; Kron, T.; Laatiaoui, M.; Nothhelfer, S.; Schneider, F.; Van Duppen, P.; et al. A gas-jet apparatus for high-resolution laser spectroscopy on the heaviest elements at SHIP. *Nucl. Instrum. Methods Phys. Res. Sect. B Beam Interact. Mater. At.* **2020**, *463*, 272–276.
28. Kaleja, O.; Anđelić, B.; Blaum, K.; Block, M.; Chhetri, P.; Droese, C.; Düllmann, C.E.; Eibach, M.; Eliseev, S.; Even, J.; et al. The performance of the cryogenic buffer-gas stopping cell of SHIPTRAP. *Nucl. Instrum. Methods Phys. Res. Sect. B Beam Interact. Mater. At.* **2020**, *463*, 280–285.
29. Barzakh, A.; Chubukov, I.Y.; Fedorov, D.; Moroz, F.; Panteleev, V.; Seliverstov, M.; Volkov, Y.M. Isotope shift and hyperfine structure measurements for ^{155}Yb by laser ion source technique. *Eur. Phys. J. A Hadron. Nucl.* **1998**, *1*, 3–5.

30. Sprouse, G.; Das, J.; Lauritsen, T.; Schecker, J.; Berger, A.; Billowes, J.; Holbrow, C.; Mahnke, H.E.; Rolston, S. Laser spectroscopy of light Yb isotopes on-line in a cooled gas cell. *Phys. Rev. Lett.* **1989**, *63*, 1463.
31. Barzakh, A.; Fedorov, D.; Panteleev, V.; Seliverstov, M.; Volkov, Y.M. Measurements of charge radii and electromagnetic moments of nuclei far from stability by photoionization spectroscopy in a laser ion source. In *AIP Conference Proceedings*; American Institute of Physics: Melville, NY, USA, 2002; Volume 610, pp. 915–919.
32. Das, D.; Barthwal, S.; Banerjee, A.; Natarajan, V. Absolute frequency measurements in Yb with 0.08 ppb uncertainty: Isotope shifts and hyperfine structure in the 399-nm $^1S_0 \rightarrow {}^1P_1$ line. *Phys. Rev. A* **2005**, *72*, 032506.

Article

Resolution Characterizations of JetRIS in Mainz Using ^{164}Dy

Danny Münzberg [1,2,3,*], Michael Block [1,2,3], Arno Claessens [4], Rafael Ferrer [4], Mustapha Laatiaoui [3], Jeremy Lantis [3], Steven Nothhelfer [1,2,3], Sebastian Raeder [1,2] and Piet Van Duppen [4]

1. GSI Helmholtzzentrum für Schwerionenforschung GmbH, 64291 Darmstadt, Germany; m.block@gsi.de (M.B.); nothhelfer@uni-mainz.de (S.N.); s.raeder@gsi.de (S.R.)
2. Helmholtz-Institut Mainz, 55099 Mainz, Germany
3. Department Chemie, Johannes Gutenberg-Universität Mainz, 55099 Mainz, Germany; mlaatiao@uni-mainz.de (M.L.); jlantis@uni-mainz.de (J.L.)
4. KU Leuven, Instituut Voor Kern-en Stralingsfysica, B-3001 Leuven, Belgium; arno.claessens@kuleuven.be (A.C.); rafael.ferrer@kuleuven.be (R.F.); piet.vanduppen@kuleuven.be (P.V.D.)
* Correspondence: dmuenzbe@students.uni-mainz.de

Abstract: Laser spectroscopic studies of elements in the heavy actinide and transactinide region help understand the nuclear ground state properties of these heavy systems. Pioneering experiments at GSI, Darmstadt identified the first atomic transitions in the element nobelium. For the purpose of determining nuclear properties in nobelium isotopes with higher precision, a new apparatus for high-resolution laser spectroscopy in a gas-jet called JetRIS is under development. To determine the spectral resolution and the homogeneity of the gas-jet, the laser-induced fluorescence of ^{164}Dy atoms seeded in the jet was studied. Different hypersonic nozzles were investigated for their performance in spectral resolution and efficiency. Under optimal conditions, a spectral linewidth of about 200–250 MHz full width at half maximum and a Mach number of about 7 was achieved, which was evaluated in context of the density profile of the atoms in the gas-jet.

Keywords: JetRIS; fluorescence spectroscopy; gas-jet; de Laval nozzle; nobelium

1. Introduction

The measurement of atomic transitions via laser spectroscopy is a versatile method for determining fundamental nuclear and atomic properties [1–4]. At the GSI Helmholtzzentrum für Schwerionenforschung, Darmstadt, Germany, laser spectroscopy is used at the Separator for Heavy Ion reaction Products (SHIP) [5,6] with a focus on the heavy actinide and transactinide region [4,7,8]. The low production rates and short half-lives of these nuclides pose difficult experimental challenges and require highly sensitive techniques. Recent laser spectroscopic measurements were conducted successfully at GSI on nobelium isotopes produced through fusion-evaporation reactions at SHIP using the Radiation Detected Resonance Ionization Spectroscopy (RADRIS) technique [7,9], where reaction products are thermalized in an argon filled gas cell and collected on a tantalum filament. The ions are neutralized by collection on a metallic filament, which is subsequently heated to produce an atomic vapor for resonance ionization spectroscopy (RIS). Due to the pressure and temperature conditions in the gas cell, the spectral resolution is limited to about 3 GHz. This is often insufficient to resolve all individual hyperfine components of the studied optical transition, as, e.g., in the case of ^{253}No [10]. Additionally, species with half-lives of less than approximately one second are inaccessible to the RADRIS technique due to decay losses during recoil ion collection. To overcome both of these limitations, JetRIS has been constructed for high-resolution resonance ionization spectroscopy in a hypersonic gas-jet [10]. JetRIS combines the high resolution of the in-gas-jet laser spectroscopy technique developed at KU Leuven [11–13] with the sensitivity of the ion collection and neutral desorption from a heated filament used in the RADRIS technique [14,15]. In the new approach presented here, after neutralization, the atoms are carried through a hypersonic nozzle to form a low-temperature and low-density gas-jet, reducing the Doppler and collisional broadening effects and thus increasing the spectral resolution by an order of magnitude. The ability to transport neutral species makes it possible to run the system in a continuous mode instead of in cycles as is happening in RADRIS. The negative potential on the filament can be applied at all times in addition to heating, minimizing the before-mentioned decay losses. JetRIS is designed to achieve a spectral resolution of at least 400 MHz for the heaviest elements, allowing for a more precise determination of the nuclear moments. To understand the performance of different nozzles, we present here the characteristics of these in terms of Mach number, spectral resolution and homogeneity of the produced jet.

2. Experimental Procedure
2.1. A Technical Overview of JetRIS

JetRIS consists of a high-pressure gas cell (stagnation pressure P_0 of 80–125 mbar argon) used to stop and thermalize recoil ions from fusion-evaporation reactions after separation from the primary beam by SHIP and a lower pressure jet cell (background pressure P of 5×10^{-3} mbar–2×10^{-2} mbar), which is used for laser spectroscopy. Inside the gas cell, the thermalized ions are transported via an electric field created by a set of cylindrical electrodes toward a filament located at the front of the nozzle, as sketched in Figure 1. This filament, typically made of tantalum, is resistively heated, allowing for neutralization and desorption of atoms, which are subsequently transported by a gas flow into the jet cell through the de Laval nozzle, forming a well-collimated hypersonic gas-jet. This gas-jet features a low temperature and a low pressure, thus reducing the spectral linewidth while the collimation of the gas-jet is crucial to maintain the highest efficiency. Two laser beams are used in a cross-beam geometry to interact with the gas-jet, performing two-step resonance ionization spectroscopy. The laser for the first excitation step is propagating anticollinearly relative to the gas-jet, while the second step proceeds in a perpendicular configuration. While the perpendicular configuration reduces the power density of the laser light, it helps in avoiding ionization in the gas cell. The photo-ions are then guided around a 90° curve via a radio frequency quadrupole (RFQ) to a detector cell, where a channel electron multiplier (CEM) or silicon detector is located. A more detailed description of JetRIS can be found in [10]. In this technique, the nozzle determines the achievable resolution and the total efficiency from the collimation. Therefore, a thorough characterization is essential in understanding the performance of the setup. At KU Leuven, such nozzles are studied in detail using Laser Induced Fluorescence (LIF) in Cu I using pulsed laser radiation as well as the RIS of neutral Cu atoms [16,17].

In this study, we follow a different path by using LIF of neutral ^{164}Dy, which is illuminated by light from a cw-diode laser, propagating anticollinearly to the gas-jet as sketched in Figure 2. With this technique, three different de Laval type nozzles were investigated, and they were designed for different operation pressures and differences in their contour. All of them feature a throat diameter of 1 mm. The first nozzle is intended for usage at low stagnation pressures of $P_0 = 80$ mbar and a background pressure of $P = 2.5 \times 10^{-2}$ mbar. The diverging part of this nozzle has a length of about 1 cm as sketched in Figure 3. From fluid dynamic calculations, a jet of approximately Mach 8 was expected. The second nozzle is optimized for high stagnation pressures around $P_0 = 300$ mbar, and here, the diverging part has a length of about 3 cm. This nozzle is identical to the nozzles investigated recently at KU Leuven [16]. The third nozzle, referred to as the mid-range nozzle, has a conic contour. Here, the diverging part has a length of 2 cm. This nozzle was a prototype for operation in an intermediate pressure range while being simple to machine. No simulations were performed to optimize the design of this nozzle, and its optimal operating conditions were not previously known. To seed the atoms into the gas-jet for these tests, the tantalum filament in front of the nozzle was replaced by a tantalum strip that was previously loaded with a sample and resistively heated until a suitable fluorescence signal was observed, but the temperature of the filament was not measured. It can only be approximated from its color when glowing, with an estimated temperature of 1200 °C.

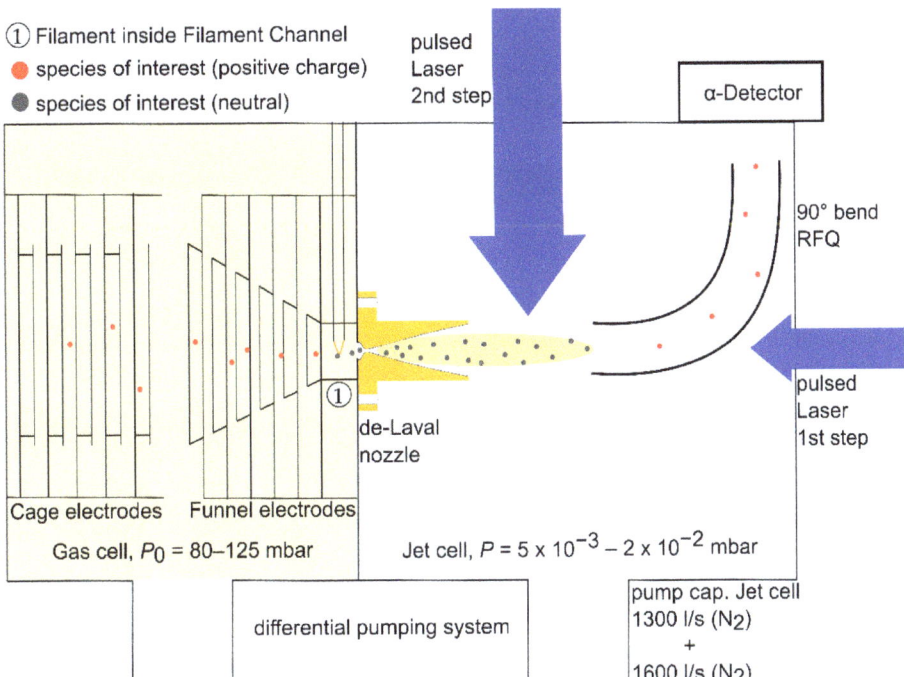

Figure 1. Schematic overview of JetRIS. On the left side are the cage and funnel electrodes. In front of the nozzle, there is a tantalum filament. After being evaporated from the filament, the atoms follow the flow of the buffer gas through the nozzle into the gas-jet. Here, two laser beams used in a cross-beam geometry resonantly ionizes the formerly neutralized species of interest. The ions are guided around a curve via a 90° bend RFQ and collected on an α-Detector.

2.2. Fluorescence Characterization

During the experiments presented in this work, we used one-step laser excitation in contrast to the two-step resonant ionization that will be used in online experiments. As no ions were produced, the RFQ structure was removed (cf. Figure 2) and the fluorescence of the seeded atoms provided a way to determine the density and homogeneity along the gas-jet. The atom source was installed next to the nozzle entrance in the gas cell, consisting of a folded piece of tantalum foil, which contained a piece of a few mg of ^{164}Dy with an isotopic purity of about 95%. The usage of an isotopically enriched sample ensured the investigation of a single atomic line as only minor contributions to the fluorescence signal from other isotopes are present and the even-even isotope features no hyperfine structure splitting. The foil was resistively heated with an electric power of 15 W to produce a dysprosium vapor, which was carried to the nozzle by the gas flow. A self-built laser with a 405 nm laser diode (Thorlabs L405P20) in an external cavity in Litrow configuration with approximately 12 mW of laser power and a sub-megahertz linewidth was used to excite the $4f^{10}6s^2 \rightarrow 4f^{10}6s6p$ transition in Dy I at a wavelength of 404.5 nm and with a transition strength of 1.92×10^8 s^{-1} [18]. The laser beam was expanded to form a circle of about 10 mm in diameter and was aligned to propagate anticollinear to the central axis of the gas-jet. A Complementary Metal-Oxide Semiconductor (CMOS) camera (Zelux® CS 165 MU) with a quantum efficiency of 50% was used to capture the fluorescence light originating from the atomic deexcitation. A bandpass filter featuring about 40% transmission at 405 nm and a bandwith of 10 nm was installed in front of the camera. Pictures of the fluorescence, as shown in Figure 4, were taken as a function of gas pressure, wavelength and exposure time, which did not exceed 26 s due to limitations of the software for the camera.

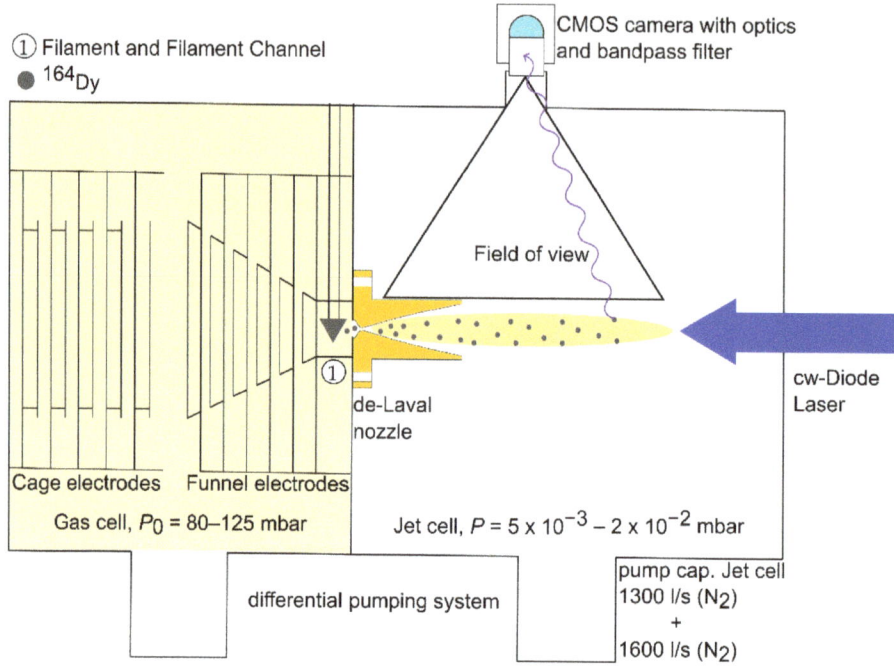

Figure 2. Schematic overview of JetRIS. On the left side are the cage and funnel electrodes, which are necessary for an online experiment but were not in use for the fluorescence measurements. In front of the nozzle, there is a tantalum filament that contains a piece of ^{164}Dy foil. After being evaporated from the filament, the atoms follow the flow of the buffer gas through the nozzle into the gas-jet. Here, a cw-diode laser beam at approximately 405 nm wavelength resonantly excites the dysprosium, and the resulting fluorescence is captured using a CMOS camera. The camera was mounted at a 45° angle relative to the field of view of this schematic.

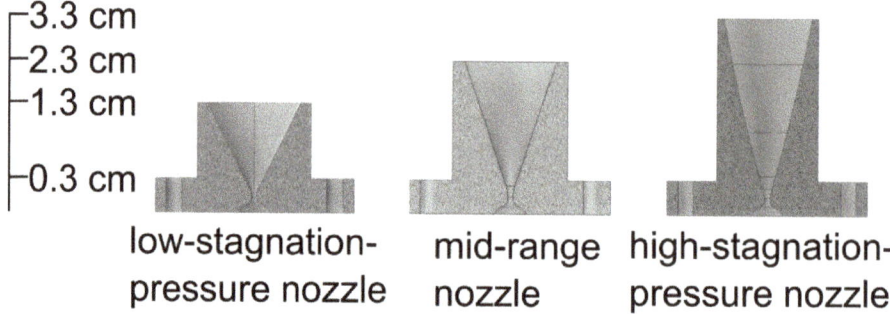

Figure 3. Cross sectional profiles of the characterized nozzles. The base and the diameter of the hole are identical for every nozzle.

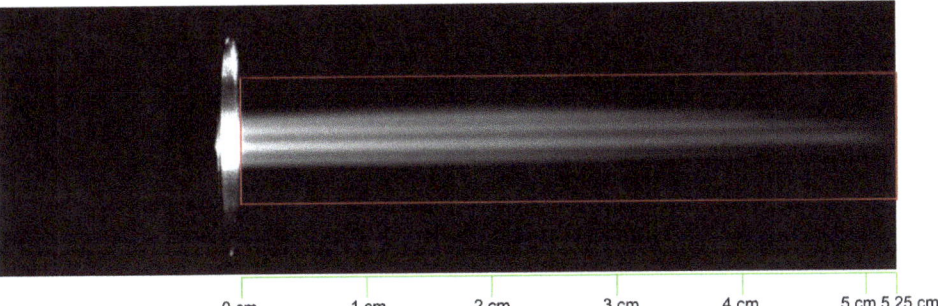

Figure 4. Example picture of the fluorescence acquired with the CMOS camera. Shown is the midrange nozzle at the centroid frequency of the transition using a stagnation pressure of 100 mbar and a background pressure of 6.47×10^{-3} mbar. The visible stripes in the jet are a property of the laser diode used. The red box indicates the region that was considered in the analysis.

The fluorescence intensity was averaged in the radial plane, normal to the flow direction, in order to obtain information of the performance characteristics along the jet. Due to averaging, the stripes visible in Figure 4 did not disrupt the analysis.

2.3. Characterization of the Gas-Jet

The recorded fluorescence intensity was used to determine the density of atoms in the gas-jet, as well as to study the effective spectral broadening and, thus, the temperature of the jet, while exciting the atoms around the resonance frequency, i.e., performing spectroscopy. The intensity was evaluated pixelwise along the length of the gas-jet with the intensity averaged across the jet for each pixel in x direction. For each pixel, the normalized fluorescence intensity was plotted as a function of the laser frequency. A Gaussian fit to the data provided the centroid frequency and the spectral linewidth of the resonance. A number typically used to describe a gas-jet is the Mach number M, which is defined as the quotient of the stream velocity and the local speed of sound. It gives us an easy-to-compare variable that convolutes the speed of the jet and the temperature. The Mach number M is calculated with the following [11].

$$M = \sqrt{\frac{2}{\gamma - 1}\left(\frac{T_0}{T} - 1\right)}. \tag{1}$$

Here, γ is the ratio of the specific heat capacities of the gas, which is 5/3 for a monoatomic gas, T is the temperature of the jet and T_0 is the initial temperature of the gas before it reaches the nozzle.

The temperature T of the jet was determined from the measured linewidth by using the following relation.

$$\Delta \nu_D = 2\sqrt{\ln(2)}\frac{\nu_{01}}{c}\sqrt{\frac{2kT}{m}}. \tag{2}$$

Here, $\Delta \nu_D$ is the contribution to the full width at half maximum (FWHM) of the Doppler broadening, ν_{01} is the transition frequency, c is the speed of light, k is the Boltzmann constant and m is the mass of ^{164}Dy. As the measured resonance features a Voigt profile, the Doppler broadening can be determined by using the following approximate relation.

$$\Delta \nu = 0.5346\, \Delta \nu_L + \sqrt{0.2166\, \Delta \nu_L^2 + \Delta \nu_D^2}. \tag{3}$$

Here, $\Delta \nu$ is the FWHM of the measured Voigt profile, and $\Delta \nu_L$ describes the Lorentzian part of the overall resolution, which contains the natural linewidth and the pressure broadening. Any contribution from power broadening is neglected.

To obtain an estimate of the temperature T_0, the connection between T_0 and the stream velocity was used [11].

$$u = \sqrt{\frac{\gamma k T_0 M^2}{m\left(1 + \left(\frac{\gamma-1}{2}\right)M^2\right)}}. \tag{4}$$

where m is the mass of the buffer gas, and u is the stream velocity of the jet, which can be obtained from the recorded centroid using the optical Doppler shift from the literature value for the transition of $\nu_{01} = 24{,}708.97$ cm^{-1} [19]. The stated reference did not mention the isotope of dysprosium for the recorded value. Therefore, the transition was measured with JetRIS by shining a laser beam perpendicular to the flow direction of the gas-jet, which yields a value free from Doppler shift. The measured value was in agreement with the literature value reported in [19].

Above Mach 5, the stream velocity reaches 95% of its maximum. Since the Mach number was expected to be around 5–8, the mean value of these ($M = 6.5$) was taken as an approximation for T_0. The deviation of the temperatures obtained with $M = 5$ and $M = 8$ from the value at $M = 6.5$ is around 3% and was considered when determining the uncertainty of the experimentally determined Mach number. A typical value of T_0 obtained from the fitting of the data is 380 K, indicating some heating of the gas from the hot filament, a fact that was already observed in previous investigations in Leuven [16].

To determine the quality of the gas-jet, a new metric was established and will be referred to as the homogeneity factor H. The photon density of the fluorescence light was used to evaluate the homogeneity of the sample atom density across the full length of the jet and was compared to a hypothetical, perfectly homogenous jet of constant light intensity. For this new factor, two different integrals have been calculated. A normalized integral of the hypothetical perfect jet $\int I_{max}$, where the intensity should be constant over the entire length of the jet and the intensity integral over the experimental intensity values $\int I$, resulting in the following equation.

$$H = \frac{\int I}{\int I_{max}}. \tag{5}$$

The boundaries of both integrals are the same and are determined by the length of the real jet. The homogeneity factor provides a simple value between 0 and 1, where 0 would mean no observed fluorescence, meaning no formation of a jet, and 1 would mean that we would observe a perfectly homogenous jet.

For an overall view on the performance of a nozzle, the spectral resolution and M were multiplied by the relative intensity, summed up and divided by the sum of the relative intensities, therefore making an intensity-weighted average. The uncertainty of these parameters was determined as the standard deviation of the individual numbers.

3. Results

3.1. Resolution

The low-stagnation-pressure nozzle is a de-Laval nozzle and was designed for a stagnation pressure of $P_0 = 80$ mbar and a background pressure of $P = 2.5 \times 10^{-2}$ mbar [20]. However, while investigating the resolution as a function of the background pressure, as shown in Figure 5a for the low stagnation pressure nozzle, a lower background pressure was found to provide the best resolution. This general trend that the resolution is improving as the background pressure drops was observed for all three nozzles. It has to be noted that the available pressure ranges are limited by the capacity of the JetRIS pumping system. At optimal parameters, the best achievable resolution was 212 ± 4 MHz for the low-stagnation-pressure nozzle, 239 ± 13 MHz for the mid-range nozzle and 311 ± 15 MHz for the high-stagnation-pressure nozzle. These values are all intensity-weighted averages of the individual values for each pixel slice along the gas-jet. It was verified whether analyzing the jet as a whole has an impact on the values relative to the pixel-by-pixel analysis, and both methods are in agreement with one another. The optimal stagnation pressure of 300 mbar for the high-stagnation-pressure nozzle could not be reached, again limited by the pumping system [16]. Under the available conditions, the low-stagnation-pressure and mid-range nozzle outperformed the high-stagnation-pressure nozzle with regards to the obtained resolution. All of the obtained spectral linewidths are smaller than the stated goal of 400 MHz [10]. The individual parameters for the measurements are summarized in Table 1.

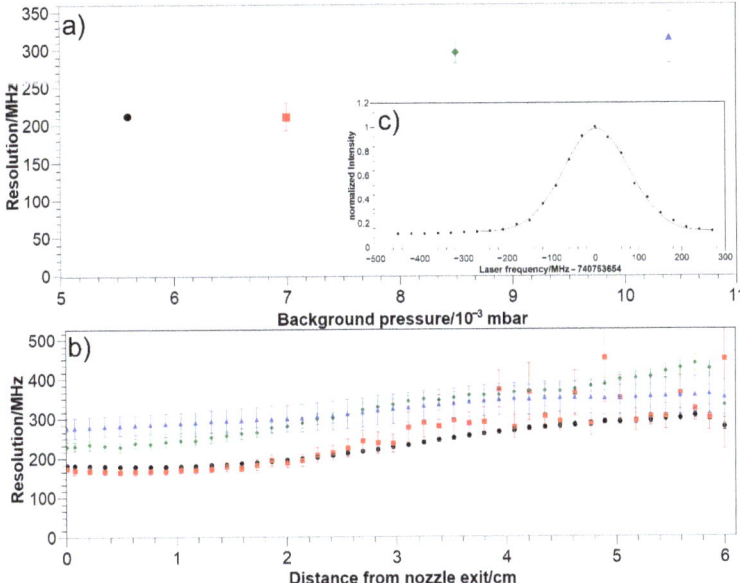

Figure 5. (a) Intensity-weighted averages of the resolution for the low-stagnation-pressure nozzle. The resolution generally improves as the background pressure is reduced. (b) Resolution along the jet for different parameters of the low-stagnation-pressure nozzle. (c) Example Gaussian fit of the intensity as a function of the laser frequency for the low-stagnation-pressure nozzle at $P_0 = 80.6$ mbar and $P = 5.6 \times 10^{-3}$ mbar. In both pictures, the parameters are as follows: black: $P_0 = 80.6$ mbar and $P = 5.6 \times 10^{-3}$ mbar; red: $P_0 = 80.6$ mbar and $P = 7.0 \times 10^{-3}$ mbar; green: $P_0 = 80.0$ mbar and $P = 8.5 \times 10^{-3}$ mbar; blue: $P_0 = 82.2$ mbar and $P = 10.4 \times 10^{-3}$ mbar.

Table 1. Intensity weighted averages of M, $\Delta\nu$ and H for the three different nozzles.

Nozzle	P_0/mbar	$P/10^{-3}$ mbar	M	$\Delta\nu$/MHz	H
Low-stagnation-pressure nozzle	80.6	5.6	7.2 ± 1.0	212 ± 30	0.40
	80.6	7.0	7.4 ± 1.0	211 ± 35	0.26
	80.0	8.5	5.0 ± 0.5	296 ± 33	0.43
	82.2	10.4	5.1 ± 0.7	316 ± 45	0.61
Mid-range nozzle	100	6.47	6.7 ± 0.9	250 ± 32	0.60
	125	7.35	7.2 ± 1.0	239 ± 33	0.67
	149	10.0	6.6 ± 0.9	259 ± 33	0.69
High-stagnation-pressure nozzle	125	9.3	4.2 ± 0.5	335 ± 31	0.84
	131	8.5	3.8 ± 0.3	352 ± 30	0.79
	154	12.2	4.6 ± 0.5	311 ± 34	0.78

3.2. Mach Number

The jet was evaluated for its Mach number as described in Section 2.3. For the determination of the gas-jet temperature from the linewidth, the spectral profiles were fitted with Gaussian profiles. The calculated linewidths were taken as the values for the overall resolution, since the fit was in good agreement with the data, as shown in Figure 5c. The natural linewidth can be calculated to be 30.5 MHz from the transition strength. The pressure broadening could not be determined; however, in the case of Cu I studied at Leuven, it was found to be approximately 3 MHz [16]. Power broadening has been neglected due to the low laser power used in the experiment. The two factors were added to a Lorentzian contribution to the linewidth of 33.5 MHz and the temperature-dependent part of the resolution was calculated according to Equation (3). With this, the Mach numbers were calculated as $M = 7.2 \pm 1.0$ for the low-stagnation-pressure nozzle, $M = 7.2 \pm 1.0$ for the mid-range nozzle and $M = 4.6 \pm 0.5$ for the high-stagnation-pressure nozzle in the best case, respectively. The Mach numbers of the high stagnation pressure nozzle are significantly lower than $M = 8$, expected from fluid-dynamics calculations and from observations at KU Leuven [16]. This was most likely due to the fact that the nozzle was used outside of its desired pressure range [21]. In this investigation, some small uncertainties in the evaluation remain, concerning the determination of the stagnation temperature T_0 and the frequency instability of the laser diode while measuring, which are expected to be reflected in the uncertainties. The presented values agree very well with the observations from previous studies at KU Leuven, albeit it has to be noted that the measurements were taken under different conditions. On one hand, the investigations in Leuven for the low-stagnation-pressure nozzle were performed using only the central 1 mm diameter of the gas-jet core with collinear illumination, while in this work the entire jet is illuminated anticollinearly, adding the jet boundary layer of the jet in the evaluation. Furthermore, the ^{164}Dy atoms used in this study are heavier than the ^{65}Cu atoms used in Leuven, which is a much lighter system that is closer to the carrier gas (^{40}Ar).

3.3. Homogeneity Factor

Finally, the homogeneity as defined in Equation (5) was evaluated, which shows a quite different behavior of the nozzles. With the best possible parameters, a value of $H = 0.33$ was achieved for the low-stagnation-pressure nozzle, compared to values of $H = 0.63$ for the mid-range nozzle and $H = 0.76$ for the high-stagnation-pressure nozzle. The corresponding intensity distributions along the jet for the three nozzles are shown in Figure 6.

Clearly, none of the investigated nozzles provide an ideal jet with a perfectly homogenous density profile and some losses from diffusion into the background gas are unavoidable. Furthermore, the intensity profile at the spectral maximum was compared with the intensity profile averaged over the spectral profile. The latter corresponds to the total density of the jet independent of the velocity distribution and shows a better homogeneity. Nevertheless, the profile at the maximum excitation frequency corresponds to the accessible fraction of the density and, thus, provides a better estimate on the expected efficiency. It shall be noted that the pulsed laser for the intended resonant ionization application features a significantly larger bandwidth of about 100 MHz compared to the sub-megahertz bandwidth of the cw diode laser used in this work [22]. This will enable addressing more atoms of the ensemble in the gas-jet and, thus, the effective homogeneity will be in between the two curves in the upper and lower panels of Figure 6, respectively.

The homogeneity factor provides a good impression about the achievable efficiency from the atom density along the gas-jet, but it does not yet provide conclusive information about the overall efficiency of JetRIS. Further measurements are planned, including the transport efficiency of atoms evaporated from the filament and transported through the nozzle to the detector at online-like conditions. For this, a radioactive recoil source will be used, since it releases ions at a known rate, allowing for a quantitative measurement, independent from ionization efficiency when using lasers.

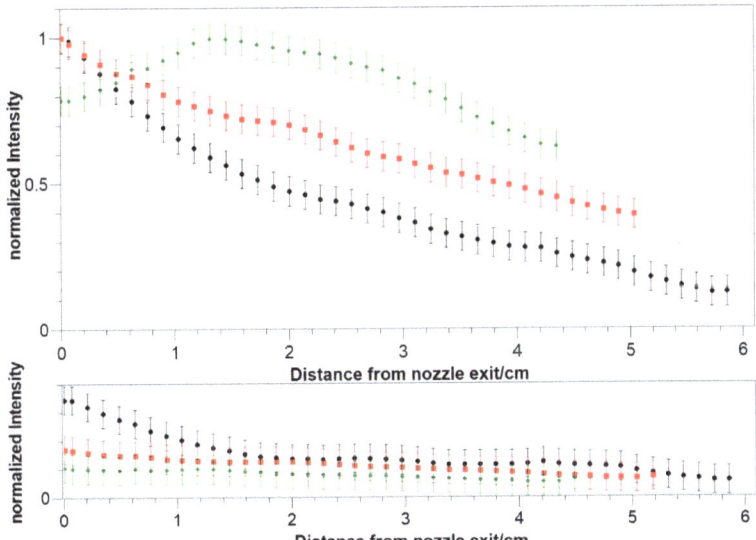

Figure 6. Intensity distribution at the centroid frequency (**upper**) and average over all frequencies (**lower**) for the best parameters of the low-stagnation-pressure nozzle (black, P_0 = 80.6 mbar, P = 5.6 × 10^{-3} mbar), mid-range nozzle (red, P_0 = 125 mbar, P = 7.35 × 10^{-3} mbar) and high-stagnation-pressure nozzle (green, P_0 = 125 mbar, P = 9.3 × 10^{-3} mbar).

4. Summary and Outlook

To enable high-resolution laser spectroscopy of the heaviest elements at GSI, Darmstadt JetRIS is under development. For an online experiment, efficiency is of paramount importance while maintaining a high spectral resolution. Therefore, fluorescence spectroscopy was performed to characterize three hypersonic nozzles in terms of spectral resolution, Mach number and homogeneity. These nozzles were designed for operation at different stagnation pressures. For each nozzle, gas pressures were identified resulting in a resolution sufficient for determining the hyperfine structure of ^{253}No, for example. The highest spectral resolution was found for the low-stagnation-pressure and the mid-range nozzle with linewidths of 211 MHz and 239 MHz, respectively, for the investigated ground-state transition at 404.5 nm in ^{164}Dy. In contrast, the high-stagnation pressure nozzle provided a linewidth of 335 MHz at the intended operation pressures of up to 125 mbar. The larger mass of ^{253}No compared to ^{164}Dy should allow achieving a higher resolution, but since the transition used for nobelium has a wavelength of 333 nm [7] compared to 405 nm for dysprosium, the resolution can be expected to be the similar in both cases. The low- and mid-range nozzle show a similar performance in terms of the Mach number as well. In terms of jet homogeneity, the high-stagnation-pressure nozzle showed the best performance. The mid-range nozzle seems to be the best overall choice, since its resolution and homogeneity are both close to the optimal values found for the other two nozzles. According to investigations at KU Leuven, the high-stagnation pressure nozzle would greatly benefit from operation at a higher stagnation pressure [16]. Nevertheless, our obtained resolution is already close to the value of 170 MHz projected in [16] for laser spectroscopy in the actinide region. Further studies will be performed offline with radioactive sources and resonance ionization spectroscopy to determine the efficiency of JetRIS before measuring online isotopes of nobelium at GSI, Darmstadt.

Author Contributions: R.F. and S.R. conceived the experiment. S.R., D.M., J.L. and S.N. set up the diode laser system. D.M., J.L. and S.N. conducted the measurements. D.M. and J.L. analyzed the data with the input from P.V.D., R.F., M.L., S.R., M.B. and A.C. The paper was written by D.M. with the input from P.V.D., M.B., A.C., R.F., J.L., M.L., S.N. and S.R. All authors have read and agreed to the published version of the manuscript.

Funding: M.L. acknowledges funding from the European Research Council (ERC) under the European Union's Horizon 2020 Research and Innovation Programme (Grant Agreement No. 819957).

Data Availability Statement: The data presented in this study are available upon request from the corresponding author.

Acknowledgments: The authors thankfully acknowledge the LARISSA group (Institut für Physik, Johannes Gutenberg-Universität Mainz) for the contribution of the laser diode cavity, as well as the target lab of GSI, Darmstadt, for the supply of enriched ^{164}Dy.

Conflicts of Interest: The authors declare no conflict of interest.

References

1. Kluge, H.-J.; Nörtershäuser, W. Lasers for nuclear physics. *Spectrochim. Acta B* **2003**, *58*, 1031–1045. [CrossRef]
2. Cheal, B.; Flanagan, K.T. Progress in laser spectroscopy at radioactive ion beam facilities. *J. Phys. G Nucl. Part. Phys.* **2010**, *37*, 113101. [CrossRef]
3. Campbell, P.; Moore, I.; Pearson, M. Laser spectroscopy for nuclear structure physics. *Prog. Part. Nucl. Phys.* **2016**, *86*, 127–180. [CrossRef]
4. Block, M.; Laatiaoui, M.; Raeder, S. Raeder. Recent progress in laser spectroscopy of the actinides. *Prog. Part. Nucl. Phys.* **2021**, *116*, 103834. [CrossRef]
5. Hofmann, S.; Münzenberg, G. The discovery of the heaviest elements. *Rev. Mod. Phys.* **2000**, *72*, 733–767. [CrossRef]
6. Münzenberg, G.; Faust, W.; Hofmann, S.; Armbruster, P.; Güttner, K.; Ewald, H. The velocity filter SHIP, a separator of unslowed heavy ion fusion products. *Nucl. Instrum. Methods* **1979**, *161*, 65–82. [CrossRef]
7. Laatiaoui, M.; Lauth, W.; Backe, W.L.H.; Block, M.; Ackermann, D.; Cheal, B.; Chhetri, P.; Düllmann, C.; Van Duppen, P.; Even, J.; et al. Atom-at-a-time laser resonance ionization spectroscopy of nobelium. *Nature* **2016**, *538*, 495–498. [CrossRef] [PubMed]
8. Backe, H.; Lauth, W.; Block, M.; Laatiaoui, M. Prospects for laser spectroscopy, ion chemistry and measurements of superheavy elements in buffer-gas traps. *Nucl. Phys. A* **2015**, *944*, 492–517. [CrossRef]
9. Lauth, W.; Backe, H.; Dahlinger, M.; Klaft, I.; Schwamb, P.; Schwickert, G.; Trautmann, N.; Othmer, U. Resonance Ionization spectroscopy in a buffer gas cell with radioactive decay detection, demonstrated using ^{208}Tl. *Phys. Rev. Lett.* **1992**, *68*, 1675–1678. [CrossRef] [PubMed]
10. Raeder, S.; Block, M.; Chhetri, P.; Ferrer, R.; Kraemer, S.; Kron, T.; Laatiaoui, M.; Nothhelfer, S.; Schneider, F.; Van Duppen, P.; et al. A gas-jet apparatus for high-resolution laser spectroscopy on the heaviest elements at SHIP. *Nucl. Instrum. Methods Phys. Res. Sect. B Beam Interact. Mater. At.* **2020**, *463*, 272–276. [CrossRef]
11. Kudryavtsev, Y.; Ferrer, R.; Huyse, M.; Bergh, P.V.D.; Van Duppen, P. The in-gas-jet laser ion source: Resonance ionization spectroscopy of radioactive atoms in supersonic gas jets. *Nucl. Instrum. Methods Phys. Res. Sect. B Beam Interact. Mater. B Beam Interact. Mater. At.* **2013**, *297*, 7–22. [CrossRef]
12. Raeder, S.; Bastin, B.; Block, M.; Creemers, P.; Delahaye, P.; Ferrer, R.; Fléchard, X.; Franchoo, S.; Ghys, L.; Gaffney, L.P.; et al. Developments towards in-gas-jet laser spectroscopy studies of actinium isotopes at LISOL. *Nucl. Instrum. Methods Phys. Res. Sect. B Beam Interact. Mater. At.* **2016**, *376*, 382–387. [CrossRef]
13. Ferrer, R.; Barzakh, A.; Bastin, B.; Beerwerth, R.; Block, M.; Creemers, P.; Grawe, H.; de Groote, R.; Delahaye, P.; Fléchard, X.; et al. Towards high- resolution laser ionization spectroscopy of the heaviest elements in supersonic gas jet expansion. *Nat. Commun.* **2017**, *8*, 14520. [CrossRef] [PubMed]
14. Laatiaoui, M.; Backe, H.; Block, M.; Chhetri, P.; Lautenschläger, F.; Lauth, W.; Walther, T. Perspectives for laser spectroscopy of the element nobelium. *Hyperfine Interact* **2013**, *227*, 69–75. [CrossRef]
15. Lautenschläger, F.; Chhetri, P.; Ackermann, D.; Backe, H.; Block, M.; Cheal, B.; Clark, A.; Droese, C.; Ferrer, R.; Giacoppo, F.; et al. Developments for resonance ionization laser spectroscopy of the heaviest elements at SHIP. *Nucl. Instrum. Methods Phys. Res. Sect. B Beam Interact. Mater. At.* **2016**, *383*, 115–122. [CrossRef]
16. Ferrer, R.; Verlinde, M.; Verstraelen, E.; Claessens, A.; Huyse, M.; Kraemer, S.; Kudryavtsev, Y.; Romans, J.; Bergh, P.V.D.; Van Duppen, P.; et al. Hypersonic nozzle for laser-spectroscopy studies at 17 K characterized by resonance-ionization-spectroscopy-based flow mapping. *Phys. Rev. Res.* **2021**, *3*, 043041. [CrossRef]
17. Zadvornaya, A.; Creemers, P.; Dockx, K.; Ferrer, R.; Gaffney, L.P.; Gins, W.; Granados, C.; Huyse, M.; Kudryavtsev, Y.; Laatiaoui, M.; et al. Characterization of Supersonic Gas Jets for High-Resolution Laser Ionization Spectroscopy of Heavy Elements. *Phys. Rev. X* **2018**, *8*, 041008. [CrossRef]

18. Wickliffe, M.; Lawler, J.; Nave, G. Atomic transition probabilities for Dy I and Dy II. *J. Quant. Spectrosc. Radiat. Transf.* **2000**, *66*, 363–404. [CrossRef]
19. Sansonetti, J.E.; Martin, W.C. Handbook of Basic Atomic Spectroscopic Data. *J. Phys. Chem. Ref. Data* **2005**, *34*, 1559–2259. [CrossRef]
20. Roelens, S. Characterization of a Hypersonic Nozzle for Laser Spectroscopy of Singly-Charged Thorium Ions. Master's Thesis, KU Leuven, Leuven, Belgium, 2021.
21. Verstraelen, E. Laser Spectroscopy of Actinides: Octupole Deformation and Gas-Jet Characterization. Ph.D. Thesis, Ku Leuven, Leuven, Belgium, 2021.
22. Verlinde, M.; Ferrer, R.; Claessens, A.; Granados, C.A.; Kraemer, S.; Kudryavtsev, Y.; Li, D.; Bergh, P.V.D.; Van Duppen, P.; Verstraelen, E. Single-longitudinal-mode pumped pulsed-dye amplifier for high-resolution laser spectroscopy. *Rev. Sci. Instrum.* **2020**, *91*, 103002. [CrossRef] [PubMed]

Article

A Progress Report on Laser Resonance Chromatography

Elisa Romero Romero [1,2,3,*], Michael Block [1,2,3], Biswajit Jana [1,2,3], Eunkang Kim [1,2,3], Steven Nothhelfer [1,2,3], Sebastian Raeder [2,3], Harry Ramanantoanina [1,2,3], Elisabeth Rickert [1,2,3], Jonas Schneider [1], Philipp Sikora [1] and Mustapha Laatiaoui [1,2,3]

1. Department Chemie—Standort TRIGA, Johannes Gutenberg-Universität Mainz, 55099 Mainz, Germany
2. Helmholtz-Institut Mainz, 55099 Mainz, Germany
3. GSI Helmholtzzentrum für Schwerionenforschung, 64291 Darmstadt, Germany
* Correspondence: eromeror@uni-mainz.de

Abstract: Research on superheavy elements enables probing the limits of nuclear existence and provides a fertile ground to advance our understanding of the atom's structure. However, experimental access to these atomic species is very challenging and often requires the development of new technologies and experimental techniques optimized for the study of a single atomic species. The Laser Resonance Chromatography (LRC) technique was recently conceived to enable atomic structure investigations in the region of the superheavy elements. Here, we give an update on the experimental progress and simulation results.

Keywords: laser spectroscopy; superheavy elements; laser resonance chromatography

1. Introduction

In the last two decades, there have been outstanding and exceptional efforts in the discovery and study of the superheavy elements [1]. One of the highlights is the completion of the seventh row in the periodic table with the addition of four new synthetic elements in 2016, including oganesson (Og, element number $Z = 118$), the last and heaviest element to date. The development of new selective and efficient techniques has had an impact on the discovery of these elements and their detailed study. Some of these elements are predicted to not behave chemically like their lighter homologs, with relativistic effects being the dominant cause of this peculiarity [2,3].

The challenges to study them are manifold. Superheavy elements are produced in nuclear fusion-evaporation reactions using powerful accelerators at extremely low rates in the presence of a huge background from primary-beam particles. In addition, they usually exist only for a few seconds after their production, which explains why their basic chemical and atomic properties are often not known [1]. Efficient gas chromatography has been used to elucidate the adsorption enthalpies. The heaviest element studied with this technique is flerovium (Fl, $Z = 114$), with a half-life ranging between one and two seconds [4–6]. A few years ago, experiments using surface-ionization techniques were successfully applied to lawrencium (Lr, $Z = 103$), aiming at establishing the element's ionization potential [7].

Deeper insights into the atomic properties and structure can be gained from optical spectroscopy. At present, in-gas-cell laser resonance ionization spectroscopy [8–10] is the most advanced method for atomic structure studies on the heaviest elements. A recent breakthrough in this research field was achieved with the spectroscopy of nobelium (No, $Z = 102$) [10] using the RAdiation-Detected-Resonance-Ionization-Spectroscopy (RADRIS) technique.

Our alternative way of optical spectroscopy, namely, Laser Resonance Chromatography, has already been proposed for optical spectroscopy of lawrencium ions and is explained in detail in Ref. [11]. Briefly, this technique combines resonant laser excitation with electronic-state chromatography [12–15] and is conducted directly on the ion in-situ,

without the need for a neutralization step. Given the fusion products are stopped and extracted from a gas catcher in a +1 charge state, a laser of a proper wavelength optically pumps the ions into a metastable state from the ionic ground state. After this step, the ions are injected into a drift tube filled with diluted helium (He) gas, where they undergo a constant drift under the influence of an external electric field. Different interactions of the ions in the different states with helium result in state-specific ion mobilities, which enable modern electronic-state chromatography, i.e., separating the ions in the ground state from the metastable ions by drift time [13,16]. In other words, the changes in the arrival time distributions caused by laser excitations give the resonance signal. Although only applicable to ions and dependent on the presence of metastable states, the method of electronic state chromatography is well established for many elemental cations of the first-, second- and third-row transition metals [17–22].

To this end, a first-generation drift tube chamber has been designed for LRC applications. This design is different from traditional ion-mobility-experiment applications since suppressing deactivation of metastable states is mandatory and is pursued by reducing the length of the tube and operating at relatively low pressures.

In the next two sections, we give a brief report on the experimental progress of the laser resonance chromatography project by presenting the experimental apparatus including the laser system, the cryogenic drift tube, and the corresponding ion trajectory simulations. Due to the scarcity of data and since scandium (Sc, $Z = 21$) can be deemed as a homolog of lutetium (Lu, $Z = 71$), the later simulations were conducted for singly charged scandium in its ground and metastable states of known ion mobilities. In the last section, we give prospects of LRC experiments on Sc^+, Lu^+ and its heavier iso-electronic system, Lr^+. A summary of the important properties of these elements is compiled in Table 1.

Table 1. Relevant electronic states in Sc^+, Lu^+, and Lr^+ ions. The experimental ion mobilities are given for a helium temperature of 295 K. Predictions are marked by $\star$.

Ion	Ground State				State to Be Probed		Metastable State		
	Config.	$\tilde{\nu}$		K_0	Config.	$\tilde{\nu}$	Config.	$\tilde{\nu}$	K_0
		(cm^{-1})		(cm^2/Vs)		(cm^{-1})		(cm^{-1})	(cm^2/Vs)
Sc^+ [a]	$3d4s\ a^3D_1$	0		22.5	$3d4p\ z^3D_1^\circ$	27,917.78	$3d^2\ a^3F_2$	4802.87	18.5
Lu^+ [b]	$6s^2\ ^1S_0$	0		16.8	$6s6p\ ^3P_1^\circ$	28,503.16	$5d6s\ ^3D_1$	11,796.24	19.5 $\star$
Lr^+ [c]	$7s^2\ ^1S_0$	0		16.8 $\star$	$7s7p\ ^3P_1^\circ$	31,540 $\star$	$6d7s\ ^3D_1$	20,846 $\star$	19.4 [d]$\star$

a: Refs. [23–25]; b: Refs. [26–28]; c: Ref. [28–30]; d: Ref. [31].

2. Experimental Approach

Laser resonance chromatography couples laser spectroscopy with ion mobility spectrometry. It is based on a population transfer between metastable ionic states in a resonant laser excitation process. A laser excites the ion, e.g., from the ground state to an intermediate level (to be optically probed) in an allowed optical transition. The intermediate level depopulates partly to lower-lying metastable states that do not easily quench to the ground state. In a simplified picture, the ion changes its size during this process, which can then be exploited for purposes of diagnostics. The resonant process is identified by a change in the characteristic arrival-time distributions of the ions on a particle detector after passing a drift tube filled with helium gas at pressures < 10 mbar. Since the mobility is function of the gas temperature and could be distinct for the different states, the operation of the drift tube at cryogenic temperatures usually provides an additional degree of freedom to optimize time resolution and state separation [19,32].

The method is generally applicable for transition-metal ions including Lu^+ and Lr^+. Promising optical pumping schemes for singly charged rutherfordium, the next-heavier element within the fourth row transition metals, have already been proposed [33]. Compared to many existing spectroscopy techniques, the LRC approach has a number of key advantages, some of which are:

- No neutralization of the thermalized fusion products is required. The ions can be manipulated and guided with high efficiency by electric fields;
- No further ionization of the ions is required. Only one laser is needed for spectroscopy;
- No radiation detection is required as in fluorescence spectroscopy. The sensitivity does not depend on the solid angle coverage of the detectors;
- A mass filter is a useful option at low ion production rates, but is not mandatory to suppress molecular sidebands or even isobars of different electronic configurations, as the drift itself provides the required ion discrimination.

2.1. The LRC Apparatus

The LRC setup is shown in Figure 1. It consists of five different pressure sections (PS) for stopping, extraction, separation, mass selection and detection of the sample ions. The ionized residual nuclei produced during the fusion-evaporation process lose most of their kinetic energy by passing through a metallic window of a few µm thickness before they are thermalized by collisions with the He buffer gas inside of the stopping cell (PS1) at a pressure of about 60 mbar. The thermalized ions are ejected through a convergent–divergent nozzle of 0.6 mm throat diameter towards a radio frequency quadrupole (RFQ) in PS2 that serves to extract and further cool the ions and to guide them towards the buncher in the next pumping section (PS3). The first-generation stopping cell of the SHIPTRAP setup together with its extraction RFQ i used for this purpose [34].

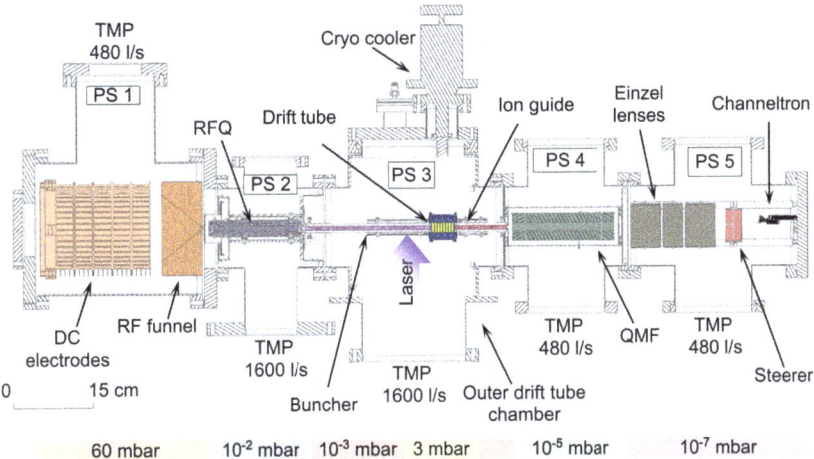

Figure 1. Schematic overview of the LRC apparatus. See text for more information.

The subsequent buncher installation enables a spatial confinement of the ions for laser spectroscopy and a precise referencing of their arrival time distributions. It consists of four stainless steel rods with diameters of 3.5 mm, each divided into 25 segments. The distance between opposite rods is $2r_0 = 3$ mm. PS3 also incorporates a cryogenic drift tube and an ion guide. The drift tube is used for electronic-state chromatography and is explained in more detail in Section 2.3. The ion guide comprises 10 segments of similar geometry as the buncher segments and is used to transport and focus the ions into the quadrupole mass filter (Extrel QMS) in the pumping section PS4, where the ions are selected based on their mass-to-charge ratio. Next, the ions are focused by einzel lenses and a X and Y steerer towards the detection system, which contains a channeltron detector (Dr Sjuts K15) installed in the last pumping section PS5.

2.2. The Laser System

One of the characteristics and a potential advantage of the LRC technique compared with conventional resonance ionization spectroscopy is the use of only one laser beam to search for optical resonances by optical pumping of metastable states. The laser system is shown in Figure 2. It consists of a 10-kHz Nd:YAG laser (Edgewave, 90 W at 532 nm) that pumps a dye laser (Sirah Credo), providing laser pulse energies between 10 and 100 µJ in the ultraviolet (UV) range from 220 up to 360 nm after frequency doubling or tripling, depending on the dye. Both lasers are installed next to the LRC apparatus and the laser beam path and optics are arranged as shown in Figure 2. The fundamental wavelength is monitored using a wavelength meter (HighFinesse WS7 UVU) featuring autocalibration via an integrated calibration source. For initial experiments and offline studies, a Nd:YAG laser (Continuum Minilite II) operated at 10 Hz repetition rate was used in addition to produce ions via ablation from primed samples inserted inside of the stopping cell (PS1).

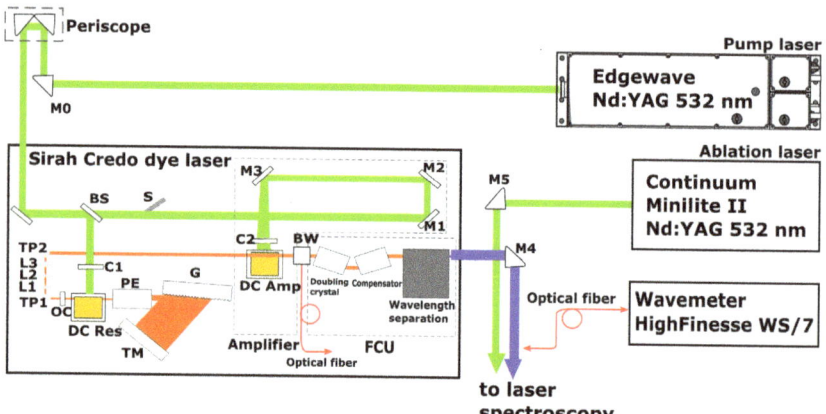

Figure 2. LRC laser system. Edgewave Nd:YAG laser pumps a Sirah Credo dye laser. Laser ablation is carried out using a Continuum Minilite II Nd:YAG laser. The wavemeter is used for wavelength monitoring. Abbreviations: M, mirror; L, lens; TP, telescopic lens; C, cylindrical lens; BS, beam splitter; BW, Brewster window; G, grating; PE, prism expander; DC Res, dye cell resonator; DC Amp, dye cell amplifier; OC, output coupler; FCU, frequency conversion unit.

2.3. The Drift Tube Outer Chamber

The main components of the drift tube section are shown in Figure 1 (PS3). The section incorporates two stainless steel chambers: The outer vacuum chamber and the cryogenic drift tube are connected to the buncher on the left side and to the ion guide on its exit on the right side. The outer chamber has a cuboid shape with edge lengths of (L × W × H) = (255 mm × 269 mm × 262 mm). A 1600 l/s turbomolecular pump (TMP, Edwards STP 1603C) is connected to this chamber via a DN-200 ConFlat flange to pump it down to pressures <10^{-8} mbar in standby mode or <10^{-2} mbar in operation mode. The chamber provides vacuum and thermal shielding for the cryogenic drift tube and features high voltage and RF feedthroughs, a gas inlet, pressure gauges, electrical feedthroughs for heaters and temperature sensors, view ports for the laser beam and a DN-63 ConFlat flange to connect a free piston Stirling cryocooler (CryoTel-CT). The latter has a cooling capacity of about 11 W at 77 K and is connected to the drift tube via four copper strands with a cross sectional area of 16 mm².

2.4. The Drift Tube Inner Chamber

The cryogenic drift tube sits at the heart of the LRC apparatus. A schematic overview of this is shown in Figure 3. The tube has a hexagonal shape with an inner diameter of 46 mm and a length of 53.5 mm. It is fixed to the outer chamber via 12 titanium spokes

(M2, DIN 975/DIN 976 Titanium Grade 2). The drift tube chamber is plated on the outside with a thin copper layer of 50–100 µm thickness to enable better heat conductance and a homogeneous distribution of the temperature over the whole drift tube during cooling and warming phases. It includes a gas inlet and outlet, a connection for a pressure gauge (Pfeiffer Vacuum PKR 360) and several tapered holes to fix heaters (high power resistors TCP100U) and temperature sensors (Lake Shore Germanium-CD). The tube has octagonal flanges at both ends that also serve to attach it to the spokes on the outer chamber.

In its interior, the drift tube chamber incorporates eight stainless steel electrodes of 20 mm inner diameter, 24 mm outer diameter and of a width of 5 mm. Six of the electrodes are enclosed by two identical end caps designed to have an electrode in one side and a diaphragm of 1 mm on the other side, serving either as injection or exit nozzle. The caps also serve as a support for the stainless steel fixation of the buncher and the ion guide; cf. Figure 3. All inner electrodes are electrically connected to each other by seven 1-MΩ resistors in series to build up a resistance of 7.15 MΩ between the end caps. The electrodes are supported via Vitronit ceramic rods of 5 mm diameter and 46.5 mm length and separated by 0.5 mm from each other with Vitronit ceramic cylindrical spacers of 5 mm length and 5 mm inner diameter. All inner electrodes plus the end caps are surrounded by a ceramic cylinder of 40 mm inner diameter, 44 mm outer diameter and length of 46.5 mm to isolate the electrodes from the grounded tube housing.

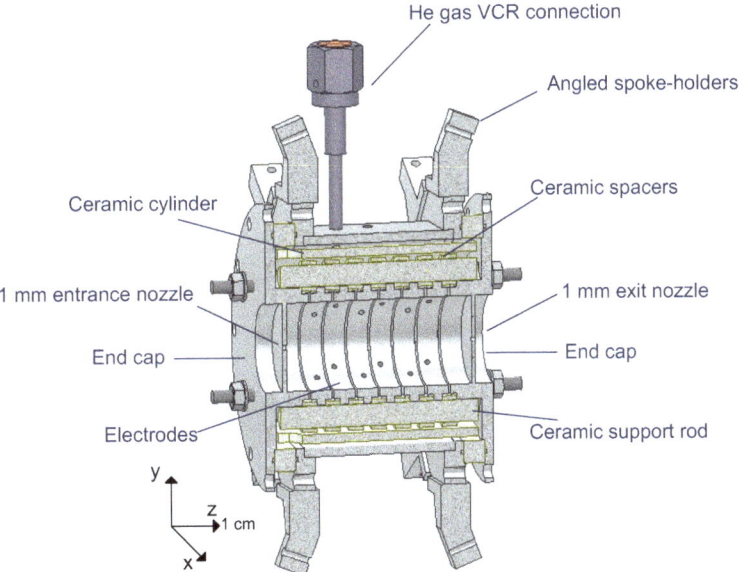

Figure 3. 3D cross-sectional view of the LRC drift tube and its components.

3. Ion Drift Simulations

Simulations were performed for the drift tube using the SIMION software package [35] in order to estimate Sc$^+$ drift times at a given He pressure and temperature and to extract suitable voltage configurations to be used in future LRC experiments. In the simulations, we considered both Statistical Diffusion (SDS) and Viscous Damping (VD) models [36]. Hard sphere model simulations could not be performed thus far due to the lack of reference data for the collision cross sections.

The reduced mobility for Sc$^+$ in the ground state and Sc^{+*} in the metastable state for the SDS and VD models were taken from [20]; cf. Table 1. We tested two configurations, one with a roughly constant electric field (unfocused beam) and a second with a gradually increasing electric field (focused beam). Ions were generated at the entrance of the drift tube and their drift times were recorded when they exited through a 1 mm or 2 mm diameter nozzle to explore the feasibility of enhancing the transmission while keeping time resolution unchanged. The two voltage configurations we used are shown in Table 2. We simulated different voltage values of U_0 in a way that the resulting average ratio of electric-field strength to gas number density, E/n_0, spanned a range between 1 and 30 Td, with 1 Td = 10^{-17} V · cm^2. For each value of U_0, 10,000 ions were generated in a 3D Gaussian distribution with a standard deviation of $\sigma_{x,y,z} = 0.2$ mm. The ion mobilities were calculated from the reduced mobilities by considering a pressure of 2 mbar of helium gas at a temperature of $T = 297$ K. Figure 4a shows ion trajectories projected on the symmetry plane obtained for the two different electric field configurations at an average reduced field of 15 Td. Using the VD model, the electric fields acting on each ion during its drift were recorded for each voltage configuration and allowed us to extract the mean electric field; cf. Figure 4b.

Table 2. Voltage configurations for unfocused (*) and focused beam (**). n is the electrode number. In the case of the unfocused beam, the voltages applied to the different electrodes were scaled by n, whereby values of U_0 between 0.1–10 V were applied in steps of 0.1 V to span a range of E/n_0 between 1–30 Td. For the focused beam, we added different offsets to the unfocused beam configurations as given in the table, where $\delta = 0.75$ V and U_0 was varied between 0.1–2.7 V to span in total an E/n_0 range between 1–30 Td.

Electrode # n	Unfocused beam Voltage (V) *			Focused beam Voltage (V) **		
1			0			0
2			0			0
3			0			0
4			0			δ
5	n · U_0	+	0	n · U_0	+	3δ
6			0			7δ
7			0			12δ
8			0			24δ

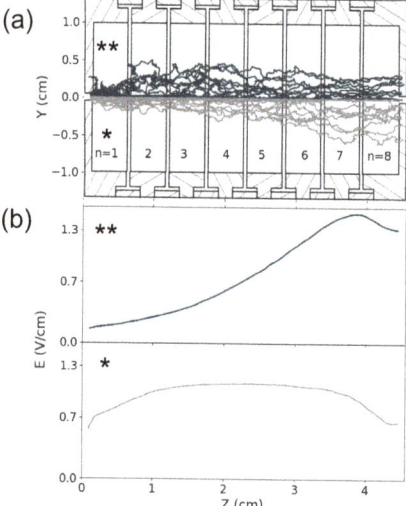

Figure 4. (a) Trajectories for $E/n_0 = 15$ Td for unfocused (*) and focused beams (**). (b) Electric fields along the electrodes for focused (**top**) and unfocused (**bottom**) beams.

Results

We made a comparison of the transmission efficiency between focused and unfocused beam configurations and between 1 mm and 2 mm exit nozzles for Sc^+ ions. To this end, we defined this efficiency as the fraction of the number of ions arriving at the exit nozzle within a radius of 0.5 mm (1 mm) from the center axis respective to the initial number of ions for 1 mm (2 mm) nozzle diameters. Figure 5 shows this transmission efficiency for the different states as function of the reduced field. For the unfocused beam using the 1 mm diameter exit nozzle, it grows quickly as the reduced field increases to reach a maximum of 3.7% at an E/n_0 value of about 8.5 Td and decreases with increasing fields to stagnate at about 2%. When using the 2 mm diameter exit nozzle, it grows even quicker as the reduced field increases to reach a maximum of 4.6% at an E/n_0 value of about 7.6 Td and stays stable up to around 20 Td to then increase again. According to the simulations, there is nearly no difference for the unfocused beam in terms of transmission efficiency between the ground and the metastable state for both 1 mm and 2 mm exit diameters below 20 Td. In the case of a focused beam using the 1 mm exit nozzle, the efficiency follows the unfocused beam up to 3 Td, then gradually increases with increasing fields, but stays below that achieved for the unfocused beam till reaching 15 Td. In the case of the 2 mm nozzle, the focused beam and the unfocused beam have similar transmission up to 10 Td. From these values onward for both nozzles, 1 mm and 2 mm, the deviation in the transmission of the two states becomes apparent. A maximum transmission efficiency of 7% for 1 mm and 20% for 2 mm nozzles in the focused beam configuration is achieved for the ground state ions at 30 Td, while the metastable state transmission stagnates at about 5% and 15% for 1 mm and 2 mm, respectively. Since the ions in the ground state exhibit a higher mobility, they can drift faster compared with the ions in the metastable states and thus are less prone to transversal diffusion losses. Theoretically, even higher efficiencies can be expected for these latter scenarios if the reduced field is increased beyond 30 Td, but only at the cost of deactivating states due to gas collisions that would degrade the metastable signal [17,37,38]. In addition, increased electric fields carry the risk of gas discharges with only a few hundred volts for 2 mbar of He gas and lead to shorter drift times due to higher velocity, which can in turn lead to both neutralization and a lower resolving power, respectively.

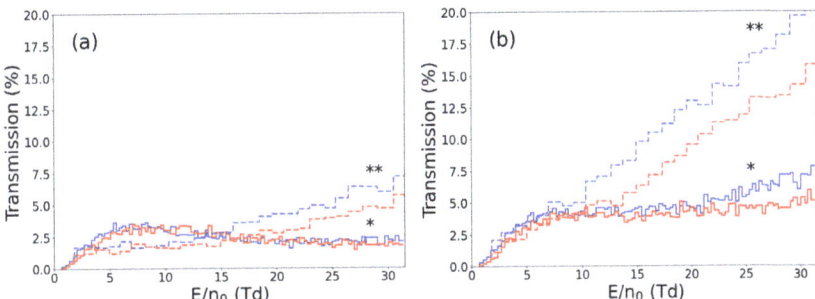

Figure 5. Ion transmission for unfocused (*) and focused (**) beams for both ground (blue) and metastable states (red) and for (**a**) 1 mm and (**b**) 2 mm exit diameter nozzles. Dash-line: focused beam; solid line: unfocused beam.

To better understand the behavior of the different electric field configurations in terms of resolution, we analyzed the drift time differences between the ground state and metastable state. Figure 6 shows the drift time for the two Sc^+ states in the different beam configurations in the case of the 1 mm nozzle; similar behavior was observed for the 2 mm exit diameter nozzle. It becomes apparent that, irrespective of the electronic states, the gradual increase of the electric field (corresponding to the beam focusing scenario) cause the ions to drift at small velocities the majority of the time and to lag behind in comparison when they are exposed to an average but rather homogeneous electric field (unfocused beam). The relative drift time differences exhibit a maximum at reduced field values between 5 Td and 10 Td in both configurations, indicating the best time resolution. However, a deeper insight is obtained by including peak broadening effects in the analysis by comparing the time histograms of the transmitted ions from the simulations. The different ionic states can be disentangled better from each other at larger reduced fields, which means at smaller absolute drift times and thus at the cost of relative drift time differences. If we compare the two different configurations, it becomes clear that, here as well, the unfocused beam provides better working conditions because it provides better time resolution over a larger range of E/n_0 values. In the case of a focused beam, the time peaks can be partly disentangled only at fields higher than $\approx$10 Td. The 2 mm configuration shows a similar trend with respect to the resolution. However, even though the larger nozzle provides higher efficiency, this latter is not so remarkably higher as to trade off the vacuum conditions inside of the PS3 section. We can consider this option for future tests.

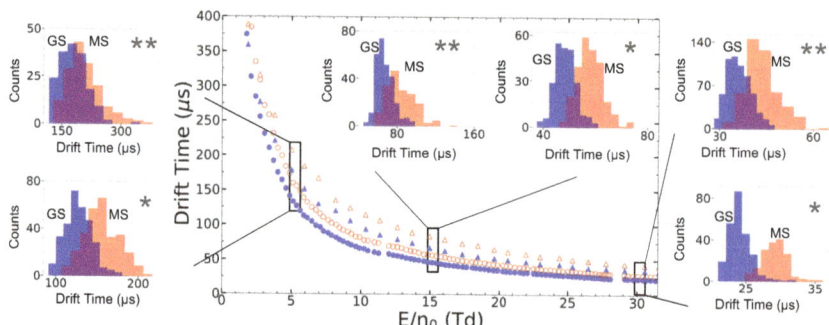

Figure 6. Absolute drift time comparison between ground and metastable states for both focused and unfocused beams. Unfocused beam: ● = ground state; ○ = metastable state. Focused beam: ▲ = ground state; △ = metastable state. Insets: selected histograms for E/n_0 = 5, 15, and 30 Td to demonstrate resolution behavior. * = unfocused beam ; ** = focused beam; blue = ground state; red = metastable state.

4. Current Status and Outlook

In the summer of 2022, the LRC setup is nearly complete and the commissioning phase has already begun with testing of the vacuum and functionality of key components such as the buffer gas stopping cell, the quadrupole mass filter and the laser systems. The cryogenic drift tube together with the miniature ion guide and buncher are being assembled and are ready for integration into the setup. Different ion sources are available, including a laser ablation source and a ^{223}Ra recoil ion source, with the latter being best suited for optimizing and quantifying the transmission efficiency through the whole apparatus.

SIMION simulations were performed for the LRC drift tube using two electric field configurations: unfocused and focused beams; and two geometry configurations: 1 mm and 2 mm exit nozzle diameters. From these simulations, we inferred that a rather homogeneous electric field enables a comparably higher ion transmission while maintaining a good resolution at relatively low E/n_0 values using a 1 mm exit diameter nozzle. In addition, it can be expected that working at lower fields minimizes the risk of gas discharges and deactivation of states. This can therefore also be very beneficial for a successful application of the LRC method. Higher transmission can be achieved when using a 2 mm exit nozzle and eventually focusing the beam into the nozzle.

Our first proof-of-principle experiments will target ^{45}Sc$^+$, cf. Table 1. These offline measurements are currently being prepared and we expect them to last for up to one year. The relative mobility difference between the ground and the metastable state is about 20% at 295 K in He [25], which should be sufficient to enable LRC measurements. The laser probing occurs inside the buncher, i.e. before the ion drift, via laser resonant excitation of the $z^3D_1^o$ state at 27,917.78 cm^{-1} to optically pump the ion into the metastable state a^3F_2 at 4802.87 cm^{-1}. Since the metastable state is energetically relatively close to the ground state, deactivation of states will likely occur during the ion-atom collisions [39]. If such collisional de-excitations dominate and entirely prevent the chromatography of Sc$^+$, we will pursue LRC experiments on ^{175}Lu$^+$, the lighter chemical homologue of Lr$^+$. In the Lu$^+$ experiments, we will probe the $^3P_1^o$ state at 28,503.16 cm^{-1} that feeds the $^3D_1$ metastable state at 11,796.24 cm^{-1}. Since this latter state is energetically high enough above the ground state, level crossings in the corresponding diabatic potential curves become unlikely. Thus, for short drift paths, as in the LRC experiments, we expect deactivation of states to be suppressed in Lu$^+$-He collisions, particularly at moderate kinetic energies. Here, one should note that in Ref. [25], the signal of the metastable state could still be observed even for Sc$^+$ drifting inside a drift tube of about 2 m length. However, since the drift tube of the LRC apparatus is only 45 mm long, the chromatography will require detailed analysis of the arrival-time distributions due to expected moderate time resolution; cf. Figure 6.

Applying the LRC technique to stable Lu ions can give us a better understanding of the trade-off we should make to achieve maximum count rates without losing the chromatography information. Once experimentally optimized for low yields, LRC can then be applied to search for atomic levels in the heavier iso-electronic system ^{255}Lr$^+$ in on-line experiments.

Author Contributions: Conceptualization, M.L.; Setup design, E.R.R and M.L.; Simulations, E.R.R.; Simulations Methodology, E.R.R. and M.L.; Formal analysis, E.R.R.; Funding acquisition, M.L.; Investigation, E.R.R. and M.L.; Project administration, M.L.; Resources, B.J., E.K., H.R., E.R. and J.S.; Software, E.R.R.; Supervision, M.B. and M.L.; Validation, E.R.R, M.B., S.R. and M.L.; Visualization, E.R.R.; Writing—original draft, E.R.R; Writing—review & editing, E.R.R., M.B., M.L., S.N., S.R. and P.S. All authors have read and agreed to the published version of the manuscript.

Funding: This project has received funding from the European Research Council (ERC) under the European Union's Horizon 2020 Research and Innovation Programme (Grant Agreement No. 819957).

Institutional Review Board Statement: Not applicable.

Informed Consent Statement: Not applicable.

Data Availability Statement: Not applicable.

Acknowledgments: We would like to thank the workshops of the Chemistry, Nuclear Chemistry, Physics and Nuclear Physics departments of the JGU Mainz.

Conflicts of Interest: The authors declare no conflict of interest.

Abbreviations

The following abbreviations are used in this manuscript:

LRC	Laser Resonance Chromatography
SHE	Super Heavy Elements
PS	Pressure Section
SDS	Statistical Diffusion Simulation
VD	Viscous Damping

References

1. Giuliani, S.A.; Matheson, Z.; Nazarewicz, W.; Olsen, E.; Reinhard, P.G.; Sadhukhan, J.; Schuetrumpf, B.; Schunck, N.; Schwerdtfeger, P. Colloquium: Superheavy elements: Oganesson and beyond. *Rev. Mod. Phys.* **2019**, *91*, 011001. [CrossRef]
2. Nazarewicz, W. The limits of nuclear mass and charge. *Nat. Phys.* **2018**, *14*, 537–541. [CrossRef]
3. Düllmann, C.E. Studying chemical properties of the heaviest elements: One atom at a time. *Nucl. Phys. News* **2017**, *27*, 14–20. [CrossRef]
4. Yakushev, A.; Gates, J.M.; Türler, A.; Schädel, M.; Düllmann, C.E.; Ackermann, D.; Andersson, L.L.; Block, M.; Brüchle, W.; Dvorak, J.; et al. Superheavy element flerovium (element 114) is a volatile metal. *Inorg. Chem.* **2014**, *53*, 1624–1629. [CrossRef]

5. Eichler, R.; Aksenov, N.; Albin, Y.V.; Belozerov, A.; Bozhikov, G.; Chepigin, V.; Dmitriev, S.; Dressler, R.; Gäggeler, H.; Gorshkov, V.; et al. Indication for a volatile element 114. *Rca-Radiochim. Acta* **2010**, *98*, 133–139. [CrossRef]
6. Yakushev, A.; Lens, L.; Düllmann, C.E.; Block, M.; Brand, H.; Calverley, T.; Dasgupta, M.; Di Nitto, A.; Götz, M.; Götz, S.; et al. First study on nihonium (Nh, element 113) chemistry at TASCA. *Front. Chem.* **2021**, *9*, 753738. [CrossRef]
7. Sato, T.K.; Sato, N.; Asai, M.; Tsukada, K.; Toyoshima, A.; Ooe, K.; Miyashita, S.; Schädel, M.; Kaneya, Y.; Nagame, Y.; et al. First successful ionization of Lr (Z = 103) by a surface-ionization technique. *Rev. Sci. Instrum.* **2013**, *84*, 023304. [CrossRef]
8. Block, M.; Giacoppo, F.; Heßberger, F.P.; Raeder, S. Recent progress in experiments on the heaviest nuclides at SHIP. *Riv. Nuovo C* **2022**, *45*, 279–323. [CrossRef]
9. Ferrer, R.; Barzakh, A.; Bastin, B.; Beerwerth, R.; Block, M.; Creemers, P.; Grawe, H.; de Groote, R.; Delahaye, P.; Fléchard, X.; et al. Towards high-resolution laser ionization spectroscopy of the heaviest elements in supersonic gas jet expansion. *Nat. Commun.* **2017**, *8*, 14520. [CrossRef]
10. Laatiaoui, M.; Lauth, W.; Backe, H.; Block, M.; Ackermann, D.; Cheal, B.; Chhetri, P.; Düllmann, C.E.; Van Duppen, P.; Even, J.; et al. Atom-at-a-time laser resonance ionization spectroscopy of nobelium. *Nature* **2016**, *538*, 495–498. [CrossRef]
11. Laatiaoui, M.; Buchachenko, A.A.; Viehland, L.A. Laser Resonance Chromatography of Superheavy Elements. *Phys. Rev. Lett.* **2020**, *125*, 023002. [CrossRef]
12. Backe, H.; Lauth, W.; Block, M.; Laatiaoui, M. Prospects for laser spectroscopy, ion chemistry and mobility measurements of superheavy elements in buffer-gas traps. *Nucl. Phys. A* **2015**, *944*, 492–517. [CrossRef]
13. Laatiaoui, M.; Backe, H.; Habs, D.; Kunz, P.; Lauth, W.; Sewtz, M. Low-field mobilities of rare-earth metals. *Eur. Phys. J. D* **2012**, *66*, 232. [CrossRef]
14. Baumbach, J. Ion mobility spectrometry in scientific literature and in the International Journal for Ion Mobility Spectrometry (1998–2007). *Int. J. Ion Mobil. Spectrom.* **2008**, *11*, 3–11. [CrossRef]
15. Mason, E.A.; McDaniel, E.W. *Transport Properties of Ions in Gases*; Wiley Online Library: Hoboken, NJ, USA, 1988; Volume 26.
16. Kemper, P.R.; Bowers, M.T. State-selected mobilities of atomic cobalt ions. *J. Am. Chem. Soc.* **1990**, *112*, 3231. [CrossRef]
17. Kemper, P.R.; Bowers, M.T. Electronic-state chromatography: Application to first-row transition-metal ions. *J. Phys. Chem.* **1991**, *95*, 5134–5146. [CrossRef]
18. Iceman, C.; Rue, C.; Moision, R.M.; Chatterjee, B.K.; Armentrout, P.B. Ion mobility studies of electronically excited states of atomic transition metal cations: Development of an ion mobility source for guided ion beam experiments. *J. Am. Soc. Mass Spectrom.* **2007**, *18*, 1196. [CrossRef]
19. Ibrahim, Y.; Alsharaeh, E.; Mabrouki, R.; Momoh, P.; Xie, E.; El-Shall, M.S. Ion mobility of ground and excited states of laser-generated transition metal cations. *J. Phys. Chem. A* **2008**, *112*, 1112–1124. [CrossRef]
20. Manard, M.J.; Kemper, P.R. Ion Mobility Mass Spectrometry: The design of a new high-resolution mobility instrument with applications toward electronic-state characterization of first-row transition metal cations. *Int. J. Mass Spectrom.* **2016**, *402*, 1–11. [CrossRef]
21. Manard, M.J.; Kemper, P.R. Characterizing the electronic states of the second-row transitionmetal cations using high-resolution ion mobility mass spectrometry. *Int. J. Mass Spectrom.* **2016**, *407*, 69–76. [CrossRef]
22. Manard, M.J.; Kemper, P.R. An experimental investigation into the reduced mobilities of lanthanide cations using high-resolution ion mobility mass spectrometry. *Int. J. Mass Spectrom.* **2017**, *423*, 54–58. [CrossRef]
23. Lawler, J.E.; Dakin, J.T. Absolute transition probabilities in Sc I and Sc II. *J. Opt. Soc. Am. B* **1989**, *6*, 1457. [CrossRef]
24. Kramida, A.; Ralchenko, Y.; Reader, J. *NIST Atomic Spectra Database (Ver. 5.7.1)*; National Institute of Standards and Technology: Gaithersburg, MD, USA, 2020. [CrossRef]
25. Manard, M.J.; Kemper, P.R. Reduced mobilities of lanthanide cations measured using high-resolution ion mobility mass spectrometry with comparisons between experiment and theory. *Int. J. Mass Spectrom.* **2017**, *412*, 14. [CrossRef]
26. Quinet, P.; Palmeri, P.; Biémont, E.; McCurdy, M.M.; Rieger, G.; Pinnington, E.H.; Wickliffe, M.E.; Lawler, J.E. Experimental and theoretical radiative lifetimes, branching fractions and oscillator strengths in Lu II. *Mon. Not. Royal Astron. Soc.* **1999**, *307*, 934. [CrossRef]
27. Arifin. Lutetium Ion Spectroscopy. Bachelor's Thesis, Department of Physics, National University of Singapore, Singapore, 2014.
28. Visentin, G.; Laatiaoui, M.; Viehland, L.A.; Buchachenko, A.A. Mobility of the Singly-Charged Lanthanide and Actinide Cations: Trends and Perspectives. *Front. Chem.* **2020**, *8*, 438. [CrossRef] [PubMed]
29. Kahl, E.V.; Berengut, J.C.; Laatiaoui, M.; Eliav, E.; Borschevsky, A. High-precision ab initio calculations of the spectrum of Lr^+. *Phys. Rev. A* **2019**, *100*, 062505. [CrossRef]
30. Ramanantoanina, H.; Borschevsky, A.; Block, M.; Laatiaoui, M. Electronic Structure of Lr+ (Z = 103) from Ab Initio Calculations. *Atoms* **2022**, *10*, 48. [CrossRef]
31. Ramanantoanina, H.; Borschevsky, A.; Block, M.; Laatiaoui, M. State specific mobility of Lr^+ ion in He. *Phys. Rev. A* 2022, *Manuscript in preparation*.
32. Buchachenko, A.A.; Visentin, G.; Viehland, L.A. Gaseous transport properties of the ground and excited Cr, Co and Ni cations in He: Ab initio study of electronic state chromatography. *J. Chem. Phys.* **2022**, *in press*. [CrossRef]
33. Ramanantoanina, H.; Borschevsky, A.; Block, M.; Laatiaoui, M. Electronic structure of Rf^+ ($Z = 104$) from ab initio calculations. *Phys. Rev. A* **2021**, *104*, 022813. [CrossRef]

34. Neumayr, J.B.; Beck, L.; Habs, D.; Heinz, S.; Szerypo, J.; Thirolf, P.G.; Varentsov, V.; Voit, F.; Ackermann, D.; Beck, D.; et al. The ion-catcher device for SHIPTRAP. *Nucl. Instrum. Methods Phys. Res. B* **2006**, *244*, 489. [CrossRef]
35. Scientific-Instrument-Services. SIMION 8.0. Available online: https://simion.com/ (accessed on 9 July 2022).
36. Appelhans, A.D.; Dahl, D.A. SIMION ion optics simulations at atmospheric pressure. *Int. J. Mass Spectrom.* **2005**, *244*, 1–14. [CrossRef]
37. Wilkins, C.L.; Trimpin, S. *Ion Mobility Spectrometry-Mass Spectrometry: Theory and Applications*; CRC Press: Boca Raton, FL, USA, 2010.
38. Loh, S.; Fisher, E.; Lian, L.; Schulz, R.; Armentrout, P. State-specific reactions of Fe+ (6D, 4F) with O2 and c-C2H4O: D° 0 (Fe+-O) and effects of collisional relaxation. *J. Phys. Chem.* **1989**, *93*, 3159–3167. [CrossRef]
39. Chhetri, P.; Ackermann, D.; Backe, H.; Block, M.; Cheal, B.; Düllmann, C.E.; Even, J.; Ferrer, R.; Giacoppo, F.; Götz, S.; et al. Impact of buffer gas quenching on the $^1S_0 \rightarrow {}^1P_1$ ground-state atomic transition in nobelium. *Eur. Phys. J. D* **2017**, *71*, 195. [CrossRef]

Article

Extending Our Knowledge about the ^{229}Th Nuclear Isomer

Benedict Seiferle *, Daniel Moritz, Kevin Scharl, Shiqian Ding †, Florian Zacherl, Lilli Löbell and Peter G. Thirolf *

Faculty of Physics, Ludwig-Maximilians University München, Am Coulombwall 1, 85748 Garching, Germany;
daniel.moritz@physik.uni-muenchen.de (D.M.); K.Scharl@physik.uni-muenchen.de (K.S.);
dingshq@gmail.com (S.D.); Zacherl.Florian@physik.uni-muenchen.de (F.Z.);
Lilli.Loebell@physik.uni-muenchen.de (L.L.)
* Correspondence: benedict.seiferle@physik.uni-muenchen.de (B.S.);
peter.thirolf@physik.uni-muenchen.de (P.G.T.)
† Current Address: Department of Physics, Tsinghua University, Beijing 100084, China.

Abstract: The first nuclear excited state in ^{229}Th possesses the lowest excitation energy of all currently known nuclear levels. The energy difference between the ground- and first-excited (isomeric) state (denoted with ^{229m}Th) amounts only to ≈8.2 eV (≈151.2 nm), which results in several interesting consequences: Since the excitation energy is in the same energy range as the binding energy of valence electrons, the lifetime of ^{229m}Th is strongly influenced by the electronic structure of the Th atom or ion. Furthermore, it is possible to potentially excite the isomeric state in ^{229}Th with laser radiation, which led to the proposal of a nuclear clock that could be used to search for new physics beyond the standard model. In this article, we will focus on recent technical developments in our group that will help to better understand the decay mechanisms of ^{229m}Th, focusing primarily on measuring the radiative lifetime of the isomeric state.

Keywords: Th-229; nuclear clock; hyperfine structure spectroscopy; ion trap

Citation: Seiferle, B.; Moritz, D.; Scharl, K.; Ding, S.; Zacherl, F.; Löbell, L.; Thirolf, P.G. Extending Our Knowledge about the ^{229}Th Nuclear Isomer. *Atoms* **2022**, *10*, 24. https://doi.org/10.3390/atoms10010024

Academic Editor: Camillo Mariani

Received: 31 December 2021
Accepted: 31 January 2022
Published: 14 February 2022

Publisher's Note: MDPI stays neutral with regard to jurisdictional claims in published maps and institutional affiliations.

Copyright: © 2022 by the authors. Licensee MDPI, Basel, Switzerland. This article is an open access article distributed under the terms and conditions of the Creative Commons Attribution (CC BY) license (https://creativecommons.org/licenses/by/4.0/).

1. Introduction

The nuclear first excited state in ^{229}Th is in the focus of nuclear as well as atomic physics research. Due to its low excitation energy in the range of ≈8.2 eV (we took the mean value of the two most recent energy determinations [1,2]), the first nuclear excited state plays an exceptional role with the possibility to be excited by laser light. This led to the proposal to use the ^{229}Th nucleus as a basis for a nuclear optical clock [3]. It has been predicted that a nuclear clock could potentially reach a relative frequency uncertainty in the range of 10^{-19} [4]. Therefore, such a nuclear clock could complement current atomic clocks. It could especially be employed in the search for new physics beyond the standard model [5].

The reader is referred to the references [6–8] for a detailed overview of the topic.

The exceptionally low excitation energy plays an important role when one considers the possible decay channels of the isomer: The isomer potentially decays to its ground state via four decay channels: γ decay, internal conversion (IC), bound internal conversion (BIC) [9] and electronic bridge (EB) [10]. In the gamma decay channel, the isomer decays by emitting a photon that carries the excitation energy. The partial lifetime of this decay channel has been predicted to be in the range of 10^3 to 10^4 s [11,12].

The γ-decay channel competes with the internal conversion decay channel, whose lifetime has been measured in neutral atoms to be in the range of several microseconds [13], making it orders of magnitude faster than the γ decay. During the internal conversion decay, the energy of the isomeric state is transferred to the electronic shell and an electron is emitted into the vacuum. A prerequisite for the IC decay to occur is that the binding energy of one of the bound electrons (which is given by the ionization potential) is below the isomeric excitation energy. For the specific case of ^{229m}Th, the IC decay is already energetically forbidden for ^{229m}Th^{1+} ions with an ionization potential of ≈12 eV.

Another possible decay channel is bound internal conversion, where the decay energy is also transferred to the electronic shell. Instead of an electron being emitted, as in the internal conversion decay, an electronic state is excited. A requirement for electronic bridge decay is the presence of a transition in the electronic shell that is in resonance with the isomeric ground-state transition. This strong requirement is relaxed in the electronic bridge channel, where the isomer decays by exciting a virtual state in the electronic shell, which subsequently decays to a real electronic state. The excess energy is then carried away in the form of photons.

In the following, we focus on prospects to measure the radiative decay channel in a new setup currently being arranged at LMU Munich.

2. Towards Radiative Lifetime Measurements

For the measurement of the radiative lifetime it is envisaged to monitor the number of ^{229}Th ions in the isomeric state ^{229m}Th over time. The measurement of the radiative lifetime requires the complete suppression of all the other competing decay channels, such as internal conversion and bound internal conversion. The suppression of internal conversion can be achieved by preventing ^{229m}Th ions from neutralizing, since IC is energetically forbidden in Th ions. Therefore, the ions are confined in an ion trap. The trap is operated under cryogenic conditions to achieve the high vacuum quality that is needed to realize long storage times in the range of the expected radiative lifetime.

The appearance of BIC and EB can be excluded by measuring the lifetime in different electronic states. For a successful measurement of the lifetime, the storage time of the $^{229(m)}$Th ions (the m in brackets indicates that we are dealing with a cloud of ions in the nuclear ground state and the nuclear isomeric state) in the ion trap needs to be at least in the range of the expected lifetime, i.e., several 1000 s. This requires optimum vacuum conditions that can only be achieved under cryogenic conditions at temperatures around 4 K.

The general concept of the setup is shown in Figure 1. $^{229(m)}$Th^{3+} ions extracted from a buffer gas stopping cell are loaded axially (from the left side in Figure 1) into a cryogenic linear Paul trap. $^{229(m)}$Th^{3+} ions are used due to their favorable electronic level scheme exhibiting a rather simple alkali-like structure of an inert Rn core and a single valence electron, providing a closed three-level Lambda system suitable for for laser excitation and fluorescence detection. There, they are sympathetically cooled by ^{88}Sr ions, which are provided by an ion source and are axially loaded into the same linear Paul trap from the opposite side (i.e., the right side in Figure 1).

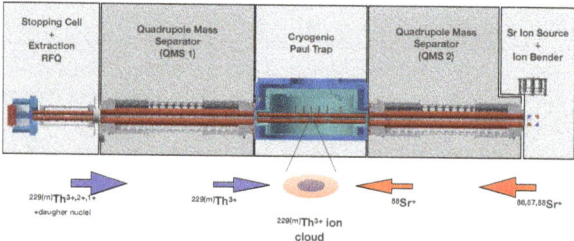

Figure 1. Visualization of the experimental setup and concept. A detailed explanation is provided in the text. $^{229(m)}$Th ions are produced in the α-decay of ^{233}U and extracted by a buffer-gas stopping cell and an extraction radio frequency quadrupole (RFQ). A quadrupole mass separator (QMS) allows for the selection of a specific charge state, which enables the loading of $^{229(m)}$Th $^{3+}$ into a cryogenic Paul trap. Sr ions produced by an ion dispenser source are bent by 90° by an electrostatic ion bender and are then injected into a QMS that selects ^{88}Sr$^+$ from other naturally occurring Sr isotopes. ^{88}Sr$^+$ ions are loaded into the cryogenic Paul trap and can be laser cooled.

The Sr ion source is placed 90° off axis, and the ions are bent by 90° using an electrostatic bending quadrupole in order to prevent the cryogenic stages from being exposed to the heated ion source and thereby reducing the heat load to the cold stages. This geometry also allows for a direct line of sight along the central axis of the setup (e.g., to align lasers along the axis for Doppler cooling and spectroscopy).

2.1. Stopping Cell and Extraction RFQ

$^{229(m)}$Th ions are produced in the α decay of ^{233}U, where the isomeric state is fed by a 2% decay branch. For this reason, a ^{233}U α recoil source with an activity of 10 kBq is placed in a buffer-gas stopping cell. The source consists of a Si wafer disk with a diameter of 30 mm. ^{233}U is deposited onto the disk by electroplating. $^{229(m)}$Th ions leaving the source material with a kinetic energy of $\approx$84 keV are stopped in 32 mbar catalytically purified helium. The ions are guided by an RF-DC funnel towards a de-Laval nozzle (nozzle diameter $\emptyset$ = 0.4 mm) that connects the high-pressure stopping cell to another vacuum chamber.

The RF-DC funnel consists of concentrically stacked ring electrodes, whose inner diameter is reduced linearly with the distance from the source, thus, creating a funnel-like shape. A DC gradient along the funnel electrodes guides the ions axially towards the de-Laval nozzle. Sinusodial RF-fields that are varying in phase by 180° between neighboring funnel electrodes prevent the ions from hitting the electrodes. The electrical potentials together with the funnel-like geometry allow the transport of ions that are far from the central axis towards the nozzle exit.

In the vicinity of the de-Laval nozzle, a gas flow drags the ions through the nozzle and injects them into the subsequent chamber. The formed supersonic gas jet is generated by a pressure difference between the buffer-gas stopping cell (typically at 32 mbar) and the subsequent chamber, which is typically pumped to a pressure in the range of 10^{-3}–10^{-4} mbar.

This chamber houses an axially segmented radio-frequency quadrupole (RFQ). A voltage gradient along the axis drags the ions through the remaining buffer gas, while the applied RF voltage keeps the ions on the central axis. This enables the formation of a cooled ion beam.

2.2. Quadrupole Mass Separators

The setup contains two quadrupole mass separators (QMS 1 and 2). QMS 1 is used to generate an isotopically pure $^{229(m)}$Th^{3+} ion beam that can be injected into the Paul trap and is located between the extraction RFQ and the cryogenic Paul trap. The second QMS (QMS 2) is placed between the cryogenic Paul trap and the ^{88}Sr ion source. QMS 2 serves two purposes: First, it is used to select ^{88}Sr ions from the ion beam generated by the Sr ion source.

In addition to other naturally occurring Sr isotopes, the ion beam may also contain elements other than Sr (such as K, Rb or Cs) due to the production process of the source. Secondly, QMS 2 can be used to investigate a possible formation of molecules of the Th ions after being trapped in the Paul trap. The QMS modules follow the design of [14], which was also used in earlier experiments [1,13,15]. In order to achieve the required mass resolving power, the RF-voltage amplitudes are actively stabilized by an FPGA-based circuit. For further details, see [16].

2.3. Cryogenic Paul Trap

The central structure of the setup is a Paul trap that is designed to be operated at cryogenic conditions. The design of the Paul trap follows closely the design used in [17,18]. For further details, see [16].

2.4. Sr Ion Source and Ion Bender

The Sr ion source is a commercially available heated dispenser ion source. The source is typically heated to a temperature above 1000 °C by applying a current of $\approx$2.2 A to a heating filament that is part of the source assembly.

The ions that are emitted from the source are extracted and focused by two ring electrodes. An electrostatic ion bender, consisting of four quarter cylinders that form a quadrupole potential, bends the ions by 90° towards QMS 2. Before entering QMS 2, the ions pass three more ring electrodes that help to efficiently inject them into QMS 2.

2.5. Cooling Lasers and HFS Lasers

To resolve the hyperfine-structure (HFS) shifts that are used to distinguish between the nuclear ground and nuclear isomeric state the $^{229(m)}$Th^{3+} ions need to be cooled.

Direct laser cooling of $^{229(m)}$Th^{3+} has already been achieved [19]. In our setup, $^{229(m)}$Th^{3+} ions are sympathetically cooled by ^{88}Sr ions, whose mass-to-charge ratio (88 u/e) is close to that of $^{229(m)}$Th^{3+} (76.3 u/e). The lack of hyperfine-structure shifts in ^{88}Sr ions provides a simpler cooling scheme than for $^{229(m)}$Th^{3+}. Doppler cooling can be performed on the $^2S_{1/2} \to\ ^2P_{1/2}$ transition at 422 nm [20]. The ions are re-pumped from the $^2D_{3/2}$ to the $^2P_{1/2}$ state with 1091 nm radiation (see the left part of Figure 2). The discrimination between the nuclear ground state and nuclear isomeric state is performed by measuring the HFS of $^{229(m)}$Th^{3+}.

The HFS will be probed on the $^2F_{5/2} \to\ ^2D_{5/2}$ transition at 690 nm. An additional re-pumping laser at 984 nm is needed to pump from the $^2F_{7/2}$ level back to $^2D_{5/2}$. The level scheme is shown in the right panel of Figure 2. $^{229(m)}$Th^{3+} exhibits a rich hyperfine structure; therefore, in order to avoid pumping into (hyperfine) dark-states, corresponding sidebands are generated with electro-optic modulators (EOMs). All central wavelengths are provided by external cavity diode lasers.

The 422 nm laser is locked to a close-by transition in Rb and shifted with an acousto-optical modulator (AOM) by approximately 440 MHz in order to drive the transition in ^{88}Sr [21]. The remaining lasers will be stabilized by either using a scanning transfer cavity or a commercial wavelength meter.

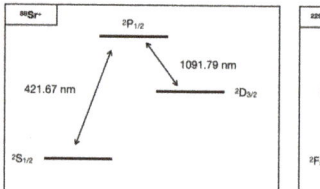
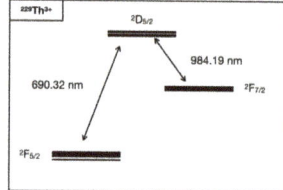

Figure 2. The relevant level schemes of singly charged ^{88}Sr and triply charged ^{229}Th. The presence of the hyperfine structure is indicated by the broadened width of the bars.

2.6. Measurement Scheme

The measurement scheme involves two stages. Ions are loaded into the trap and cooled down in a first stage. The second stage involves the measurement of the lifetime. First, $^{229(m)}$Th^{3+} ions are loaded into the trap. The ions are extracted from a buffer gas stopping cell. We estimate the number of extracted ions by scaling the number of $^{229(m)}$Th^{3+} ions extracted from a similar buffer-gas stopping cell and a similar source geometry [15] with the source activity. In Ref. [15], the number of extracted $^{229(m)}$Th^{3+} ions was on the order of 10^4 ions per second with a source activity of 290 kBq. Therefore, we expect an extraction rate in the range of 10^2 ions per second.

This number, however, requires experimental verification, as the exact extraction rate is influenced by several factors, such as the buffer gas cleanliness. We expect a small number of $^{229(m)}$Th^{3+} ions in the range between 10 and 100 to be loaded into the trap. It is envisaged to form an ion crystal by sympathetic cooling and to identify the nuclear state of the trapped ions by measuring their hyperfine structure. When there is at least one isomer confined in the trap, the lifetime measurement is started. This involves imaging the fluorescence radiation of individual ions onto an (EM)CCD camera.

This allows for identification of the decay of the isomer by tagging ions in the isomeric state on the camera image via their HFS fluorescence and registering their decay to the ground state; the lasers are set to exclusively drive HFS transitions that correspond to the isomeric state. When the isomeric state decays to the ground state, the respective thorium ion turns dark on the camera.

In order to double-check that the ion was not lost due to any other process (i.e., neutralization or molecule formation), the laser is set to drive nuclear ground-state HFS transitions immediately after the ion has turned dark. If the ion is still present in the trap, the time of the decay event can then be recorded and used for data analysis.

It is possible that the isomeric radiative lifetime is affected by the electronic state. For cross-checks, the duty-cycle of the 690 nm laser can be varied. This will leave the ions in the electronic ground-state for a variable amount of time. Additionally, by varying the duty cycle of the re-pumping laser (984 nm), it is possible to pump the ions into the $^2F_{7/2}$ electronic state and investigate the isomeric lifetime for ions in this electronic excited state.

3. Conclusions

We presented a setup that is able to measure the radiative lifetime of ^{229m}Th in the absence of the internal conversion decay channel. For this purpose, triply charged $^{229(m)}$Th ions are confined in a cryogenic Paul trap. $^{229(m)}$Th is cooled sympathetically by a laser-cooled cloud of ^{88}Sr ions. The number of ^{229m}Th ions is monitored over time by measuring the hyperfine-structure shifts specific for ^{229m}Th.

Author Contributions: The original draft was prepared by B.S. with input from B.S., D.M., K.S., S.D., F.Z., L.L. and P.G.T.; supervision, P.G.T. All authors have read and agreed to the published version of the manuscript.

Funding: This work is part of the 'ThoriumNuclearClock' project that received funding from the European Research Council (ERC) under the European Union's Horizon 2020 Research and Innovation Programme (Grant Agreement No. 856415) and by the European Union's Horizon 2020 Research and Innovation Programme under grant agreement No 664732 "nuClock".

Institutional Review Board Statement: Not applicable.

Informed Consent Statement: Not applicable.

Data Availability Statement: Not applicable.

Acknowledgments: We thank J. R. Crespo López-Urrutia, E. Peik, M. Okhapkin, J. Thielking, J. Weitenberg and L. v.d. Wense for fruitful discussions and their support.

Conflicts of Interest: The authors declare no conflict of interest.

References

1. Seiferle, B.; von der Wense, L.; Bilous, P.V.; Amersdorffer, I.; Lemell, C.; Libisch, F.; Stellmer, S.; Schumm, T.; Düllmann, C.E.; Pálffy, A.; et al. Energy of the ^{229}Th nuclear clock transition. *Nature* **2019**, *573*, 243–246. [CrossRef] [PubMed]
2. Sikorsky, T.; Geist, J.; Hengstler, D.; Kempf, S.; Gastaldo, L.; Enss, C.; Mokry, C.; Runke, J.; Düllmann, C.E.; Wobrauschek, P.; et al. Measurement of the ^{229}Th Isomer Energy with a Magnetic Microcalorimeter. *Phys. Rev. Lett.* **2020**, *125*, 142503. [CrossRef] [PubMed]
3. Peik, E.; Tamm, C. Nuclear laser spectroscopy of the 3.5 eV transition in Th-229. *Europhys. Lett.* **2003**, *61*, 181. [CrossRef]
4. Campbell, C.J.; Radnaev, A.G.; Kuzmich, A.; Dzuba, V.A.; Flambaum, V.V.; Derevianko, A. Single-Ion Nuclear Clock for Metrology at the 19th Decimal Place. *Phys. Rev. Lett.* **2012**, *108*, 120802. [CrossRef] [PubMed]
5. Peik, E.; Schumm, T.; Safronova, M.S.; Pálffy, A.; Weitenberg, J.; Thirolf, P.G. Nuclear clocks for testing fundamental physics. *Quantum Sci. Technol.* **2021**, *6*, 034002. [CrossRef]
6. Thirolf, P.G.; Seiferle, B.; von der Wense, L. The 229-thorium isomer: Doorway to the road from the atomic clock to the nuclear clock. *J. Phys. B At. Mol. Opt. Phys.* **2019**, *52*, 203001. [CrossRef]
7. Thirolf, P.G.; Seiferle, B.; von der Wense, L. Fundamental Constants: Improving Our Knowledge on the 229mThorium Isomer: Toward a Test Bench for Time Variations of Fundamental Constants (Ann. Phys. 5/2019). *Ann. Der Phys.* **2019**, *531*, 1800381. [CrossRef]
8. Beeks, K.; Sikorsky, T.; Schumm, T.; Thielking, J.; Okhapkin, M.V.; Peiket, E. The thorium-229 low-energy isomer and the nuclear clock. *Nat. Rev. Phys.* **2021**, *3*, 238–248. [CrossRef]
9. Karpeshin, F.F.; Trzhaskovskaya, M.B. Bound internal conversion versus nuclear excitation by electron transition: Revision of the theory of optical pumping of the ^{229m}Th isomer. *Phys. Rev. C* **2017**, *95*, 034310. [CrossRef]

10. Strizhov, V.F.; Tkalya, E.V. Decay channel of low-lying isomer state of the Th-229 nucleus. Possibilities of experimental investigation. *Sov. Phys. JETP* **1991**, *72*, 387.
11. Tkalya, E.V.; Schneider, C.; Jeet, J.; Hudson, E.R. Radiative lifetime and energy of the low-energy isomeric level in ^{229}Th. *Phys. Rev. C* **2015**, *92*, 054324. [CrossRef]
12. Minkov, N.; Pálffy, A. Reduced Transition Probabilities for the Gamma Decay of the 7.8 eV Isomer in ^{229}Th. *Phys. Rev. Lett.* **2017**, *118*, 212501. [CrossRef] [PubMed]
13. Seiferle, B.; von der Wense, L.; Thirolf, P.G. Lifetime Measurement of the ^{229}Th Nuclear Isomer. *Phys. Rev. Lett.* **2017**, *118*, 042501. [CrossRef] [PubMed]
14. Haettner, E.; Plaß, W.R.; Czok, U.; Dickel, T.; Geissel, H.; Kinsel, W.; Petrick, M.; Schäfer, T.; Scheidenberger, C. A versatile triple radiofrequency quadrupole system for cooling, mass separation and bunching of exotic nuclei. *Nucl. Instrum. Methods A* **2018**, *880*, 138–151. [CrossRef]
15. von der Wense, L.; Seiferle, B.; Laatiaoui, M.; Neumayr, J.B.; Maier, H.-J.; Wirth, H.-F.; Mokry, C.; Mokry, J.; Eberhardt, K.; Düllmann, C.E.; et al. Direct detection of the ^{229}Th nuclear clock transition. *Nature* **2016**, *533*, 47–51. [CrossRef] [PubMed]
16. Moritz, D.; Scharl, K.; Ding, S.; Seiferle, B.; von der Wense, L.; Zacherl, F.; Löbell, L.; Thirolf, P.G. A cryogenic Paul trap setup for the determination of the ionic radiative lifetime of ^{229}Th^{3+}. 2022, *in preparation*.
17. Schwarz, M.; Versolato, O.O.; Windberger, A.; Brunner, F.R.; Ballance, T.; Eberle, S.N.; Ullrich, J.; Schmidt, P.O.; Hansen, A.K.; Gingell, A.D.; et al. Cryogenic linear Paul trap for cold highly charged ion experiments. *Rev. Sci. Instrum.* **2012**, *83*, 083115. [CrossRef] [PubMed]
18. Leopold, T.; King, S.A.; Micke, P.; Bautista-Salvador, A.; Heip, J.C.; Ospelkaus, C.; Crespo López-Urrutia, J.R.; Schmidt, P.O. A cryogenic radio-frequency ion trap for quantum logic spectroscopy of highly charged ions. *Rev. Sci. Instrum.* **2019**, *90*, 073201. [CrossRef] [PubMed]
19. Campbell, C.J.; Radnaev, A.G.; Kuzmich, A. Wigner Crystals of ^{229}Th for Optical Excitation of the Nuclear Isomer. *Phys. Rev. Lett.* **2011**, *106*, 223001. [CrossRef] [PubMed]
20. Removille, S.; Dubessy, R.; Dubost, B.; Glorieux, Q.; Coudreau, T.; Guibal, S.; Likforman, J.-P.; Guidoni, L. Trapping and cooling of Sr+ ions: Strings and large clouds. *J. Phys. B At. Mol. Opt. Phys.* **2009**, *42*, 154014. [CrossRef]
21. Madej, A.A.; Marmet, L.; Bernard, J.E. Rb atomic absorption line reference for single Sr+ laser cooling systems. *Appl. Phys. B* **1998**, *67*, 229–234. [CrossRef]

Article

First Offline Results from the S³ Low-Energy Branch

Jekabs Romans [1,*,†], Anjali Ajayakumar [2], Martial Authier [3], Frederic Boumard [4], Lucia Caceres [2], Jean-François Cam [4], Arno Claessens [1], Samuel Damoy [2], Pierre Delahaye [2], Philippe Desrues [4], Antoine Drouart [3], Patricia Duchesne [5], Rafael Ferrer [1], Xavier Fléchard [4], Serge Franchoo [5], Patrice Gangnant [2], Ruben P. de Groote [1], Sandro Kraemer [1], Nathalie Lecesne [2], Renan Leroy [2], Julien Lory [4], Franck Lutton [2], Vladimir Manea [5], Yvan Merrer [4], Iain Moore [6], Alejandro Ortiz-Cortes [2], Benoit Osmond [2], Julien Piot [2], Olivier Pochon [5], Blaise-Maël Retailleau [2], Hervé Savajols [2], Simon Sels [1], Emil Traykov [7], Juha Uusitalo [6], Christophe Vandamme [4], Marine Vandebrouck [3], Paul Van den Bergh [1], Piet Van Duppen [1], Matthias Verlinde [1], Elise Verstraelen [1] and Klaus Wendt [8]

1. KU Leuven, Instituut voor Kern- en Stralingsfysica, B-3001 Leuven, Belgium; arno.claessens@kuleuven.be (A.C.); rafael.ferrer@kuleuven.be (R.F.); ruben.degroote@kuleuven.be (R.P.d.G.); sandro.kraemer@kuleuven.be (S.K.); simon.sels@kuleuven.be (S.S.); paul.vandenbergh@kuleuven.be (P.V.d.B); piet.vanduppen@kuleuven.be (P.V.D.); matthias.verlinde@kuleuven.be (M.V.); elise.verstraelen@kuleuven.be (E.V.)
2. GANIL, CEA/DRF-CNRS/IN2P3, B.P. 55027, F-14076 Caen, France; anjali.ajayakumar@ganil.fr (A.A.); lucia.caceres@ganil.fr (L.C.); samuel.damoy@ganil.fr (S.D.); pierre.delahaye@ganil.fr (P.D.); patrice.gangnant@ganil.fr (P.G.); nathalie.lecesne@ganil.fr (N.L.); renan.leroy@ganil.fr (R.L.); franck.lutton@ganil.fr (F.L.); alejandro.ortiz-cortes@ganil.fr (A.O.-C.) benoit.osmond@ganil.fr (B.O.); julien.piot@ganil.fr (J.P.); blaise-mael.retailleau@ganil.fr (B.-M.R) herve.savajols@ganil.fr (H.S.)
3. IRFU, CEA, Université Paris-Saclay, F-91191 Gif sur Yvette, France; martial.authier@cea.fr (M.A.); antoine.drouart@cea.fr (A.D.); marine.vandebrouck@cea.fr (M.V.)
4. Normandie Université, ENSICAEN, UNICAEN, CNRS/IN2P3, LPC Caen, F-14000 Caen, France; boumard@lpccaen.in2p3.fr (F.B.); cam@lpccaen.in2p3.fr (J.-F.C.); desrues@lpccaen.in2p3.fr (P.D.); flechard@lpccaen.in2p3.fr (X.F.); lory@lpccaen.in2p3.fr (J.L.); merrer@lpccaen.in2p3.fr (Y.M.); vandamme@lpccaen.in2p3.fr (C.V.)
5. IJCLab, Université Paris-Saclay, CNRS/IN2P3, F-91405 Orsay, France; patricia.duchesne@ijclab.in2p3.fr (P.D.); serge.franchoo@ijclab.in2p3.fr (S.F.); vladimir.manea@ijclab.in2p3.fr (V.M.); olivier.pochon@ijclab.in2p3.fr (O.P.)
6. Department of Physics, University of Jyväskylä, P.O. Box 35 (YFL), FI-40014 Jyväskylä, Finland; iain.d.moore@jyu.fi (I.M.); juha.uusitalo@jyu.fi (J.U.)
7. IPHC, Université de Strasbourg, CNRS, F-67037 Strasbourg, France; emil.traykov@iphc.cnrs.fr
8. Institut für Physik, Johannes Gutenberg-Universität Mainz, 55128 Mainz, Germany; Klaus.Wendt@uni-mainz.de
* Correspondence: jekabs.romans@kuleuven.be
† Current address: Bd Henri Becquerel, B.P. 55027, CEDEX 05, F-14076 Caen, France.

Citation: Romans, J.; Ajayakumar, A.; Authier, M.; Boumard, F.; Caceres, L.; Cam, J.-F.; Claessens, A.; Damoy, S.; Delahaye, P.; Desrues, P.; et al. First Offline Results from the S³ Low-Energy Branch. *Atoms* **2022**, *10*, 21. https://doi.org/10.3390/atoms10010021

Academic Editor: Alexander Kramida

Received: 7 January 2022
Accepted: 3 February 2022
Published: 9 February 2022

Publisher's Note: MDPI stays neutral with regard to jurisdictional claims in published maps and institutional affiliations.

Copyright: © 2022 by the authors. Licensee MDPI, Basel, Switzerland. This article is an open access article distributed under the terms and conditions of the Creative Commons Attribution (CC BY) license (https://creativecommons.org/licenses/by/4.0/).

Abstract: We present the first results obtained from the S³ Low-Energy Branch, the gas cell setup at SPIRAL2-GANIL, which will be installed behind the S³ spectrometer for atomic and nuclear spectroscopy studies of exotic nuclei. The installation is currently being commissioned offline, with the aim to establish optimum conditions for the operation of the radio frequency quadrupole ion guides, mass separation and ion bunching, providing high-efficiency and low-energy spatial spread for the isotopes of interest. Transmission and mass-resolving power measurements are presented for the different components of the S³-LEB setup. In addition, a single-longitudinal-mode, injection-locked, pumped pulsed-titanium–sapphire laser system has been recently implemented and is used for the first proof-of-principle measurements in an offline laser laboratory. Laser spectroscopy measurements of erbium, which is the commissioning case of the S³ spectrometer, are presented using the $4f^{12}6s^2\ ^3H_6 \rightarrow 4f^{12}(^3H)6s6p$ optical transition.

Keywords: resonance ionization laser spectroscopy; gas cell; hypersonic gas jets; radio frequency quadrupoles; nuclear ground state properties; isotope shift; hyperfine structure

1. Introduction

The Super Separator Spectrometer (S^3) [1] is a fusion–evaporation recoil separator, which is currently under construction at the SPIRAL2 facility in GANIL, aiming to study exotic neutron-deficient isotopes in the actinide and super-heavy element regions, and in the $N = Z$ region around ^{100}Sn [2]. The fusion–evaporation reactions will be produced by an intense heavy ion beam, impinging on a thin target. The low-production cross-sections and the available primary beam intensities at various facilities worldwide limits the production rates, and thus the amount of experimental data of very exotic nuclear systems. To overcome this obstacle, the superconducting LINAC of the SPIRAL2 facility has been developed to produce stable ion beams from He to U with energies from 0.75 up to 14.5 MeV/u, and intensities from 1pµA up to Ni [1]. Primary beams of such high intensities will make SPIRAL2-S^3 and its low-energy branch (S^3-LEB) a prominent place to study the ground and isomeric state properties of exotic nuclei [3]. For a detailed description of the SPIRAL2 project, one can refer to [4].

The S^3-LEB will be installed at the S^3 final focal plane for some of the first experimental campaigns, and it will deploy a variety of low-energy measurement techniques (laser spectroscopy, decay spectroscopy and mass spectrometry). The underpinning working principle of the S^3-LEB setup is the in-gas laser ionization and spectroscopy (IGLIS) technique [5,6], which aims to perform laser spectroscopy measurements to extract the isotope shifts and hyperfine parameters of radioactive isotopes. This experimental data can give access to differences in mean square charge radii $\delta \langle r^2 \rangle$, magnetic dipole μ and electrical quadrupole Q moments, as well as nuclear spins I, which are crucial for validating atomic and nuclear models, and for improving our understanding of the atomic and nuclear structure in poorly explored regions of the nuclear chart. However, the access to I and Q can be highly case-dependent, due to line-broadening mechanisms. One such example is the predicted existence of the island of stability of super-heavy elements [7].

Together with the hot-cavity laser ion sources used at ISOL facilities [8,9], IGLIS belongs to the broader class of laser ion source and laser spectroscopy techniques which probe the radioisotopes very close to the production or stopping area. These techniques allow the production of element-selective ion beams with high efficiencies. Nevertheless, their spectral resolution is typically limited by broadening mechanisms. The hot-cavity spectroscopy is dominated by a large Doppler broadening, induced by the $T \sim 2000$ °C temperature of the laser beam–atom interaction region. At ISOL facilities, it is thus common to study radioactive beams after reacceleration and mass separation using high-resolution collinear fluorescence [10,11] or resonance ionization spectroscopy (RIS) [12]. Recently, new approaches for improving the spectral resolution of hot-cavity laser spectroscopy have also been explored, with promising results (such as the use of perpendicular illumination [13] and Doppler-free, two-photon spectroscopy [14]).

With the IGLIS method, one first thermalizes and neutralizes the reaction products in the buffer gas of a gas cell that is kept under a constant gas flow. Performing laser ionization spectroscopy in such an environment results in spectral line widths of several GHz, due to collisional broadening. A crucial upgrade for the IGLIS technique has been the use of a de Laval nozzle at the exit of the gas cell, which creates a collimated and homogeneous hypersonic gas jet of low temperature T and low density ρ [6], containing the products of interest. Such an environment allows for laser spectroscopy with reduced broadening mechanisms by about an order of magnitude, while maintaining a high selectivity and efficiency [5].

The S^3-LEB setup has been developed by a collaboration between KU Leuven, SPIRAL2-GANIL, LPC Caen, IJCLab, University of Jyväskylä and University of Mainz. The setup is currently being commissioned at the GANIL Ion Source using Electron Laser Excitation (GISELE) [15] and LPC Caen. In this paper, the S^3-LEB setup will be described and some first results from the offline commissioning tests will be presented.

2. The S^3 Low-Energy Branch

2.1. Gas Cell, RFQ Ion Guides and Mass Spectrometer

The starting point of the S^3-LEB setup is a gas cell, in which the S^3 fusion–evaporation recoils will enter via a thin window. A 3D image of the gas cell is presented in Figure 1. The next point of the setup is the beam transport, mass separation, bunching and cooling stages. This is achieved by the static and alternating electric fields created by a set of radio frequency quadrupole (RFQ) structures. An image of the full RFQ chain is presented in Figure 2.

Once stopped in the buffer gas environment, neutralization and thermalization of recoils will occur by interactions with the gas atoms and the electron density created by the stopped ion beam. The gas cell follows closely the design currently used at KU Leuven [16]. It is designed to be operated with argon gas at 200–500 mbar under constant flow, which exits the cell through a de Laval nozzle, having typically a 1 mm throat diameter. Gas flow simulations using COMSOL [16,17] have been performed in order to optimize the gas cell geometry and find an optimal volume providing an efficient stopping and extraction of the S^3 beam, while maintaining minimal extraction time. The resulting internal cross-section of the gas cell has a 30 mm depth and a 70 mm width. With this geometry, simulations give an average extraction time from the stopping area to the exit hole of about 500 ms for a 1 mm throat diameter.

A feedthrough in the gas cell body allows the insertion of two filaments that are resistively heated for evaporating an element used in the offline tests or as an online reference. The gas cell body and filament holder flange are water-cooled and the entire gas cell can be baked by resistively heated cartridges inserted in the gas cell body. The temperature is monitored by PT100 sensors. Just before the exit of the gas cell, two ion-collector electrodes are installed for removing non-neutralized ions in online experiments.

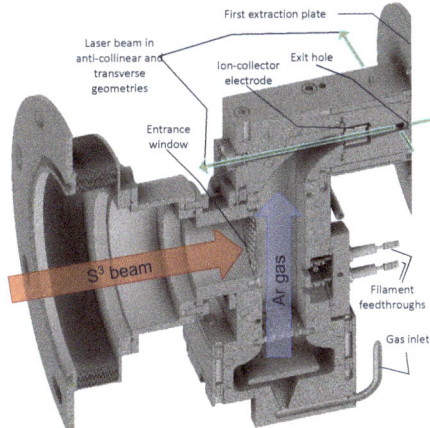

Figure 1. 3D cross-sectional view of the S^3-LEB gas cell.

The gas cell has three laser windows, two just before the exit, facing each other, and one opposite and concentric to the exit hole. At the gas cell exit, a de Laval nozzle is installed, the geometry of which is optimized using the calculations performed by the Von Karman Institute for Fluid Dynamics (VKI, Belgium) [18]. On the exit side of the gas cell, aligned with the nozzle, two extraction plates—one on ground potential and the other on a slightly positive potential—provide an initial guiding field for the ions towards the RFQ chain.

The RFQ design follows the initial concept from KU Leuven [19], with further adaptations. For each RFQ, the RF voltage is impedance-matched using a specially designed transformer with a tunable capacitor connected to the secondary circuit. DC voltage gradients are applied via voltage divider resistor chains across the RFQs.

First, the ions enter a segmented S-shape RFQ (SRFQ), which has the purpose of extracting the ions from the jet and decoupling the laser and ion beam axes. The SRFQ is located in the same vacuum chamber as the gas cell; thus, it is in a relatively high-pressure environment for RFQ operation ($\sim 10^{-2}$–10^{-1} mbar). The SRFQ has two injection plates that can be biased, and a linear DC gradient is applied on top of the RF voltage, to drag the ions through it. At the end of the first straight section of the SRFQ, a mirror fixed on top of the structure guides the laser light longitudinally into the gas cell.

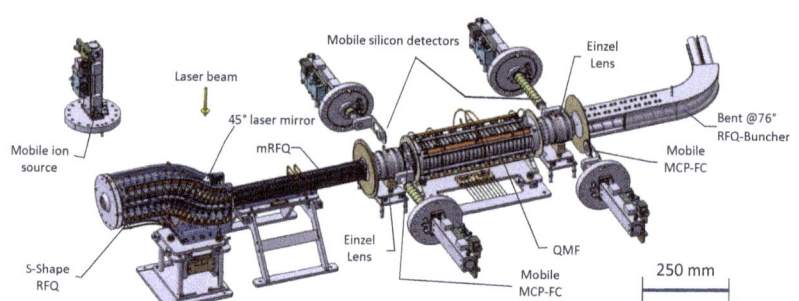

Figure 2. Full S^3-LEB ion guide layout. From left to right: mobile ion source, SRFQ, mRFQ, QMS and RFQ$_{cb}$. See text for details.

After the SRFQ, the ions enter the mini-RFQ (mRFQ), which serves as a differential pumping stage and hence stands between two areas of approximately two orders of magnitude different vacuum levels. The vacuum chambers of the SRFQ and of the mRFQ only communicate through a 3 mm-radius bore of the latter. The gas load in the SRFQ area is pumped by an Edwards GXS450 screw pump, while in the mRFQ area, a Pfeiffer STPiXA3306C turbo pump, coupled to an Edwards GXS160F screw pump for pre-vacuum, are used to remove the remaining gas.

Next, ions enter the quadrupole mass filter (QMF), which was designed to reach a mass-resolving power $m/(2\Delta m)$ of ~ 50. The first and last QMF segments can be DC biased independently from the rest, allowing it to act as a Brubaker lens [20].

After the QMF, the ions enter the cooler–buncher RFQ (RFQ$_{cb}$), which is a two-section system. In the cooler section, which is surrounded by a metallic housing, the ions are cooled by helium gas, which is injected at the center of the RFQ. This minimizes the longitudinal and transversal emittance of the beam. In the following buncher section, the ions are bunched using a potential well created by a series of segments that are connected to high-voltage switches. After a predefined trapping time in the buncher, the extraction takes place by switching the trapping voltages to an extraction ramp, which accelerates the ions out of the RFQ$_{cb}$. Differential pumping stages separate the QMF from the poor intermediate pressure areas of both the mRFQ and the cooler.

Once the cooled and bunched ion beam leaves the RFQ chain, it enters the pulse up (PU) drift tube. The tube is used for ion beam reacceleration up to ~ 3–3.5 keV kinetic energy, which is the design voltage for the final point of the S^3-LEB setup, consisting of a multi-reflection, time-of-flight (MR-TOF) mass spectrometer. When the ions enter the PU drift tube, its electrode is biased at ~ -1.5 kV. When the ions are at its center (typical flight times from the buncher are between 5 and 10 µs), the electrode voltage is switched to $\sim +1.5$ kV. This gives the ions a relative kinetic energy gain of ~ 3 keV.

Further beam purification and detection will be performed by the MR-TOF mass spectrometer, called Piège à Ions Linéaire du GANIL pour la Résolution des Isobares et la mesure de Masse (PILGRIM). In this device, the ion beam is reflected between two electrostatic mirrors until it is separated in time of flight, leading to a mass-resolving power $R = m/(2\Delta m) \approx 10^5$ [21]. The setup will expand in its capabilities by a decay spectroscopy setup called *Spectroscopy Electron Alpha in Silicon bOx couNter* (SEASON). In a later phase, a transport line to the future DESIR facility [22] is foreseen.

The ion beam detection is performed at multiple locations using micro-channel plate detectors (MCP$_{1,2}$) at the QMF entrance and exit, and after the PU electrode (MCP$_3$). All 3 MCPs have 10 % transmission grids allowing attenuation of intense beams and also detection of ion currents. The MCP$_3$ detector has an additional phosphor screen for ion beam imaging. Additional detection sites are located around the MR-TOF mass spectrometer [23]. It is also possible to install silicon detectors on linear actuators at the QMF entrance and exit.

The S^3-LEB setup with the gas cell, ion guides and PILGRIM mass spectrometer is currently installed in a test room at the LPC Caen institute. All components have been coupled and aligned.

2.2. The GISELE Laser Laboratory

The purpose of the GISELE laboratory is to perform offline laser ionization and spectroscopy experiments with the elements of interest for the S^3-LEB facility. A part of the GISELE laser system has been coupled to the S^3-LEB setup at LPC where it is currently being tested. The layout of the full GISELE laser system can be seen in Figure 3. An Nd:YAG laser, working at 10 kHz repetition rate and in the second harmonic, pumps several titanium:sapphire (Ti:sa) lasers with a power distribution achieved by implementing $\lambda/2$ retardation plates and polarizing beam splitter (PBS) cubes. Intra-cavity and extra-cavity higher harmonic generation can be achieved using nonlinear crystals. The Ti:sa laser beams are overlapped and guided towards an atomic beam unit (ABU) with a high-temperature oven ($T_{max} \sim 2000\ °C$).

In the future, a dye laser system is foreseen to be implemented to complement the Ti:sa wavelength coverage [24]. Recently, studies of a single-longitudinal-mode, pumped pulsed-dye amplifier have been carried out for high-resolution and high repetition rate spectroscopy applications, when using the dye laser system [25].

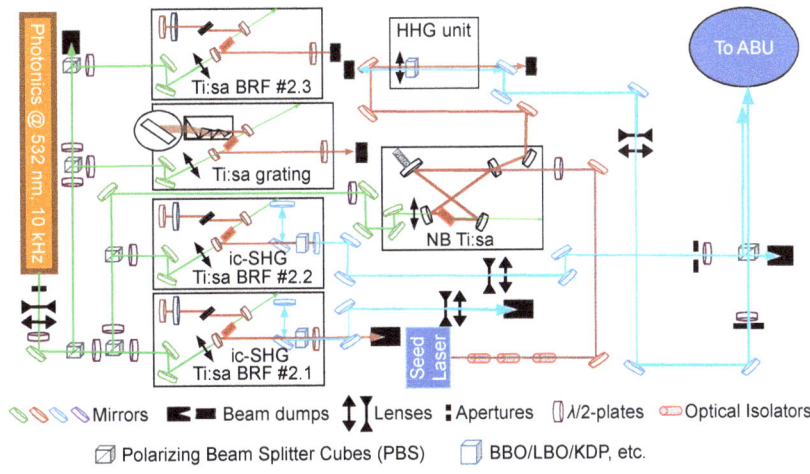

Figure 3. Typical GISELE laboratory layout. See text for details.

Monitoring and synchronizing the laser pulse time profiles is ensured by picking up a reflection or a fraction of each output laser beam and detecting it with a photodiode, the output of which is connected to an oscilloscope. The temporal overlap of the different

Ti:sa laser beams can be controlled either by modifying the gain using the focusing of the pump light into the crystal, or by Pockels cells. The wavelength is measured using a HighFinesse WS7 wavemeter. A Labview control and acquisition system is used to operate the lasers, record power and wavelength values, count ions in the ABU and perform wavelength scans.

The Z-type Ti:sa cavities of GISELE (see Figure 3) are broadband (BB) cavities, having either a birefringent filter (BRF) plus etalon, or grating as wavelength selective elements and achieving a typical linewidth $\Delta f_{laser-fund}$ of 5–10 GHz of the fundamental output frequency [26,27]. A Z-type cavity using two etalons is available, for achieving a narrower linewidth $\Delta f_{laser-fund}$ of 1.5–2 GHz [28]. For narrowband (NB) spectroscopy, an injection-locked pulsed-Ti:sa ring laser is available, seeded by an external cavity diode laser (ECDL), achieving linewidths, $\Delta f_{laser-fund}$, of $\leq$50 MHz [29]. The ECDL system requires feedback protection, which is provided by optical isolators. Typical output powers with standard 10 W pumping power of these Ti:sa systems are 2.2–2.7 W.

The design of the resonators is optimized so that any astigmatism from the surfaces of the Ti:sa crystal and the curved mirrors at both sides of the crystal cancel each other. The resonator is designed for high repetition rate operation (up to 10–15 kHz).

The ABU consists of an oven, apertures, ion optics and a MCP detector that is kept under vacuum. The atomic beam diffuses in the upward direction and it is collimated by multiple apertures before it reaches the photon–atom interaction region. This helps to minimize the transverse Doppler width of the atomic ensemble, as well as to constrain the interaction volume. To deflect the surface ions, two electrode pairs, located below the photon–atom interaction region, can be biased.

Once ions are created by the photon–atom interaction, an electric field gradient guides the ions towards an MCP located ~50 cm away from the interaction region. The gradient is optimized in order to obtain a time focus on the MCP allowing mass resolving powers on the order of $R = 200$.

The MCP signal is pre-amplified, then sent to a constant fraction discriminator and, finally, a time to digital converter (TDC) with maximum resolution of 4 ns/bin. The TDC is triggered by a TTL signal synchronized to the Q-switch trigger of the pump laser. The obtained TDC signal is sent to the Labview acquisition system.

3. Results

3.1. RFQ Offline Tests

The voltage optimization and the transmission and resolution tests were performed separately for the SRFQ/mRFQ and QMF/buncher. To set the voltages and monitor/control vacuum parameters, a CVI control system with Python interfaces was used. The MCP signals were recorded by a National Instruments 9402 counter and the ion currents by a Keithley 6487 picoampere meter unit.

For the tests of the SRFQ/mRFQ section, a ^{133}Cs source was inserted on a linear actuator in the designed area for the gas jet formation (in front of the SRFQ entrance). The total source current could be measured on a 10% transmission grid covering the source emission area. To achieve the operating pressure in online conditions, argon was injected directly in the gas cell vacuum chamber. The RF driving frequency of the ion guiding RFQs was set to 500 kHz, to allow operation with lower RF amplitudes and avoid discharges. The DC voltages on the mRFQ and SRFQ electrodes were then optimized to enhance transmission. The beam was detected on a Faraday cup placed behind the mRFQ. The transmission tests were performed aiming for the range of background pressures between 10^{-2} mbar and 10^{-1} mbar, that would correspond to online conditions for the creation of a matched jet of Mach number ~ 8 by the corresponding nozzles operated at different stagnation pressure regimes.

The optimum SRFQ and mRFQ settings result in a transmission of $\geq$80(15)% after mRFQ for more than an order of magnitude change in pressure p, centered around the region of interest for S^3-LEB experiments (see Figure 4). The error bars have been fixed to a

10% value, which is typical beam current uncertainty obtained in our measurements with a picoampere meter. In the same figure a comparison with SIMION simulations [30], using the hard-sphere (HS1) collision model and the same RF, DC and p settings, is presented. For these simulations, the ion source was assumed to be a 2π emitter from a disk, having 6.5 mm diameter of the used ^{133}Cs source and the energy distribution compatible to the thermal energy of a $T \approx 1000\,°C$ ensemble. The collisional cross-section σ_{col} with argon atoms was estimated from the ionic radius of ^{133}Cs and the Van der Waals radius of argon to be $4.25 \times 10^{-19}\,m^2$. The experiments revealed that the SRFQ and mRFQ have a very high transmission efficiency (75–100(10)%) within the pressure region of interest for creating a matched hypersonic jet of Mach number 7–8. The simulations indicate 60–85% transmission efficiency. The underestimation in the simulations for high pressures can be explained by the limitations of the HS1 collision model or an inaccuracy in the chosen collision cross section. The qualitative trend is nevertheless reproduced well.

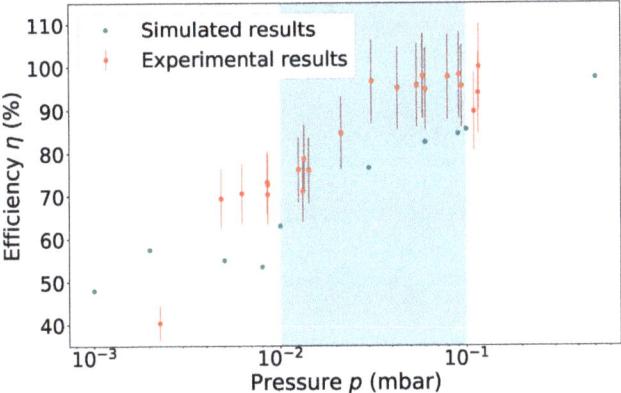

Figure 4. Experimental and simulated SRFQ and mRFQ transmission efficiency as a function of pressure p. Necessary p conditions for a matched hypersonic jet of Mach number 7–8 are highlighted by the region of interest in light blue.

The QMF/buncher ensemble was tested with a rubidium surface ion source installed in front of the QMF, providing a mixture of ^{85,87}Rb with the natural abundance. In ion guide mode (no quadrupole DC field), the transmission was close to 100%. When a DC voltage in combination with the RF voltage was applied (filtering mode), the QMF transmission efficiency was checked by a 2D scan of the DC and RF voltages leading to a resolving power on the order of $m/(2\Delta m_{FWHM}) \approx 40$ and a transmission of about 40%. For lower resolving powers, the transmission efficiency is above 80%.

In order to give a more explicit estimate of the mass resolving power, a series of scans were performed also while keeping a constant DC to RF voltage ratio, the so-called load–line scan. Knowing the inner radius $r_0 = 10$ mm of the QMF, it was possible to calculate for each RF amplitude the optimal ion mass corresponding to a Mathieu q parameter of 0.706 (the tip of the stability diagram). The load–line scan was thus converted into a mass scan, for different DC-RF ratios. In Figure 5, we present one such scan performed with a DC/RF amplitude ratio of 0.166. The mass axis is recalibrated so that the left peak corresponds to ^{85}Rb. This configuration shows a complete separation of ^{85}Rb$^+$ and ^{87}Rb$^+$ and allows the possibility of also separating the intermediate mass $A = 86$, with a suppression factor of the side bands, which remains to be determined experimentally. This resolving power is, however, limiting for the separation of heavier masses. With the first production of ions in the gas cell or jet, which will have a different emittance from the beam used in this test, the resolving power figure will be updated. Further improvements can be achieved by a better control of the symmetry of the RF field between the positive and negative phase, which is currently on the order of 1%.

In the same figure SIMION simulations of the QMF transmission are performed with the same settings as in the experiments. The incident ion beam is modeled as a cone matching the diameter of the ion-source collimator of 6 mm and having a half-angle of 2.5°, which leads to the experimental transmission efficiency through the QMF with a DC voltage of 100 V and optimal RF amplitude (which are the standard settings). One notices that the experimental resolving power is well reproduced.

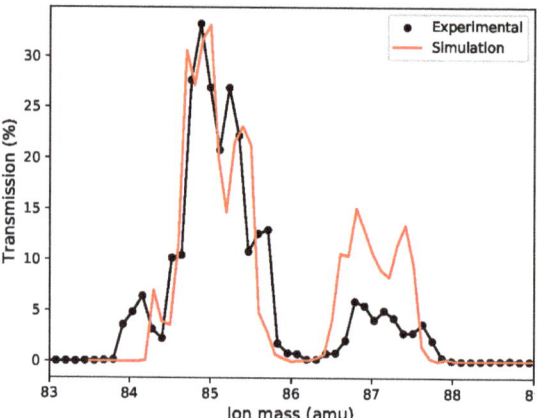

Figure 5. Experimental load–line scan of the QMF for a fixed DC to RF amplitude ratio of 0.166, compared with a SIMION simulation performed with the same parameters. The mass axis is calibrated so that the left peak corresponds to ^{85}Rb.

The transmission through the RFQ$_{cb}$ was tested under the same conditions as during the QMF tests, being optimized both in continuous and bunching mode. The helium flow rate injected in the buncher was from 75 to 105 mL/min, the latter being the limit due to the resulting pressure of 1×10^{-5} mbar in the PU electrode area, preventing the proper operation of MCP$_3$. However, an increase in flow rate from 75 to 105 mL/min achieved only 25% relative increase in the transport efficiency, making 75 mL/min already close to the optimal pressure. A comparison of ion spots on the phosphor screen showed similar radial distributions between 75 mL/min and 90 mL/min; however, for flow rates < 75 mL/min, a significant degradation of the ion spatial distribution was observed.

The 10% transmission grid on MCP3 was hardwired to the ground potential; therefore, it did not allow us to measure the continuous ion beam through the buncher in continuous mode. For this type of measurement, the beam was collected on the negatively biased PU electrode and read out with the picoampere meter. With the optimum RF, DC and He injection settings, a transport efficiency of the buncher in continuous mode of about 85% was measured on the PU electrode with an uncertainty ∼ 10%. In order to test the buncher in pulsed mode, it was necessary to accelerate the ion bunches to MCP$_3$ using the PU electrode, thus giving them sufficient energy for efficient detection.

The bunched-mode efficiency was tested both in continuous accumulation mode and using a beam gate (BG) to limit the number of ions per bunch and ensure the same cooling time for all ejected ions. A BG was created by switching the injection electrode of the QMF, in order to block the ion beam, with the exception of a short time, controlled by a TTL trigger. The transport efficiency was tested using a BG of 1 ms and a cooling time of 10 ms, leading to a transmission value of 30(10)%. This value was, however, obtained with a low-resolution (50 ns) ion-counting system with an average intensity of one ion per bunch or less. A test with a high-resolution counting system will allow eliminating any potential pile-up effects.

In addition to the transport efficiency, the bunch TOF distribution was recorded using an oscilloscope and its averaging function with 75 mL/min flow rate. This result is presented in Figure 6, left panel, where one observes two overlapping bunches corresponding to the two Rb isotopes already separated in TOF on the MCP$_3$. The fact that the double-peak structure corresponds to the two isotopes was validated by using the QMF at a DC voltage of 100 V and suitably chosen RF amplitude, to select one or the other isotope. The heights of the two individual peaks were normalized to match the corresponding isotopic abundances.

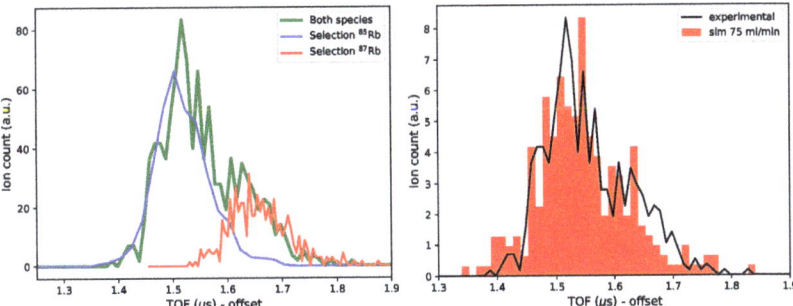

Figure 6. (**Left**) Time-of-flight distribution of rubidium ions behind the RFQ$_{cb}$ in three configurations: without any selection from the QMF (green); with QMF selecting ^{85}Rb$^+$ (blue); with QMF selecting ^{87}Rb$^+$ (red). The blue and red curves are normalized to ^{85,87}Rb relative abundance. (**Right**) Comparison of the simulated (red) TOF distribution of a ^{85}Rb$^+$-^{87}Rb$^+$ mixture with 75 mL/min helium flow rate to the experimentally measured one (black).

Simulations of the RFQ$_{cb}$ using the SIMION software and the HS1 algorithm were carried out following the same principles as those described for the SRFQ, mRFQ and QMF. Simple conductance calculations knowing the aperture diameters, the pumping power and some of the gauge pressures (corrected for helium) were performed to estimate the true pressure in the buncher. The simulations were started in front of the QMF extraction lens. The ion energy distribution chosen was identical to the one giving the best reproduction of the QMF behavior. For the entire simulation, the experimental voltages were used as input. Two helium flow rates were tested: one set to the experimental value most commonly used (75 mL/min) and one set to a slightly higher value (125 mL/min). The ions were injected all at once, allowed to cool for either 2, 5 or 10 ms, and then extracted towards the MCP$_3$. The simulations showed transmission efficiencies in the experimental pressure range of 20–40%, compatible with the experimental findings.

Furthermore, the simulated TOF distribution of a mixture of ^{85}Rb$^+$ and ^{87}Rb$^+$ with the correct elemental abundance was compared to the measurement using the same helium flow rate, and is presented in the right panel of Figure 6. The TOF offset was not measured experimentally with the oscilloscope and thus the simulation TOF was shifted by an arbitrary amount to match the centroid of the experimental spectrum. However, one notes that the experimental width and separation of the peaks is well described.

One must note, however, that all the values described in this section are obtained for the alkali ion source, the emittance (and divergence) of which should be significantly larger than that of the laser-ionized beam.

3.2. Laser Ion Source Offline Tests

Erbium atoms were chosen for the offline studies based on the fact that during the S^3 commissioning it is planned to use ^{152}Er. The goal of the Er I RIS offline measurements at GISELE is to measure the isotope shift (IS) and hyperfine structure (HFS) by a two step RIS scheme of stable erbium isotopes (^{164,166,167,168,170}Er), and to compare these results with the literature in order to quantify the performance of the equipment and the expected online performance. Stable erbium atoms are deposited in solution form (Er$_2$O$_3$ in 5 % HNO$_3$) on a tantalum foil, which then is placed inside the ABU oven.

The left panel of Figure 7 shows the ionization scheme used in the presented study. The excitation step (415.2 nm) was reported in [31] and, recently, precise Rydberg and auto-ionizing state, and ionization potential measurements, were carried out, starting from the same level at 24,083.2 cm^{-1} [32]. From the latter work, the most efficient A.I. state transition of 25,210.4 cm^{-1} was chosen for the ionization energy. Moreover, the strength of the excitation step has been determined to be $A_{ki} = 9.6 \times 10^7$ s^{-1} [33].

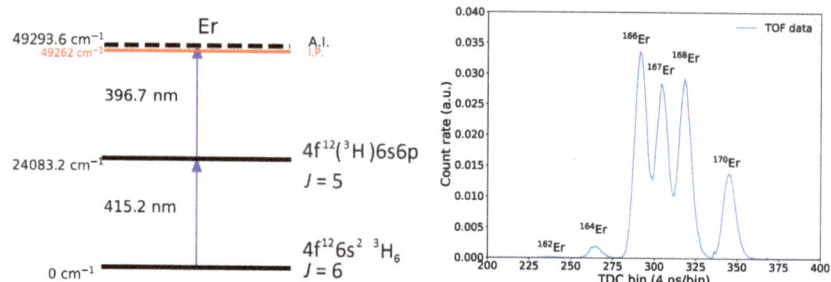

Figure 7. (**Left**) Er I two-step ionization scheme used for NB RIS measurements [32]. On the left hand side of the diagram, the excited state, the ionization potential (I.P.) energy and the populated auto-ionizing (A.I.) state levels are presented, on the right hand side, electron configuration and total angular momentum J are shown. (**Right**) TOF spectrum of the Er ions observed with the NB Ti:sa system using the scheme shown in the left panel.

In these measurements, the NB Ti:sa system with a fundamental output linewidth $20 \leq \Delta f \leq 50$ MHz was used for the excitation step and a BB Z-type Ti:sa cavity was used for the ionization step. The ABU TOF resolution with stable erbium atoms was $R = \text{TOF}/(2 \times \text{FWHM}) \sim 260$, with TOF = 21.4 µs and FWHM$_{170\text{Er}}$ = 40 ns. An acquired TOF spectrum resolving all stable Er isotopes following their natural abundances is shown in the right panel of Figure 7.

The wavelength adjustment of the excitation step was performed using the Labview control and acquisition system, which adjusts the ECDL master laser output wavelength. For each scan step the corresponding TOF spectra is saved. An individual resonance of each isotope can then be extracted from the full TOF spectra by choosing a region of interest.

After the frequency doubling stage, once the NB Ti:sa system beam reached the ABU, the measured full power after the two ABU windows varied between 30 and 100 mW. The Z-type Ti:sa BRF cavity used intra-cavity second harmonic generation and produced 40–100 mW of power at the ABU.

Before the IS and HFS measurements, the saturation power level P_0 of the excitation step was measured. In these measurements, both lasers were on resonance and the ionization step was kept at full power. Neutral density filters were used to reduce the laser power. The spatial alignment of both beams was performed by using the TDC count rate and a pair of ABU entrance/exit window apertures. The results are represented in Figure 8. The data set has been fitted by using the following equation:

$$I(P) = A + C \times (P/P_0)/(1 + (P/P_0)), \tag{1}$$

with A, C, P and P_0 being an offset describing influence from surface- and non-resonant ionization, the maximum resonant ionization rate, measured power and saturation power, respectively. The fit results were: A = 0.5(10) cps, C = 110(10) cps. The extracted saturation power P_0 was 145(40) µW. The beam spot diameter was about 1 mm.

Moreover, to observe the saturation effect more precisely, scans at several excitation step powers P were performed. In the measurements shown here the power was reduced until no more influence on the full-width at half-maximum (FWHM) was observed. This was the case at about 10–20 µW resulting in a resonance linewidth Δf_{res} of $\sim$120 MHz. The expected natural linewidth is ∼15 MHz. The saturation power from previous work [32] was 2.1(1) mW, compared with the present result of 0.145(40) mW. The reduction of the saturation power in our case can be explained by the reduced linewidth of the NB Ti:sa system ($20 \leq \Delta f \leq 50$ MHz) in comparison to the BB Z-type Ti:sa cavity ($\Delta f \sim 5$ GHz) and by possible differences in beam spot diameter used in [32].

IS and HFS measurements were performed for the different stable erbium isotopes. A detailed analysis of the data will be presented in a forthcoming paper [34], where the IS and HFS parameters will be represented.

Fitting of the raw data was carried out by a χ^2 procedure in SATLAS [35]. An IS result from a single scan of ^{166,170}Er is presented in the left panel of Figure 9. The RIS measurements were performed with 10–20 µW power levels for the excitation step and at 20–90 mW for the ionization step.

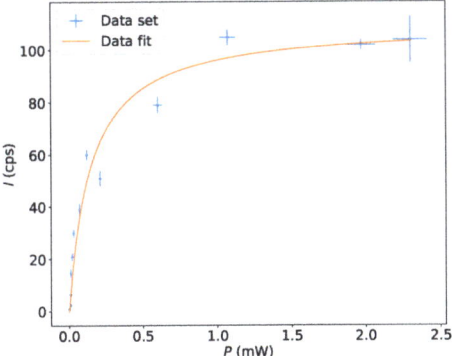

Figure 8. Measured count rate I as a function of excitation step power P for the RIS scheme presented in Figure 7. The orange curve represents a fit to the measured data.

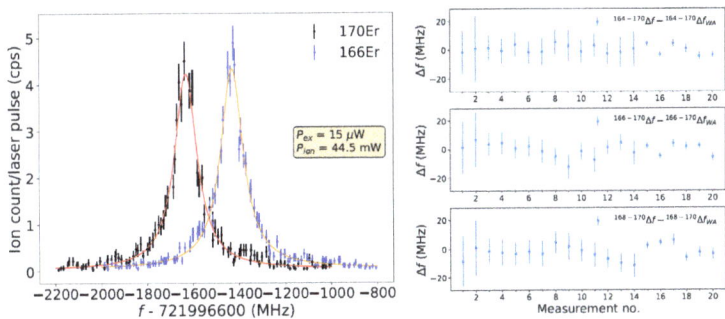

Figure 9. (**Left**) Normalized IS measurements of $^{166-170}$Er I (red/orange curve—SATLAS [35] χ^2 fit of the data; $f_0 = 721.9966$ THz; excitation and ionization step powers are represented in the text box). (**Right**) Scattering of individual IS (Δf) measurements around the weighted average IS (Δf_{WA}) from all NB RIS measurements. The used RIS scheme is presented in Figure 7.

A scatter of the IS data from 20 measurements is presented in the right panel of Figure 9, with the weighted average subtracted from all values. The individual uncertainties of the data points represent statistical uncertainties, multiplied by $\sqrt{\chi^2_{red}}$ to correct for non-statistical scattering effects. The source of the larger data scattering is still under investigation.

Owing to the narrow spectral linewidth of the NB Ti:sa system, the HFS spectra of the odd–even ^{167}Er isotope could also be measured. The total angular momentum of the ground state (g.s.) $J_{g.s.} = 6$ and nuclear spin $I = 7/2$, results in 8 g.s. HFS components ranging from $F = 5/2$ to $19/2$. The excited state (e.s.) has angular momentum of $J_{e.s.} = 5$, also with 8 HFS components ranging from $F = 3/2$ to $17/2$ (all J values taken from [33]). By applying selection rules, this results in 21 possible transitions. The splitting of the g.s. components has been measured by A. Frisch et al. [36]. The e.s. hyperfine constants A and B are unknown.

The HFS information was extracted from 11 scans, performed below the saturation power level. The g.s. A_l and B_l coefficients were fixed to the the literature values $-120.487(1)$ and $-4552.984(10)$ MHz [36], respectively. The nuclear magnetic octupole moment coefficients C_l and C_l for the g.s. and e.s. were set to 0. The fit result for a single scan is represented in Figure 10. The spectrum corresponding to all 21 HFS components has been recorded and fitted. In the presented fitting procedure, the peak intensities are left as free variables.

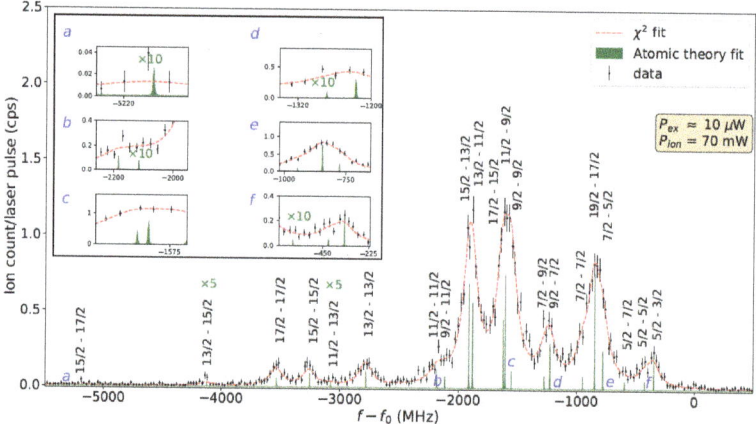

Figure 10. Normalized single HFS measurement of ^{167}Er I with an inset in the top left corner containing details of the least intense/clearly resolved HFS components $a - f$ (red/green curve—SATLAS [35] χ^2 data fit/atomic resonance positions based on input parameters; the weakest peaks according to atomic theory have been magnified for visualization purpose and are presented in the insets, with a multiplication factor added to the HFS component; $f_0 = 721.9966$ THz; text box presents the used excitation and ionization step powers P_{ex} and P_{ion}; the used RIS scheme is presented in Figure 7).

4. Outlook and Conclusions

The commissioning of the S^3-LEB setup is entering the offline test phase of the entire installation, in which the the gas cell, RFQ chain and the MR-TOF mass spectrometer are connected and the laser system is coupled to the gas cell.

The commissioning tests performed separately for the RFQ tandems of the setup (SRFQ/mRFQ and QMF/RFQ$_{cb}$) have shown promising results, both in terms of transmission and resolving power/bunching capability. Work is ongoing with the cooling and bunching section to improve the performance before the first ion injection into the MR-TOF mass spectrometer will take place.

The Ti:sa-based GISELE offline laser laboratory at GANIL has been successfully developed for the high-resolution spectroscopy requirements of S^3-LEB. The laser systems are adapted for both in-gas-cell and in-gas-jet spectroscopy methods. Using one of the possible Er I RIS schemes, new narrowband IS measurements of $^{164,166,168-170}$Er have been performed, and the stability of the system between different measurements has been illustrated. With the same RIS scheme, first high-resolution HFS spectra with stable ^{167}Er has been measured.

Author Contributions: Conceptualization, J.R., A.A., M.A., F.B., L.C., J.-F.C., A.C., S.D., P.D. (Pierre Delahaye), P.D. (Philippe Desrues), A.D., P.D. (Patricia Duchesne), R.F., X.F., S.F., P.G., R.P.d.G., S.K., N.L., R.L., J.L., F.L., V.M., Y.M., I.M., A.O.-C. , B.O., J.P., O.P., B.-M.R., H.S., S.S., E.T., J.U., C.V., M.V. (Marine Vandebrouck), P.V.d.B., M.V. (Matthias Verlinde), E.V. and K.W; methodology, J.R., A.A., P.D. (Pierre Delahaye), R.F., X.F., S.F., V.M., P.V.D. and A.O.-C.; software, V.M. and C.V.; validation, J.R., A.A., L.C., R.F., X.F., S.F., N.L., V.M., H.S., S.S., P.V.D. and A.O.-C.; formal analysis, J.R., A.A., V.M. and A.O.-C.; investigation, J.R., L.C., R.F., X.F., N.L. and V.M.; resources, R.F., N.L. and P.V.D.; data curation, J.R., A.A., V.M. and A.O.-C.; writing—original draft preparation, J.R.; writing—review and editing, L.C., R.P.d.G., R.F., X.F., N.L., V.M., I.M., H.S., P.V.D. and K.W.; visualization, J.R. and V.M.; supervision, N.L., R.F. and P.V.D.; project administration, N.L., R.F., V.M. and P.V.D.; funding acquisition, N.L. and P.V.D. All authors have read and agreed to the published version of the manuscript.

Funding: S^3 has been funded by the French Research Ministry, National Research Agency (ANR), through the EQUIPEX (EQUIPment of EXcellence) reference ANR-10EQPX- 46, the FEDER (Fonds Europeén de Developpement Economique et Reǵional), the CPER (Contrat Plan Etat Reǵion), and supported by the U.S. Department of Energy, Office of Nuclear Physics, under contract No. DE-AC02-06CH11357 and by the E.C.FP7-INFRASTRUCTURES 2007, SPIRAL2 Preparatory Phase, Grant agreement No.: 212692. S^3-LEB: This project has received funding from the French Research Ministry through the ANR-13-B505-0013, the Research Foundation—Flanders (FWO)—under the International Research Infrastructure program (nr. I002219N), the Research Coordination Office—KU Leuven—-the European Research Council (ERC-2011-AdG-291561-HELIOS) and the European Union's Horizon 2020 research and innovation program under grant agreement No 654002.

Institutional Review Board Statement: Not applicable.

Informed Consent Statement: Not applicable.

Data Availability Statement: The data presented in this study are available on request from the corresponding author.

Acknowledgments: This setup results from the collaborative work of the IGLIS newtork, grouping many research centers and universities such as CEA-Saclay (IRFU), CERN (CRIS), GANIL, IBS-RISP, IJCLab, IMP, JAEA, Johannes Gutenberg-Universität Mainz (Institut für Physik/LARISSA), JINR (GALS), JYFL (IGISOL/MARA), KEK (KISS), KU Leuven, MSU, Nagoya University, Normandie Université (LPC Caen), Peking University, RIKEN (SLOWRI/PALIS), TRIUMF (TRILIS), Université de Strasbourg (IPHC), University of Manchester, University of Tsukuba and Laboratoire de Physique des 2 infinis Irène Joliot-Curie (IJCLab) (for more details about IGLIS collaboration please refer to our network page [37]).

Conflicts of Interest: The authors declare no conflict of interest.

References

1. Déchery, F.; Savajols, H.; Authier, M.; Drouart, A.; Nolen, J.; Ackermann, D.; Amthor, A.M.; Bastin, B.; Berryhill, A.; Boutin, D.; et al. The Super Separator Spectrometer S^3 and the associated detection systems: SIRIUS & LEB-REGLIS3. *Nucl. Instruments Methods Phys. Res. Sect. B Beam Interact. Mater. Atoms* **2016**, *376*, 125–130. [CrossRef]
2. Savajols, H.; Drouart, A.; Nolen, J. Physics avenue with the super separator spectrometer (S^3) at the SPIRAL2 facility. In Proceedings of the 6th Workshop on Nuclear Fission and Spectroscopy of Neutron-Rich Nuclei, Chamrousse, France, 20–24 March 2017.
3. Ferrer, R.; Bastin, B.; Boilley, D.; Creemers, P.; Delahaye, P.; Liénard, E.; Fléchard, X.; Franchoo, S.; Ghys, L.; Huyse, M.; et al. In gas laser ionization and spectroscopy experiments at the Superconducting Separator Spectrometer (S3): Conceptual studies and preliminary design. *Nucl. Instruments Methods Phys. Res. Sect. B Beam Interact. Mater. Atoms* **2013**, *317*, 570–581. [CrossRef]
4. Déchery, F.; Drouart, A.; Savajols, H.; Nolen, J.; Authier, M.; Amthor, A.M.; Boutin, D.; Delferriére, O.; Gall, B.; Hue, A.; et al. Toward the drip lines and the superheavy island of stability with the Super Separator Spectrometer S^3. *Eur. Phys. J. A* **2015**, *51*, 1–16. [CrossRef]
5. Ferrer, R.; Barzakh, A.; Bastin, B.; Beerwerth, R.; Block, M.; Creemers, P.; Grawe, H.; de Groote, R.; Delahaye, P.; Fléchard, X.; et al. Towards high-resolution laser ionization spectroscopy of the heaviest elements in supersonic gas jet expansion, 1–9. *Nat. Commun.* **2017**, *8*. [CrossRef]

6. Kudryavtsev, Y.; Ferrer, R.; Huyse, M.; Van den Bergh, P.; Van Duppen, P. The in-gas jet laser ion source: Resonance ionization spectroscopy of radioactive atoms in supersonic gas jets. *Nucl. Instruments Methods Phys. Res. Sect. B Beam Interact. Mater. Atoms* **2013**, *297*, 7–22. [CrossRef]
7. Chapman, K. The transuranic elements and the island of stability. *Philosophical Trans. R. Soc. A Math. Phys. Eng. Sci.* **2020**, *378*. [CrossRef]
8. Marsh, B.A.; Andel, B.; Andreyev, A.N.; Antalic, S.; Atanasov, D.; Barzakh, A.E.; Bastin, B.; Borgmann, C.; Capponi, L.; Cocolios, T.E.; et al. New developments of the in-source spectroscopy method at RILIS/ISOLDE. *Nucl. Instruments Methods Phys. Res. Sect. B Beam Interact. Mater. Atoms* **2013**, *317*, 550–556. [CrossRef]
9. Prime, E.J.; Lassen, J.; Achtzehn, T.; Albers, D.; Bricault, P.; Cocolios, T.; Dombsky, M.; Labrecque, F.; Lavoie, J.P.; Pearson, M.R.; et al. TRIUMF resonant ionization laser ion source : Ga, Al and Be radioactive ion beam development. *Hyperfine Interact.* **2006**, *171*, 127–134. [CrossRef]
10. Neugart, R.; Billowes, J.; Bissell, M.L.; Blaum, K.; Cheal, B.; Flanagan, K.T.; Neyens, G.; Nörtershäuser, W.; Yordanov, D.T. Collinear laser spectroscopy at ISOLDE: New methods and highlights. *J. Phys. G Nucl. Part. Phys.* **2017**. *44*, 064002. [CrossRef]
11. Cheal, B.; Forest, D.H. Collinear laser spectroscopy techniques at JYFL. *Hyperfine Interact.* **2014**, *223*, 63–71. [CrossRef]
12. Cocolios, T.E.; Al Suradi, H.H.; Billowes, J.; Budinčević, I.; De Groote, R.P.; De Schepper, S.; Fedosseev, V.N.; Flanagan, K.T.; Franchoo, S.; Ruiz, R.F.G.; et al. The Collinear Resonance Ionization Spectroscopy (CRIS) experimental setup at CERN-ISOLDE. *Nucl. Instruments Methods Phys. Res. Sect. B Beam Interact. Mater. Atoms* **2013**, *317*, 565–569. [CrossRef]
13. Heinke, R.; Kron, T.; Raeder, S. High-resolution in-source laser spectroscopy in perpendicular geometry: Development and application of the PI-LIST. *Hyperfine Interact.* **2017**, *238*, 6. [CrossRef]
14. Chrysalidis, K.; Wilkins, S.G.; Heinke, R.; Koszorus, A.; De Groote, R.; Fedosseev, V.N.; Marsh, B.; Rothe, S.; Garcia Ruiz, R.; Studer, D.; et al. First demonstration of Doppler-free 2-photon in-source laser spectroscopy at the ISOLDE-RILIS. *Nucl. Instruments Methods Phys. Res. Sect. B Beam Interact. Mater. Atoms* **2020**, *463*, 476–481. [CrossRef]
15. Lecesne, N.; Alvès-Condé, R.; Coterreau, E.; De Oliveira, F.; Dubois, M.; Flambard, J.L.; Franberg, H.; Gottwald, T.; Jardin, P.; Lassen, J.; et al. GISELE: A resonant ionization laser ion source for the production of radioactive ions at GANIL. *Rev. Sci. Instruments* **2010**, *81*, 02A910. [CrossRef]
16. Kudryavtsev, Y.; Creemers, P.; Ferrer, R.; Granados, C.; Gaffney, L.P.; Huyse, M.; Mogilevskiy, E.; Raeder, S.; Sels, S.; Van Den Bergh, P.; et al. A new in-gas-laser ionization and spectroscopy laboratory for off-line studies at KU Leuven. *Nucl. Instruments Methods Phys. Res. Sect. B Beam Interact. Mater. Atoms* **2016**, *376*, 345–352. [CrossRef]
17. COMSOL-Software for Multiphysics Simulation. Available online: https://www.comsol.com/ (accessed on 6 January 2022).
18. Ferrer, R.; Verlinde, M.; Verstraelen, E.; Claessens, A.; Huyse, M.; Kraemer, S.; Kudryavtsev, Y.; Romans, J.; Van den Bergh, P.; Van Duppen, P.; et al. Hypersonic nozzle for laser-spectroscopy studies at 17 K characterized by resonance-ionization-spectroscopy-based flow mapping. *Phys. Rev. Res.* **2021**, *3*, 043041. [CrossRef]
19. Sels, S.; Ferrer, R.; Dockx, K.; Buitrago, C.G.; Huyse, M.; Kudryavtsev, Y.; Kraemer, S.; Raeder, S.; Van Den Bergh, P.; Van Duppen, P.; et al. Design and commissioning of an ion guide system for In-Gas Laser Ionization and Spectroscopy experiments. *Nucl. Instruments Methods Phys. Res. Sect. B Beam Interact. Mater. Atoms* **2020**, *463*, 148–153. [CrossRef]
20. Brubaker, W.M. An Improved Quadrupole Mass Analyzer. *Adv. Mass Spectrosc.* **1968**, *4*, 293–299.
21. Retailleau, B.M. PILGRIM: Un Spectromètre de Masse Par Temps de vol Pour S^3, et Brisure de Symétrie D'isopin Dans le 38K. Ph.D. Dissertation, Normandie Université, Paris, France, 2021.
22. Thomas, J.-C.; Blank, B. The DESIR facility at SPIRAL2. *Nucl. Struct. Probl.* **2012**, 224–229. [CrossRef]
23. Chauveau, P.; Delahaye, P.; De France, G.; El Abir, S.; Lory, J.; Merrer, Y.; Rosenbusch, M.; Schweikhard, L.; Wolf, R.N. PILGRIM, a Multi-Reflection Time-of-Flight Mass Spectrometer for Spiral2-S^3 at GANIL. *Nucl. Instruments Methods Phys. Res. Sect. B Beam Interact. Mater. Atoms* **2016**, *376*, 211–215. [CrossRef]
24. Raeder, S.; Ferrer, R.; Granados, C.; Huyse, M.; Kron, T.; Kudryavtsev, Y.; Lecesne, N.; Piot, J.; Romans, J.; Savajols, H.; et al. Performance of Dye and Ti: Sapphire laser systems for laser ionization and spectroscopy studies at S^3. *Nucl. Inst. Methods Phys. Res. B* **2020**, *463*, 86–95. [CrossRef]
25. Verlinde, M.; Ferrer, R.; Claessens, A.; Granados, C.A.; Kraemer, S.; Kudryavtsev, Y.; Li, D.; Van Den Bergh, P.; Van Duppen, P.; Verstraelen, E. Single-longitudinal-mode pumped pulsed-dye amplifier for high-resolution laser spectroscopy. *Rev. Sci. Instrum.* **2020**, *91*, 103002. [CrossRef] [PubMed]
26. Mattolat, C.; Rothe, S.; Schwellnus, F.; Gottwald, T.; Raeder, S.; Wendt, K. An all-solid-state high repetiton rate titanium: Sapphire laser system for resonance ionization laser ion sources. *AIP Conf. Proc.* **2009**, *1104*, 114–119. [CrossRef]
27. Moore, I.D.; Nieminen, A.; Billowes, J.; Campbell, P.; Geppert, C.; Jokinen, A.; Kessler, T.; Marsh, B.; Penttilä, H.; Rinta-Antila, S.; et al. Development of a laser ion source at IGISOL. *J. Phys. G Nucl. Part. Phys.* **2005**, *31*, S1499. [CrossRef]
28. Rothe, S.; Fedosseev, V.N.; Kron, T.; Marsh, B.A.; Rossel, R.E.; Wendt, K.D. Narrow linewidth operation of the RILIS titanium: Sapphire laser at ISOLDE/CERN. *Nucl. Instruments Methods Phys. Res. Sect. B Beam Interact. Mater. Atoms* **2013**, *317*, 561–564. [CrossRef]
29. Sonnenschein, V.; Moore, I.D.; Raeder, S.; Reponen, M.; Tomita, H.; Wendt, K. Characterization of a pulsed injection-locked Ti: Sapphire laser and its application to high resolution resonance ionization spectroscopy of copper. *Laser Phys.* **2017**, *27*, 085701. [CrossRef]
30. Dahl, D.A. SIMION for the personal computer in reflection. *Int. J. Mass Spectrom.* **2000**, *200*, 3–25. [CrossRef]

31. Meggers, W.F.; Corliss, C.H.; Scribner, B.F. *Tables of Spectral-Line Intensities Part I—Arranged by Elements Part II—Arranged by Wavelengths*, 2nd ed.; National Bureau of Standards: Washington, DC, USA, 1975; pp. 65–75.
32. Studer, D. Resonanzionisationsspektroskopie Hochliegender Zustände in Dysprosium und Erbium zur Entwicklung effizienter Anregungsschemata und Bestimmung des Ersten Ionisationspotentials. Master's Thesis, Johannes Gutenberg-Universitat Mainz, Mainz, Germany, 2015.
33. Kramida, A.; Ralchenko, Y.; Reader, J.; NIST ASD Team. NIST Atomic Spectra Database (ver. 5.9), [Online]. National Institute of Standards and Technology, Gaithersburg, MD, 2021. Available online: https://physics.nist.gov/asd (accessed on 21 November 2021).
34. Romans, J. Commissioning of the S^3-LEB. Bd Henri Becquerel, B.P. 55027, Caen, France. 2022, *Manuscript in preparation*.
35. Gins, W.; de Groote, R.P.; Bissell, M.L.; Buitrago, C.G.; Ferrer, R.; Lynch, K.M.; Neyens, G.; Sels, S. Analysis of counting data: Development of the SATLAS Python package. *Comput. Phys. Commun.* **2018**, *222*, 286–294. [CrossRef]
36. Frisch, A.; Aikawa, K.; Mark, M.; Ferlaino, F.; Berseneva, E.; Kotochigova, S. Hyperfine structure of laser-cooling transitions in fermionic erbium-167. *Phys. Rev. A* **2013**, *88*, 032508. [CrossRef]
37. In-Gas Laser Ionization and Spectroscopy NETwork (IGLIS-NET) Home Page, 2021. Available online: https://research.kek.jp/group/wnsc/iglis-net/ (accessed on 3 November 2021).

Article

The NEXT Project: Towards Production and Investigation of Neutron-Rich Heavy Nuclides

Julia Even [1,*], Xiangcheng Chen [1], Arif Soylu [1], Paul Fischer [2], Alexander Karpov [3], Vyacheslav Saiko [3], Jan Saren [4], Moritz Schlaich [5], Thomas Schlathölter [1], Lutz Schweikhard [2], Juha Uusitalo [4] and Frank Wienholtz [5]

1. Faculty of Science and Engineering, University of Groningen, 9701 BA Groningen, The Netherlands; xiangcheng.chen@rug.nl (X.C.); a.soylu@rug.nl (A.S.); t.a.schlatholter@rug.nl (T.S.)
2. Institut für Physik, Universität Greifswald, 17487 Greifswald, Germany; paul.fischer@uni-greifswald.de (P.F.); lschweik@physik.uni-greifswald.de (L.S.)
3. Joint Institute for Nuclear Research, 141980 Dubna, Russia; karpov@jinr.ru (A.K.); saiko@jinr.ru (V.S.)
4. Department of Physics, University of Jyväskylä, 40014 Jyväskylä, Finland; jan.saren@jyu.fi (J.S.); juha.uusitalo@jyu.fi (J.U.)
5. Institut für Kernphysik, Technical Univeristy of Darmstadt, 64289 Darmstadt, Germany; mschlaich@ikp.tu-darmstadt.de (M.S.); fwienholtz@ikp.tu-darmstadt.de (F.W.)
* Correspondence: j.even@rug.nl; Tel.: +31-50-363-3618

Abstract: The heaviest actinide elements are only accessible in accelerator-based experiments on a one-atom-at-a-time level. Usually, fusion–evaporation reactions are applied to reach these elements. However, access to the neutron-rich isotopes is limited. An alternative reaction mechanism to fusion–evaporation is multinucleon transfer, which features higher cross-sections. The main drawback of this technique is the wide angular distribution of the transfer products, which makes it challenging to catch and prepare them for precision measurements. To overcome this obstacle, we are building the NEXT experiment: a solenoid magnet is used to separate the different transfer products and to focus those of interest into a gas-catcher, where they are slowed down. From the gas-catcher, the ions are transferred and bunched by a stacked-ring ion guide into a multi-reflection time-of-flight mass spectrometer (MR-ToF MS). The MR-ToF MS provides isobaric separation and allows for precision mass measurements. In this article, we will give an overview of the NEXT experiment and its perspectives for future actinide research.

Keywords: NEXT; neutron-rich nuclei; mutlinucleon transfer; solenoid separator; mass spectrometer

1. Introduction

Access to the heaviest elements in the periodic table is limited. While elements up to einsteinium and fermium are still available in macro-amounts, all heavier elements are only accessible in accelerator-based experiments on a one-atom-at-a-time scale. Workhorses for the production of the transfermium elements are fusion–evaporation reactions [1], which are restricted by the availability of target materials and ion beams, as well as by the reaction cross-sections. An alternative reaction mechanism that can be applied and that gives access to isotopes further on the neutron-rich side are deep inelastic collisions resulting in multinucleon transfer [2–6]. Multinucleon transfer reactions have been known for decades as a means for accessing neutron-rich transfermium isotopes. However, their application in studying transfermium isotopes is still limited.

Similar to experiments using fusion reactions, an intense ion beam (of typically 0.5 particle nA up to 2 particle μA) impinges on a target foil with a thickness of a few microns. The various products of the fusion–evaporation reactions continue flying in beam direction and can be separated by an electromagnetic separator. In deep inelastic collisions, a neck is formed between the projectile and the target nucleus. Nucleons are exchanged; the system rotates and splits again. The reaction products are emitted in a large polar angle of 30° to 60°

with respect to the beam axis, which limits the collection of multinucleon transfer products for subsequent precision studies. Electromagnetic separators such as SHIP [2], VAMOS [7], or PRISMA [8] cannot cover the whole solid angle and are only able to capture a fraction of the products. Studies of transfer products using radiochemical separation techniques are limited to long-lived isotopes [4]. In recent years, new experiments, in which gas-cells are directly placed behind the target to stop and capture a large fraction of the transfer products, have been developed, such as the KISS experiment [9], the $N = 126$ factory [10], and experiments at IGISOL [11] and at the FRS gas-catcher [12]. All these experiments require an additional separation step. In the case of the KISS experiment, laser ionization of the products is applied.

Here, we report about a new setup called NEXT that is currently being built at the AGOR cyclotron in Groningen. The NEXT setup shall fulfill the following requirements:

- a large angular acceptance to capture the vast majority of the target-like transfer products and achieve good focusing;
- good suppression of the primary beam and lighter transfer products;
- separation and identification of isobaric nuclides;
- isotope identification independent from chemical properties
- sensitivity to isotopes of a broad range of half-lives.

To achieve this demand, the heavy target-like transfer products are pre-separated by their magnetic rigidity from the primary beam and the light projectile-like products within a superconducting solenoid magnet [13]. The target-like products are focused towards the end of the solenoid, where they are stopped in a gas-catcher [14]. The transfer products are extracted and bunched by a stacked-ring ion guide [15] before they are injected into a multi-reflection time-of-flight mass spectrometer (MR-ToF MS) [16–18] for isobaric separation and mass measurements. Figure 1 shows a schematic overview of the setup.

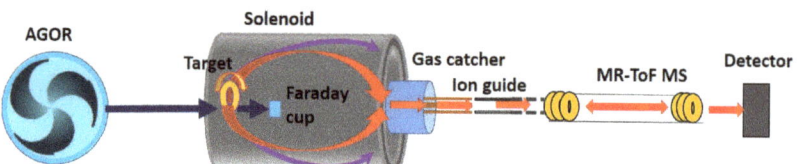

Figure 1. Schematic overview of the NEXT setup. The dark arrows indicate the primary beam. The red arrows indicate the trajectories of target-like fragments, while the purple arrows indicate the trajectories of the projectile-like fragments.

2. The NEXT Setup

2.1. AGOR Cyclotron

The primary intense ion beam is delivered by the AGOR cyclotron in Groningen [19]. AGOR is a superconducting cyclotron with a cyclotron K value (bending limit) of 600 MeV that is capable of accelerating light and heavy ions in a range of energies, from 5 MeV/u for heavy ions and up to 190 MeV for protons, as practically continuous beams. It is equipped with an electron cyclotron resonance (ECR) ion source, which provides a broad range of stable beams up to lead. Beam intensities depend on the desired projectiles and range from an particle nA to a few particle μA [20]. Based on the experience with various projectiles and ion-source tests, we expect beam currents at the target position of the NEXT experiment in the order of hundreds of particles nA.

2.2. The Solenoid Separator

The primary beam from AGOR is focused on the target, which is located inside a solenoid magnet. The un-reacted beam is collected by a Faraday cup behind the target. The target can be moved along the central axis of the magnet. The magnet had previously been part of a magnetic resonance imaging apparatus. Its total length is 160 cm, and the inner diameter is about 90 cm. It provides a magnetic flux density of $B = 3$ T. The trajectories of the transfer-product ions recoiling out from the target are bent depending on the emitting angle and the magnetic rigidity $B\rho = \frac{p}{q}$ of the ions, where ρ is the gyroradius of the ion due to the magnetic field, p is its momentum, and q is its charge state.

In order to optimize the transmission of target-like products towards the gas-catcher and their separation from projectile-like fragments, two model reactions were chosen:

- ^{136}Xe + ^{198}Pt at an energy of 6 MeV/u to produce nuclei around $N = 126$ [21];
- ^{48}Ca + ^{251}Cf at an energy of 6.1 MeV/u to produce transfermium nuclei [22].

To simulate the trajectories of the reaction products, the differential cross-section, the emitting angle from the target, the kinetic energy, and the charge-states of the ions of interest are required as input data. The differential cross-section of the various isotopes, the emitting angle, and the kinetic energies of the ions are taken from predictions made by a dynamical model based on the Langevin equations [21,22]. This model provides a continuous description of the time evolution of the system of colliding nuclei, starting from the approaching stage of the projectile and the target in the entrance channel of the reaction, and up to the formation of the final reaction products. The stochastic nature of the interaction between two colliding nuclei is taken into account in this model. This leads to the formation of products in a wide range of masses, energies, and scattering angles. The model gives a reasonable description of various characteristics of the products of multinucleon transfer reactions that was verified on a large set of available experimental data. The mean charge states of the ions were calculated using an empirical charge state formula for heavy ions, according to reference [23]. The distributions of the charge states were calculated according to reference [24]. Figure 2 shows two examples of the resulting acceptance region of the solenoid separator. The green areas indicate the emitting angle and magnetic rigidity of ions that will be transmitted from a target towards the gas-catcher. Ions emitted in a small angle are stopped by a cylindrical Faraday cup of 6.2 cm radius and 12.4 cm length, which is placed a few centimeters behind the target. By changing the target position, the acceptance region can be adjusted. As an example for neutron-rich transfermium nuclei ^{261}Md produced in the reaction ^{48}Ca + ^{251}Cf at an energy of 6.1 MeV/u was chosen. The magnetic rigidity and angular distribution of ^{261}Md (Z = 101) is indicated by the solid lines in Figure 2A. They overlap, to a large degree, with the acceptance region of the magnet. The transmission efficiencies of the target-like products of the model reaction ^{48}Ca + ^{251}Cf are summarized in Figure 3. The figure shows the suppression of recoiling nuclei that are close to the nuclear mass and charge of the target material. The transfer products, which are heavier than the target material, are emitted within the acceptance region of the solenoid and, therefore, high-transmission yields around 80% can be achieved.

In order to optimize for $N = 126$ nuclei, the transmission of the products of the reaction ^{136}Xe + ^{198}Pt at an energy of 6 MeV/u was investigated. The magnetic rigidity of $N = 126$ nuclei is higher than the rigidity of the transfermium isotopes produced in ^{48}Ca + ^{251}Cf, and, thus, they lie only partially within the acceptance region of the magnet (see Figure 2B). The optimum target position for the reaction ^{136}Xe + ^{198}Pt was determined to be 70 cm inside the solenoid, and typical transmission yields of about 15% could be reached. The projectile-like fragments lie, to a large degree, outside the acceptance region; thus, they are efficiently suppressed by the solenoid separator.

2.3. Gas-Catcher, Ion Guide, and MR-ToF MS

The transmitted target-like transfer products pass the titanium entrance window of the gas-catcher [14] placed behind the solenoid. The ions are slowed down by collisions with the gas atoms inside the gas catcher, which has a length of 45 cm and a diameter of 40 cm. The ions are guided by a direct current (DC) gradient towards the backside of a gas-catcher, where a radiofrequency (RF) carpet is located. The RF carpet is a printed circuit board with concentric ring electrodes and an electrode gap of 0.125 mm. The ions are transported by a DC gradient of 3 V/cm and an RF potential of 80 V peak-to-peak and at a frequency of 5.7 MHz towards the center, from where they are extracted through a hole of 0.45 mm diameter by a supersonic gas flow. The ions are, thus, emitted from the gas-catcher as a continuous, divergent beam with energies of a few electron volts. In order to inject the ions into the MR-ToF MS, the beam needs to be transformed into well-focused ion bunches with energies of a few kiloelectron volts. To this end, an ion guide consisting of a stack of rings has been developed.

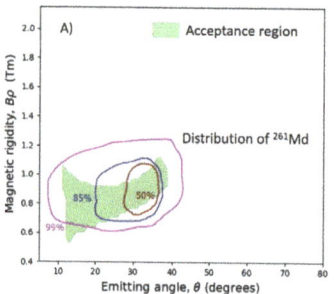
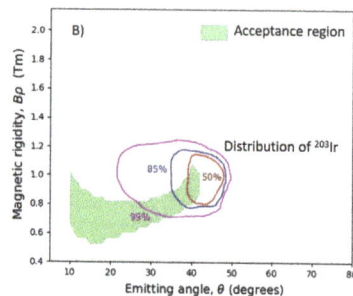

Figure 2. Acceptance plots of the solenoid separator. The green areas indicate the acceptance region of the solenoid magnet. Ions with corresponding magnetic rigidities and emitting angles that are released from a target placed behind the solenoid will reach the entrance window of the gas-catcher. (**A**) shows the acceptance region when the target is placed 53 cm inside the magnet. The distance between the target and the Faraday cup is 32 cm, and the distance between the gas-catcher and the end of the solenoid is 70 cm. The solid lines represent the distribution of ^{261}Md ions produced in the reaction ^{48}Ca + ^{251}Cf at an energy of 6.1 MeV/u. (**B**) shows the acceptance region when the target is placed 69 cm inside the magnet. The distance between the target and the Faraday cup is 32 cm, and the distance between the gas-catcher and the end of the solenoid is 72 cm. The solid lines represent the distribution of ^{203}Ir ions produced in the reaction ^{136}Xe + ^{198}Pt at an energy of 6.0 MeV/u.

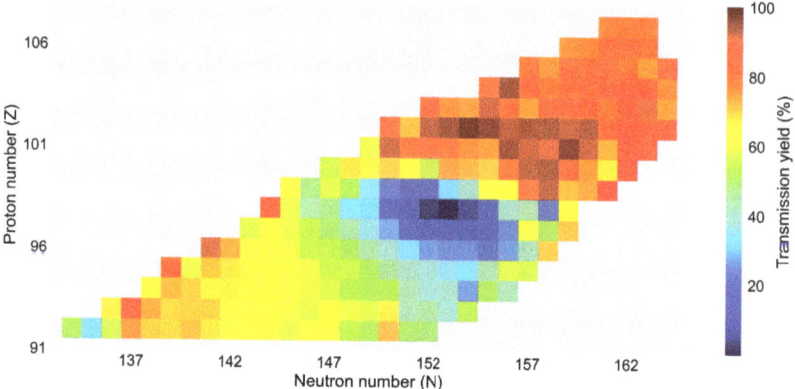

Figure 3. Transmission yields of nuclides produced in the reaction ^{48}Ca + ^{251}Cf at an energy of 6.1 MeV/u.

Figure 4 shows the model of the novel stacked-ring ion guide. Details concerning its design and the simulation of the ion transmission efficiency can be found in reference [15]. The ion guide consists of a stack of 78 ring electrodes. The ions are confined radially by an RF potential. To capture the divergent beam from the gas-catcher, the first ring has the widest inner diameter (14 mm). The inner diameters over the first eight rings decrease in order to focus the ions. Behind the focusing section of the ion guide, the thermalization section follows (see Figure 4), which consists of 60 identical rings. Here, the ions reach thermal equilibrium by interaction with the buffer gas and are transported by a travelling wave of bias voltages. From the thermalization section, the ions enter the refocusing section consisting of five rings with decreasing inner diameters. From there, the ions reach the bunching section, which consists of five rings. Here, the ions are accumulated until they are ejected as an ion bunch by disconnecting the last four rings from the RF voltage and applying optimized ejecting voltages. According to our simulations, the transmission efficiency of the ion guide is 80%. The energy and time spreads of ion bunches at the one-sigma level are 3.66 eV and 0.06 µs, respectively.

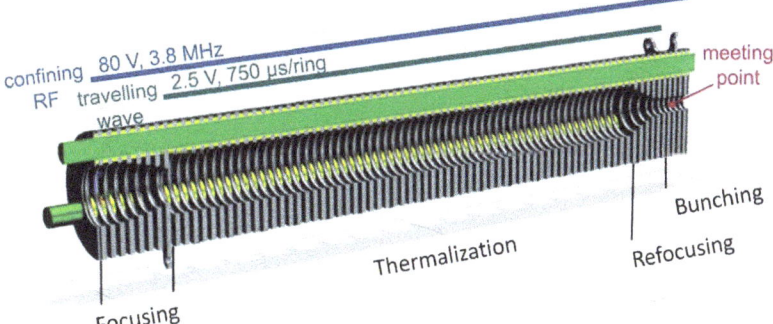

Figure 4. Design of the stacked-ring ion guide. The ions leaving the gas-catcher are captured in the focusing section. They are transported by a travelling wave towards the refocusing and the bunching section, from where they are ejected.

Figure 5 shows the model of the gas-catcher, the ion-guide section, and the MR-ToF MS. The gas-catcher is operated at a pressure of 50 mbar. The gas streaming through the exit hole of the gas-catcher is pumped away by a turbo-molecular pump with a pump capacity of 2200 L/s (pump 1, Figure 5), resulting in a pressure of about 10^{-3} mbar at the ring ion guide section. The operation of the MR-ToF MS requires a vacuum in the order of 10^{-9} mbar. Therefore, differential pumping is implemented. The ion guide section is separated by a 2 mm wide pulsed drift tube from a set of ion lenses. In this section, a turbo molecular pump with a capacity of 350 L/s (pump 2) is installed, and a pressure of 10^{-7} mbar is reached. This section is separated by an iris from the section of the MR-ToF analyzer, where another pump with a capacity of 700 L/s (pump 3) is installed in order to reach 10^{-9} mbar.

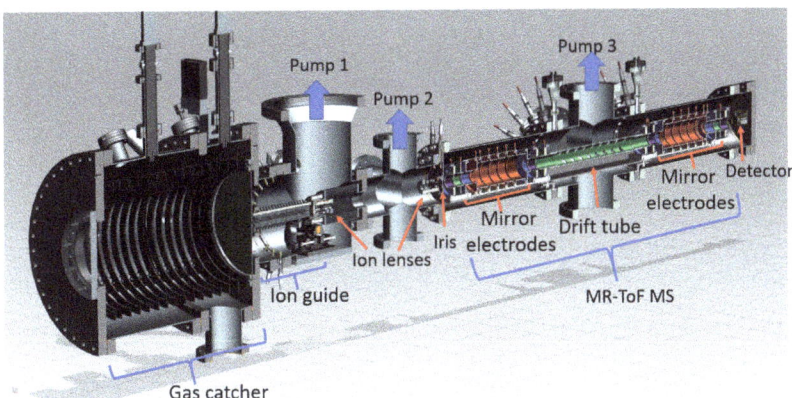

Figure 5. Drawing of the gas-catcher coupled by the ion guide to the MR-ToF MS.

The ion bunches ejected from the ring ion guide are refocused by the set of lenses; they pass the iris and are injected into the MR-ToF MS.

The MR-ToF MS has been developed at the Technical University of Darmstadt [16] and is currently under construction. It consists of two electrostatic ion-optical mirrors which are connected by a 70 cm long drift tube with a pulsable potential. For the injection and ejection of the ions, the "in-trap potential lift method" will be used [25]: the ions are injected into the MR-ToF MS, while the drift tube is on high potential. When the ions are inside, the potential of the drift tube is lowered and the ions are trapped between the mirrors and are reflected multiple times. By increasing the potential of the drift tube, the ions are ejected in mass-separated bunches and sent to a multichannel plate (MCP) detector to determine the time of flight. The MR-ToF method allows for mass measurements with a resolving power of several hundred thousands [17,18], as well as for isobaric separation to prepare purified samples for decay spectroscopy. Due to their different velocities, the ions of interest can be separated even from isobaric species, either during the storage period [26] or by the timing and duration of the ejection pulse [27]. For the spectroscopy, the MCP detector will be replaced by a silicon detector that is sensitive to alpha particles and fission fragments. The detection station is designed in such a way that it can be easily upgraded and the detectors can be exchanged.

3. Status and Planned Experimental Program

Currently, the NEXT experiment is in the late design phase. The machining and installation of several parts has already started. The ion guide and MR-ToF components are under construction, and the solenoid magnet will arrive at AGOR in Summer 2022.

NEXT will open the door to nuclei around the third waiting point for the r-process of nucleosynthesis at the neutron shell closure around $N = 126$ [28]. These nuclei will be accessed through ^{136}Xe-induced reactions, and their mass will be determined by the MR-ToF MS. The expected rates of ^{203}Ir and neighboring isotopes and isotones lie in the order of a few hundred ions per second at the focal point of the solenoid. The first mass-measurement campaigns at NEXT will focus on this region of the nuclear chart. Furthermore, NEXT will study neutron-rich nuclei in the transfermium region. These will be accessible through asymmetric reactions with actinide targets. The focus of the first experiments will lie in the mendelevium region towards the neutron subshell closure at $N = 162$, where we expect rates of a few ions per minute at the focal plane of the solenoid. For the simulations, we focused on the medium-mass projectile ^{48}Ca. However, as day-one experiments, we plan to also use beams that are easier to develop, such as ^{18}O and ^{22}Ne. After commissioning, we plan to focus on the masses and fission half-lives of the neutron-rich isotopes in the transfermium region.

4. Conclusions

NEXT will provide a new step to the neutron-rich side of the chart of nuclei. It will give access to isotopes that are difficult to reach at other facilities. The solenoid separator will allow for the separation of target-like transfer products from the primary beam and projectile-like fragments. The coupling to the MR-ToF MS through a gas-catcher and stacked-ring ion guide will prepare samples for decay studies and will allow the mass measurements of very exotic isotopes with high precision.

Author Contributions: Conceptualization, J.E.; simulation and design of the solenoid separator, A.S., J.S., J.U. and J.E.; theoretical predictions of the nuclear reactions/nuclear input data for the simulations, A.K. and V.S.; simulation and design of the ion guide, X.C., J.E. and T.S.; design and development of the MR ToF MS, M.S., F.W., L.S. and P.F.; writing—original draft preparation, J.E.; writing—review and editing, all authors; visualization, A.S., X.C. and J.E.; supervision, J.E.; project administration, J.E.; funding acquisition, J.E. All authors have read and agreed to the published version of the manuscript.

Funding: This research was funded by the European Research Council Executive Agency (ERCEA), under the powers delegated by the European Commission through a starting grant number 803740—NEXT—ERC-2018-STG.

Institutional Review Board Statement: Not applicable.

Informed Consent Statement: Not applicable.

Data Availability Statement: Data of the simulation are available upon request.

Acknowledgments: We would like to thank Nathanael Moorrees and Henk Smit for their technical support and help with the drawings. Furthermore, we would like to thank the workshops at the PARTREC facility at UMCG, Groningen, for their support.

Conflicts of Interest: The authors declare no conflict of interest.

Abbreviations

The following abbreviations are used in this manuscript:

NEXT	Neutron-rich, EXotic, heavy nuclei produced in multi-nucleon Transfer reactionss
MR-ToF MS	Multi-reflection time-of-flight mass spectrometer
SHIP	Separator for heavy ion reaction products
VAMOS	Variable mode spectrometer
KISS	KEK isotope separation system
IGISOL	Ion guide isotope separation on-line
FRS	Fragment separator
AGOR	Accélérateur Groningen–Orsay
ECR	Electron cyclotron resonance
N	Neutron number
DC	Direct current
RF	Radiofrequency
MCP	Multichannel plate

References

1. Türler, A.; Pershina, V. Advances in the production and chemistry of the heaviest elements. *Chem. Rev.* **2013**, *113*, 1237–1312. [CrossRef] [PubMed]
2. Devaraja, H.M.; Heinz, S.; Ackermann, D.; Göbel, T.; Heßberger, F.P.; Hofmann, S.; Maurer, J.; Münzenberg, G.; Popeko, A.G.; Yeremin, A.V. New studies and a short review of heavy neutron-rich transfer products. *Eur. Phys. J. A* **2020**, *56*, 224. [CrossRef]
3. Loveland, W.D. The Synthesis of New Neutron-Rich Heavy Nuclei. *Front. Phys.* **2019**, *7*, 1–8. [CrossRef]
4. Kratz, J.V.; Loveland, W.; Moody, K.J. Syntheses of transuranium isotopes with atomic numbers $Z \leq 103$ in multi-nucleon transfer reactions. *Nucl. Phys. A* **2014**, *944*, 117–157. [CrossRef]
5. Zagrebaev, V.I.; Greiner, W. Cross sections for the production of superheavy nuclei. *Nucl. Phys. A* **2014**, *944*, 257–307. [CrossRef]
6. Corradi, L.; Szilner, S.; Pollarolo, G.; Montanari, D.; Fioretto, E.; Stefanini, A.M.; Valiente-Dobón, J.J.; Farnea, E.; Michelagnoli, C.; Montagnoli, G.; et al. Multinucleon transfer reactions: Present status and perspectives. *Nucl. Instrum. Methods Phys. Res. Sect. B Beam Interact. Mater. Atoms.* **2013**, *317*, 743–751. [CrossRef]
7. Golabek, C.; Heinz, S.; Mittig, W.; Rejmund, F.; Villari, A.C.C.; Bhattacharyva, S.; Boilley, D.; de France, G.; Drouart, A.; Gaudefroy, L.; et al. Investigation of deep inelastic reactions in 238U + 238U at Coulomb barrier energies. *Eur. Phys. J. A* **2010**, *43*, 251–259. [CrossRef]
8. Vogt, A.; Birkenbach, B.; Reiter, P.; Corradi, L.; Mijatovic, T.; Montanari, D.; Szilner, S.; Bazzacco, D.; Bowry, M.; Bracco, A.; et al. Light and heavy transfer products in ^{136}Xe + ^{238}U multinucleon transfer reactions. *Phys. Rev. C Nucl. Phys.* **2015**, *92*, 1–12. [CrossRef]
9. Watanabe, Y.; Hirayama, Y.; Imai, N.; Ishiyama, H.; Jeong, S.; Miyatake, H.; Clement, E.; de France, G.; Navin, A.; Rejmund, M.; et al. Study of collisions of ^{136}Xe + ^{198}Pt for the KEK isotope separator. *Nucl. Instrum. Methods Phys. Res. Sect. B Beam Interact. Mater. Atoms.* **2013**, *317*, 752–755. [CrossRef]
10. Savard, G.; Brodeur, M.; Clark, J.A.; Knaack, R.A.; Valverde, A.A. The N = 126 factory: A new facility to produce very heavy neutron-rich isotopes. *Nucl. Instrum. Methods Phys. Res. B Beam Interact. Mater. Atoms* **2020**, *463*, 258–261. [CrossRef]
11. Spătaru, A.; Balabanski, D.L.; Beliuskina, O.; Constantin, P.; Dickel, T.; Hornung, C.; Kankainen, A.; Karpov, A.V.; Nichita, D.; Plass, W.; et al. Production of exotic nuclei via MNT reactions using gas cells. *Acta Phys. Pol. B* **2020**, *51*, 817–822. [CrossRef]
12. Dickel, T.; Kankainen, A.; Spătaru, A.; Amanbayev, D.; Beliuskina, O.; Beck, S.; Constantin, P.; Benyamin, D.; Geissel, H.; Gröf, L.; et al. Multi-nucleon transfer reactions at ion catcher facilities—A new way to produce and study heavy neutron-rich nuclei. *J. Phys. Conf. Ser.* **2020**, *1668*, 012012. [CrossRef]
13. Dvorak, J.; Block, M.; Düllmann, C.; Heinz, S.; Herzberg, R.D.; Schädel, M. IRiS—Exploring new frontiers in neutron-rich isotopes of the heaviest elements with a new Inelastic Reaction Isotope Separator. *Nucl. Instrum. Methods Phys. Res. Sect. A Accel. Spectrometers Detect. Assoc. Equip.* **2011**, *652*, 687–691. [CrossRef]
14. Mollaebrahimi, A.; Anđelić, B.; Even, J.; Block, M.; Eibach, M.; Giacoppo, F.; Kalantar-Nayestanaki, N.; Kaleja, O.; Kremers, H.R.; Laatiaoui, M.; et al. A setup to develop novel Chemical Isobaric SEparation (CISE). *Nucl. Instrum. Methods Phys. Res. Sect. B Beam Interact. Mater. Atoms.* **2020**, *463*, 508–511. [CrossRef]

15. Chen, X.; Even, J.; Fischer, P.; Schlaich, M.; Schlathölter, T.; Schweikhard, L.; Soylu, A. Stacked-ring ion guide for cooling and bunching rare isotopes. *Int. J. Mass Spectrom.* **2022**, *477*, 116856. [CrossRef]
16. Schlaich, M. Development and Characterization of a Multi-Reflection Time-of-Flight Mass Spectrometer for the Offline Ion Source of PUMA. Master's Thesis, Technische Universität Darmstadt, Darmstadt, Germany, 2021.
17. Wolf, R.N.; Wienholtz, F.; Atanasov, D.; Beck, D.; Blaum, K.; Borgmann, C.; Herfurth, F.; Kowalska, M.; Kreim, S.; Litvinov, Y.A.; et al. ISOLTRAP's multi-reflection time-of-flight mass separator/spectrometer. *Int. J. Mass Spectrom.* **2013**, *349–350*, 123–133. [CrossRef]
18. Wienholtz, F.; Beck, D.; Blaum, K.; Borgmann, C.; Breitenfeldt, M.; Cakirli, R.B.; George, S.; Herfurth, F.; Holt, J.D.; Kowalska, M.; et al. Masses of exotic calcium isotopes pin down nuclear forces. *Nature* **2013**, *498*, 346–349. [CrossRef]
19. Brandenburg, S.; Ostendorf, R.; Hofstee, M.; Kiewiet, H.; Beijers, H. The irradiation facility at the AGOR cyclotron. *Nucl. Instrum. Methods Phys. Res. Sect. B Beam Interact. Mater. Atoms.* **2007**, *261*, 82–85. [CrossRef]
20. Brandenburg, S.; Hevinga, M.A.; Nijboer, T.W.; Vorenholt, H. Beam loss monitoring and control for high intensity beams at the AGOR-facility. In Proceedings of CYCLOTRONS 2010, Lanzhou, China, 6–10 September 2010; pp. 227–229.
21. Karpov, A.; Saiko, V. Production of neutron-rich nuclides in the vicinity of N = 126 shell closure in multinucleon transfer reactions. *EPJ Web Conf.* **2017**, *163*, 27. [CrossRef]
22. Karpov, A.; Saiko, V. Synthesis of Transuranium Nuclei in Multinucleon Transfer Reactions at Near-Barrier Energies. *Phys. Partic. Nucl. Lett.* **2019**, *16*, 667–670. [CrossRef]
23. Shima, K.; Ishihara, T.; Mikumo, T. Empirical formula for the average equilibrium charge-state of heavy ions behind various foils. *Nucl. Instrum. Methods Phys. Res.* **1982**, *200*, 605–608. [CrossRef]
24. Nikolaev, V.; Dmitriev, I. On the equilibrium charge distribution in heavy element ion beams. *Phys. Lett. A* **1968**, *28*, 277–278. [CrossRef]
25. Wolf, R.N.; Marx, G.; Rosenbusch, M.; Schweikhard, L. Static-mirror ion capture and time focusing for electrostatic ion-beam traps and multi-reflection time-of-flight mass analyzers by use of an in-trap potential lift. *Int. J. Mass Spectrom.* **2012**, *313*, 8–14. [CrossRef]
26. Fischer, P.; Knauer, S.; Marx, G.; Schweikhard, L. In-depth study of in-trap high-resolution mass separation by transversal ion ejection from a multi-reflection time-of-flight device. *Rev. Sci. Instrum.* **2018**, *89*, 015114. [CrossRef]
27. Wienholtz, F.; Kreim, S.; Rosenbusch, M.; Schweikhard, L.; Wolf, R.N. Mass-selective ion ejection from multi-reflection time-of-flight devices via a pulsed in-trap lift. *Int. J. Mass Spectrom.* **2017**, *421*, 285–293. [CrossRef]
28. Cowan, J.J.; Sneden, C.; Lawler, J.E.; Aprahamian, A.; Wiescher, M.; Langanke, K.; Martinez-Pinedo, G.; Thielemann, F.K. Origin of the heaviest elements: The rapid neutron-capture process. *Rev. Mod. Phys.* **2021**, *93*, 15002. [CrossRef]

MDPI
St. Alban-Anlage 66
4052 Basel
Switzerland
Tel. +41 61 683 77 34
Fax +41 61 302 89 18
www.mdpi.com

Atoms Editorial Office
E-mail: atoms@mdpi.com
www.mdpi.com/journal/atoms

www.ingramcontent.com/pod-product-compliance
Lightning Source LLC
LaVergne TN
LVHW070642100526
838202LV00013B/861